more ...

TOKYO FOR FREE

SUSAN POMPIAN

with

a Foreword by
Ambassador **Michael H. Armacost**

KODANSHA INTERNATIONAL
Tokyo • New York • London

PHOTO CREDITS

The author and publisher would like to express their gratitude to each of the institutions, organizations, museums, universities, places of worship, and shops that kindly allowed us to reproduce their photographs in this volume. Thanks are also due to the following for their generous assistance: the Japan National Tourist Organization (JNTO), the Japan Traditional Craft Center, the Budokan, and the Sumida City Office for providing a number of photographs; The House of Councillors, *Asahi Shinbun*, Kozo Sekiya (p 305), Meiji University Archaeology Museum, Meiji University Criminal Museum, Musashino Academia Musicae's Museum of Musical Instruments, the Bank of Japan's Currency Museum, the Japan Foundation, and *Minzoku Geinou 76*; the artists and photographers whose work appears in chapter 14: Vincent David Feldman (p 364), Mitsuru Okada (p 365), Fukuo Yuminamochi (p 367), Kaoru Ijima (p 370), Ivica Tanaskovic (p 372), Yonosuke Natori (p 373), Susumu Saiga (p 374), Masato Seto (p 377), Yusuke Yoshi (p 381, top), Rie Iguchi (p 381, bottom), Saburo Ota (p 383), Yutaka Toriyama (p 385), Michiyo Kamei (p 387), Toshihiro Uchihira (p 387), Mariko Isozaki (p 390), Shinoda Toko (p 398), Takanori Ogisu (p 399), and Koichi Namekawa (p 402); and the Irish Network and Heather McAuliffe.

The jacket photography and nearly half of the interior shots were taken by the author.

Maps by Tadamitsu Omori
Additional fact-checking: Kazuko Matsuzaki

Distributed in the United States by Kodansha America, Inc., and in the United Kingdom and continental Europe by Kodansha Europe Ltd.

Published by Kodansha International Ltd., 17–14 Otowa 1-chome, Bunkyo-ku, Tokyo 112–8652, and Kodansha America, Inc.

Dedicated to my sister
Sandra for the book we never had
a chance to write together

ACKNOWLEDGMENTS

I wish to express my appreciation to all those people who patiently answered my never-ending questions and helped me compile the material for this book. To Mike Marklew for his expert professional advice; to Alan Brender for his editorial assistance; to my research assistant and translator, Keiko Hirano, for her patience and perseverance, and for accompanying me on what seemed like endless treks through uncharted territory; and to Michiko Uchiyama for her fact-checking and map work. A special thanks to the Japan National Tourist Office for their generosity in allowing me to use their lovely slides of Tokyo.

Special appreciation to Barry Lancet, my Executive Editor at Kodansha International, for his editorial direction and for believing in the concept of the book from the very beginning and giving me the opportunity to turn it into a reality. And, last but not least, to my dear friend Ethan for all his help—and without whose patience and understanding over the last few years this book would never have been written.

CONTENTS

FOREWORD

Tokyo is a city rich in history and culture. It has fantastic gardens, an abundance of temples, fascinating shops, and interesting neighborhoods. It offers to visitors a rich menu of artistic and sporting events, and an extraordinary range of other sources of enlightenment, entertainment, and amusement.

Susan Pompian has provided a service of incalculable value to both the casual visitor and long-time resident of Tokyo by developing this resourceful guide to the city. And since Tokyo remains an expensive city—particularly for foreigners—this guide is all the more valuable for its tips on the way one can see much of the best Tokyo has to offer without busting one's budget.

There is something here for everyone. Reading through this guide brought many fond memories of the seven years my own family lived in Tokyo and its environs. It offers many practical suggestions that would have been particularly useful when we were serving on the faculty of International Christian University in the 1960s, struggling to make ends meet on a teacher's salary, yet exposing ourselves and our children to the rich heritage of Tokyo.

In looking through the book, I was surprised and pleased at how many of the places and events my family and I managed to visit over the years. We could have done so more knowledgeably, and certainly more economically, had we had the benefit of this extremely useful book.

Ambassador Michael H. Armacost
President, The Brookings Institution

INTRODUCTION

Tokyo is one of the most important and exciting cities in the world today. But unlike Paris, New York, or London, specific information is still lacking. Tokyo is generally perceived as being so prohibitively expensive that people are afraid to venture to this part of the world. This is unfortunate, for in reality Japan's capital is a delightful, enriching city with much to offer, even for those on a limited budget.

As a long-term resident of Japan who enjoys traveling, I find myself spending a great deal of time answering questions and explaining to people in other countries what Tokyo is "really like." I have discovered that people are very familiar with Japanese products—but not with Japan itself. One day I learned of an American survey in which respondents were asked to name some well-known Japanese people. The most frequent replies were: Yoko Ono, Godzilla (yes, the fictitious movie-monster), and Bruce Lee (the Chinese martial arts expert).

I started to wonder if there was something I might do to remedy this lack of information about Japan—and at the same time help overcome people's "fear of coming to Tokyo" that seemed to prevail so strongly. I began to search out attractions and activities with a "zero yen" price tag on them, intending to write a travel article about spending time in Tokyo without spending a fortune. Well, I found more than I bargained for, and soon *Tokyo for Free* took on a life of its own. There is no question that the book was out there, just waiting to be written. And I feel very fortunate to have been the one who was given the opportunity to do so.

I certainly don't claim to cover everything there is to know about Tokyo in this book (that would take volumes), but I sincerely hope that my effort will offer you a little insight into the simple pleasures that make up the day-to-day lifestyle of the city. For isn't that what determines what a city is "really like," after all? I hope you will enjoy *Tokyo for Free* and appreciate the spirit in which it was written—with much love for one of the world's most intriguing cities.

GETTING AROUND—TIPS TO GET YOU STARTED

Yes, all the places and events in this book are free—but in order to enjoy them, you are going to have to get yourself to them. Finding your way around Tokyo may seem like a formidable task at first, especially since the address system is so complex, but it is actually quite easy to navigate by public transportation—once you know the basics.

In chapter 1 (see both the Introduction and the Tourist and Travel Information) I list some valuable resources that are waiting for you from the moment you arrive at Narita Airport. So look these over, pick up a free English subway/train map, and let the adventure begin.

Train Basics

The trains and subways of Tokyo are among the cleanest, safest, and perhaps most efficient in the world. Here is how they work. Tickets are purchased from dispensers located in the stations. If you can't decipher the overhead map that lists the fares, a simple rule is to buy the least expensive ticket and pay any difference owed at the other end. Prepaid "Metrocards" that automatically deduct the fare of each trip can be purchased at the newer subway ticket machines—press the SF button to buy one. Japan Railway also sells an "IO Card" that whisks you through the turnstiles without the bother of digging for change.

To enter the platform area, insert your ticket or Metrocard into the turnstile slot. Keep it in a safe place during your journey, for you will need it to exit when you reach your destination. Station names are written in both English and Japanese at most stations, and trains generally run from around 5:30 AM to midnight. Hours vary slightly from line to line—schedules are posted on each train platform. Note that Tokyo subways and JR (Japan Railway) train lines are independent of each other, and transferring from one to the other requires purchasing a new ticket.

Printed information on passes and excursion tickets is available from the Tourist Information Center, but using these can be a bit tricky, since there are a number of different train lines—each with its own system.

Bus Basics

Tokyo buses actually have set routes, although at times they appear to meander all over the city. But not to worry—if you need to take a bus to a destination in this book, the bus number and the place to board it are clearly indicated in the "Access" section of each entry.

Here are the basic rules for riding a bus in Tokyo. Board through the front door and deposit your money into the fare box located next to the driver's seat. The fare will be clearly marked—a flat ¥200 (¥100 for children) as of this writing. It is usually a good idea to state your destination to the driver upon boarding. This assures that you are on the right bus, and it also lets the driver know where you want to get off. Then stay as close to him as possible so that he can indicate when your stop is coming up. (It helps to be near enough to communicate, since all announcements are made in Japanese, and the driver doesn't normally stop the bus unless someone pushes the stop-request button.) Exit the bus from the rear door.

NOTE: Buses in the outlying areas sometimes operate a little differently, in that fares are based on a zone system. You board through the rear door, take a numbered zone voucher, and pay as you leave by the front door. Watch what the other people do, and follow their example.

Help Along the Way

There is help waiting for you en route, too. The very large maps on the subway station walls (just outside the ticket turnstiles) offer a good orientation to the area around the station. Important landmarks are generally labeled in both English and Japanese—

and your destination may even be pinpointed as well. Establishing your route visually before setting out makes following directions a lot easier when you start making your lefts, rights, and jogs through the tiny streets of the city.

Often the station attendant on duty will have small maps of the immediate area that he can give you. And he might even trace out the route with a colored pen if he is familiar with your destination. (Show him the name in Japanese.)

And please become familiar with the local police boxes (*koban*) that are found all over the city. The policemen in them are miracle workers who can pinpoint any address for you on a big map of their district. Suddenly it doesn't matter that the streets have no names—your destination has been made a reality.

As far as the listings in this book are concerned, I have tried to clarify access to them as much as possible. I have even included detailed walking directions from the most convenient train station or bus stop right up to their front door. By the way, I walk at a pretty fast pace. Please keep this fact in mind and adjust the printed walking times accordingly when accompanied by children or strolling leisurely.

SOME IMPORTANT BASICS TO LEARN BEFORE YOU BEGIN YOUR TOKYO ADVENTURE

Be Aware of Closing Times and Customs

As a general rule, just about every place is closed for several days over the New Year holidays. On the other hand, many places remain open on a national holiday and then close the following day if the holiday falls on their regular closing day.

During the Golden Week holidays in early May and the *Obon* season in August, some places close while others stay open more days than usual. Many places also have irregular closing days throughout the year for company holidays, taking inventory, and various other reasons. It is probably best to check first to make sure your destination will be open on the day you want to go. And keep in mind that entry to museums, gardens, and other places often stops one-half hour before the posted closing times.

Understanding the Term "Foreigner"

Contrary to what you may have experienced in other parts of the world, the word "foreigner" is not a derogatory or insulting term in Japan. It simple means non-Japanese. The Japanese word is *gaijin*, which translates literally as "outside person." This fact will become clearer when you see signs in shops and restaurants that declare "foreigners welcome," or "tax-free for foreigners."

And don't be offended if you happen to see a sign that reads "no foreigners." This doesn't mean that they don't like you or that they are anti-foreigners. It usually means that the pricing system used by that establishment would be misunderstood (considered a rip-off) by those unfamiliar with some Japanese pricing practices. So be happy for the warning—it saves everyone a lot of headaches.

* * *

Although the information contained in *Tokyo for Free* was current at press time, time marches on and things change. Some events may no longer be held, and some places may cease to exist. So it is best to call and confirm.

I am always on the lookout for new places and activities for inclusion into the next edition of this book. So please feel free to send any comments, updates, or wonderful new discoveries to:

Susan Pompian/*Tokyo for Free*
c/o Kodansha International, Ltd.
17–14 Otowa 1-chome, Bunkyo-ku, Tokyo 112–8652, Japan

My greatest hope is that *Tokyo for Free* will serve its intended purpose—to inform visitors and residents alike (and armchair travelers, too) of the many free treasures and pleasures in Tokyo—one of the most fascinating cities on earth. So good luck, have fun, and most of all, enjoy Tokyo—for free!

Please Mind Your Manners

When visiting any of the locations listed in this book, please be courteous. Whether the sites and activities are run by companies, nonprofit or government organizations, or private individuals, they monitor responses. They want visitors to come and enjoy themselves, and will often bend over backwards to accommodate guests, particularly those from outside Japan. Volunteers and paid staff spend their time and energy to make your experience enjoyable, but if the privilege is abused they may be inclined to add restrictions in the future. So be polite and gracious.

When paying a visit to a *dojo* (martial arts practice center), the home of a craftsperson, or any other live demonstration, please be quiet and attentive. Those with children should keep a strict eye on them, reminding them in advance to be on their best behavior. During a martial arts session, keep your feet tucked underneath you and out of the way. Always bear in mind that you are an invited guest. The hosts were kind enough to extend an invitation to you, so please return the favor and don't spoil it for those who will come after you.

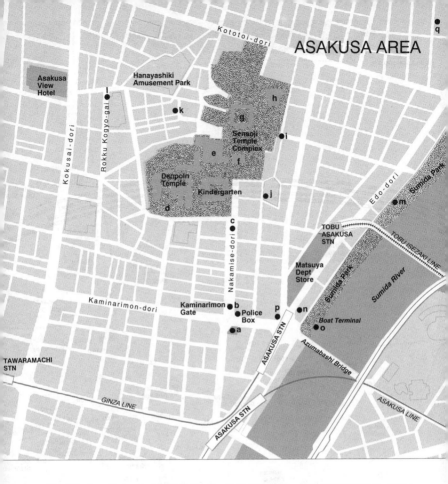

ASAKUSA AREA

The following places can all be found in chapter 3, Old Things—Shitamachi/Asakusa. If they have been written up in more detail in other chapters, the chapter is cited.

SPECIAL DESTINATIONS (ch 3)

a Asakusa Cultural and Sightseeing Center
b Kaminarimon Gate
c Nakamise-dori (ch 9)
d Denpoin Temple Garden (ch 7)
e Five-Storied Pagoda (Goju-no-to)
f Hozomon "Treasure House" Gate
g Asakusa Kannon Temple (Sensoji)
h Asakusa Shrine (Asakusa Jinja)
i East Gate (Nitenmon)
j The Bell of Time (Toki-no-Kane)

k Asakusa Kannon Onsen (hot springs bath)
l Rokku Kogyo-gai (Sixth District Entertainment Area)
m Sumida Park (see also ch 4—Yabusame)
n Riverside Gallery
o Tokyo Cruise Boat Terminal (Boats to Hinode Pier and Odaiba Beach Area)
p Kamiya Bar
q Miyamoto Studio (see also ch 11—Taiko Drumming)

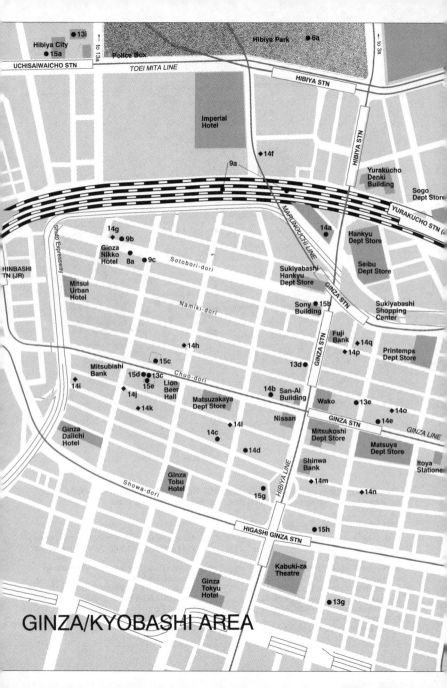

GINZA/KYOBASHI AREA

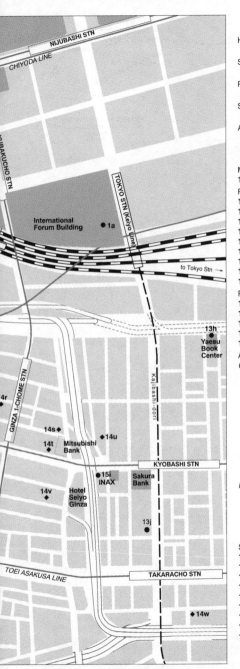

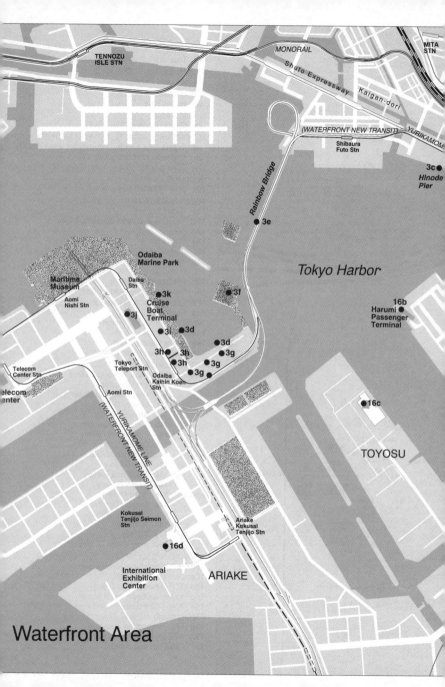

MITA STN

TENNOZU ISLE STN

MONORAIL

Shuto Expressway

Kaigan-dori

(WATERFRONT NEW TRANSIT)

YURIKAMOME

Shibaura Futo Stn

● 3c
Hinode Pier

Rainbow Bridge

● 3e

Odaiba Marine Park

Tokyo Harbor

Maritime Museum

Daiba Stn

Aomi Nishi Stn

● 3k
Cruise Boat Terminal

● 3f

16b
Harumi ●
Passenger Terminal

● 3j

● 3i

● 3d

● 3d

Telecom Center Stn

Tokyo Teleport Stn

3h ●

● 3h

● 3h

● 3g

● 3g

● 3g

Telecom Center

Aomi Stn

Odaiba Kaihin Koen Stn

● 16c

TOYOSU

YURIKAMOME LINE (WATERFRONT NEW TRANSIT)

Kokusai Tenjijo Seimon Stn

Ariake Kokusai Tenjijo Stn

● 16d

International Exhibition Center

ARIAKE

Waterfront Area

SPECIAL DESTINATIONS (ch 3)

3a Tsukiji Fish Market
3b Asahi Shinbun (Communications in Japan)
3c Hinode Pier (Shitamachi/Asakusa and Odaiba Beach Areas)
3d Odaiba Beach and Park Area
    3e Rainbow Bridge
    3f Ruins of the Shogun's Fortress
    3g Sunset Beach Restaurant Row and *Spirits of the East, West, and Hope* Public Art Sculptures (ch 14—Public Art)
    3h *Twisted Headband* and *25 Porticos* Public Art Works (ch 14—Public Art)
    3i Decks Tokyo Beach Complex
    3j Fuji Television Headquarters Building
3k Cruise Boat Terminal (Boats to Hinode Pier and Asakusa)

PARKS (ch 6)

6a Shiba Park

TEMPLES AND SHRINES (ch 8)

8a Tsukiji Honganji Temple
8b Nami-Yoke Inari Shrine
8c Zojoji Temple

MUSEUMS (ch 10)

10a Tsukiji Fish Information Center and Museum

ART GALLERIES (ch 14)

14a The Tolman Collection

VIEWS (ch 16)

16a St. Luke's Tower
16b Tokyo Harumi Passenger Terminal
16c Gas Science Center
16d Tokyo Big Sight/Ariake International Exhibition Center

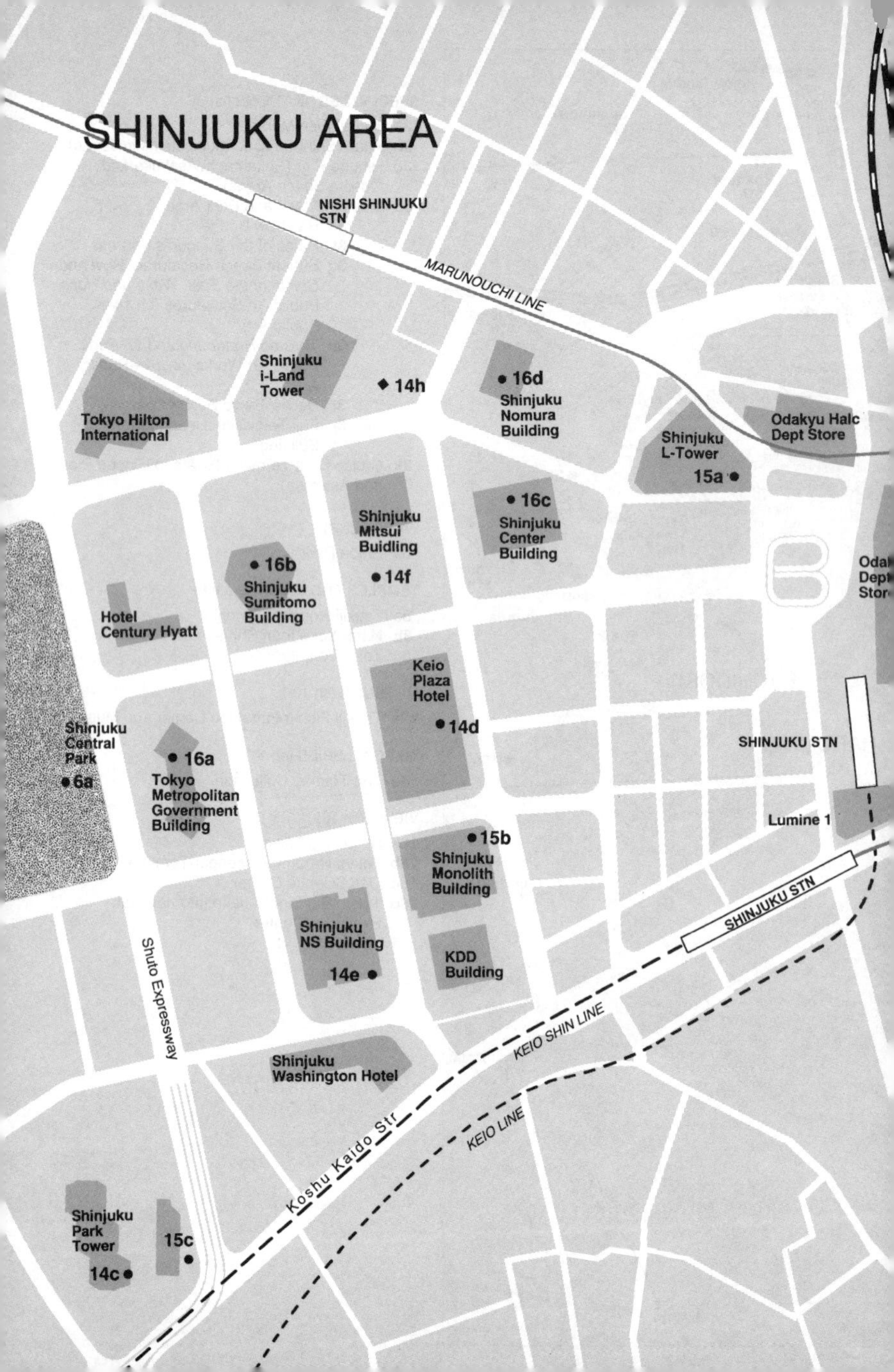

SHINJUKU AREA

NISHI SHINJUKU STN

MARUNOUCHI LINE

Shinjuku i-Land Tower

◆ 14h

● 16d
Shinjuku Nomura Building

Tokyo Hilton International

Odakyu Halc Dept Store

Shinjuku L-Tower

15a ●

● 16c
Shinjuku Center Building

Shinjuku Mitsui Buidling

● 14f

Odak Dept Stor

● 16b
Shinjuku Sumitomo Building

Hotel Century Hyatt

Keio Plaza Hotel

● 14d

SHINJUKU STN

Shinjuku Central Park

● 6a

● 16a
Tokyo Metropolitan Government Building

Lumine 1

● 15b
Shinjuku Monolith Building

SHINJUKU STN

Shinjuku NS Building

14e ●

KDD Building

KEIO SHIN LINE

Shuto Expressway

Shinjuku Washington Hotel

Koshu Kaido Str

KEIO LINE

Shinjuku Park Tower

15c ●

14c ●

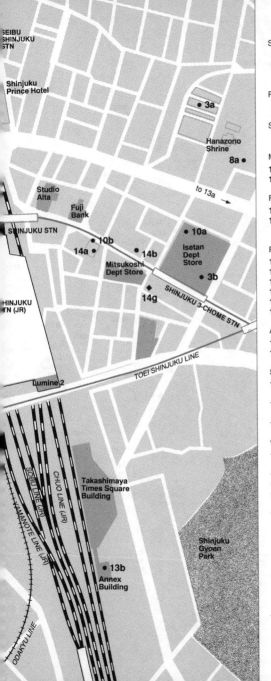

SPECIAL DESTINATIONS (ch 3)

3a Golden Gai
3b Isetan Food Basement Tour (Small Stuff)

PARKS (ch 6)

6a Shinjuku Central Park

SHRINES (ch 8)

8a Hanazono Shrine

MUSEUMS (ch 10)

10a Isetan Museum of Art
10b Konica Camera Museum

FREE READS (ch 13)

13a Tibet House*
13b Kinokunia Bookstore (Takashimaya Times Square Annex Building)

PHOTO EXHIBITION SHOWROOMS (ch 14)

14a Konica Plaza
14b Minolta Photo Space
14c Galley One
14d Shinjuku Nikon Salon
14e Nikon Mini Gallery
14f Pentax Forum

ART GALLERIES (ch 14)

14g Gallery Shinjuku Takano
14h Shinjuku i-Land

SHOWROOMS (ch 15)

15a TOTO and INAX showrooms (L-Tower Building)
15b NAIS Showroom Shinjuku (Shinjuku Monolith Building)
15c TSS—Tokyo Gas Shinjuku Showroom

VIEWS (ch 16)

16a Tokyo Metropolitan Government Building Observatories
16b Shinjuku Sumitomo Building
16c Shinjuku Center Building
16d Shinjuku Nomura Building

* just off map

Meiji Shrine ● 8a

Yoyogi Park
● 6a

HARAJUKU
STN

to 14a

Togo
Shrine

Takeshita-dori

● 9a

Palais
France

MEIJI
JINGUMAE
STN

National
Gymnasium

8b ● ● 15a   Laforet 2

Laforet
Harajuku

Kishi Kinen
Taiikukan
● 4a

15b ●
Kiddyland ● 9b ● 16b

Meiji-dori

Oriental ● 9c
Bazaar

Omotesando

14b

8d ●   ● 8c
● 16a

Cafe
de
Flore
16b ●   Cafe
des Pres
9d ●
Hanae
Mori
Building

14h ◆   ◆ 14g

Fuji
Bank

YAMANOTE LINE (JR)

Kinokunia
Supermarket

Seibu
Dept
Store

14f ●   ◆ 14e
13b ● ● 12b
12a ●
● 13c
Citibank

● 14d
Spiral
Building

United
Nations
University

Kotto-dori (Antique road)

Aoyama-dori

SHIBUYA STN

Aoyama Gakuin
University

Shuto Expressway

AOYAMA/ HARAJUKU AREA

SPORTS (ch 4)
4a Kishi Kinen Taiikukan

PARKS (ch 6)
6a Yoyogi Park

GARDENS (ch 7)
7a Nezu Institute of Fine Arts Garden

TEMPLES, SHRINES, AND CHURCHES (ch 8)
8a Meiji Shrine
8b Tokyo Central Church of Seventh Day Adventists
8c Tokyo Union Church
8d First Church of Christ, Scientist Tokyo

ANTIQUES, FOLKCRAFTS, AND FLEA MARKETS (ch 9)
9a Togo Shrine Antique Flea Market
9b Fuji Torii (antiques)
9c Oriental Bazaar
9d Antique Market (Hanae Mori Building)
9e Japan Traditional Craft Center
9f Kotto-dori (Antique Road)

LECTURES, CLASSES, AND EDUCATIONAL EVENTS (ch 12)
12a United Nations University (talks on Asia)
12b Eri Hara's Poetry Workshops (Tokyo Women's Plaza)

FREE READS (ch 13)
13a On Sundays (Watari-um Museum Bookstore)
13b Aoyama Book Center
13c United Nations University (Information Centre)

ART GALLERIES (ch 14)
14a Okazaki Tamako Gallery
14b Gallery Tao
14c Gallery 360°
14d Spiral Garden (Spiral Building)
14e Fairy (*see* Art Galleries intro)
14f Galeria Building (*see* Art Galleries intro)
14g Mizuma Art Gallery
14h Las Chicas Restaurant and Gallery (*see* Art Galleries intro)
14i AKI-EX Gallery

SHOWROOMS (ch 15)
15a Furusato Plaza Tokyo
15b Cosmetic Garden—Shiseido

FANTASTIC FREE VIEWS (ch 16)
16a Omotesando during the Christmas season
16b Pedestrian Overpasses

SHIBUYA AREA

NHK

Shibuya Public Hall

Tobu Hotel

Parco II

Parco III · Parco I

Tokyu Hands

15a

13e · Shibuya Beam Building

Bunkamura

Tokyu Dept Store

14c · 13d

15b

14a

14b

13c

Tower Records

Miyashita Park

10b

Koen-dori

Seibu Dept Store

13b

Inokashira-dori

Bunkamura-dori

10a

109 Building

109-2 Building

Dogenzaka

SHIBUYA STN

Hachiko Exit

SHIBUYA STN

HANZOMON LINE

GINZA LINE

9a

Aoyama-

Meiji-dori

SHIN TAMAGAWA LINE

KEIO INOKASHIRA LINE

Tokyu Plaza · 13a

YAMANOTE LINE (JR)

TOKYU TOYOKO LINE

Shuto Expressway

Tamagawa-dori

ANTIQUES, FOLKCRAFTS, AND FLEA MARKETS (ch 9)

9a Beniya Craft Shop

MUSEUMS (ch 10)

10a Eyeglass Museum
10b Tokyo Metropolitan Children's Hall

FREE READS (ch 13)

13a Kinokunia Bookstore (Tokyu Plaza)
13b Taiseido Bookstore
13c Tower Records Bookstore

13d Maruzen Art Bookstore
13e Plaza Equus Library (Shibuya Beam Building)

PHOTO EXHIBITIONS AND ART GALLERIES (ch 14)

14a Egg Gallery (photography)
14b Doi Photo Plaza
14c Bunkamura Gallery (art)

SHOWROOMS (ch 15)

15a Plaza Equus (Shibuya Beam Building)
15b TEPCO Electric Energy Museum

1

HELP!

TOURIST AND TRAVEL INFORMATION

- Tourist Offices

  Tourist Information Center (TIC)

  Information Bureaus of Tokyo

- Additional Resources

  Teletourist Information

  Japan Travel-Phone

  JR East Infoline

  Narita Airport Information

  Haneda Airport Information

  Tokyo City Air Terminal (TCAT)

  AT&T Communications Services Japan

  Postal Information Service

  Telephone Information Services

HELPLINES AND IMPORTANT INFORMATION CENTERS

- Helplines
- Emergency, Hospital, and Medical Information
- Life Safety Learning Centers
- Support Groups
- Other Assistance

  Foreign Residents' Advisory Services

  Human Rights Assistance

  Immigration Information

  Tax Consultation

  Counseling on Labor and Employment Matters

  Police Counseling

FREE SERVICES AND GIVEAWAYS

- Welcoming Services
- Government Services and Offerings
- Free Publications
- Free Classified Ads
- Bulletin Boards
- Shopping Services
- Free Toy Repair
- Free Furniture and Appliances
- Free Pets
- Free Identity Photos
- Giveaways—Where to Find Them

INTRODUCTION

*A*re you finding it difficult to get oriented in Tokyo? Discovering that it is hard to function in a place where everything is written in little squiggles you can't quite decipher? Are you feeling a little frustrated or maybe even completely lost?

Well, don't give up—there is help available. In fact, there is a plethora of services offering information, advice, and assistance that can help make your stay in Tokyo go much smoother. And that is what this chapter is all about.

From the moment you arrive at Narita (New Tokyo International Airport), help is within reach. You can have your questions answered and pick up lots of brochures and maps at the Tourist Information Center (TIC) located on the 1F of Passenger Terminal 2, right next to customs Exit A. TIC can even supply information on accommodations if needed and explain how to get into the city by bus or train.

Of course, there is a Tourist Information Center in the city as well, located near Yurakucho Station. Information is also available at the Information Bureaus of Tokyo, located at Shinjuku and Tokyo train stations. (See the Tourist and Travel Information section of this chapter for details.)

Another great source of information is the free guide Living in Tokyo, *an essential booklet for those planning to stay in Tokyo for an extended period. It contains lots of useful information for short-timers too, including the* invaluable Railway Lines in Tokyo and Its Suburbs *map, which charts all the subway and railway lines in the Tokyo area. I have found this map to be an indispensable aid and always carry it with me wherever I go. The booklet is available in five languages from any of the twenty-three ward* (ku) *offices and sometimes at the Information Bureaus of Tokyo. (See Government Services and Offerings in this chapter for more information.)*

I have found that just knowing assistance is easily available helps to keep the panic level down. You will no doubt discover this to be the case, too, once you learn how much help is actually out there for you—an important factor in this often bewildering city of streets with no names.

TOURIST AND TRAVEL INFORMATION

TOURIST OFFICES

TOURIST INFORMATION CENTER (TIC)
(Japan National Tourist Organization)

国際観光振興会 （Kokusai Kanko Shinkokai）

Narita (New Tokyo International Airport) Office

> Passenger Terminal 2, 1F
>
> Narita, Chiba 286–0000
>
> ☎ 0476–34–6251
>
> 千葉県成田市　新東京国際空港第2旅客ターミナル1階
> （郵便は第2郵便局私書箱2204　〒286-0000）

Tokyo Office

> Tokyo International Forum, B1
>
> 3–5–1 Marunouchi, Chiyoda-ku, Tokyo 100–0005
>
> ☎ 3201–3331
>
> 東京都千代田区丸ノ内3-5-1　東京国際フォーラム地下1階
> 〒100-0005
>
> ✉ http://www.jnto.go.jp

There is a wealth of free information available at the TIC. Their *Calendar Events* lists major happenings in the Tokyo area each month, and the *Tokyo Subway System Map* helps you to get there. *Japan—Your Traveling Companion* is a booklet with lots of tips for the budget traveler, and *Walking Courses in Tokyo* contains suggested city walks, with maps and information on the many interesting sights along the way.

Information on festivals, gardens, sports, cultural events, and free industrial tours are just a few of the many other leaflets and pamphlets available. Material is available in English and a number of European and Asian languages. Utilize this plentiful source of information.

NOTE: Their multilingual staff can also assist you with travel plans throughout Japan, including reservations at inexpensive accommodations.

Hours: Tokyo TIC: 9 AM–5 PM Mon–Fri and 9 AM–noon Sat. Clsd Sun and national hols. But telephone inquiries are taken daily (including wknds and hols) at the Narita Airport Information Center. Narita TIC: 9 AM–8 PM every day of the year.

Access: The Tokyo TIC is directly across from JR Yurakucho Stn (Yamanote and Keihin Tohoku lines), Kokusai (International) Forum Exit, and adjacent to Exit A4b of the Yurakucho subway line at the same station. It is also a 5-min walk via the underground concourse from Tokyo Stn (Yamanote and other lines). Exit from the Marunouchi side of the station and follow the signs to the Keiyo Line. When you reach it, a sign will direct you up the staircase to your right. TIC is on your immediate right as you enter the Forum Building. For access from Hibiya Stn (Hibiya, Chiyoda, and Mita lines), follow the underground signs to the Yurakucho Line, Exit A4b. (See address above for access to the Narita airport TIC.)

INFORMATION BUREAUS OF TOKYO
(Tokyo Metropolitan Government)
東京インフォメーション ビューロー
Main Office

Tokyo International Forum, 1F

3–5–1 Marunouchi, Chiyoda-ku, Tokyo 100–0005

☎ 5221–9084

東京都千代田区丸ノ内3-5-1　東京国際フォーラム1階
〒100-0005

Shinjuku Station Office—Shinjuku Station Building

Tourist and travel information as well as publications on a variety of essential matters such as medical and postal services can be found at these three information bureaus.

Hours: Both offices are open 10 AM–6:30 PM daily. The main office can be found of 1F of the Tokyo International Forum. For directions see the access information for TIC in the previous entry. (Clsd New Year hols.)

Access: Look for the small letter "i" inside a circle. The **Shinjuku bureau** is located at the East Exit of Shinjuku Stn (Yamanote and other lines), 1F.

ADDITIONAL RESOURCES

TELETOURIST INFORMATION ☎ 3201–2911
A tape gives information around the clock regarding events and festivals taking place in and around Tokyo for the current week.

JAPAN TRAVEL-PHONE ☎ 3201–3331, 0088–22–4800 (toll free)
This toll-free service of the Japan National Tourist Organization (JNTO) provides travelers with transportation schedules, accommodation assistance, shopping information, and other travel-related items. They can also tell you the location of your nearest tourist office, no matter where in Japan you may be. Call from anyplace in the country.
Hours: 9 AM–5 PM every day.

JR EAST INFOLINE ☎ 3423–0111
English information on train schedules, fares, routing, sightseeing, and whatever else you need to know about traveling by train in Japan is provided.
Hours: 10 AM–6 PM daily (clsd New Year hols).

NARITA AIRPORT INFORMATION ☎ 0476–34–5000

HANEDA AIRPORT INFORMATION ☎ 5757–8111

TOKYO CITY AIR TERMINAL (TCAT) ☎ 3665–7111

AT&T COMMUNICATIONS SERVICES JAPAN
  ☒ http://atthotel.att.co.jp
This "AT&T Hotel Home Page" on the Internet provides not only information on hotels, but also flight information that is updated hourly, and information on access to the airport and Tokyo train services—all in English.

■ Postal Information Service
MINISTRY OF POSTS AND TELECOMMUNICATIONS
☎ 5472–5851/2

Consultation is provided in English regarding postal services.
Hours: 9:30 AM–4:30 PM Mon–Fri. Clsd hols.

■ Telephone Information Services
DIRECTORY ASSISTANCE
At press time there was no Tokyo local directory assistance line in English, but NTT does provide free English telephone directories. You can pick up a copy of *Townpage* at your nearest NTT office or call ☎ 3356–8511 (in English) to order one. Phone numbers can also be obtained for a service charge through NTT Japanese directory assistance by dialing ☎ 104 (24 hours). Ask for an English-speaking operator and be patient.

Overseas Information in English (KDD) ☎ 0057 (toll-free 24 hours)

Overseas Operator-assisted calls in English (KDD) ☎ 0051 (toll-free 24 hours)

Customer Consultation Center in English (NTT) ☎ 0120–364–463 (toll free) 9 AM–5 PM Mon-Fri. Clsd Sat, Sun, national hols, and New Year hol.

Telephone Information in Japanese

Directory Assistance ☎ 104 (24 hours). For a service charge.

Time ☎ 117 (24 hours). Charged as a local call.

Weather ☎ 177 (24 hours). Charged as a local call.

HELPLINES AND IMPORTANT INFORMATION CENTERS

HELPLINES

TOKYO ENGLISH LIFE LINE (TELL)
☎ 5774-0992 (daily: 9 AM–4 PM, 7 PM–11 PM)

Face-to-face counseling: ☎ 3498-0231 (for appointments)

HELP!

Office: ☎ 3498–0261, Fax: 3498–0272
☺ www.telljp.com

Tokyo English Life Line (TELL) is a nonprofit organization serving the international community since 1973. TELL provides the following services: free, nonjudgmental telephone counseling and crisis intervention (Life Line); subsidized face-to-face counseling (psychotherapy) in English, Japanese, French, and Spanish; educational workshops and presentations.

TELL is affiliated with Life Line International, a worldwide telephone counseling advisory body, and in Japan with the Federation of Inochi no Denwa. Face-to-face counseling services are accredited to ensure that the highest clinical standards are maintained. All life line volunteer phone counselors undergo extensive training, and therapists are experienced and qualified.

Additional activities include the TELL information/survival guide calendar, the Charity Walk/Runathon in May, and the Charity Auction in November. For more information on services, volunteer opportunities, or donations, please call the TELL office or visit the TELL website.

JAPAN HELPLINE

☎ 0120–46–1997 (toll free)

The Japan Helpline can be dialed toll-free from anywhere in Japan twenty-four hours a day. They offer help in any area, from simple questions to emergency assistance—in about fourteen languages. Keep this number with you wherever you go.

TOKYO FAMILY NETWORK

☎ 3715–3240

This center provides Tokyo residents with introductions to others in their area with similar interests and needs, and also supplies information on their neighborhood. Guidance for families already living in Tokyo, Japanese families returning from overseas, bi-cultural families, and newcomers. (Newcomers should also see the Welcoming Services section in this chapter.)

Hours: 4 PM–7 PM Tue, Wed, and Fri—but you can leave a message anytime and someone will return your call.

EMERGENCY, HOSPITAL, AND MEDICAL INFORMATION

FIRE, AMBULANCE ☎ 119 (24 hours in Japanese)
POLICE ☎ 110 (24 hours in Japanese)

At green or gray phones, push the emergency button located on the telephone before dialing emergency numbers. If you are speaking a language other than Japanese, they will connect you with an interpreting service that will relay the information to them.

FIRE DEPARTMENT TELEPHONE INFORMATION SERVICE

☎ 3212–2323

This 24-hour service can help you with English information on hospitals, including proximity to you, facilities and capabilities, emergency information, and which hospital a patient was taken to if you supply them with his/her name. And did you know that ambulance service is free in Japan? English and Japanese are spoken; Korean on an irregular basis.

ASSOCIATION OF MEDICAL DOCTORS OF ASIA (AMDA)

International Medical Information Center

☎ 5285–8088

Information on the Japanese medical system and an introduction to doctors who speak your language can be obtained here.

Hours: *English, Chinese, Korean, Thai, and Spanish*: 9 AM–5 PM Mon–Fri. *Portuguese*: 9 AM–5 PM Mon, Wed, and Fri. *Tagalog*: 9 AM–5 PM Wed. *Persian*: 9 AM–5 PM Mon.

TOKYO METROPOLITAN HEALTH AND MEDICAL INFORMATION CENTER

☎ 5285–8181 (Regular Services), 5285–8185 (After-hour Emergency Medical Interpretation)

Information regarding Japan's medical system in general as well as which institutions provide services in foreign languages is available in English, Chinese, Korean, Spanish, and Thai.

HELP!

Hours: Regular services are available 9 AM–8 PM Mon–Fri. Emergency medical interpretation services are available 5 PM–10 PM Mon–Fri, and 9 AM–10 PM wknds and hols.

■ AIDS Hotlines

JAPAN HIV CENTER ☎ 5259–0256

Human Rights Information Center
Hours: *English*: 11 AM–2 PM Sat.

JAPAN HELPLINE AIDS INFORMATION

☎ 0120–46–1995 (toll free)
Hours: 24 hours a day.

TOKYO METROPOLITAN GOVERNMENT AIDS TELEPHONE SERVICE

Recorded information on AIDS prevention, 24-hour toll-free.
☎ *English*: 0120–085–812. *Thai*: 0120–494–812.

Counseling. ☎ 5320–4485, 9 AM–5 PM Mon–Fri. 3292–9090, 6 PM–9 PM Mon–Fri and 2 PM–5 PM, weekends and holidays.

Free anonymous HIV-antibody tests at the Tokyo Metropolitan Testing and Counseling Office. Call ☎ 3377–0811, 4 PM–6 PM Mon–Fri. Tests can be taken between 3 PM and 8 PM on weekdays.

LIFE SAFETY LEARNING CENTERS (BOSAI-KAN)

Do you know how to activate that fire extinguisher you pass every day? If smoke suddenly filled the hallways of your building, would you know what to do? Are you prepared at your home and office for an earthquake? According to statistics, your answers to these questions are probably no.

But help is available at free training sessions offered at Tokyo's Life Safety Learning Centers (Bosai-kan). To teach you what to do in an actual emergency, you can practice escaping from a smoke-filled room, responding to a magnitude 7 earthquake jolt, and administering first aid.

Training is generally offered in Japanese, with provisions for non-Japanese-speaking participants. I attended the Honjo Bosai-kan, which supplied individual interpreting devices to translate the realistic 3-D orientation film and introductory videos for each section. And since a great deal of the program is participatory, show overshadows tell. The three centers listed below are sponsored by the Tokyo Fire Department. Some ward (*ku*) offices offer training as well. Check for the center nearest you, then pay them a visit—real soon. I promise you will not forget what you learn there.

HONJO BOSAI-KAN (In the Honjo Fire Station)
本所防災館（本所消防署）

   4–6–6 Yokokawa, Sumida-ku, Tokyo 130–0003
   ☎ 3621–0119
   東京都墨田区横川4-6-6　〒130-0003

Three-hour training sessions are given at 9:15, 10:15, 11:15, 1:15, 2:15, and 3:15. The course includes a 3-D movie, an earthquake simulation, and training in what to do in an emergency—such as how to extinguish fires, help injured people, and escape from a smoke-filled room. An English pamphlet is available and some English is spoken. Appointments are preferred. Individuals can go without an appointment, but there is no guarantee that there will be space in the session.

Hours: 9 AM–5 PM (enter by 4 PM). Clsd Wed, 3rd Thurs, and New Year hol.

Access: A 10-min walk from Kinshicho Stn, North Exit (JR Sobu Line). Turn right from the station exit, and left at the main street (Yotsume-dori). Walk down for about 8 min until you reach Kuramae Bashi-dori. One block past the next traffic light (a gas station is on the corner), turn right and you will see the Honjo Fire Station and Life Safety Learning Center in front of you. The building stands out: it is a cross between an Egyptian pyramid and a silver spaceship.

IKEBUKURO BOSAI-KAN (In the Ikebukuro Fire Station)
池袋防災館（池袋消防署）

2–37–8 Nishi Ikebukuro, Toshima-ku, Tokyo 171–0021

☎ 3590–6565

東京都豊島区西池袋2-37-8　〒171-0021

Two-hour training sessions are offered. Reservations are needed for more than five people. Some English is spoken and English pamphlets are usually available.

TACHIKAWA BOSAI-KAN (Next to Tachikawa Fire Station)
立川防災館（立川消防署のとなり）

1156–1 Izumicho, Tachikawa-shi, Tokyo 190–0015

☎ 0425–21–1119

東京都立川市泉町1156-1　〒190-0015

Tours are offered in English, but require a one-month advance notice.

SUPPORT GROUPS

There are a number of English-language support groups in Tokyo. You can usually find the numbers for organizations such as Alcoholics Anonymous (AA), Adult Children of Alcoholics (ACA), Overeaters Anonymous (OA), and Emotions Anonymous (EA) in *Tokyo Classified* and other foreign-language publications. The Tokyo English Life Line (TELL) also keeps a listing (☎ 3968–4099).

OTHER ASSISTANCE

■ Foreign Residents' Advisory Services

FOREIGN RESIDENTS' ADVISORY CENTER
東京都庁外国人相談室 (Tokyo Tocho Gaikokujin Sodanshitsu)

Metropolitan Government No. 1 Building, South Tower, 3F

2–8–1 Nishi Shinjuku, Shinjuku-ku, Tokyo 163–8001

☎ *English*: 5320–7744, Mon–Fri. *Chinese*: 5320–7766, Tues and Fri. *Korean*: 5320–7700, Wed. *French*: 5320–7755, Thurs. *Spanish*: 5320–7730, Thurs.

東京都新宿区西新宿2-8-1　東京都庁第一庁舎3階　〒163-8001

Consultation is available on matters regarding life in Japan: alien registration, taxes, legal dealings, education, medical services, etc.

Hours: 9:30 AM—noon and 1 PM—4 PM. Clsd hols.

Access: 10-min walk from West Exit of Shinjuku Stn (Yamanote and other lines). Follow the signs through the underground passageway to the high-rise district. After emerging from the tunnel, you can see the huge building complex on the left side just beyond the Keio Plaza Hotel. Go up the steps and enter the building from the plaza.

CONSULTATION SERVICES are also offered by local ward/city offices. Check with the nearest one for availability, times, and days.

■ Human Rights Assistance

TOKYO LEGAL AFFAIRS BUREAU
(Human Rights Counseling Center)
法務局人権擁護部 (Homukyoku Jinken Yogobu)
Otemachi Common Government Office No. 3 Building, 6F
1–3–3 Otemachi, Chiyoda-ku, Tokyo 100–0004
☎ 3214–6231 ext. 2423
東京都千代田区大手町1-3-3大手町合同庁舎3号館6階　〒100-0004

Counseling is given here for legal matters and the infringement of human rights of foreigners. Advice is also given on such matters as international marriage, divorce, adoption, etc.

Hours: 1:30 PM—4 PM (enter by 3:30 PM). Clsd hols. *English*: Tues and Thurs. *German*: Tues and Thurs. *Chinese*: Mon.

Access: 3 min from Otemachi Stn, Exit C2 (various subway lines). Walk straight out from the station and cross the street. You will be in front of the Regional Taxation Bureau Building (Bldg. No. 2). Walk in the same direction to the end of it and turn left. Building No 3 will be straight ahead of you alongside the highway—it's the only building there.

LEGAL COUNSELING CENTER (Tokyo Bar Association)

法律相談センター (Horitsu Sodan Senta)

> Bar Association Building
>
> 1–1–3 Kasumigaseki, Chiyoda-ku, Tokyo 100–0013
>
> ☎ 3581–2302 (Taped Information)
>
> 3581–1511 (Appointment in Japanese)
>
> 東京都千代田区霞ヶ関1-1-3　弁護士会館　〒100-0013

Confidential legal counseling regarding visa status, over-stays, working conditions, unpaid wages, and similar problems is provided on Thursday for foreign residents who can't afford legal fees. If it is determined that legal assistance is needed, they will handle the case at no charge. English and Chinese are spoken; bring an interpreter for other languages.

Hours: 1 PM–4 PM Thurs (reception closes at 3 PM). Clsd national and New Year hols.

Access: In front of Kasumigaseki Stn, Exit B1 (Marunouchi, Chiyoda, and Hibiya lines).

■ Immigration Information

IMMIGRATION INFORMATION CENTER

東京入国管理局インフォメーション センター

(Tokyo Nyukoku Kanrikyoku Infomation Senta)

> Tokyo Regional Immigration Bureau,
>
> Otemachi Common Government Office No. 1 Building, 2F
>
> 1–3–1 Otemachi, Chiyoda-ku, Tokyo 100–0004
>
> ☎ 3213–8523/7, 5458–0370 (Shibuya Branch Office)
>
> 東京都千代田区大手町1-3-1　大手町合同庁舎1号館2階　〒100-0004

Information regarding visa and immigration matters can be obtained here, and counseling is provided.

Hours: *English, Spanish, Portuguese, and Chinese*: 9:30 AM–noon and 1 AM–4 PM Mon–Fri. *Korean and Thai*: 9:30 AM–noon and 1 PM–4 PM Mon, Wed, and Fri. Clsd national hols.

Access: 1 min from Otemachi Stn, Exit C2 (various subway lines). Walk straight out from the station, cross the street, and make a left turn. It will be on the right side about halfway down the block.

■ Tax Consultation

TOKYO REGIONAL TAXATION BUREAU

国税局資料調査5課 (Kokuzeikyoku Shiryo Chosa 5-ka)

    Otemachi Common Government Office No. 2 Building, 3F

    1–3–2 Otemachi, Chiyoda-ku, Tokyo 100–0004

    ☎ 3216–6811 ext. 2472/5

    東京都千代田区大手町1-3-2大手町合同庁舎2号館3階　〒100-0004

English tax consultation is given for foreign workers in room 302.

Hours: 9 AM–noon and 1 PM–5 PM Mon–Fri.

Access: Across from Otemachi Stn, Exit C2 (various subway lines). Walk straight out from the station and cross the street. You will be in front of the building.

■ Counseling on Labor and Employment Matters

ADVISORY FOR FOREIGN WORKERS

東京労働基準局監督課 (Tokyo Rodo Kijunkyoku Kantoku-ka)

    Tokyo Labor Standards Office, Korakuen Kaikan Building, 3F

    1–7–11 Koraku, Bunkyo-ku, Tokyo 112–0004

    ☎ 3814–5311 ext. 326

    東京都文京区後楽1-7-11　後楽園会館3階　〒112–0004

English consultation is available to foreign workers on labor and employment matters.

Hours: 10–noon and 1–3 PM Mon, Tues, Thurs, and Fri.

Access: 5-min walk from Korakuen Stn, Exit 1 (Marunouchi and Nanboku lines). Turn right from the exit and walk between Tokyo Dome and the station building. In a few minutes you will see a street on the left that forms a "T" intersection in front of the Satellite Hotel. Cross over and walk down that street to the second building on the right.

LABOR ADVISORY SERVICE CENTER FOR FOREIGN WORKERS

Counseling in English is given to foreign workers by the Tokyo Metropolitan government between 2 PM and 4 PM at the following locations and days:

Chuo Labor Administration Office—Mon–Fri
(☎ 5543–6110)

Shibuya Labor Administration Office—Mon and Thurs
(☎ 3770–6110)

Shinagawa Labor Administration Office—Mon and Thurs
(☎ 3776–6110)

Shinjuku Labor Administration Office—Mon only
(☎ 3203–6110)

Tachikawa Labor Administration Office—Mon and Thurs
(☎ 0425–25–6110)

▪ Police Counseling

FOREIGNERS' HOTLINE
外国人ホットライン
Tokyo Metropolitan Police Department
警視庁（Keishicho）
　☎ 3503–8484

Consultation is provided regarding personal problems and matters requiring police protection, such as forced prostitution and violence. Help offered in English, French, German, Spanish, Portuguese, Russian, Chinese, Korean, Thai, Tagalog, Persian, and Urdu.
Hours: 8:30 AM–5:15 PM Mon–Fri. Clsd wknds and hols.

FREE SERVICES AND GIVEAWAYS

WELCOMING SERVICES

WELCOME FUROSHIKI ☎ 5472–7074
This is a free welcoming service for new arrivals to Japan. Just call them, and they will send someone to visit your home or office bearing gifts—useful information, maps, sample products, and material related to your new community—all smartly wrapped in a *furoshiki*, the traditional Japanese carrying cloth. During the one-hour visit, the person will be happy to answer any questions you may have about living in Japan.

KNOW BEFORE YOU GO—ROB'S JAPAN FAQ
(Frequently Asked Questions)

⊜ http://www.gol.com/jguide/rob.html

This is a valuable Internet site for people planning to go to Japan, for it anticipates your questions about the country and answers them. The free service is hosted by the Japan Web Guide and includes lots of useful information about flights and customs; getting set up in an apartment; banking and finance; mail; cars and transport; going home and so on.

GOVERNMENT SERVICES AND OFFERINGS

The metropolitan and local governments have a number of offerings to keep you informed and advised. The Tokyo government sponsors three Information Bureaus at Tokyo and Shinjuku Stations. (See Tourist and Travel Information above.) And the ward (*ku*) offices are plentiful sources—though often untapped—of helpful printed material and useful services.

Publications abound. The free *Living in Tokyo* guide answers many basic questions about day-to-day life and contains important telephones numbers (i.e., for emergency services and foreign embassies). It even includes a map of emergency refuge centers throughout the city, and a hard-to-find but easy-to-read map of all the subway and railway lines in Tokyo and its surrounding areas. It is an indispensable aid for those who like to explore on their own. Other publications cover cultural assets, festivals, events, museums, local customs, and the logistics of living in Japan. Each ward office carries detailed street maps of the surrounding area and other basic survival information.

Other free government offerings at the ward offices may include Japanese language and cultural classes, libraries, translation and guidance services, sightseeing tours, exhibitions, cultural exchanges, health services, sports programs and facilities, and assistance with housing. Check with the Public Relations Department or Foreign Residents Information Section at your ward office to see what it offers. The answers may surprise you!

NOTE: There may be a minimal expense connected with some of the mentioned services, such as an inexpensive text for free Japanese lessons.

FREE PUBLICATIONS

Free Newspapers, Magazines, Periodicals

Tokyo has a number of free English-language publications that contain interesting articles and stories—and are also excellent sources of information for what is going on in Tokyo. These can be found at the Tourist Information Center, major hotels, embassies, international schools, and many restaurants and stores frequented by Tokyo's expatriate community.

Look for *EL,* the *Tokyo Weekender,* and *The Nippon View. Tokyo Classified*, originally a weekly listing of classified ads, now contains feature stories as well. New free publications are appearing all the time. Keep your eyes open for them.

On Your Own in Japan

This delightful little book was written for newcomers and old-timers alike. Subtitled "Everything you need to know to survive and thrive," it is full of helpful little tips and important information. Published by ITJ-0041 (otherwise known as International Telecom Japan), it is available at no cost by calling ITJ's 24-hour toll-free customer service line at ☎ 0120–440–041.

The Japan Foundation Newsletter

This substantial monthly newsletter is offered free of charge to "individuals and organizations interested in Japanese Studies and international cultural exchange." It covers topics such as religion, economics, history, and culture in Japan. Book reviews and updates on foundation activities are regular features, too. (Also see ch 13, Libraries.) To obtain a subscription, please contact:

The Editor, The Japan Foundation Newsletter
Media Department, The Japan Foundation
ARK Mori Building, West Wing, 20F
1–12–32 Akasaka, Minato-ku, Tokyo 107–6090
☎ 5562–3532 (Media Dept)
東京都港区赤坂1-12-32　アーク森ビル西館20階
国際交流基金編集局　〒107-6090

Volunteering in Tokyo Area Directory

This directory lists over seventy nonprofit organizations that can use your help—right now. The environment, crisis support, human rights, education, and animal welfare are only some of the areas that this comprehensive volume explores. The book is free, but you are asked to send ¥390 in stamps to cover mailing costs to:

Volunteering in Tokyo Area Directory

c/o Jeanne Vass, 1–12–6–202 Shoto, Shibuya-ku, Tokyo 150–0046

☎ Fax: 3481–6667 or 3460–3689

東京都渋谷区松濤1-12-6-202 〒150-0046

Jeanne Vass方ロボランティアリスト請求

MIPRO Publications

For those interested in doing business in Japan, a number of helpful English booklets dealing with the Japanese market and the importation of foreign products are available from MIPRO (Manufactured Imports Promotion Organization). They are updated yearly and include not only facts and figures on Japan, but also interesting insights into the Japanese culture. For example, *Penetrating the Japanese Market* explores such topics as the Japanese gift market (big business in Japan), how to give an effective presentation to potential Japanese customers (i.e., what's really important), and an explanation of the Japanese style of communicating—such as understanding the possible meanings of silence and the word *hai* (yes).

Some other publications available in English are *A Survey on Consumer's Awareness of Imported Goods, The Role of Imports under the Strong Yen and Changes of the Distribution System,* and a series entitled *Information on Best Selling Products* (covering toys, women's wear, men's wear, tableware, and other topics). The organization also sponsors trade fairs and workshops. For more information regarding its offerings, contact:

MIPRO

ミプロ

World Import Mart Building, 6F

3–1–3 Higashi Ikebukuro, Toshima-ku, Tokyo 170–6006
☎ 3984–5960 (some English spoken). Fax: 3984–4205
東京都豊島区西池袋3-1-3　ワールド インポートマート6階
〒170-6006

Japan National Tourist Organization

The Tourist Information Center (TIC) is a primary source for printed information on free things to do in and around Tokyo and throughout the country. (See Tourist and Travel Information above.)

Government Office Publications

Tokyo ward (*ku*) and city government offices stock a number of valuable publications in English and other languages. Check with their public relations and foreign residents sections for booklets, maps, pamphlets, and newsletters that cover such topics as how things work in Tokyo, general safety tips, earthquake emergency procedures, and cultural assets and events—and they sometimes supply a bag to carry it all home in! (See Government Services and Offerings above.)

FREE CLASSIFIED ADS

The Daily Yomiuri offers free classified listings in their Wednesday "Reader to Reader Section" and *The Japan Times* runs free recycle ads. *Tokyo Classified* lists noncommercial and employment ads at no charge. The *Tokyo Journal* prints information on organizations and their events gratis. And don't forget about the free advertising on bulletin boards (see below).

BULLETIN BOARDS

As a free service to the foreign community, bulletin boards have been set up at foreign-food supermarkets, churches, and other places where the foreign population congregates. Those who wish to post a notice, an announcement, or an advertisement may do so free of charge.

I adore bulletin boards. No matter how much of a hurry I may be in, I cannot help but pause for a look each time I spot one. "Read me, read me," it seems to chant silently. I quickly glance over the usual listings of sayonara sales, language lessons, and roommates wanted in search of the real treasures—the unexpected.

Sometimes I am rewarded. Once I found a curious request for people to participate in a "living art" performance at one of Tokyo's major art museums. The plan was for people from forty nations to concurrently shout out a series of numbers in their native tongues—all under the direction of an artist. It was scheduled to be part of a show that featured—you guessed it—numbers! So you see, in addition to being a good source of information, bulletin boards can also be signpost to new experiences.

SHOPPING SERVICES

ISETAN DEPARTMENT STORE "I CLUB"

伊勢丹アイ クラブ

Foreign Customer Service, 7F
3–14–1 Shinjuku, Shinjuku-ku, Tokyo 160–8011
☎ 3225–2514
東京都新宿区新宿3-14-17　〒160-8011

There was a time when just about every major department store featured a service to assist foreign residents and visitors. Discounts, shopping assistance, and other special services were among their offerings. Today Isetan stands pretty much alone with its "I Club," a valuable service for the international community in Tokyo.

To become a member of the "I Club," all you have to do is fill out a simple form. Membership is free and has lots of nice little perks built in—like store discounts, two hours of free parking each time you visit, a monthly English newsletter, and complimentary tickets to their Museum of Art—which features some of the best shows in Tokyo. (See ch 10.)

Hours: Store hours are 10 AM–7:30 PM. Clsd some Wed.
Access: On Shinjuku-dori, above Shinjuku-sanchome Stn, Exit B5

(Marunouchi or Toei Shinjuku lines), or a 5-min walk from JR Shinjuku Stn (Yamanote and other lines).

■ Free Delivery

National Azabu (☎ 3442–3186/7) and **Meidi-ya Hiroo** (☎ 3444–6221), both in Hiroo (Hiroo Stn, Hibiya Line), offer free delivery services. Call for specific information. Validated parking is also available.

FREE TOY REPAIR

SHOHISHA CENTER
消費者センター
> Oi 1-chome Building, 1F
> 1–14–1 Oi, Shinagawa-ku, Tokyo 140–0014
> ☎ 5718–7181
> 東京都品川区大井1-14-1 大井1丁目共同ビル1階 〒140-0014

Toy Hospital Volunteers repair broken toys for free at the Shohisha Center every Saturday afternoon. Most can be fixed the same day. Sponsored by the Shinagawa Ward Office.

Hours: 1 PM–3:30 PM Sat, except hols. Clsd New Year hols.
Access: 4 min from JR Oimachi Stn, West Exit (Keihin Tohoku Line). Cross the street in front of station and walk right until you reach Sumitomo Bank at the 2nd light. It is in the next building.

FREE FURNITURE AND APPLIANCES

Foreign Language Publications
Check *Tokyo Classified*'s "For Free" section and *The Daily Yomiuri* "Giveaways" column in their Wednesday Reader-to-Reader Market classified ads. A wide variety of items, such as pianos, computers, refrigerators, heaters, beds, VCRs, stereos and even aquariums have been among their listings.

Kurukuru Recycle Information Magazine
Furniture and electric appliances available for free are listed in this magazine, which is published in Japanese on the first day of each month for ward residents and available in Shinagawa at

the ward (*ku*) office, libraries, post offices, and culture center. If you cannot find a copy, drop by the Shohisha Center (listed on the facing page) for a copy. Please note that not all the items are free. For obvious reasons, it is best to call at the beginning of the month when the magazine first comes out. Some English is spoken, but it would be better to have someone call in Japanese.

FREE PETS

The foreign population of Tokyo is pretty transient, and people don't want their Tokyo pets to go through a long quarantine period when they return home. Consequently there are always a lot of animals available for the asking.

Check the classified sections of the English-language publications for a "Homes for Pets" or similarly named section. Adoption notices complete with photos (guaranteed to tug at your heart) can often be found on bulletin boards. Veterinarian offices sometimes have information on animals that are being given away, too. Dogs, cats, rabbits, guinea pigs, and other small animals can usually be found listed somewhere sooner or later, often with all the needed accessories included.

Dobutsutachi no Kai is a volunteer animal welfare organization that offers neutered/spayed, vaccinated, and vet-checked animals to responsible people. Pets can be adopted permanently, or they are sometimes given out for temporary "foster care." Call ☎ 3441–2475 for information (run by volunteers so hours are irregular) or fax Renate Herold in English, German, or Japanese at ☎ 0425–83–2908 and someone will get back to you.

NOTE: They will also neuter or spay your present dog or cat for a very small fee—usually an expensive process in Japan.

Japan Society for the Prevention of Cruelty to Animals/ JSPCA (Nihon Dobutsu Aigo Kyokai) is located in Minato-ku and keeps picture books of animals that are available for adoption. Call ☎ 3409–1821 in Japanese, 10 AM–4:30 PM weekdays.

The Tokyo Metropolitan Government Animal Protection Center (Tokyo-to Dobutsu Kanri Jimusho Dobutsu Aigo Senta) in Ota-ku gives puppies and kittens away to Tokyo residents who take their Wednesday course on caring for pets. You can adopt an animal from the following day. Call ☎ 3790–0861 in Japanese on weekdays.

FREE IDENTITY PHOTOS

Did you know that the photos you need for your Alien Registration Card can be taken free of charge at the Regional Immigration Bureau, its branch offices, or local immigration stations? I had mine done at the Otemachi Bureau of Immigration—in color on a digital camera. And the clerk didn't even print out the image until I was happy with the results!

GIVEAWAYS

Somebody is always giving something away in Tokyo. The foreign publications are a constant source of freebies, usually obtainable by simply sending in a postcard. It might be smart to have a stock of postcards ready to mail in for all the goodies that interest you. Winners are chosen by lottery if the demand exceeds the supply.

Most of the English-language newspapers feature giveaways. Frequently offered by companies to celebrate an event or to promote a new product, they can range from a simple telephone card to a ¥780,000 silk kimono. (This was an actual giveaway to commemorate a ladies golf tournament.) *The Asahi Evening News* features a "Presents" column in their Thursday Weekend Bulletin Board, and the *Mainichi Daily News* runs a "Winners Wanted" box in their Monday Japanofile Section. *The Daily Yomiuri* has a "Giveaways" Column in their Wednesday Classified Reader-to-Reader Market that offers furniture and such. The "Giveaways" and "Miscellaneous" columns (the latter is in their Thursday Weekend Section) offer tickets and other freebies and sometimes interesting little tidbits like free entrance to a major amusement park for people willing to dress in a *yukata* and dance for one minute in front of the park's main gate. Hey, why not?

The *Tokyo Journal* monthly magazine has a page devoted to free goodies for its readers every issue. T-shirts, books, albums, haircuts, whiskey, beer, and perfume are often among the monthly choices.

The *Tokyo Weekender* on occasion announces giveaways. When Burger King opened its first drive-through restaurant in Japan, they gave away meal coupons—and Perche Men's Shop (specializing in large men's sizes) offered large-sized sweaters in four colors to the first twenty people who brought in copies of the *Weekender*.

City Life News contains a "Freebies" column, a "Contests" column, and other offerings throughout the magazine—a free culture class on *Kuruma ningyo* (traditional Japanese puppetry on wheels) was one of these. Sometimes they offer free giveaways in articles introducing various areas of Japan to their readers.

Tokyo Classified has lots of freebies as well. Furniture and other giveaways are listed in their "For Free" column—and unique free opportunities, like aikido practice, traditional Japanese music lessons, and training on the abacus can often be found in other columns, such as "Learning." Language exchange lessons are listed in the "Language Exchange" column.

InterFM Radio Station (76.1 FM) gives away goodies, too—sometimes very substantial ones. A free trip to Hawaii for two was awarded to one lucky listener, and another time they even gave away cars! Listen for details.

The ultimate giveaway—and one that provides instant gratification—is the free tissue handed out around town. As long as you are in Tokyo you will never have to buy another little pack of tissues, I promise. For they are a very popular form of advertising in Japan—perfectly suited to a country that has no paper towels in the bathrooms and often no toilet paper in the public toilets. Needless to say, tissues can come in very, very handy. The best places to cash in on this free tissue bonanza are just outside the major train stations. Here, whatever the weather, great numbers of "tissue people" await you—eager to give you something that will make your life happier, easier, and definitely more comfortable. Now who could ask for anything nicer.

HELP!

2

CREATING
YOUR OWN
ITINERARY

FOR A SHORT STAY

Tsukiji Fish Market • Asakusa/Shitamachi Area • View from the Tokyo Metropolitan Government Building • Visit a Sumo Stable • Pay a Call on a Japanese Family • East Garden of the Imperial Palace • Golden Gai

FOR BUSINESS PEOPLE

Tsukiji Fish Market • The National Diet (Parliament) • The Tokyo Stock Exchange • Technology in Japan • Japanese Auto Showrooms • Communications in Japan • Talks on Asia and Related International Matters

FOR FAMILIES WITH YOUNGSTERS

Entertainment Spaces • Odaiba Beach Area • View from the Top of the Tokyo Metropolitan Government Building • Bike Riding and Other Sports • Spend Some Time in a Park • Festivals

FOR NATURE ENTHUSIASTS

Exquisite Gardens • Wonderful Parks • Mt. Takao • Tama River • Urban Oasis

FOR HISTORY BUFFS

Shitamachi/Asakusa Area • Sengakuji Temple • The Imperial Palace/East Garden • Remains of the Tokugawa Shogun's Castle • Fort at the Odaiba Beach Area • Kodaira Furusato Mura • Golden Gai • Japanese Festivals

FOR ART LOVERS

Art Galleries, Public Art, and Photo Exhibitions • Art Museums • Museums of Ueno Park • Buddhist Art of Gokokuji Temple • Archaeology • Architecture • Music and Dance • Antiques, Folkcrafts, and Flea Markets • Prefectural Showrooms • Visit Traditional Craftsmen

FOR SPORTS FANS

Sumo • Judo, Karate, Aikido and Other Martial Arts • Cycling, Running, and Horses

INTRODUCTION

*G*etting to know a city is a personal thing. It should be done at one's own pace, which can vary greatly from person to person. For example, one person might want to visit many places in a short period, while another may prefer to spend a whole day at one destination. Some may have a few weeks, others a few days, and still others just a few hours to spend exploring. Consequently, rather than create rigid itineraries and schedules, I have suggested a variety of choices for specific categories of interest. This frees you to mix-and-match according to your own timetable, tastes, needs, feelings at the moment, and—not to forget that very unpredictable variable— the weather.

Before you begin visiting the sites, I strongly recommend that you check with the Tourist Information Center. They have a recorded hotline that tells you what is currently on, and two numbers where you can speak to staff and have your questions answered. If you visit their office at Yurakucho Station (or Narita Airport upon your arrival), you can pick up brochures, booklets, maps, schedules, and lots of other useful information about Tokyo and the rest of the country as well. (See ch 1—Introduction and Travel and Tourism sections for more details.) Good luck and happy exploring!

FOR A SHORT STAY

Tsukiji Fish Market
An early-morning adventure to the liveliest spot in town before dawn breaks (ch 3).

Shitamachi/Asakusa Area
History lives. A visit back to old Edo before it became Tokyo (ch 3).

View from the Tokyo Metropolitan Government Building
Just one of over a dozen locations throughout the city where you can take in the vast Tokyo area from high above (ch 16).

Visit a Sumo Stable
Yes, you can actually go and watch the famed wrestlers work out just about any morning they are in town. You just need to call and make a reservation (ch 4).

Pay a Call on a Japanese Family
A rare treat. Spend an evening experiencing the Japanese domestic lifestyle first-hand (ch 3).

East Garden of the Imperial Palace
Officially part of the Imperial Palace grounds, this beautiful and historic garden is open to the public. Don't miss the ruins of the Tokugawa shogun's castle and the Museum of the Imperial Collection (ch 7 and 10).

Golden Gai
Rows of tiny, traditional drinking establishments nestled in a very unlikely location. The real thing (ch 3).

FOR BUSINESS PEOPLE

Tsukiji Fish Market
The most happening place in town when you wake up at 5 AM with jetlag (ch 3).

The National Diet (Parliament)

See where the laws of Japan are made and the room where the emperor meets with the speakers of both houses before each Diet session convenes (ch 3).

The Tokyo Stock Exchange

Watch the hubbub of the stock market going on below from the visitors' mezzanine (ch 3).

Technology in Japan

There are a number of showrooms where you can see and explore state-of-the-art Japanese technology. Here are some: **TEPIA Foundation Showroom and Library** (ch 13 and 15), **NEC Computer Showroom C&C Plaza** (ch 15), and **Sony Building** (ch 15). And don't forget about **Akihabara** (Tokyo's electronics carnival-land), where you can play with all the latest gadgets that are on display. Just go to Akihabara Station and follow the crowd into "Electric City." (See ch 3–Ueno Park.)

Japanese Auto Showrooms

Sit inside the latest model cars and mount a motorcycle for size, too (ch 15).

Communications in Japan

The *Asahi Shinbun* newspaper offers an English tour of their facilities, but bring along an interpreter to see the TV stations (ch 3).

Talks on Asia and Related International Matters

Why not check out lectures, classes, or events going on while you are in Tokyo (ch 12).

FOR FAMILIES WITH YOUNGSTERS

Entertainment Spaces

There are great places in Tokyo for kids to learn about technology and crafts in a fun way. Some of these are **Fujita Vente Amusement Space** (ch 15), **Tokyo Metropolitan Children's Hall** (ch 10), **Amlux Toyota Auto Salon Showroom** (ch 15), **Sony Building** (ch 15), and the **TEPIA Foundation Showroom** (ch 15).

Odaiba Beach Area

Run on the beach and watch people windsurfing, with the Rainbow Bridge spanning Tokyo Bay as a backdrop. Stunning views, great atmosphere, and more (ch 3).

View from the top of the Tokyo Metropolitan Government Building or another of Tokyo's skyscrapers. The kids (and grownups too) will marvel at the vastness of the city as it stretches out seemingly forever in every direction (ch 16).

Bike Riding and Other Sports

You can pedal past the Imperial Palace, along the Tama River, or through a park on a free loan bicycle. Then you can watch some martial arts sessions—or take a pony ride. (All in ch 4.)

Spend Some Time in a Park

Tokyo's parks are wonderful places. There are bird sanctuaries, animals, lakes, beaches, historic structures, and more (ch 6).

Festivals

Be sure to check with the Tourist Information Center to see if there is a festival or special event going on (ch 1 and 5)!

FOR NATURE ENTHUSIASTS

Nature lovers are in luck. For Tokyo has **exquisite gardens** (ch 7), **wonderful parks** (ch 6), and a mountain with hiking trails—**Mt. Takao** (ch 3). Or you may wish to take a peaceful bike ride along the **Tama River** (ch 4).

A very special indoor space you might want to check out is **Fujita Vente Urban Oasis** (ch 15).

FOR HISTORY BUFFS

Tokyo is packed with history that could fill volumes, but you might want to check out some of the following as starters: **Shitamachi/Asakusa Area** (ch 3), **Sengakuji temple**—and a number of other temples and shrines (ch 8), **The Imperial Palace/East Garden** (ch 3 and 7), **Remains of the**

Tokugawa Shogun's Castle (ch 3 and 7) and his **Fort at the Odaiba Beach Area** (ch 3), **Kodaira Furusato Park** (ch 6), **Golden Gai** (ch 3). And by all means, check with the Tourist Information Office (ch 1) right away to see if there are any **Japanese festivals** (ch 5) going on during your stay. These wonderful celebrations and the events that accompany them are a living history in themselves.

FOR ART LOVERS

Information on **art galleries, public art, and photo exhibitions** can be found in chapter 14, while **art museums** are listed in chapter 10. The **Museums of Ueno Park** are described in chapter 3, and the unique **Informuse** is in chapter 15. And don't miss the incredible **Buddhist Art of Gokokuji temple** and that of other temples and shrines (ch 8).

Impressive collections can be seen at the **archaeology museums** of International Christian University (ICU), Kokugakuin University, and Meiji University. All are described in chapter 10.

Architecture fans are sure to enjoy **Gallery Ma** (ch 14), and the **TOTO Aqua Library** in the same building (ch 13) has a nice collection of international architecture magazines and other publications. The **Tokyo Gas Ginza Pocket Park Showroom** (ch 15) also features architectural-based exhibitions, and carries magazines on architecture dating back to the 1960s and 1970s. Some well-known structures created by famous **Japanese architect Kenzo Tange** are the unusual stainless-steel-and-concrete St. Mary's Cathedral (ch 8), the Tokyo Metropolitan Building—be sure to catch the view from there (ch 16)—and the Fuji TV Headquarters Building in the popular Odaiba Beach Area (ch 3).

Music and dance fans will be interested in information on **performances and the arts** (ch 11), and should see the fabulous **Musical Instruments Museum** at Musashino Academia Musicae (ch 10). If you are going to Ueno Park (ch 3), stop in at the **Tokyo Metropolitan Festival Hall Music Library and**

Listening Rooms. And do check to see if there are any **festivals** currently on (ch 5). The **Theater Museum** at Waseda University (ch 10) is the center for information on theater in Japan.

There is a lot of information on **antiques, folkcrafts, and flea markets** in ch 9. See original crafts from the various areas of Japan at the **prefectural showrooms** (ch 15). Or you can **visit traditional craftsmen** in their workshops or homes (see Little Museums of Sumida-ku in ch 3).

FOR SPORTS FANS

Did you know that you can go and watch **sumo** wrestlers working out at the stables where they live? And that there are plenty of opportunities in Tokyo to attend **martial arts** demonstrations and practices year round? There is lots of information on **cycling** and **horses**, too. Choose from your favorite **martial arts and sports** (ch 4).

3

SOME VERY
SPECIAL
DESTINATIONS

THE HEART OF THE JAPANESE PEOPLE

- *The Imperial Palace*
  Where the Japanese Emperor and Empress Reside
- *Japanese Home Visit*
  Experience Domestic Life
- *Ueno Park*
  Japan's Very First—and One of Its Most Important Parks

THE POWER CENTERS

- *The National Diet (Parliament)*
  Home of Japanese Government
- *Tokyo Stock Exchange*
  Monetary Center of Japan
- *Communications in Japan: Asahi, Mainichi, Yomiuri, and Fuji*
  Japanese Print and Broadcast Media
- *Tsukiji—Tokyo Central Wholesale Fish Market*
  Fish Power!

EXCURSIONS

Big Stuff

- *Daibutsu of Jorenji*
  Tokyo's Very Own Big Buddha
- *Go Climb a Mountain*
  Mt. Takao and Takao Natural Science Museum

Small Stuff

- *Little Museums of Sumida-ku*
  See Traditional Craftsmen at Work
- *Golden Gai*
  Step into Another Time of Tinier Places
- *Department Store Basements*
  Lots of Little Things to Try Here

Old Stuff

- *Shitamachi/Asakusa*
  Explore the Streets of Old Edo

New Stuff

- *Yebisu Garden Place*
  Playground for Grown-ups
- *Odaiba Beach Area*
  Could This Really Be Tokyo?

INTRODUCTION

*Y*es, I understand that everything in Tokyo is special and it may seem redundant to choose a few things and label them as such. But these places are unique—most of them don't fit into any of the general categories in the book. (I guess that's part of what makes them special.)

I would like to think of the offerings in this chapter as being among some of the most intriguing experiences available in the city. I hope you will partake of them at your leisure. With the possible exception of Golden Gai, most of them should be around for a while.

THE HEART OF THE JAPANESE PEOPLE

THE IMPERIAL PALACE
皇居 （Kokyo）

Administrative Section, Maintenance and Works Division
Imperial Household, 1–1 Chiyoda-ku, Tokyo 100–8111
☎ 3213–1111 ext. 485 (Visitor's Office, Sankan-gakari)
東京都千代田区1-1　宮内庁管理部管理課参観係　〒100-8111

There is a certain mystique connected with places considered "forbidden" or "off limits" to the common person. Such is the case with the Imperial Palace. Surrounded by thick stone walls and a number of moats, it is a well-guarded fortress few are allowed to penetrate. And understandably so, for this is the home of the emperor and empress of Japan. So you can imagine my surprise when I discovered that it was possible to tour this modern-day "Forbidden City" that has origins dating all the way back to the 15th century.

Japan's imperial residence was relocated from the ancient capital of Kyoto to its present location in Edo (today's Tokyo) after the Meiji Restoration of 1868 and the overthrow of the Tokugawa shogunate. A new Imperial Palace was built upon the grounds of the former shogun's castle—said to have been one of the largest in the world at the time. Ruins of this castle can still be seen on the palace grounds today, adding an interesting historical twist to the visit.

The one-and-a-half-hour excursion begins with an introductory video (in Japanese with English subtitles) that shows the interior of the palace and the various ceremonies and events held there. A walk through the palace grounds follows. Chowaden Hall—from where the imperial family greets visitors twice a year (on the emperor's birthday and Jan 2)—is on the itinerary, as is a glimpse of the Imperial Household Agency and other official buildings. A stroll through the East Garden is also included, where a small wooden ceremonial structure used in the emperor's 1990 Daijosai ceremony (one of the Shinto rituals required for ascending the throne) still stands.

Some of the Edo-period (1600–1868) sights are Fujimi-yagura, a beautifully preserved three-story castle keep dating from 1659; Nishihane-bashi, the bridge marking the inner citadel of the shogun's castle that could be drawn up in defense against invading enemies; and Honmaru Tenshukaku-ato, the foundation for the castle's central tower, which can be climbed and explored.

If you are not able to take the tour, the garden and its historical sites are open to the public year round (see ch 7). The palace atmosphere can also be enjoyed by cycling alongside it on free loan bicycles on Sundays—or jogging around it anytime (see ch 4 for both).

Procedure: Arranging for a tour is not a simple process—nor should it be—but it is possible. Call the Palace Visitors Office at ☎ 3213–1111 ext. 485 to make a reservation. (English is okay.) Then, at least one day in advance, go to the Head Office of the Imperial Household (through the Sakashitamon Gate) to fill out an application and receive your permit. Bring your passport along. You will be given further instructions and a map at that time.

NOTE: The tour is in Japanese, but an English pamphlet with a map and photos is given to foreign visitors. Photography is permitted, but smoking is not.

Hours: The Imperial Household Agency is open 9 AM–4:30 PM Mon–Fri. Clsd Sat, Sun, hols, and official agency occasions.

Access: Sakashitamon Gate is a 10-min walk from Tokyo Stn, Marunouchi Central Exit (Yamanote and other lines), or a 5-min walk from either Nijubashimae Stn, Exit 6 (Chiyoda Line) or Otemachi Stn, Exit D2 (Hanzomon, Mita, Marunouchi, or Tozai lines).

JAPANESE HOME VISIT
Tourist Information Center (TIC)
国際観光振興会 （Kokusai Kanko Shinko-kai）
　　　(Japan National Tourist Organization)
　　　Tokyo International Forum Building, B1
　　　3–5–1 Marunouchi, Chiyoda-ku, Tokyo 100–0005

☎ 3201–3331
東京都千代田区丸ノ内3-5-1　東京国際フォーラム地下1階
〒100-0005
⊜ JNTO: http://www.jnto.go.jp.

Many people live in Japan for years without ever seeing the inside of a Japanese home. They just accept this as being the nature of the culture. However, if you are interested in learning more about the domestic lifestyle of the Japanese, I have some good news for you. It is possible to visit a Japanese family in their home. The Tourist Information Center can arrange it for you—and all they ask is at least one day's notice. Here's how it works.

Just fill out a form at the TIC between the hours of 9 AM and 4 PM, Mon–Fri. Applications are not accepted after 4 PM because it takes about an hour to make the arrangements and prepare the information regarding your host family. You and up to three friends (Japanese homes are small) will be welcomed by a Japanese family on the evening of your choice. This generally takes place after dinner, from about 7 PM to 9 PM. There is no set schedule or format; each family welcomes guests in their own way. But you will get a first-hand glimpse of domestic Japanese life—a rare treat in this country.

The Japanese home visit is often perceived as being only open to short-term visitors in Japan, but the tourist office says that long-termers are just as welcome, since people who have been here for a while can often appreciate even more what a wonderful opportunity this is to gain personal insight into the culture—and to have some questions answered at the same time. English is the language generally spoken, but sometimes it might be possible to visit a family that speaks another language.

Note: Although there is no charge for the visit, it is customary to bring a small gift (perhaps something from your own country) for the host family.

Hours: TIC accepts applications for a home visit 9–12 AM and 2–4 PM on wkdys (except national hols).

Access: The Tokyo TIC is directly across from JR Yurakucho Stn, Kokusai (International) Forum Exit (Yamanote and Keihin Tohoku lines), and adjacent to Exit A4b of the Yurakucho subway line at the same station. It is also a 5-min walk via the underground concourse from Tokyo Stn (Yamanote and other lines). Exit from the Marunouchi side of the station, then follow the signs to the Keiyo Line. When you reach it, a sign will direct you up the staircase to your right. TIC is on your immediate right as you enter the Forum Building. For access from Hibiya Stn (Hibiya, Chiyoda, and Mita lines), follow the underground signs to the Yurakucho Line and take Exit A4b.

UENO PARK

上野公園 （Ueno Koen）

> 5–20 Ueno Koen, Taito-ku, Tokyo 110–0007
> ☎ 5685–1181 (Park Information Center)
> 3828–5644 (Park Office)
> 東京都台東区上野公園5-20　　〒110-0007

There is a plethora of free things to see and do in and around Ueno Park. You could easily spend several days here. Founded in 1873 as Japan's first city park, it is still one of the largest and most important in the country. To get the most from your visit, your first stop should be the **Park Information Center**, located at the main entrance to the park (across from JR Ueno Station). Their free color brochure, *Guide to Ueno Imperial Park,* contains pictures and descriptions of the park's main attractions, and their separate park map provides an easy-to-understand depiction of the area. Both are available in English. Two additional free guides that can be obtained beforehand are the TIC's *Walking Courses in Tokyo* leaflet that details a self-guided walking tour of Ueno Park and vicinity, and the colorful pamphlet, *Shitamachi—Guide for Sightseeing Around Asakusa, Ueno, Shitaya, and Yanaka*. The former is available at the main Tourist Information Center (ch 1), and generally both can be found at the Asakusa Cultural and Sightseeing Center (see Shitamachi below).

Historical Aspects: Ueno Park has quite an interesting history. It was founded on the grounds of the former Kaneiji temple, the powerful guardian temple against evil spirits for the Tokugawa shogun's center of power—Edo. In its heyday, this huge and influential temple complex was made up of numerous structures that included impressive mausoleums of deceased shoguns as well as thirty-six subsidiary temples. Most of Kaneiji

SOME VERY
SPECIAL
DESTINATIONS

was destroyed during the 1868 Meiji Restoration that marked the overthrow of the Tokugawa shogunate, but the structures that were left standing—**Kiyomizu Kannondo temple,** the **five-storied pagoda**, and **Toshogu shrine** (dedicated to the first Tokugawa shogun)—can still be visited today (see ch 8). And don't forget about **Bentendo temple** located in the middle of Ueno Park's Shinobazu Pond—it is dedicated to the Indian goddess of good fortune, happiness, and prosperity.

Cultural Aspects: Today Ueno Park serves as a major center for the arts, for many of its attractions are cultural in nature. At the main entrance (across from the Park Information Center) is the **Tokyo Metropolitan Festival Hall** (Tokyo Bunka Kaikan). On its 4F are great free **music library and listening rooms** (see ch 13) where you can read music-related books (1,000 in foreign languages), play records and CDs, or watch recorded performances in their thirty-station listening room. Just beyond the hall is the **Japan Art Academy**, a national honorary institute that holds free exhibitions of works by people who have been presented special awards in the arts (see ch 10). Next in line is the **Ueno Royal Museum,** free about 20–30% of the time when *shodo* (Japanese calligraphy) exhibitions are held. Admission is charged at other times. Beyond **the Grand Fountain** in the center of the park is the **Tokyo Metropolitan Art Museum.** It holds numerous exhibitions by art groups, many of which are free (see ch 10). On its first floor is the **art library** where you can sit and browse through 3,000 beautifully illustrated art books (see ch 13). Behind this museum is the **art museum of the prestigious Tokyo National University of Fine Arts and Music** (see ch 10). Still on the campus, but across the road, free **classical music concerts** are given Thursday mornings mid-May through mid-July—and at other times throughout the year as well (see ch 11).

Other Attractions: Nature is an important part of Ueno Park too. The lovely **Shinobazu Pond** provides a home for water birds, turtles, and lotus plants, and in one section you can rent boats to take out for a row or paddle. Each spring, 1,300 cherry trees burst into bloom along the wide path that runs through the

park on its way to the **Grand Fountain**. Azaleas, peonies, and other flowers soon follow. There is even a **Greenery Information Bureau** located behind the Park Information Center that holds nature-related art exhibitions and periodically shows nature videos. It also contains a topographical model of the entire Ueno Park area.

Each March/April the park is the site of the biggest **cherry blossom bash** you could ever imagine, and from mid-July to mid-August it hosts the grand **Ueno Summer Festival**, which features a seemingly endless string of free entertainment, including parades, traditional dances, and a nightly series of outdoor concerts at the Waterside Music Hall alongside Shinobazu Pond (see ch 5).

A well-known meeting place on the upper level of the park is the **bronze statue of General Takamori Saigo**, famous Meiji-period (1868–1912) politician and a leader of the revolt against the Tokugawa shogun. Unlike many statues of warriors who are portrayed on horseback in full military regalia, he is depicted in a very casual pose wearing a *yukata* (summer kimono) and standing next to his dog.

The area surrounding the park contains many things to do as well. Across the street is **Ameya Yokocho (Ameyoko) Street**—a colorful area of narrow shopping lanes where you can see vendors hawking everything from fresh fish to watches at bargain prices. And just down Chuo-dori (the main street) is the popular discount electronics carnival-land of **Akihabara**, where you can try out all the latest gadgets in many of its 600 stores.

The Ueno Park area is part of Shitamachi, the preserved "downtown" section of the city (see Old Stuff—Shitamachi below for more information on this fascinating part of Tokyo).

Hours: **Ueno Park**—5 AM–11 PM daily. **Ueno Park Information Center**—9 AM–6 PM daily (☎ 5685–1181). **Tokyo Metropolitan Festival Hall Music Library and Listening Rooms**—12 noon–8 PM Tues–Sat, and noon–5 PM Sun and hols. Clsd Mon, 2nd Sun, and sometimes other Sun too, so check first (☎ 3828–2111). **Japan Art Academy**—10 AM–noon and 1 PM–4 PM between July and Feb when shows are on. Call for days open ☎ 3821–7191. **Ueno Royal Museum**—10 AM–5 PM daily (enter by 4:30 PM). Clsd New Year hols (☎ 3833–4191). **Tokyo Metropolitan Art Museum and Art Reading Room**—10 AM–5 PM Mon–Sat. 9 AM–5 PM Sun and hols. Clsd 3rd Mon (Tues if hol), and New Year and museum hols ☎ 3823–6921. **Tokyo University of Fine Arts and Music-Art Museum**—10 AM–4 PM Mon–Fri. Usually clsd on wknds, Jan–March, and national and school hols (☎ 5685–7744, museum). **Greenery Information Bureau**—9 AM–5 PM. Clsd Mon (Tues if hol) ☎ 5685–3330.

Access: The main entrance to the park is across from JR Ueno Stn, Ueno Park Exit (Yamanote and other lines). Also accessible via Ueno Stn on the Ginza and Hibiya lines.

THE POWER CENTERS

THE NATIONAL DIET

国会議事堂（Kokkai Gijido）

1–7–1 Nagatacho, Chiyoda-ku, Tokyo 100–8961

☎ 3581–3111 Ask for Tour Information (Kengaku Annai)

東京都千代田区永田町1-7-1　〒100-8961

"The Diet shall be the highest organ of state power," declares the Japanese constitution. As I stood in front of this commanding building, gazing up at its high central tower flanked by two symmetrical wings, it was exciting to think that soon I would be walking around inside the political center of one of the world's major economic powers. For I was on my way to tour Japan's National Diet (Parliament) Building, home of the legislative branch of the Japanese government.

Established in 1890 under the Meiji government (1868–1912) following the overthrow of the Tokugawa shogunate, this lawmaking body was originally called the Imperial Diet. It consisted of aristocratic and appointed members who served as advisors to the emperor. But following World War II, a new constitution went into effect that created the National Diet in its current form.

Today the Diet is composed of two elected houses—the House of Representatives (500-member lower house) and the House of Councilors (252-member upper house).

It is in this building that the laws of Japan are established, the prime minister is chosen from among its members, and both domestic and international affairs are planned and carried out. A special invitation is needed to visit the House of Representatives, but the House of Councilors (a mirror-image wing that contains a few extra features) will be happy to accommodate you on a tour when it is not in session. The ordinary sessions begin each January and last for approximately 150 days, while extraordinary and special sessions may be called at any time.

On the tour, the layout of the building and the basics of Japanese government are explained while you sit and absorb the architectural details of the House of Councilors' chamber—the magnificently carved zelkova wood walls and the stained glass ceiling fashioned in an arabesque design, among others. You will be shown the location of the throne from which the emperor convenes each new session, along with the seats of political leaders and the balconies for the imperial family and important state guests. The throne and special balconies are unique to the House of Councilors Chamber, and are not found in the House of Representatives.

Other areas you will see are the large Central Hall that lies under the Central Tower, the Grand Imperial Staircase, and the special room where the emperor meets with the speakers of both houses before each Diet session convenes. Among the features of this luxurious room are a thick, hand-woven silk carpet and gold-thread brocade–covered walls. The entire building was created from domestic materials, and took 17 years to complete. Opened in 1936, it is over 206 m (675 ft) long, has a 65.5-m (215-ft) central tower, and contains 53,466 sq m (577,433 sq ft) of floor space.

An interesting fact I learned on the tour was that one of the members of the House of Councilors represented Japan in seven Olympics between 1988 and 1996—in both speed skating and bicycling—and even brought back a bronze medal from

Albertville in 1992. This Diet member's name? Seiko Hashimoto—
a Japanese woman.

NOTE: A visit to the nearby Parliamentary Museum (see ch 10) is a nice supplement to your tour. It is located in the Diet Front Park, which also contains both Japanese and Western gardens open to the public. The National Diet Library (see ch 13) is also in the area, and is open to everyone over twenty years of age.

Procedure: You may go between 9:30 AM and 4 PM Mon–Fri, fill out an application form, and take a tour on days when the Diet is not in session, but it is best to call the above number to make sure tours are being offered that day. Depending on the availability of English-speaking staff, you will either be assigned a guide or given an audio tape tour of the building. Each tour lasts about 40 min. Groups of twenty or more need to make a reservation.

Hours: 9:30 AM–4 PM Mon–Fri, except when the Diet is in session. Clsd on wknds and national hols.

Access: The tour entrance for the House of Councilors is located in the rear of the National Diet building, across the street from Exit 1 of Nagatacho Stn (Yurakucho and Hanzomon lines). If traveling by the Hanzomon Line, exit through the Yurakucho Line to reach Exit 1.

THE TOKYO STOCK EXCHANGE

東京証券取引所 (Tokyo Shoken Torihikijo)

2–1 Nihonbashi Kabutocho, Chuo-ku, Tokyo 103–8220

☎ 3666–0141 (Visitors Section, Office of Public Relations)

東京都中央区日本橋兜町2-1 〒103-8220

Although the frantic pace of the "bubble economy" is no longer the driving force behind the Tokyo Stock Exchange, it is still a very exciting place to visit. For it is one of the "big three" stock exchanges in the world, alongside those of London and New York.

It is possible to pay a visit on your own if you would like. Or you can join a one-hour English tour if you make a reservation. The tour begins with an English introductory video that explains the basics of trading in a very clear and precise manner. This is followed by a visit to the trading floor mezzanine where the flurry of activities going on below can be viewed. The frantic hand signaling, the constantly changing numbers on the display boards, and the jobs of the 800 or so workers in various-colored jackets scurrying around the floor are explained, and questions regarding them are answered.

Next is a visit to the computer-assisted trading rooms, where the activities of all but the 150 most active stocks are handled. The tour then goes to the second floor Exhibition Plaza, where you will be given a brief introduction to its offerings, then turned loose to explore on your own. I spent a lot of time in front of a wonderful lifesize robot that demonstrates the hand signals used on the trading floor—some of which were quite funny. There is also a 3-D "Air Vision" movie, a video library section, and a "Kabuto" puppet theater for children of all ages that answers basic questions about finance and the stock market. Many other bilingual interactive displays and games are located here too.

If you decide to visit the exchange on your own, you can still experience most of the features offered on the tour. The English introductory video is available at the Exhibition Plaza video library, and the workings of the stock trading floor are explained by telephone guides at the viewing stations in English, French, German, Chinese, Korean, and Japanese.

Flanking the information desk on the main floor are four bronze statues representing the major aspects of the Japanese economy: agriculture, commerce, manufacturing, and transportation/communications. In the Stock Exchange Museum on the same floor (see ch 10) you can learn about the history of the Japanese stock market and other interesting facts, such as the origin of the area's name—Kabuto-cho. It seems to have come from a rock resembling a helmet (*kabuto* in Japanese) found in the garden of the former samurai owner of this land that now encompasses the entire financial district of the city of Tokyo.

NOTE: Flash photography, smoking, and eating are not allowed.

Hours: The building is open 9 AM–4 PM Mon–Fri (except hols). Trading hours are 9 AM–11 AM and 12:30 PM–3:00 PM English tours are offered at 1:30 PM. Call the above number for a reservation.

Access: 4 min from Kayabacho Stn, Exit 11 (Tozai and Hibiya lines). Turn right from the exit and right again just before the highway. The Stock Exchange is the last building on the right at the end of that street. Enter through the visitors' entrance.

THE ASAHI SHINBUN/ASAHI EVENING NEWS

朝日新聞／朝日イブニング ニュース

   5–3–2 Tsukiji, Chuo-ku, Tokyo 104–8011

   ☎ 5540–7724 (Tour Office for reservations, English okay)

   東京都中央区築地5-3-2　〒104-8011

Visiting a newspaper office is exciting. The air is charged with the urgency of upcoming deadlines that are always looming. For quite some time I had wanted to see first-hand how a newspaper was put together. So when I learned that the *Asahi Shinbun* offered tours in English (a courtesy not extended by the other newspapers), I called and made a reservation.

After a 15-min introductory video in English, the tour started where the newspaper began—at a beautiful but obsolete 7,000 *kanji*-character typewriter keyboard used to typeset the handwritten manuscripts reporters would turn in during the early days of the publication, which was founded in 1879.

In the production department, ads are laid out on large, vertically oblong computer screens made to accommodate the writing system of the Japanese language. In the editorial department, many teams of computer operators and editors work side-by-side making up the individual pages, each machine identified with a page number clearly marked on its side.

The *Asahi Shinbun* has a circulation of about 12.5 million nationwide, among the highest in the world. After watching the newly created newspaper being run off at the incredible speed of twenty copies per second in the printing/mailing section, we were presented with our very own "hot off the press" edition— and it really was warm!

One of the things learned on the tour was that as early as 1980 this innovative newspaper was already computerized. After working in close association with IBM and other companies over a twenty-year period, the *Asahi Shinbun* developed NELSON (New Editing and Layout System of Newspapers), a new computer technology that revolutionized the newspaper industry.

The *Asahi Shinbun*'s Tokyo headquarters building is located across the street from Tsukiji Fish Market, so you might consider combining the two into a full morning of sightseeing. (See Tsukiji Fish market below.)

NOTE: Photography is not allowed in the editorial or production departments.

Hours: 1-hour tours are given three times a day (at 11 AM, 12:45 PM, and 2:15 PM), Mon–Fri except hols.

Access: 10-min walk from Tsukiji Stn, Exit 2 (Hibiya Line). Walk straight out of the exit and continue along Shin Ohashi-dori for about 10 min. When you reach the third traffic light, cross the street and walk right. The entrance to the building complex will be on the left side. Enter and go up the escalator. The tour departs from the Visitor Information Center on the second floor of the Main Building.

THE MAINICHI SHINBUN/MAINICHI DAILY NEWS

毎日新聞／毎日デイリー ニュース

1–1–1 Hitotsubashi, Chiyoda-ku, Tokyo 100–0051

☎ 3212–0193 (in Japanese)

東京都千代田区一ツ橋1-1-1　〒100-0051

Tours are offered in Japanese twice a day (12:15 PM and 1:15 PM), Mon–Fri to groups of any size (no minimum and up to thirty maximum). They will accommodate you on short notice if they are not full.

YOMIURI SHINBUN/DAILY YOMIURI

読売新聞／デイリー読売

1–7–1 Otemachi, Chiyoda-ku, Tokyo 100–0050

☎ 3217–8399 (in Japanese)

東京都千代田区大手町1-7-1　〒100-0050

Tours in Japanese (with an English video) are given four times a day: 11 AM, noon, 1 PM, and 2 PM), Mon–Fri. From one person to very large groups can be accommodated, but you need to make a reservation ten days in advance.

FUJI TELEVISION—Channel 8

フジテレビ—8チャンネル

Headquarters Building

2–4–8 Daiba, Minato-ku, Tokyo 137–8088

☎ 5500–8888 Ask for Tour Information (Kengaku Annai), 0180–993–180 (Telephone Service in Japanese)
東京都港区台場2-4-8　フジテレビ本社ビル　〒137-8088

Fuji Television offers free 1-hour tours of their new studios, opened in the spring of 1997 in the popular Odaiba Beach area of Tokyo. They can accommodate groups of five to twenty people. The tour covers facilities, equipment, the newsroom, and technical control room, but no live broadcasts are seen. However, you will have the opportunity to see yourself "live" on the TV monitors as you sit at the special studio set of a news desk. Bring along a camera to record the moment. Tours are conducted in Japanese, so they request that you bring an interpreter if you do not understand Japanese. Please be aware that this is a very popular new area, and at press time it was necessary to make reservations several months in advance for the studio tour.

Be sure to visit the 7F Fuji Television Art Gallery (ch 14). See Odaiba Beach Area below for information on other nearby attractions.

NOTE: You can visit the "Sphere" skydeck on the 24F afterward for a spectacular view of the entire area (¥500). Access it via the special elevators that depart from the 7F roof garden. The "Sphere" skydeck is open 10 AM to 10 PM (last elevator up at 9:30 PM). Clsd Mon (Tues if Mon is a hol).

Hours: **Studio tours** are offered Mon–Fri at 1:30 PM and 3:30 PM. **Fuji Television Art Gallery**—11 AM–7 PM. Clsd Mon.

Access: The Fuji Television Headquarters Building is located next to Daiba Stn on the Yurikamome Transit System, which originates from Shinbashi Stn (Yamanote and other lines).

TSUKIJI FISH MARKET

築地魚市場・東京中央卸売市場
（Tokyo Chuo Oroshiuri Ichiba）
5–2–1 Tsukiji, Chuo-ku, Tokyo 104–0045
☎ 3542–1111
東京都中央区築地5-2-1　東京中央卸売市場　〒104-0045

A lot of fish is eaten in Japan—about 200 gm (7.1 oz) per person every day. This may not sound like much, but it is five times more than the fish-and-chips–loving British, and ten times more than is consumed in the United States or Germany. Yes, fish has long been a major source of protein for the people of Japan, a nation completely surrounded by water.

Tokyo's Tsukiji serves as the main fish market for the entire country of Japan. As many as 70,000 people are found here on busy days, and transactions for 2,900 tons of marine products bring in ¥2.8 billion (approximately U.S. $25 million) every day. That's mighty powerful stuff!

The history of Tsukiji goes back about 400 years. Moved to its present location after the Great Kanto Earthquake of 1923, today it covers an area of 230,000 sq m (2.5 million sq ft)—a maze of tiny little lanes teeming with activity. Pull-carts, loading trucks, bikes, scooters, and people all buzz back and forth as workers prepare their fish for market, and vendors hawk their wares. There are lots of restaurants and tiny food stalls too—with people lined up waiting to eat in them as early as 7 AM. Many of these small establishments have only three to five seats at their counters, and they fill up fast. But you can take your food to the nearby makeshift tables made from crates and loading machinery that line the perimeter of Shin Ohashi-dori, the street in front of the market.

You are welcome to wander about freely and take in all the action. The fish auction begins in the inner market about 5 AM and is followed by one for fruits and vegetables. But even if you can't make it down that early, there is still plenty to see for several hours following the auctions. And in the outer market there are colorful stalls selling a large variety of food and market-related goodies. Although it is officially open until 3 PM, many shops close between noon and 2 PM. So it is best to go before noon.

Don't miss the colorful Nami-yoke Inari shrine, with its giant 3.3-m (10.8 ft) -wide lion's head on display, and its monuments to the fish (including one to sushi) that sacrificed themselves to feed us humans. The striking Indian-style Tsukiji Honganji temple is located nearby too (see ch 8 for both). To see live swimming fish, visit the Tsukiji Fish Information Center and Museum—located right on the premises of the fish market (see ch 10).

Visiting the market is a great thing to do when you have just arrived in Tokyo and are suffering from jet lag. Its raw energy is

NOTE: It gets pretty wet around the marketplace, so be sure to wear shoes that won't mind a little water. And if you plan to take pictures, use a film speed that requires no flash to avoid disturbing the market workers.

very invigorating and will leave you much more prepared to face the day than if you had stayed in bed and tossed and turned. So when your eyes pop open in the wee hours of the morning and you know there is no chance of going back to sleep, throw on some clothes and head for Tsukiji. It's the most happening place in town at that hour!

Hours: 5 AM–3 PM Mon–Sat (but best before noon). Clsd Sun, hols, every 2nd and 4th Wed, and New Year and summer hols.

Access: A 2-min walk from Tsukiji Stn, Exit 1 (Hibiya Line). Turn left from the station and walk to the next corner to reach the outer perimeter of the market. The early-morning action is back behind the shops in the inner market, and as the morning progresses the focus of activity shifts to the outer market shops.

EXCURSIONS

BIG STUFF

■ Daibutsu of Jorenji

JORENJI TEMPLE

乗蓮寺 (Jorenji)

5–28–3 Akatsuka, Itabashi-ku, Tokyo 175–0092

☎ 3975–3325/6

東京都板橋区赤塚5-28-3　〒175-0092

The large Buddha images (*daibutsu*) in the ancient Japanese capitals of Nara and Kamakura have achieved worldwide recognition. But few people are aware that Tokyo has its own Big Buddha—the **Jorenji Daibutsu**, a beautiful bronze statue that ranks as the third-largest Buddhist image in all of Japan. Only 1/2 m (19 in) shorter than its famous Kamakura cousin, the 13-m- (42.6-ft-) high image is located on the grounds of a noted temple—and creates quite an impressive sight. Originally of a gold color, the 22-ton (19,954-kg) image has undergone the natural transformation of metal exposed to the elements, so that its façade now has a shiny black patina. Its calm countenance radiates an aura of peace and tranquillity as you gaze up at it, taking in the smell of the incense burning nearby.

The Sekichosan Jorenji temple complex in which the Buddha sits has quite a long and interesting past. It was founded about 800 years ago during the Kamakura period (1185–1333) along the well-traveled Nakasendo Highway, where it became known throughout the country. During Edo times (1600–1868), it was a favorite resting spot for the Tokugawa shoguns who came here to relax and dine after their hawking expeditions. The elegant serving tables and dining ware that they used have been preserved as part of the temple's treasury.

When an expressway replaced the old Nakasendo Highway in 1973, the temple was relocated to its present spot amidst the ruins of Akatsuka Castle. Since this had been the site of many fierce battles fought in defense of the castle, concerns for the spirits of the soldiers who died there gave rise to the construction of the Daibutsu in 1977, in the hopes of consoling their souls.

Scattered around the temple grounds are a number of other smaller statues, including three of the seven deities of good fortune—Ebisu, Daikoku, and a marvelously roly-poly Hotei. The latter can be seen on the right side as you enter the temple grounds. A lovely little carp pond bordered by a small garden sits next to the main temple, and a bell that can be struck on New Year's Eve as a part of the purification ritual is located next to the temple's main gate.

A visit to the Daibutsu can be a day's outing, for there are a number of other attractions in the immediate area. If you turn right upon leaving the temple you will be at the **Akatsuka Botanical Garden** (☎ 3975–9127). Plants, flowers, and trees from every season can be found here in a variety of environments, so there is sure to be something in bloom whenever you go (see ch 7).

A left turn from the temple and 5-min walk downhill on Tokyo Daibutsu-dori will bring you to a small park with a pond where you can usually see people fishing. Here you will find two museums sponsored by Itabashi Ward.

The **Itabashi Historical Museum** (☎ 5998–0081) offers a well-executed visual glimpse into the area's past. Artifacts, fossils dating back 30,000 years, and local folklore items are just some of the things that you can see here. Make sure to go out back and look at the 170-year-old authentic farmhouse with its *kamado* (stone cooking oven) inside, and all-wooden well outside. An adjoining shack houses old farming tools and a rice-cleaning machine. You can also walk across a re-creation of the original Itabashi Bridge, reconstructed from documents and old paintings for an expo in Osaka, and relocated here afterward. The Akatsuka Castle, dating from 1455, was once located behind the present museum.

The **Itabashi Art Museum** (☎ 3979–3251) was Tokyo's first city museum. It holds both community exhibitions, special showings, and maintains its own collection of Edo-period (1600–1868) art as well as more recent avant-garde works from the Showa period (1926–89). Admission is free about 40 percent of the time. A free shuttle bus service to and from the museum is offered daily from Aug 10 to Sept 8, and on weekends and hols the rest of the year. It operates from 9 AM–4:30 PM between the museum and Narimasu Stn (Tobu Tojo Line), and between the museum and Takashimadaira Stn (Mita Line). Call the museum (in Japanese) for the schedule and pickup location.

Hours: **Jorenji temple**—8 AM–4:30 PM (Apr–Sept), 8 AM–4 PM (Oct–March) daily. **Akatsuka Botanical Garden**— 9 AM–4:30 PM (March–Nov), 9 AM–4 PM (Dec–Feb) daily. **Itabashi Historical Museum**—9 AM–4:30 PM Tues–Sun. Clsd Mon (Tues if hol) and between exhibitions. **Itabashi Art Museum**—9 AM–4:30 PM Tues–Sun. Clsd Mon (Tues if Mon is hol).

Access: Narimasu Stn, North Exit (Tobu Tojo Line from Ikebukuro). Special express train does not stop here. Board Bus No. 2 heading for Akabane Stn (from Bus Stand No. 1) at the bottom of the station steps. It is a short bus ride to the Akatsuka 8-chome (Tokyo Daibutsu-mae) stop. (It is best to tell the bus driver where you are headed, so he will be sure to stop.) Turn and walk back to the corner, where you will see a "Tokyo Daibutsu-dori" street sign. Walk to the right down the hill for about 4 min. Pass the next traffic signal and turn left into the second small street. The temple is on your right. Or a 20-minute walk from either Shimo Akatsuka Stn (Tobu Tojo Line), Eidan Akatsuka Stn (Yurakucho Line), or Nishi Takashimadaira Stn (Mita Line). See above for information on the shuttle bus.

■ Go Climb a Mountain

MT. TAKAO

高尾山 (Takaosan)

> Mt. Takao Visitor's Center
> 2176 Takao-machi, Hachioji-shi, Tokyo 193–0844
> ☎ 0426–64–7872
> 東京都八王子市高尾町2176　高尾山ビジター センター　〒193-0844

TAKAO NATURAL SCIENCE MUSEUM

東京都高尾自然科学博物館
(Tokyo-to Takao Shizen Kagaku Hakubutsukan)

> 2436 Takao-machi, Hachioji-shi, Tokyo 193–0844
> ☎ 0426–61–0305
> 東京都八王子市高尾町2436　〒193-0844

A train from the center of town will whisk you right to the foothills of Mt. Takao, where the temperature is cooler, and the air a whole lot cleaner. Yes, this is still Tokyo, less than an hour away from the city center but light-years away from its hectic pace.

A clear mountain stream runs alongside the station— follow the small road that goes off to the right between the stream and station for a few minutes to the nearby Takao Natural Science Museum. (Look for the sign in English directing you to turn left over a small bridge.) At the museum you can get a free introduction to the flora and fauna of the area, and a visual orientation of the topography and hiking trails before you embark upon your journey up the mountain. The captions are in Japanese, but the displays speak for themselves.

The wide road that you crossed en route to the museum will lead you up to the base of the mountain and the trail head. The various routes are color-coded on a large outdoor map, and a simple-but-free English map is available at the base building office. (Tokyo's downtown Tourist Information Center has information on Mt. Takao that includes a map with information on the hiking trails and train routes, and a listing of some inexpensive local accommodations.)

Route No. 1 is a 90-min course that winds past the chair lift and cable car stations found part-way up the mountain. (These offer another way up for the elderly, those with small children, or anyone seeking to enjoy the scenery without the rigors of a hike—see specifics below.)

But whatever method you choose, plan to pass through the ancient temple of Yakuoin (about a 15-min walk past the upper cable car station). Established by an edict of the emperor Shomu as the official "guardian temple of peace for the Eastern part of Japan," it dates back to the year 744. Its establishment secured the mountain as a sacred one, enabling it to remain in the pristine state in which it has been preserved to this day.

Yakuoin enshrines both Buddhist and Shinto deities, and the joining together of the practices of the two religions led to the emergence of the *Yamabushi*, mountain ascetics who practiced healing exorcism. The temple devotees worship nature and engage in ascetic practices such as bathing in cold waterfalls and fire-walking. Every second Sunday in March a popular "Fire-walking Festival" (*Hiwatari*) is held at the foot of the mountain not far from the Natural Science Museum—during which the public (this means you) can take part in a walk across hot coals (after they have cooled down a bit, of course).

Yakuoin sits very near the top of the mountain. So about a 20-min hike upward from the center of the temple grounds will bring you to the 600-m- (2,000-ft-) high mountain summit, lookout, and Visitors' Center. Designated as "Meiji-no-Mori National Park" (Imperial Forest of the Meiji Period), the mountain is well known for its natural beauty, clean air, and nice views. You might try looking for Yokohama's Bay Bridge, the skyscrapers of Shinjuku, the Nikko mountain range, or the ever-elusive Mt. Fuji. Unfortunately, summers can be a bit foggy. The clearest time to visit is December or January, but dress warmly. It is also very beautiful during May and November, the most popular times, but don't expect to be alone at the top. I went in April and it was lovely—but it did get quite cool later in the day.

If you choose to return via Trail Route No. 6, this 3.3-km (2.1-mi) course will take you down along Takao's southern edge past Biwataki Falls, which is often used for religious rituals. It takes about 80 min to reach the bottom.

The cable car and chair lift run about 6/8 AM–5:30/8 PM daily (times vary with the season), and cost ¥470 one way or ¥900 round trip (tickets are sold at separate ticket windows). The cable car was built in 1927 and has the steepest climb in Japan (32 degrees), while the chair lift was constructed for the 1964 Olympics and is the longest pair lift in the country (872 m/2,860 ft). The Takao Natural Animals and Plants Garden (¥500—☎ 0426–61–2381) is also located near the upper cable car station.

NOTE: *Day Walks Near Tokyo*, by Gary D'A. Walters, would be a very handy little guide to have along. In addition to a map and basic introduction to the area, it offers information on the trails and buildings in the temple compound and covers the surrounding environs in adjoining chapters.

Hours: **Takao Visitor's Center**—10 AM–4 PM daily except Mon. **Takao Natural Science Museum**—9 AM–5 PM daily (9 AM–4 PM *Dec–March*). Clsd 1st and 3rd Mon, Christmas, and New Year hols.

Access: Mt. Takao is little less than 1 hour from Shinjuku on the Keio Line. Take an express or limited express train bound for Takaosan-guchi, which is the final station. Do not get off at Takao, which is one stop earlier. And ask if you have any questions, since some trains split en route and go in different directions. Mt. Takao can also be reached by taking the JR Chuo Line to Takao Stn, then transferring to the Keio Line for one stop to Takaosan-guchi. Once you arrive, follow the directions in paragraphs two and three above.

SMALL STUFF

■ Little Museums of Sumida-ku

The museums of Sumida-ku may be tiny, but the talent represented here isn't. For many of these museums are in the homes and workshops of local craftsmen who work to preserve the traditional arts and crafts of Tokyo. In acknowledgment of their

SOME VERY
SPECIAL
DESTINATIONS

NOTE: The Sumida City Office publishes a free bilingual book that describes all these delightful museums individually and includes a clear map and directions to each one. It can be obtained either at the museums or by sending a request for the *Little Museum Guide Map* along with your name and address and a ¥190 stamp (at the time of this printing) for postage to the address below. If you have specific questions, call the Sumida City Office at ☎ 5608–6186. They will transfer you to an English-speaking person if you don't speak Japanese. Write to: The Sumida City Office, Commerce and Industry Department, Economic Affairs Division, Economic Development Section, 1–23–20 Azumabashi, Sumida-ku, Tokyo 130–8640.

NOTE: Please be aware that the name of the "Arakawa" Station on the Keisei Line has now been changed to "Yahiro."

efforts, Sumida-ku has bestowed upon them the title of "Sumida Meisters" ("Meister" being German for master craftsmen). It is part of a program inaugurated in 1987 and known as the 3M Campaign—museums, model shops, and meisters. The program gives recognition to the noted local craftsmen and makes their work accessible to the public.

There are other museums in the program too. For example, the Sumida River has been the site of the most popular fireworks display in Tokyo each summer since Edo times (1600–1868), so there is a Fireworks Museum. And since the headquarters for sumo wrestling (the Kokugikan) is located in Sumida-ku, there are sumo-related museums as well—the Sumo Photograph Museum, the Tabi Museum, and the official Sumo Museum. A fun time to go small museum-hopping in the area is during one of Tokyo's January, May, or September sumo tournaments, when you will be treated to the sight of *rikishi* (wrestlers) in *yukata* (cotton kimono) and *geta* (wooden clogs) wandering through the streets. The Kokugikan (Sumo Hall) is next to Ryogoku Station and many of the "stables" in which the wrestlers live and train are in the vicinity. (Did you know that you can visit these stables and watch morning training sessions for free? See ch 4 for details.) But keep in mind that while the tournaments are on, the Sumo Museum located in the Kokugikan may only be visited by ticket holders to the matches.

But back to crafts. The making of Japanese dolls, Noh masks, and *tabi* (traditional Japanese socks) are just a few of the many arts and crafts you can learn about first-hand from the master craftsmen at their little museums. I have written about these three so that you might get a feeling for the museums, and have listed the basics on the others. Please pick up a copy of the wonderful *Little Museum Guide Map*, a booklet put out by the Sumida City Office for full details (see note). It would be a good idea to give a quick courtesy call before heading over to some of the smaller museums, especially the ones located in craftsmen's homes. When in doubt about the location of a museum, look for the lively six-colored logo on the sign outside that identifies it.

KOBAYASHI DOLL MUSEUM

小林人形資料館 （Kobayashi Ningyo Shiryokan）

6–31–2 Yahiro, Sumida-ku, Tokyo 130–0041

☎ 3612–1644

東京都墨田区八広6-31-2　小林人形工房　〒131-0041

Wending your way through this very old neighborhood to find the museum is an adventure. And when you enter the little house Kobayashi-san and his brother use as a workshop, he will stop what he is doing, jump up, and cheerfully take you on an animated tour of their precious treasures upstairs. It's all in Japanese, but no matter—the basics are listed here and your eyes will do the rest of the work. In addition to some very old heads and other pieces of dolls that may seem eerie to some, there is one of the famous "blue-eyed dolls" that were sent to Japan as a gesture of friendship from the United States in 1927, and one of the Japanese dolls sent to America in return. Unfortunately, most of these were destroyed when relations between the two countries worsened several years later during the 1930s. You can also see what the "honorable dolls" presented to kamikaze pilots looked like, as well as the doll that was a gift to General Douglas MacArthur following World War II. Don't miss the collection of tiny doll wigs that show the various hairstyles worn during the Edo period (1600–1868).

Downstairs is the Kobayashi brothers' workshop, where they create their beautiful handmade dolls and send them to shops around the county. Their doll-making process can be viewed with prior arrangements.

Hours: 10:30 AM–5 PM every Fri, Sat, and Sun.

Access: 3 min from Yahiro (formerly Arakawa) Stn (Keisei Line). From the front of the train coming from the city center, cross over the tracks and leave by the only exit. Turn right and go down the first set of stairs on the right side. At the bottom of the steps, go left, then turn right into the second small lane of houses. The museum will be in the final house on the left side before the traffic light. The entrance is around the front. Check for the six-colored logo.

SOME VERY
SPECIAL
DESTINATIONS

NOH MASK MUSEUM

能面博物館 （Nomen Hakubutsukan）

    5–10–5 Narihira, Sumida-ku, Tokyo 130–0002

    ☎ 3623–3055

    東京都墨田区業平5-10-5　墨田住宅センター　〒130-0002

Another winner. When I climbed up the steep staircase and entered Kaneko-san's second-floor living room/workshop, I was taken aback by the display of fifty exquisitely hand-carved Noh masks that line its walls. I had seen copies of Noh masks in souvenir stores before, but seeing real masks so close up was a totally different experience. The emotion contained by each one is astounding. Kaneko-san, a very sweet and unassuming man, proceeded to go through the steps of mask-making for me. Even if you don't understand Japanese, you can't help but understand the process when there are twenty-five photos before you clearly illustrating each step along the way—from a slab of mud to an incredibly expressive Noh mask. All the raw materials used in the process, clay replicas and molds, and samples of various stages of the mask-making process are in a display case—and long blocks of wood for future masks lay on the floor alongside the case.

Only natural material is used for the coloring—boiled pods from a tree create the facial stain, carbon from candle burnings on the bottom of a plate is brushed on to create eyebrows, and gold leaf covers the teeth and eyeballs of the more dramatic characters. Hair from a horse's mane is used for beards, hair, and eyebrows. No matter what your knowledge was about Noh masks before you arrive, you can't help but leave with a greater appreciation for the art.

Hours: 9 AM–5 PM every Tues, Sat, and the 4th Sun.

Access: A 5-min walk from Oshiage Stn, Exit A2 (Toei Asakusa Line). Turn left from the exit and walk down Asakusa-dori. Turn right into the first small street after the second light. It is the first entrance on the left side. Look for the six-colored logo.

TABI MUSEUM

足袋資料館 （Tabi Shiryokan）

Kikuya Tabi Shop
1–9–3 Midori, Sumida-ku, Tokyo 130–0021
☎ 3631–0092
東京都墨田区緑1-9-3　喜久や足袋本舗　〒130-0021

Miyauchi-san, the proprietor of the 250-year-old Kikuya, greets us with a big smile as we slide open the door and step inside his tiny shop. He sits working merrily away in the same exact spot where ten generations of his family sat before him, creating made-to-order *tabi* (split-toed socks worn with kimono) for the famous sumo wrestlers who frequent his shop. Does this sound like the opening of an intriguing novel? Could very well be—but it's real!

And so is Miyauchi-san. As he works away on what he has been doing for the past forty years, he explains (in Japanese) all about *tabi*-making to us. There are twenty-four stages to the process, which involves taking a myriad of measurements to assure a proper fit. He points these out to us. Rare tools of his trade that he has carefully collected over the years are on display in his window, and the outlines of some very famous feet can be seen on the walls of his shop—Akebono and Konishiki, for example, and the brothers Wakanohana and Takanohana. Even the feet of John Wayne and the King of Tonga are represented!

And all the while that he was relating the history of his shop and his craft, Miyauchi-san never once stopped smiling. Sumida-ku seems to have a monopoly on charming, friendly, and very special craftsmen.

Hours: Irregular hours within the time frame of 9 AM–6 PM daily except Sun and hols. Call first to confirm.

Access: An 8-min walk from Ryogoku Stn, East Exit (Sobu Line). Walk left from the exit and follow the train tracks until you reach Kiyosumi-dori. Cross over the pedestrian overpass and walk away from the tracks for about another 4 or 5 min. A few doors after Sanwa Bank, look for the display of tabi in the showcase window on the left.

SOME VERY
SPECIAL
DESTINATIONS

ALLOY CASTING MUSEUM
合金鋳物博物館 （Gokin Imono Hakubutsukan）
403, Lions Mansion Oshige,3–4–13 Narihira, Sumida-ku, Tokyo 130–0002
☎ 3624–2494
東京都墨田区業平3-4-13　ライオンズマンション押上403　〒130-0002

BATTLEDORE MUSEUM
羽子板資料館 （Hagoita Shiryokan）
Kogetsu Battledore, 5–43–25 Mukojima, Sumida-ku, Tokyo 131–0033
☎ 3623–1305
東京都墨田区向島5-43-25　羽子板の鴻月　〒131-0033

CIGARETTE LIGHTER MUSEUM *(See ch 10 for write-up)*
ライター博物館 （Raita Hakubutsukan）
Ivy Antique Gallery, 3F
1–27–6 Mukojima, Sumida-ku, Tokyo 131–0033
☎ 3622–1649
東京都墨田区向島1-27-6　アイビー アンティック ギャラリー3階
〒130-0002

CONSTRUCTION TOOLS/WOODEN FRAME MUSEUM
建築道具・木組資料館 （Kenchiku Kogu Kigumi Shiryokan）
Morishita Co., 1–5–3 Kikukawa, Sumida-ku, Tokyo130–0024
☎ 3633–0328
東京都墨田区菊川1-5-3　(株)森下工務店　〒130-0024

DRY WOODWORK MUSEUM
乾燥木材工芸資料館 （Kanso Mokuzai Kogei Shiryokan）
Kansomokuzai Kogei Building
2–9–11 Kinshi, Sumida-ku, Tokyo 130–0013
☎ 3625–2401
東京都墨田区錦糸2-9-11　乾燥木材工芸ビル　〒130-0013

EARTHQUAKE MUSEUM
東京復興記念館 （Tokyo Fukko Kinenkan）
2–3–25 Yokoami, Sumida-ku, Tokyo 130–0015
☎ 3622–1208
東京都墨田区横網32-3-25　〒130-0015

EDO-TOKYO MUSEUM

江戸東京博物館 （Edo-Tokyo Hakubutsukan）

    1–4–1 Yokoami, Sumida-ku, Tokyo 130–0015

    ☎ 3626–8000 (Recorded Information) 3626–9974

    東京都墨田区横網1-4-1　〒130-0015

This is not one of the "little museums," but it's right in the middle of them, and one that you should be aware of. They have a wonderful video library, where you can watch culture and craft videos for free (ch 13), and a nice museum shop that features unique Edo-period (1600–1868) goods. See ch 9 for details. (There is a charge to see the museum's exhibition.)

FIREWORKS MUSEUM *(See ch 10 for write-up)*

両国花火資料館 （Ryogoku Hanabi Shiryokan）

    Sumitomo Fudosan Ryogoku Building, 1F

    2–10–8 Ryogoku, Sumida-ku, Tokyo 130–0026

    ☎ 5608–1111 ext. 3406

    東京都墨田区両国2-10-8　住友不動産両国ビル1階　〒130-0026

KAWASHIMA KNIT MUSEUM

川島編物博物館 （Kawashima Amimono Hakubutsukan）

    3–9–8 Mukojima, Sumida-ku, Tokyo 131–0035

    ☎ 3622–6350

    東京都墨田区向島3-9-8　川島メリヤス製作所　〒131-0035

KO-IMARI POTTERY MUSEUM (Porcelain)

古伊万里資料館 （Ko-Imari Shiryokan）

    A-S Motors Co., 2F, 5–23–9 Yahiro, Sumida-ku, Tokyo 131–0041

    ☎ 3619–3867

    東京都墨田区八広5-23-9　エーエス自動車2階　〒131-0041

MUSEUM OF BOOKS ON GLASSWARE

ガラスの本の博物館 （Garasu no Hon no Hakubutsukan）

    Shotoku Garasu Co., 4–10–4 Kinshi, Sumida-ku, Tokyo 130–0013

    ☎ 3625–3755

    東京都墨田区錦糸4-10-4　松徳硝子(株)2階　〒130-0013

PORTABLE FOLDING SCREEN MUSEUM

屏風博物館（Byobu Hakubutsukan）

Kataoka Byobu Co., 1–31–6 Mukojima, Sumida-ku, Tokyo 131–0033

☎ 3622–4470

東京都墨田区向島1-31-6　(株)片岡屏風店　〒131-0033

RUBBER BASEBALL EXHIBITION HALL

軟式野球資料室（Nanshiki Yakyu Shiryoshitsu）

Nagase Kenko Co., 2–36–10 Sumida, Sumida-ku, Tokyo 131–0031

☎ 3614–3501

東京都墨田区墨田2-36-10　ナガセケンコー(株)　〒131-0031

SAFE AND KEY MUSEUM

金庫と鍵の博物館（Kinko to Kagi no Hakubutsukan）

Sugiyama Kinko Shop, 3–4–1 Chitose, Sumida-ku, Tokyo 130–0025

☎ 3633–9151

東京都墨田区千歳3-4-1　(有)杉山金庫店　〒130-0025

SUMO MUSEUM *(See ch 10 for write-up)*

相撲博物館（Sumo Hakubutsukan）

Kokugikan, 1–3–28 Yokoami, Sumida-ku, Tokyo 130–0015

☎ 3622–0366

東京都墨田区横網1-3-28　国技館内　〒130-0015

SUMO PHOTOGRAPH MUSEUM

相撲写真資料室（Sumo Shashin Shiryokan）

Kudo Photo Shop, 3–13–2 Ryogoku, Sumida-ku, Tokyo 130–0026

☎ 3631–2150

東京都墨田区両国3-13-2　工藤写真館　〒130-0026

SUZUKI WOODWORK MUSEUM

鈴木木工博物館（Suzuki Mokko Hakubutsukan）

6–38–15 Higashi Mukojima, Sumida-ku, Tokyo 131–0032

☎ 3616–5008 or 3611–5008

東京都墨田区東向島6-38-15　鈴木製作所　〒131-0032

TAKINAMI GLASSWARE MUSEUM *(See ch 10 for write-up)*
タキナミ ガラス博物館 （Takinami Garasu Hakubutsukan）

Takinami Glass Factory

1–18–19 Taihei, Sumida-ku, Tokyo 130–0012

☎ 3622–4141

東京都墨田区大平1-18-19　瀧波硝子(株)　〒130-0012

TORTOISE SHELL WORK MUSEUM
べっ甲博物館 （Bekko Shiryokan）

2–5–5 Yokoami, Sumida-ku, Tokyo 130–0015

☎ 3625–5875

東京都墨田区横網2-5-5　磯貝べっ甲専門店　〒130-0015

TRADITIONAL WOOD SCULPTING MUSEUM
伝統木彫刻資料館 （Dento Mokuchokoku Shiryokan）

4–7–8 Higashi Komagata, Sumida-ku, Tokyo 130–0005

☎ 3623–0273

東京都墨田区東駒形4-7-8　大野伝統木彫刻工房　〒130-0005

WOOD CARVING MUSEUM
木彫資料館 （Mokucho Shiryokan）

Matsumoto Wood Carving, 1–13–3 Ishihara, Sumida-ku, Tokyo 130–0011

☎ 3622–4920

東京都墨田区石原1-13-3　松本彫刻店　〒130-0011

WOODEN HOUSE MUSEUM
墨田住宅センター木造建築資料館

（Sumida Jutaku Senta, Mokuzo Kenchiku Shiryokan）

1–7–16 Tsutsumi-dori, Sumida-ku, Tokyo 131–0034

☎ 3612–7724

東京都墨田区堤通り1-7-16　(有)山孝工務店　〒131-0034

WORSHIPPER'S CARD MUSEUM
千社札博物館 （Senjafuda Hakubutsukan）

Hayashi Co., 2–10–9 Kyojima, Sumida-ku, Tokyo 131–0046

☎ 3612–1691

東京都墨田区京島2-10-9　林塗装(株)　〒131-0046

■ Golden Gai

The first time I stumbled upon Golden Gai, I could only stare in amazement. "How could this be?" I remember thinking. For smack in the middle of the neon-clad, carnival-town of Shinjuku is an area that hasn't changed a bit in the last fifty years. More than 200 tiny traditional drinking establishments (*nomiya*) line the alleyways of this mazelike enclave known as Golden Gai. And when you enter the maze, it's easy to get lost—in time. This compact little entertainment district was built in the years directly following World War II in a style common at the time: a series of tiny row shops with the owners' living quarters overhead, accessed by the ladderlike staircases running alongside. The area deserves to be designated a tangible cultural property.

Most of the tiny *nomiya* are only able to accommodate a few people at a time, and are said to be frequented by a mixture of writers, artistic types, intellectuals, and *yakuza* (gangsters). The great majority consider themselves to be "members' clubs," which means strangers are generally not welcome, but there are exceptions, of course. There are two larger bars on the corner closest to Yasukuni-dori, Bons (☎ 3209–6334) and the upstairs Hungry Humphrey (☎ 3200–6156), where you can sit comfortably and have a drink (and perhaps learn about another place or two where you might be welcome in the lanes). One night I met someone wandering through the alleyways who told us of a spot that welcomed foreigners, and we climbed the steep staircase to a second-floor bar for a very atmospheric drink and chat with the owner in English. So it can be done.

If you want to get a glimpse of what life in Japan was like during the postwar years of the late 1940s, take a stroll down the narrow alleys of Golden Gai. But go soon—because for years now the powers-that-be have been threatening to "redevelop" the area. Of course, there are a few other places in Tokyo where you can experience these long rows of *nomiya,* but Golden Gai has such a wonderful feeling of community that it deserves a special mention. Smaller clusters of *nomiya* can sometimes be found near train stations, like Shibuya's *Nonbei Yokocho* (Drunkard's Alley). Although smaller than Golden Gai, the basics still apply. They are a charming tour through the past.

Hours: Hours vary, but the nomiya of Golden Gai are only open in the evening. Some of the later ones remain open until about 5 AM. Clsd Sun and hols.

Access: Golden Gai is near the intersection of Yasukuni-dori and Meiji-dori, a 7- min walk from JR Shinjuku Stn, East Exit (Yamanote and other lines). Walk over to Yasukuni-dori, cross the street and turn right. You will soon see Shinjuku Promenade Park (a winding little marble pavement veering off to the left). You can enter here and turn into the first row of nomiya on your right, or you can continue along Yasukuni-dori to the next small street and turn left. Bons and Hungry Humphrey are down this street on the left, just past the police box (koban).

NOTE: The neighborhood proprietors request that you refrain from taking pictures. It may have a historical appeal, but privacy is cherished.

■ Department Store Basements

Here is something definitely worth knowing about if you don't already—the Japanese department store basements specialize in food. All kinds of food. And since there is so much of it, each vendor wants to entice you to buy his or her own special goods. So they put out samples. Lots of samples. In fact, you can wander through a department store basement and nibble on everything from pickled vegetables, tofu, and other local offerings to bite size pieces of meat, chicken, and fish prepared a great variety of ways. Sweets galore await you, and sometimes Korean, Chinese, Thai, and other ethnic food nibblings as well. This is the perfect way to try unknown Japanese foods—of which there is such a bewildering variety—and add the ones you like to your dinner table.

Isetan Department Store in Shinjuku ranks among the best food basements in Tokyo. And guess what? They offer free English tours of this space twice a year (every March and September). I signed up and spent a very enjoyable couple of hours exploring a mind-boggling variety of food. We learned what the different offerings were, how they were prepared, and what to do with them. The tour even took us behind the scenes to watch the preparation of tofu. (We returned later to taste the finished product—delicious creamy samples with a custard-like quality.) We were given a talk on saké, and sampled various grades of the brew. A listing and pictures of the main foods used in Japanese cooking were included in our courtesy packet, which also had recipes to try out at home (sukiyaki, miso soup, and spinach with sesame dressing were some of these). We came away with presents from the vendors too—like crunchy cookies and a set of wooden saké cups.

NOTE: The tours fill up quickly, so sign up as soon as you receive the announcement in the mail.

To partake in this adventure in food, all you have to be is a member of Isetan's "I Club," which is free and easy to join (see ch 1).

OLD STUFF

■ Shitamachi/Asakusa

Before Tokyo Was Tokyo

Tokyo's older areas—the traditional "downtown" sections of the city where the "common folk" lived—are collectively known as Shitamachi. To walk through Shitamachi is to immerse yourself in the past, for here the traditions of old Edo, as Tokyo was known, are preserved and very much alive. It is a glimpse into what life was like before Tokyo was Tokyo.

A good place to begin your exploration of old Edo is in Asakusa. Like the other areas that make up Shitamachi, it percolates with living history. The people at the **Asakusa Cultural and Sightseeing Center** across from the main entrance to the Asakusa Kannon temple will be happy to supply you with literature, maps, and information in English (and eight other languages) 10 A.M.–5 P.M. daily. Their *Walking Courses in Tokyo* details a self-guided walking tour of Asakusa and includes a clear map with good directions, and the colorful pamphlet entitled *Shitamachi—Guide for Sightseeing Around Asakusa, Ueno, Shitaya, and Yanaka* illustrates the highlights of Asakusa and its surrounding areas. There is also an interactive bilingual computer available 9:30 AM–8 PM that offers visual previews and printouts of important places and events of the area. (Asakusa Kannon temple puts out its own excellent English pamphlet that you might try and obtain from one of the temple buildings later.)

You are now ready to cross the street and pass through the big red **Kaminarimon Gate** to **Nakamise-dori**, the lively, 300-m- (275-yd-) long arcade leading up to the Asakusa Kannon Temple. It's so easy to get caught up in the rows of small shops selling traditional Japanese items. Edo-style (1600–1868) straw sandals, kimono, oiled-paper umbrellas, masks, fans, dolls, toys, and traditional sweets can all be found here. They even carry elaborate geisha wigs (with elaborate price tags) and samurai hairpieces as well. You can watch rice crackers being made out in the open and sold fresh off the grill. It's a fun, energetic atmosphere and it may take you a while to make your way through to reach the temple. But after all, you are here to see everything, right?

Off to the side of bustling Nakamise-dori is the serene **Denpoin garden**, with origins dating back to the 7th century. Opened to the public only a few years ago, it can now be visited by obtaining permission from the office in the **five-storied pagoda** (goju-no-to) next to the main temple building. It is not always open, so call ahead (see ch 7).

You're getting closer. Pass underneath the huge **Hozomon "Treasure House" Gate** (storage place for the temple's rare 14th-century sutras) to reach the very heart of the entire Asakusa area—the **Asakusa Kannon temple** (**Sensoji**), named for the 5-cm (2-in) Kannon Goddess of Mercy statue that is enshrined here. The story goes that in the 7th century two local fishermen caught the tiny golden image in their nets while fishing in the nearby Sumida River. The head of their village recognized it as an object of worship and enshrined it. As the word spread, the area grew in importance—centered around the temple and its Kannon Goddess. Today over 30 million people come here each year to pray and immerse themselves in the healing smoke from the incense burning in front of the temple.

The next-door **Asakusa shrine** (**Sanja Gongen**) was built by the third Tokugawa shogun in honor of the two fisherman and their village head. It is nicknamed "Sanja-sama,"

which means "Three Holy Shrines." Many of the buildings in the complex were destroyed by fire and other disasters over the years and had to be rebuilt, but this shrine and the temple's **East Gate** (**Nitenmon**) that sits next to it managed to survive. They have both been designated as Important Cultural Assets by the government of Japan.

I was delighted to discover that many of the buildings in the complex are user-friendly—which means you may walk inside (if you take off your shoes, of course). For example, you can walk behind the wire mesh of Sensoji temple to see the Buddhist images up close if the little inside gate at the far right is open. You may also enter the Asakusa shrine's tatami-matted Outer Hall at the top of the red steps to study the details of the colorful prancing dragons and birds on its walls. Enter via the small gate at the right. (Once again—shoes off!)

If you walk straight out from the Asakusa shrine, in about 1 min you will come to a small hill on your left side with a large bell on it. This is the **Bell of Time** (**Toki-no-Kane**), one of nine bells that kept the people of Edo informed of the time every day from the 1600s. It is still rung at 6 AM every day to mark the opening of the temple, and 108 times at midnight on New Year's Eve as a purification ritual for the New Year. Numerous festivals are held in Asakusa, including the very popular mid-May *Sanja Matsuri* (festival), when over one hundred portable shrines (*mikoshi*) are carried through the streets by men and women sporting Edo-style *happi*-coats and headbands. And each July, people come from all over to watch Tokyo's most spectacular display of fireworks light up the skies over the nearby Sumida River—as they have been doing for nearly 400 years. A complete listing of the many activities that take place in this active area is available at the Asakusa sightseeing center.

To the left (as you face the temple) are other buildings in the complex, including the **five-storied pagoda** that contains relics of Buddha in its upper reaches. If you turn left and follow the road that runs in front of the temple, you will soon reach a shopping arcade. Just to the right of the arcade entrance is the **Asakusa Kannon Onsen**, where (for ¥700) you can enter and experience a traditional Japanese hot springs–style public bath. (Soap is ¥40 and refundable towel deposit is ¥100.) The water has a slightly brown tint and comes from a spring underneath the building. Scrub down with soap and rinse off thoroughly at one of the little stations around the perimeter of the room before you *even think of* getting into the bath. No, it's not communal—men and women are separated.

A little further on in that same direction is the old **Rokku Kogyo-gai (Sixth District)** entertainment area. Although the area is a mere shadow of its former incarnation when Asakusa was the uncontested hottest spot in town, it still hosts a number of movie theaters and playhouses that include performances of *rakugo*—a kind of comic storytelling that has been popular since Edo times. Explore the small streets of the area for shops selling traditional goods, and stalls and restaurants serving traditional foods.

Back on the other side of the temple is the **Sumida River**, flanked by **Sumida Park** along its banks. A number of events are held at the park, including a spectacular cherry blossom festival each spring and a *yabusame* (**archery on horseback**) competition each April (see ch 4). Its underground **Riverside Gallery** often holds exhibitions related to traditional Japan as well. And while you are in the area you might want to visit **Tokyo's oldest Western bar**, built in 1880. The **Kamiya Bar** is above Asakusa Station, on the corner of Edo-dori, just across from the Azumabashi Bridge. It is a friendly place with a big, beer-hall feel to it.

Note: If this small taste of Shitamachi has gotten you hooked and you'd like to explore it further, *More Foot-loose in Tokyo* (and also *Foot-loose in Tokyo*) by Jean Pearce and *Old Tokyo: Walks in the City of the Shogun* by Sumiko Enbutsu delve deeper into this fascinating aspect of Tokyo with self-guided walking tours. Another option is to join one of Mr. Nobuo Oka's English-language walks through old Tokyo. Mr. Oka is a long-time international tour guide who has now made it his mission to keep the spirit of old Edo alive. For information on his walks and fees, call ☎ 0422–51–7673 after 7 PM.

Hours: **Asakusa Cultural and Sightseeing Center**—Assistance is available 10 AM–5 PM daily, but the center itself (and the friendly computer) is open 9:30 AM–8 PM (☎ 3842–5566). **Nakamise-dori**—Shops generally open between 9 AM and 10 AM and close between 6 PM and 8 PM. Each store keeps its own hours. **Asakusa Kannon Temple (Sensoji)**—6 AM–5 PM daily (☎ 3842– 0181). **Denpoin Garden**—9 AM–3 PM when available for viewing. Clsd Sun and when premises are in use

NOTE: When you leave the area, an option is to take the ferry from the terminal at Azumabashi Bridge that travels underneath the Eleven Bridges of the Sumida River to Hinode Pier. Here you can either transfer to other boats (one goes to Odaiba Beach Area, see below) or walk to the JR Hamamatsucho Stn (Yamanote Line). See posted schedule or call ☎ 3841–9178 in Japanese for information.

(☎ 3842–0181—ask for Denpoin). **Sumida Park**—Open 24 hours (☎ 3871– 1528). **Riverside Gallery**—9 AM–5 PM daily (☎ 3841–7971). **Asakusa Kannon Onsen** (¥700)—6:30 AM–6 PM. Clsd Thurs (☎ 3844–4141). **Kamiya Bar** (not free)—11:30 AM–10 PM. Clsd Tues (☎ 3841–5400).

Access: 1-min walk straight out from Asakusa Stn (Ginza Line) Exit 1 for Kaminarimon Gate, or Exit 2 for the Sightseeing Center. Also accessible by the Asakusa Line.

NEW STUFF

YEBISU GARDEN PLACE
恵比寿ガーデン プレース
4–20–3 Ebisu, Shibuya-ku, Tokyo 150–6090
☎ 5423–7111
東京都渋谷区恵比寿4-20-3 〒150-6090

Yebisu Garden Place is one of several newly-created areas in Tokyo known as "multipurpose developments," a combination of office and residential space harmoniously integrated along- side cultural and entertainment facilities. The 8.3-hectare (20.5- acre) complex was opened in 1994 on the site of the former Sapporo Beer Factory (parent company of Yebisu Beer), which operated here for over one hundred years between 1887 and 1988. And its legacy lives on. In 1906 the newly constructed down-the-street train station took on the name Ebisu, and in 1928 a town by the same name was incorporated. ("Yebisu" and "Ebisu" are two spellings of the same word, the second being a modified version of the original.)

The grounds of Yebisu Garden Place have a very European feel. There's plenty of greenery, fountains, and benches—and you are never far from the soothing sound of running water. **Twenty works of art** are scattered throughout, including Auguste Rodin's bronze *Genie du Repos Eternel.* In keeping with this atmosphere is the **Chateau Restaurant Taillevent- Robuchon**, modeled after a Louis XVth French chateau. It was created from a merger of two top Paris establishments (hence the name), and great care was taken to ensure an authentic French atmosphere. Antique stone and woodwork were even imported from France for use in the construction of the building. The creators, Taillevent's Jean-Claude Vrinat and celebrity "Chef of the Century" Joel Robuchon, still return to Tokyo several times a year to update the menu and make sure all is running well.

Many other restaurants are scattered throughout the complex, including an outdoor beer garden and the 500-seat **Grand Beer Hall**—fashioned after a German beer hall with large fermentation vats in the middle of the floor. Its entrance overlooks the whole scene from above.

The lively **Beer Museum Yebisu** offers a free tour through the now-defunct beer factory via multimedia exhibits. It even includes a **Virtual Brewery Adventure**, where you are taken on a virtual reality journey through one of the four beer-making processes—brewing, fermentation, filtration, or bottling. Starting from a broad landscape of Japan, you proceed to zoom in smaller and smaller until you are actually inside one of the processes—where you can fly over the "mountain peaks" of fermentation or go inside the tiny bubbles of the brewing process. (At the end is a tasting room where you can sample Yebisu beer for a reasonable ¥200.) The museum is located behind Mitsukoshi Department Store. Easiest access is through the B1 central exit of the store (see ch 10).

The **Contemporary Sculpture Center** is an art gallery that presents the works of guest artists as well as its permanent collection. Sculpture in stone, metal, and other media can be seen here. A striking exhibition of Auguste Rodin bronzes was on display during one visit, and another time sculptures of metal and paper were featured. There is no charge for the gallery, which is located on 1F of the Nibankan Building, just beyond the Beer Museum (see ch 14).

See-through express elevators whisk you to the "**Top of Yebisu**," where a dramatic, unobstructed northern view of Tokyo that encompasses Shibuya, Shinjuku, and points beyond awaits you on the 39F at no charge. Board 1F elevators from the north end of Yebisu Garden Place Tower—the tallest building on the grounds. (See ch 16.)

When darkness descends, the buildings (and artwork) light up and the area presents a different face. The smaller structures around **Marionette Clock Square** at the entrance take on a pleasant "Disneyesque" atmosphere. Don't miss the performance of the Marionette Clock: its marching band, prancing horses, and twirling dance figures mark the magical hours of noon, 3 PM, and 6 PM daily.

NOTE: Some non-free offerings located on the site include the Tokyo Metropolitan Museum of Photography (¥500—clsd on Mon), a movie theater complex, a number of facilities for concerts and other events, the elegant Westin Hotel, and Mitsukoshi Department Store. Not bad for a former beer factory!

The complex even has its own, tiny resident shrine. Peacefully nestled between the Beer Museum and the Contemporary Sculpture Center, **Ebisu Shrine** offers a quiet space to pause for a little solace and serves to remind us that we are, after all, still in Japan.

Hours: **Information Counter**—Located on B1 of the Entrance Pavilion and open 9:30 AM–6 PM daily. **Beer Museum Yebisu**—10 AM–6 PM (enter by 5 PM) Tues–Sun. Clsd Mon and New Year hols (☎ 5423–7255). **Contemporary Sculpture Center**—10 AM–6 PM. Clsd Sun and hols (☎ 5423–3001). **Top of Yebisu**—11 AM and 11 PM daily (☎ 5423–7111). **Marionette Clock Square**—Performances by the clock marionettes can be seen at noon, 3 PM, and 6 PM daily.

Access: 7 min from JR Ebisu Stn (Yamanote Line) via the Skywalk from the East Exit, which takes you directly to Yebisu Garden Place. You can either take the escalators at the end of the walkway down to the B1 level of the Entrance Pavilion (and the Information Counter), or cross the street and enter Marionette Clock Square. It is also accessible from the Hibiya Line's Ebisu Stn.

■ Odaiba Beach Area
(Waterfront City Subcenter/Rinkai Fukutoshin)

ODAIBA BEACHSIDE PARK

御台場海浜公園 〔Odaiba Kaihin Koen〕

Cruise Boat Terminal Building, 2F

1–4–1 Daiba, Minato-ku, Tokyo 135–0091

☎ 5531–0851 (Park Office)

東京都港区台場1-4-1　〒135-0091

FUJI TELEVISION HEADQUARTERS BUILDING

フジテレビ本社ビル（Fuji Terebi Honsha Biru）

2–4–8 Daiba, Minato-ku, Tokyo 135–0091

☎ 5500–8888 (For tour information, ask for Kengaku-annai),
5500–5930 (Art Gallery)

東京都港区台場2-4-8　〒135

TOKYO "BIG SIGHT"—TOWER BUILDING

東京ビッグサイト（Tokyo Biggu Saito）

Tokyo International Exhibition Center (Ariake)

3–21–1 Ariake, Koto-ku, Tokyo 135–0063

☎ 5530–1111

東京都江東区有明3-21-1　東京国際展示場　〒135-0063

The first stage of Tokyo's newest reclaimed waterfront area has been completed and contains some great free things to do. And they can all be reached by the driverless, computer-run Yurikamome Transit System. The ride is not free, of course, but it offers an unobstructed view of the area as it whisks you across the Rainbow Bridge and drops you off at these newly developed spots that *are* free—and definitely worth a visit.

The first stop over the bridge is the 1,450-m- (4,750-ft-) long beach area known as **Odaiba Beachside Park**. This part of Tokyo originally came into being when the Tokugawa shogun built a series of six island fortifications (*daiba*) to protect Edo (old Tokyo) from invasion by those nasty foreign ships. Two of these remain. No. 3 (Daisan Daiba) is now known as Daiba Park and contains ruins of the shogun's fortress. It is connected to the far end of the beach. No. 6 (Dairoku Daiba) is still an offshore island.

Ironically, today the area sports a very international atmosphere. The sidewalk cafes along **Sunset Beach Restaurant Row** have a definite European ambiance, and the fantastic views of the **Rainbow Bridge** stretching out across Tokyo Bay are quite reminiscent of San Francisco, New York, or Sydney. You can walk along the sand or the boardwalk and listen to the waves splashing gently on the shore, or watch people wind surfing and fishing in the bay.

SOME VERY
SPECIAL
DESTINATIONS

The area remains active even after dark as traditional plea-sure boats host floating parties on the water and people stroll along the multiple levels of the **Decks Tokyo Beach** complex to catch the stunning view of the bridge against the backdrop of city lights twinkling in the distance. It is a popular spot for dates, and offers restaurants to suit every taste. The Decks complex also houses Decks Tokyo Brewery, maker of the local Daiba Beer that can be purchased in the brewery's restaurant on the premises. The **Searea Odaiba Art Project** features Daniel Buren's *25 Porticos* that lead down to the beach area, as well as other playful works that can be found in various spots near the station (see ch 14).

Another area attraction is the super-modern **Fuji Televi-sion Headquarters Building** designed by renowned architect Kenzo Tange and located next door to the Decks complex. Its offerings include a visit to the **Fuji Television Art Gallery** (see ch 14), a tour of the **new broadcasting facilities** (see above), and a spectacular view of the entire area from its twenty-fourth-floor **"Sphere" skydeck** (for a fee).

Opened in 1996, the **Ariake International Exhibition Center**, or **Tokyo Big Sight** (see ch 16), offers a 360-degree view of both land and water from the viewing platform that wraps around the top of the inverted-pyramid-shaped Tower Building. Keep an ear tuned for new developments in the area. There are sure to be more fabulous attractions coming up.

Hours: **Odaiba Beachside Park** does not close, but most beachside shops are open about 11 AM to 9 PM. Restaurants hours are gen-erally between 11 AM and 11 PM daily, although some remain open until very late on wknds and the day before a hol (particu-larly the ones on Sunset Beach Restaurant Row). **Fuji Televi-sion Art Gallery** hours are 11 AM–7 PM. Clsd Mon. **Fuji TV Studio Tours** are offered Mon through Fri at 1:30 PM and 3:30 PM. **The "Sphere" skydeck** is open 10 AM to 10 PM (last eleva-tor up is 9:30 PM). Clsd Mon (Tues if Mon is a hol). **Tokyo Big Sight** outside observation platform is open 10 AM–5/6 PM daily (weather permitting), and the glass-enclosed interior remains open until the adjoining restaurant closes about 9 PM.

Access: The Yurikamome Transit System originates at Shinbashi Stn (Yamanote and other lines). **Beach Area**—Odaiba Kaihin Koen Stn. **Fuji Television Headquarters Building**—Daiba Stn (or walk along the beach from Odaiba Kaihin Koen Stn). To reach the **art gallery** or **"Sphere,"** take the covered escalator to the 7F. To continue on to the "Sphere" skydeck, board the special elevators from the seventh-floor roof garden. **Tokyo Big Sight**—Kokusai Tenjijo Seimon Stn. The area is also accessible by boat from Hinode Pier, located near JR Hamamatsucho Stn (Yamanote and Keihin Tohoku lines), or from the Asakusa area (see the Shitamachi section above). Call ☎ 3841–9178 in Japanese for information.

4

MARTIAL ARTS
AND SPORTS

SEE FOR YOURSELF

- Nippon Budokan and Budokan Gakuen—*Center for Traditional Japanese Martial Arts*
- Judo—*The Gentle Way*
- Karate—*Empty Hand*
- Kendo, Jukendo, and Naginata—*The Way of the Sword*
- Aikido—*Meeting of the Spirits*
- Shorinji Kenpo—*Working Together in Harmony*
- Kobudo—*Original Forms of Classical Martial Arts*
- Kyudo and Yabusame—*The Way of the Bow*
- Sumo—*The National Sport*
  - –Visit a Stable
  - –Shrines and Festivals
  - –Sumo Related

DO IT YOURSELF

- Bicycling
  Imperial Palace Cycling Course
  Meiji Shrine Outer Garden Cycling Course
  Tama River Cycling Course
  Bicycle Related
- Jogging and Walking
  Jog around the Imperial Palace
  Tokyo International Walk Rally
  Just Get Out There and Do It!

HORSES, MORE HORSES, AND PONIES TOO

- Horse Racing
  Japan Racing Association (*Off-Track Facilities*)
  Plaza Equus Showroom
  Horse Racing Museum
- Horse Shows
  Baji Koen
- Free Rides for Kids
  Baji Koen, Ponylands, and Higashi Itabashi Park

INTRODUCTION

*Martial arts and sports are alive and well in Tokyo. Proof of this can be seen in the numerous dojo (martial arts practice halls) and other sports facilities found throughout the city. Even the more traditional sports such as archery on horseback (*yabusame*) and the original forms of classical martial arts (*kobudo*) that are no longer commonly practiced can still be seen at festivals and special events throughout the year. And did you know that October 10 of each year is designated as "Sports Day"—a legal holiday in Japan?*

In this chapter I have listed a number of places in Tokyo where you can watch martial arts and sports at no charge. Be sure to check current festivals and events listings in the English-language publications for additional activities, and contact the Tourist Information Center for any specific requests you might have.

I have also offered some suggestions for taking in a little exercise yourself. In addition, you might want to get in touch with the nearest city or ward office to discover what kind of sports activities and facilities they sponsor.

SEE FOR YOURSELF

NIPPON BUDOKAN AND BUDOKAN GAKUEN

BUDOKAN

日本武道館 （Nippon Budokan）

> 2–3 Kitanomaru Koen, Chiyoda-ku, Tokyo 102–8321
>
> ☎ 3216–5100 (Main number in Japanese), 3216–5134 or Fax: 3216–5117 (English Information—Attention: Mr. Goto, Promotion Department). E-mail: budokan@oak.ocn.ne.jp.
>
> 東京都千代田区北ノ丸公園2-3 〒102-8321

If you are interested in Japanese martial arts (*budo*), the Nippon Budokan is a good place with which to become familiar. Every year about fifty free martial arts exhibitions and demonstrations are held here. Built for the 1964 Olympics, this octagonal-shaped, 14,130-seat arena is an important center for eight Japanese martial arts (judo, karate, *kendo*, *naginata*, aikido, *shorinji kenpo*, *jukendo*, and *kyudo*), which train the mind and spirit as well as the body. The Budokan is located in lovely Kitanomaru Park, the historical site that was once the northern citadel for the Tokugawa shogun's Edo Castle (see ch 6).

Two of the many special events that can be seen here at no charge are the Children's Kendo Competition and the January *"Kagami Biraki"* ceremony. About 5,000 children from all over Japan participate in the former, and the latter is a grand ceremonial event during which men dressed in full samurai gear perform a number of rituals dating from the 15th century. It includes the traditional New Year "pounding of the rice cake" ceremony.

NOTE: At other times the Budokan is the site of many international cultural events, concerts, and conventions

Mr. Shoji Goto in the Promotion Department can answer questions in English about sporting events by email, telephone or fax (email is preferred). You are also free to visit their office for information.

Hours: Office hours are 9 AM–5 PM.

Access: 1 min from Kudanshita Stn, Exit 2 (Hanzomon, Tozai, or Toei

Shinjuku lines). Walk straight out from the exit and you will see a bridge spanning the moat to your left. This is the entrance to Kitanomaru Park. The road just inside the historic double Tayasumon Gate will lead you past the Budokan, which is the large building on your left.

BUDOKAN GAKUEN
武道館学園

> 2–3 Kitanomaru Koen, Chiyoda-ku, Tokyo 102–8321
> ☎ 3216–5143 (in Japanese for class information)
> 東京都千代田区北ノ丸公園2-3　〒102-8321

Besides all the events held at the Budokan main arena (see above), it is also possible to drop in and watch practice sessions/classes at their school (the Budokan Gakuen), located on the premises. This is a more casual way to see the martial arts— and a good opportunity to watch them at closer range at the same time.

A nice feature of the school is that it has three *dojos* on the same floor. So you will usually have the opportunity to see more than one type of martial art during your visit. There are even children's classes where you can observe how the kids are taught from a very early age.

Hours: Classes are generally held from about 5 PM–8 PM on weeknights and 2 PM–6:30 PM on Sat. Sometimes this timetable varies slightly, so call for specifics (in Japanese). There is a printed class schedule available in Japanese as well. Clsd on Sun, national, New Year, and spring hols, and from late July through Aug.

Access: Same as for Budokan above, except that as soon as you come through the second large Tayasumon Gate, make an immediate left. After you walk down some steps, turn left again and enter the first door you come to on your left. Take the stairs down to the B2 level, where the school is located.

JUDO

A method of self-defense known as *jujutsu* developed in Japan as a result of samurai grappling, or wrestling, on the battlefield.

It became a popular martial art during Edo times (1600–1868). In 1882, its various schools were reorganized into what is known today as modern judo. Based on the premise of maintaining suppleness and utilizing your opponent's strength to your own advantage, judo has today become a world-famous martial art and Olympic sport. In addition to the Budokan (see above), the Kodokan also hosts judo.

KODOKAN
講道館

> 1–16–30 Kasuga, Bunkyo-ku, Tokyo 1112–0003
> ☎ 3818–4172 (Kodokan)
>   3818–4199 (All-Japan Judo Federation)
> 東京都文京区春日1-16-30　〒112-0003

The Kodokan Judo Hall is the headquarters of judo in Japan. It is home to the All-Japan Judo Federation, which controls judo activities throughout the country. This includes the programs at schools, businesses, all the *dojo* (practice halls)—and the police and self-defense forces as well. The Kodokan Judo Hall has a free spectators' gallery from which you can watch practice on the floor below, which is usually filled with people working out in their all-white *judogi* (training gear).

Hours: Spectators' gallery is open 4 PM–8 PM Mon–Sat. Clsd Sun and hols. The action starts about 6 PM.

Access: 1 min from Kasuga Stn, Exit A1 (Mita Line). Turn right from the exit and walk to the end of the second building. You will see "Kodokan International Judo Center" written in English above the doorway. Take the elevator to the spectators' gallery on the 8F.

KARATE

The self-defense art of karate originated long ago in China, where it was a synthesis of physical, mental, and spiritual aspects. About the year 1500 it traveled to Okinawa, where it became more combat-oriented, and in the 1920s it was introduced to the rest of Japan as modern karate. It incorporates punching and kicking, and as is the case in judo no weapons are used. Karate can be observed in the Budokan (see above), the Japan Karate Association, and other places.

JAPAN KARATE ASSOCIATION

日本空手協会 （Nihon Karate Kyokai）

　　2–23–15 Koraku

　　Bunkyo-ku, Tokyo 112–0004

　　☎ 5800–3091 (English or Japanese)

　　東京都文京区後楽 2-23-15　〒112-0004

The Japan Karate Association is the world's largest karate network. Training and classes may be viewed through the *dojo*'s glass window when they are in session.

Hours: Generally open Mon–Sat, 10:30 AM–11:30 AM, and then again from 5–8 PM (4–8 PM on Sat). Clsd Sun. Call to confirm.

Access: Takanawadai Stn, Exit A2 (Toei Asakusa Line). Turn left and follow the main street for about 5 min. It is on the left side between a large parking lot and the Hotel Mate.

For information only

JAPAN KARATEDO FEDERATION

全日本空手道連盟 （Zen Nihon Karatedo Renmei）

　　No. 2 Senpaku Shinko Building, 6F

　　1–11–2 Toranomon, Minato-ku, Tokyo 105–0001

　　☎ 3503–6640 (English or Japanese)

　　東京都港区虎ノ門1-11-2　第2船舶振興ビル6階　〒105-0001

There are several main styles of karate, which are in turn divided into many subcategories. If you are interested in a specific style, the Japan Karatedo Federation can advise you on where to see it.

Hours: Call 9 AM–5 PM Mon through Fri.

KENDO, JUKENDO, AND NAGINATA

Kendo, or "the Way of the Sword," is the Japanese style of fencing that uses two hands instead of one (as in Western swordsmanship). A long wooden Japanese sword and, more commonly,

a bamboo version are used. Once an ancient Japanese martial art, *kendo* is now practiced as a sport. Opponents wear masks and protective clothing and are only allowed to strike each other on four parts of the body, the head, torso, forearms, and throat.

Jukendo is Japanese bayonet fencing, derived from "the Art of the Spear." *Naginata,* or fencing with a graceful long bamboo pole, was invented by soldier monks who wanted to find a way to defend themselves without harming their opponent. Today the sport is very popular with women. You can see these martial arts at the Budokan, where the All-Japan Kendo Federation is based.

ALL-JAPAN KENDO FEDERATION

全日本剣道連盟 （Zen Nihon Kendo Renmei）
   c/o Nippon Budokan
   2–3 Kitanomaru Koen, Chiyoda-ku, Tokyo 102–8321
   ☎ 3211–5804 (Mrs. Chiba speaks a little English)
   東京都千代田区北ノ丸公園2-3　日本武道館内　〒102-8321

Hours: Call to confirm class sessions. Kendo: 5:20 PM–8 PM Mon, Wed, and Fri. Naginata: 6:30 PM–7:30 PM Tues.
Access: See directions for Budokan Gakuen above.

For information only
ALL-JAPAN NAGINATA FEDERATION (Tokyo Office)

全日本なぎなた連盟 （Zen Nihon Naginata Renmei）
   Kishi Memorial Hall (Kishi Kinen Taiikukan)
   1–1–1 Jinnan, Shibuya-ku, Tokyo 150–8050
   ☎ 3481–2411
   東京都渋谷区神南1-1-1　岸記念体育館　〒150-8050

AIKIDO

Aikido, or "Meeting of the Spirits," is often described as being half sport and half religion. Although it sounds like an ancient art, aikido was developed in Japan in the early 20th century and combines principles of traditional judo, karate, *kendo*, and other old art forms into a unique and spiritual martial art. It is non-aggressive, and muscular strength is not an important factor. In aikido, the spirit power (*ki*) comes strongly into play.

The key is to use as little physical effort as possible to throw your opponent, which is sometimes said to be accomplished by masters without physical contact. In addition to the Budokan (see above), aikido can be seen at the International Aikido Federation.

INTERNATIONAL AIKIDO FEDERATION
合気道本部道場 （Aikido Honbu Dojo）
   17–18 Wakamatsucho, Shinjuku-ku, Tokyo 162–0056
   ☎ 3203–9236 (Mr. Somemiya speaks English—available Mon and Thurs only)
   東京都新宿区若松町17-18　〒162-0056

You are welcome to come and watch aikido sessions here, but you are requested to remain quiet and to keep your legs underneath you. (Do not stick your feet out.)

Hours: Call to confirm. General Practice Sessions: 1-hour lessons Mon–Sat, 6:30–9 AM, 3–8 PM and Sun mornings 9–11:30 AM. Beginners' Classes: 1-hour lessons Mon–Sat 7–8 AM and Mon, Wed, Fri 5:30–8 PM (call for more information).

Access: Take bus No. 76 from Shinjuku Stn (Yamanote and other lines), West Exit, headed toward Iidabashi. Board alongside the corner of the Subaru Showroom Building, just beyond the bus terminals. Get off at Nuke-benten stop (about a 10-min ride). Continue walking in the same direction to the traffic signal, turn left and walk about 150 m (35 yd). It is a four-story building set back slightly on the left.

SHORINJI KENPO

Shorinji kenpo was founded in Japan in 1947, following the devastation of World War II. It was created as a means of encouraging people to rebuild their war-torn country, and instilling a sense of pride and values. It combined a new type of Zen philosophy with a boxing style of martial arts that originated with the Indian monk Bodhidharma and was practiced by the priests at a Buddhist temple in 6th-century China. Physical force is not emphasized here, but rather a working together in harmony. *Shorinji kenpo* can be seen at the Budokan (see above).

MARTIN ARTS
AND
SPORTS

For information only

**WORLD SHORINJI KENPO ORGANIZATION
(Tokyo Office)**

小林寺拳法連盟 （Shorinji Kenpo Renmei）

    1–3–5 Uehara, Shibuya-ku, Tokyo 151–0064

    ☎ 3481–5191

    東京都渋谷区上原1-3-5　〒151-0064

KOBUDO

Kobudo are the original forms of the classic martial arts that gained prominence in Japan during feudal times. Based on techniques necessary for survival on the battlefield, they are the roots of today's martial arts. Although not easily found today, free demonstrations can be seen at the following places: **River-side Sports Center in Sumida Park** (☎ 3872–3181)— Performed here yearly on the 3rd Sat in April. **Meiji Shrine** (☎ 3379– 5511)—Every Nov 3 (Culture Day). **Yasukuni Shrine** (3261–8326)—Performed here three times a year at the shrine's spring (April), summer (July), and autumn (Oct) festivals.

For information only

NIPPON KOBUDO ASSOCIATION

日本古武道協会 （Nippon Kobudo Kyokai）

    Nippon Budokan

    2–3 Kitanomaru Koen, Chiyoda-ku, Tokyo 102–8321

    ☎ 3216–5114

    東京都千代田区北ノ公園2-3　日本武道館　〒102-8321

JAPAN KOBUDO PROMOTION ASSOCIATION

日本古武道振興会 （Nihon Kobudo Shinkokai）

    Room 805, 4–17–1 Kami Takada, Nakano-ku, Tokyo 164– 0002

    ☎ 3386-4764 (Japanese)

    東京都中野区上高田4-17-1　805号室　〒164-0002

This very old, traditional society is dedicated to the preservation of *kobudo*.

KYUDO AND YABUSAME

■ Kyudo

Kyudo means "the Way of the Bow," and is one of the oldest traditional martial arts in Japan. This Japanese-style archery had its origins in hunting, and from the 10th century on became important in military endeavors as well (until warfare techniques changed drastically after the introduction of guns into the country in the 16th century). It features flexible, slender bows that are 2 m (6 ft) long.

Kyudo maintains a close association with Zen and requires an extreme amount of discipline since every movement is predetermined and leaves no room for improvisation. Yet it has maintained a wide following among Japanese students, who continue to join school *kyudo* clubs affiliated with shrines or temples that sponsor demonstrations and competitions. Each spring a *kyudo* competition is held at the Budokan (see above), and the All-Japan Kyudo Federation sometimes sponsors competitions as well. Watch the festivals and events listings too.

For information only
ALL-JAPAN KYUDO FEDERATION
全日本弓道連盟 （Zen Nihon Kyudo Renmei）
    Kishi Memorial Hall (Kishi Kinen Taiikukan)
    1–1–1 Jinnan, Shibuya-ku, Tokyo 150–8050
    ☎ 3481–2387
    東京都渋谷区神南1-1-1　岸記念体育館　〒150-8050

■ Yabusame

Yabusame (archery on horseback) dates back to the Heian (794–1185) and Kamakura (1185–1333) periods, when it was practiced by warriors. Its popularity continued under the rule of the shoguns, and it can still be seen today at festivals and special events. It is very exciting to watch, since the riders ready their bows and shoot at targets while astride horses galloping at full speed, *Yabusame* can be seen at the following places each year (check current festival and events listings for other sites):

Sumida Park (☎ 3871–1528)—Held on the 3rd Sat in April (following day in case of rain) alongside the Sumida River next to Asakusa Stn (Ginza Line). Information available from the Taito Ward Office (☎ 5246–1151). **Baji Koen** (☎ 3429–5101)—Every Sept 23 (Autumn Equinox Holiday). *Yabusame* can be seen as part of their annual "Equestrian Day" horse show, during which the various uses of horses in the Japanese culture are demonstrated. (See horse section in this chapter.) **Toyama Park** (☎ 3200–0066)—Each Oct 10 (Sports Day). Waseda Stn, Exit 2 (Tozai Line). Walk left to the next intersection (police box on corner) and turn left. The park is at the following intersection. Sponsored by the Ana-Hachiman shrine (☎ 3203–7212). **Meiji Shrine** (☎ 3379–5511)—Every Nov 3 (Culture Day) during their annual autumn festival. (See ch 8.)

SUMO

Sumo is the national sport of Japan. Its origins date back to an ancient Shinto religious ritual that determined the harvest for that year according to the will of the gods. Two wrestlers (*rikishi*) wearing only loincloths (*mawashi*) square off inside a 4.5-m- (15-ft-) diameter clay ring. The object is to push the opponent outside of it, or to have some part of his body other than his feet touch the ground. True to its ancient connections with Shinto, the sport is filled with a tremendous amount of ritual and tradition. Even today, sumo matches are held under a hanging roof built in the architectural style of a Shinto shrine, and the ring is sprinkled with salt to purify it before each contest. The referee is still dressed as an ancient nobleman, whose gear includes a fan to represent his authority.

The huge wrestlers, who weigh on an average of between 90 and 165 kg (200–365 lb), live together in "stables" (*heya*) run by former high-ranking wrestlers. A number of *heya* are located around the Kokugikan sumo hall—sumo headquarters and venue for the three 15-day tournaments held yearly in Tokyo (each Jan, May, and Sept). Three additional tournaments are held in cities outside Tokyo each year as well.

For information only

JAPAN SUMO ASSOCIATION

日本相撲協会（Nihon Sumo Kyokai）

    c/o Kokugikan (Sumo Hall)

    1–3–28 Yokoami, Sumida-ku, Tokyo 130–0015

    ☎ 3623–5111

    東京都墨田区横網1-3-28　国技館内　〒130-0015

This is the governing body of professional sumo. Their offices are located in Tokyo's Ryogoku Kokugikan, headquarters for sumo wrestling in Japan.

JAPAN SUMO FEDERATION

日本相撲連盟（Nihon Sumo Renmei）

    Kishi Memorial Hall (Kishi Kinen Taiikukan)

    1–1–1 Jinnan, Shibuya-ku, Tokyo 150–8050

    ☎ 3481–2377

    東京都渋谷区神南1-1-1　岸記念体育館　〒150-8050

This governing body of amateur sumo in Japan sponsors free university sumo tournaments at Yasukuni shrine (see above) each May and September. You could possibly see a future grand champion at one of these matches.

INTERNATIONAL SUMO FEDERATION

国際相撲連盟（Kokusai Sumo Renmei）

    Oonoya Building, 7F

    2–20–1 Hyakunincho, Shinjuku-ku, Tokyo 169–0073

    ☎ 3360–3911

    東京都新宿区百人町2-20-1　大野屋ビル7階　〒169-0073

This organization was created to promote sumo worldwide.

■ Visit a Stable

For an intimate view of the action minus the pageantry, you can visit one of the stables where the mighty men live and train. Their early-morning practice sessions take place just about every day when the wrestlers are in town. The sessions are open to the public, but you need to call ahead for permission. It is a very

different experience from going to an official match, for here you sit ringside—and there is no admission charge! And you can see things you would never see in the formal circumstances of the tournaments. When a wrestler gets strongly jostled in an encounter and his topknot becomes undone, he shakes it out and fixes it right on the spot, enabling you to see how it is tied. And the impact of two huge bodies colliding in close proximity is not something you generally experience in an 11,000-seat stadium, either. It is all so much more real somehow.

The wrestlers hone their techniques at these sessions, practicing certain moves a number of times in quick succession. A visit is an education on the fighting skills behind the pageantry. The lower-ranked wrestlers begin their practice quite early, at about 6 AM. Later (9 AM or so) the major players appear. Note that these times are subject to variation and that the *rikishi* are not always in town. So have someone call ahead (in Japanese) to request permission to visit and get directions and times. It is usually okay to take photos, as long as you DO NOT USE A FLASH.

NOTE: I have listed some centrally located stables below—a complete listing can be found in *Sumo, A Pocket Guide* (see below) and other books on the sport. Also check *Sumo World* magazine's home page (⊜ http://iac.co.jp/~sumowrld/).

SUMIDA-KU STABLES

Azumazeki—3625–0033
Dewanoumi—3632–4920
Hakkaku—3621–0404
Izutsu—3634–9827
Kasugano—3634–9828
Kataonami—3623–9596
Kokonoe—5608–0404
Magaki—3623–7449

Mihogaseki—3632–4767
Miyagino—3634–6291
Nishonoseki—3631–0179
Oshima—3632–6578
Tatsunami—3631–2424
Tokitsukaze—3634–8549
Wakamatsu—5608–3223

TAITO-KU STABLES

Takasago—3876–7770

KOTO-KU STABLES

Ajigawa—3634–5514
Kitanoumi—3630–9900
Oguruma—5245–5103

Oshiogawa—3643–9797
Taiho—3820–8340
Tomozuna—3631–6390

EDOGAWA-KU STABLES

Asahiyama—3686–4950   Nakamura—3655–1808
Isenoumi—3677–6860   Takadagawa—3656–5604
Kagamiyama—3673–7339   Takashima—5607–5488

■ Shrines and Festivals

Meiji Shrine (☎ 3379–5511)—If you want to see ritual, the
Meiji shrine hosts two dedicatory sumo ceremonies each year.
One is the New Year *Hono Dezuiri* held in early January, and
the other can be seen at the end of September. Official installation ceremonies for new grand champions (*yokozuna*) take
place here as well. (See ch 8.) **Yasukuni Shrine** (☎ 3261–
8326)—Yasukuni shrine hosts a dedicatory *Hono Sumo* (or
Zumo)" ceremony each April. About 500 wrestlers participate in
this all-day event, including the top-ranked *yokozun*a grand
champions. Following the morning ceremonies, demonstrations
and matches are held, but in a much lighter vein than at formal
tournaments. Pouring water on each other's heads and playing
leapfrog are some of the antics they go through before settling
down to business. All this takes place rain or shine in the sumo
ring alongside the shrine. Only the ring area is protected by a
roof, so make sure to bring an umbrella if it looks like rain. At
lunchtime you can see the wrestlers close-up and take their pictures as they walk from their dressing room to lunch (See ch 8.)

Free university sumo tournaments are held at Yasukuni
shrine during May and September of each year as well. They are
sponsored by the Japan Sumo Federation (see above).

■ Sumo Related

SUMO MUSEUMS

The Sumo Museum, located inside the sumo headquarters
building (Kokugikan), is the official museum of the sport. (See
ch 10.) **The Sumo Photograph Museum** and **Tabi Museum**
are located nearby as well. (See ch 3—Little Museums of
Sumida-ku.)

MARTIAL ARTS
AND
SPORTS

SUMO ART

Lynn Matsuoka is an American artist who was married to a sumo wrestler. She has become quite famous for her paintings of sumo life. (See ch 14—Art Galleries, Ebisu/Hiroo area).

SUMO MONUMENTS

Tomioka Hachiman shrine (*jinja*) has two monuments to Sumo on its grounds, one for *ozeki* and one for *yokozuna*. (See ch 8.)

FOR MORE INFORMATION

Sumo, A Pocket Guide (revised and updated by David Shapiro) is a compact little guide packed with information that explains the basics of this very complex sport in easily understood language. It also includes a complete listing of stables as well as a glossary of sumo terms. *Sumo World* is a highly respected English-language magazine on sumo. Its home page on the Internet (✉ http://iac.co.jp/~sumowrld/) contains an abundance of information about the sport, its headquarters, tournaments, broadcasts in Japan and abroad, a listing of sumo stables, and other topics.

Do IT YOURSELF

BICYCLING

IMPERIAL PALACE CYCLING COURSE
皇居サイクリング道路 (Kokyo Saikuringu Doro)
1–1 Kokyo Gaien, Chiyoda-ku, Tokyo 100–0002
☎ 3211–5020 (Sundays only)
5572–6412 (Weekdays)
東京都千代田区皇居外苑1-1 〒100-0002

Did you know that it is possible to borrow a bike and ride alongside the Imperial Palace on Sundays for free? Yes, every week 500 bikes are lent out on a first-come, first-served basis to anyone six years of age or older. Just fill out a very short form (in Japanese or English), and you can choose from among their offerings—which include MTBs, road-racers, light-cycles, mini-cycles, and children's bikes.

The 3-km (2-mi) route is a very scenic one, and mainly runs along Uchibori-dori which is closed to traffic and passes in front of the Imperial Palace. Located between the two outer moats, the course cuts through the Palace Outer Garden, where row after row of finely groomed *matsu* (pine) trees that resemble large bonsai line either side of the road. After crossing in front of the palace square, the road continues along the palace moat and its Edo-style guard towers. After the turnabout at the Palace Hotel, the return route passes by the Wadakura Fountain Park, where spouting fountains "perform" for you as you pedal by.

NOTE: You might want to wander back to the Wadakura Fountain Park after you turn in your bike. It contains a rest corner where nature videos are played, and a wall map of walking routes through the area (labeled in English and Japanese). Next door is a restaurant that overlooks the fountains.

The course takes about 15 min to complete at a leisurely pace. You can go around more than once, but they ask that you fill out another short form for their records each time.

Hours: 10 AM–3 PM (last bike out 3 PM) every Sun (except when it is raining).

Access: A 3-min walk from Nijubashi-mae Stn, Exit 2 (Chiyoda Line). Walk straight ahead when you come up to street level and you will soon see the Babasakimon Police Box (koban). The registration booth and bicycles are next to it. It is also a 15-min walk from JR Tokyo Stn (Yamanote and other lines). Exit the Marunouchi side.

MEIJI SHRINE OUTER GARDEN CYCLING COURSE
神宮外苑サイクリングセンター
(Jingu Gaien Saikuringu Senta)
   10 Kasumigaoka, Shinjuku-ku, Tokyo 160–0013
   ☎ 3405–8753 (Sundays and National Holidays),
   3582–3311 (Information on Weekdays, Japan Bicycle Road Development Association)
   東京都新宿区霞岳町10 〒160-0013

The road circling the Meiji Shrine Outer Gardens is closed to auto traffic on Sunday and national hols. You only need to fill out a simple form (in Japanese or English) to borrow one of their 400 bicycles and ride around the oval 1.2-km (3/4-mi)

MARTIAL ARTS
AND
SPORTS

course. There is no age requirement, and bicycles come in all sizes, even with training wheels. The route takes about 10–15 min to complete, but no time limit is imposed (except on extremely busy days or for the use of popular bicycle models such as mountain bikes). You are requested to return the bike if you stop to take a long break.

The route passes by the Meiji Memorial Picture Gallery (Kaigakan Museum), the National Stadium (the largest in Japan and the main venue for the 1964 Summer Olympics), the Jingu Baseball Stadium (home of the Yakult Swallows), tennis courts, and lots of greenery.

NOTE: The Meiji Memorial Picture Gallery contains 80 Japanese and Western-style paintings documenting the final days of the Edo period and the life of the Meiji emperor. (¥300)

Hours: 9 AM–4 PM (last bike out 3:30 PM) Sun and national hols (except when it is raining).

Access: A 7-min walk from JR Sendagaya Stn (Sobu Line). Walk straight out from the station's only exit until you reach the next traffic signal (Mos Burger is on the corner). Turn left and walk until the road ends at Gaien Nishi-dori. Cross the street and walk right to the next traffic signal. Go left at the corner and follow the stadium around to the end of the block. The free bike rental office will be to your left. Also accessible from Gaienmae Stn (Ginza Line).

TAMA RIVER CYCLING COURSE

玉川緑地サイクリング コース

（Tamagawa Ryokuchi Saikuringu Kosu）

4–23–3 Nishi Rokugo, Ota-ku, Tokyo 144–0056

☎ 3731–9388

東京都大田区西六郷4-18-14　〒144-0056

If you don't want to wait until Sundays or holidays to go biking, there are two courses where you can cycle along the Tama River daily. You can either get your laps in on the 2.5-km (1.5-mi) track that encircles the baseball field, or ride on the 10.6-km (6.5-mi) strip running alongside the river between the Maruko-bashi and Daishibashi bridges.

About forty bikes are available for adults and kids ten years of age and older (sorry, no small children) at no charge. To borrow one, just present identification.

Hours: 9 AM–noon (last bike out 11 AM) and 1 PM–4 PM (last bike out 3 PM) daily. Clsd New Year hols. Bikes must be returned for lunch time.

Access: 3 min from Rokugodote Stn (local stop on the Keihin Kyuko Line). Walk straight out from the station's only exit, turn left at the street and left again after you pass under the next set of train tracks. At the end of the road you will see the bicycle lending office on the right side.

Bicycle Related
BICYCLE CULTURE CENTER, 2/3F
自転車文化センター 2/3階 〈Jitensha Bunka Center〉
JAPAN BICYCLE PROMOTION INSTITUTE, 6F
日本自転車産業復興協会6階 〈Nihon Jitensha Shinko Kyokai〉
> Jitensha Kaikan No. 3 Building
> 1–9–3 Akasaka, Minato-ku, Tokyo 107–0052
> ☎ 3584–4530 (Bicycle Culture Center),
> 5572–6410 (Japan Bicycle Promotion Institute)
> 東京都港区赤坂1-9-3　自転車会館3号館　〒107-0052

A bicycle museum with sixty-three interesting and unusual bicycles is on the 2F of the Bicycle Culture Center (see ch 10), and a Bicycle Information Center with lots of books, magazines, maps, and more, in English and other languages (see ch 13) is on the 3F. An information pamphlet in English about cycling throughout Japan in general can be obtained from the Japan Bicycle Promotion Institute on the 6F.

NOTE: Another good source of bicycling information is the book *Cycling Japan: A Personal Guide to Exploring Japan by Bicycle,* edited by Bryan Harrell

Hours: **The Bicycle Culture Center**—10 AM–4 PM wkdys. The **Japan Bicycle Promotion Institute**—9:30 AM–noon and 1 PM–5 PM wkdys.

Access: 7 min from Toranomon Stn, Exit 3 (Ginza Line). Walk straight out of the exit and follow the sidewalk as it curves to the left. (Don't cross the street here.) Continue walking for about five min until the road ends at a T-crossing at the Shin-Nikko Building. Turn right. When you reach the intersection, cross over. Directly across from the main entrance to the American Embassy you will see a "Bicycle Culture Center" sign in English on the side of the building. Enter there and walk back to Building No. 3.

JOGGING AND WALKING

JOG AROUND THE IMPERIAL PALACE

Tokyo's most famous jogging route encircles the Imperial Palace, where every morning you can see people taking their 20–30 min jog before heading off to work. Start anywhere along the road that circles the palace grounds.

TOKYO INTERNATIONAL WALK RALLY

東京国際ウォークラリー

 National Recreation Association of Japan
 Suidobashi Nishiguchi Building, 6F
 2–20–7 Misakicho, Chiyoda-ku, Tokyo 101–0061
 ☎ 3265–1318 (Ask for Odawara-san)
 東京都千代田区三崎町2-20-7　水道橋西口会館6階　日本国際レク
 リエーション協会　〒101-0061

Every March the National Recreation Association of Japan organizes a walk to promote international exchange. The event calls for participants to follow a course outlined on a map and solve quizzes along the way. Although there are three courses that begin at various parks throughout the city, everyone eventually ends up at the same spot. About 5,000 people take part in the event each year, which began in 1990. Children and non-Japanese participants are invited to join at no charge. A free knapsack and lunch are provided for everyone who registers.

Hours: 9 AM–3 PM on the day of the walk.
Access: The courses begin from various parks around Tokyo. Specific information will be given to you when you register.

JUST GET OUT THERE AND DO IT!

Tokyo is a great walking city. This giant metropolis is actually made up of many small and unique neighborhoods, each with its own distinct personality. This makes Tokyo an endlessly fascinating place to wander through. But please be aware that the layout of the city is quite complex, and that not many streets have actual names. So it would probably be a good idea to bring a map or guide of some kind to accompany you on your walks (although allowing yourself to get lost is another option—I have made some fascinating discoveries this way). But assuming that you want to know where you are at the end of the day, here are some suggestions for walks.

The Tourist Information Center publishes a free pamphlet entitled *Walking Courses in Tokyo*. Several interesting routes through central Tokyo are mapped out, including walks through sections of the older, more traditional areas of the city known as Shitamachi (see ch 3).

The English area-maps provided by ward offices sometimes include walking tours. For example, Bunkyo-ku publishes a map containing four courses that pass by well-known sites and gardens, such as the famous stainless-steel roofed St. Mary's Cathedral (see ch 8) and the prestigious Tokyo University.

The Ginza and Aoyama areas of the city are great places for gallery-hopping (see ch 14), and Tokyo's parks and gardens are delightful for strolls (see ch 6 and 7). So why not just start walking? Tokyo is a city filled with many unexpected surprises and rich rewards.

Horses, more horses, and ponies too

Horses have been an important part of Japanese culture since ancient times. Early on they were worshipped as deities, and it was believed that the "divine spirit" came to the human world on horseback. Evidence of horses being harnessed and ridden dates from about the 4th–6th centuries AD, during the Kofun period.

Horse racing in Japan began in the 8th century, when races were held at the Imperial Court and at shrine festivals in connection with prayers for a good harvest. Western-style horse racing was introduced in 1861, when the first races were organized in

Yokohama. Today the Japan Racing Association (a semigovernment organization) manages all the national horse racing and facilities in the country. They produce a free, nicely illustrated English guide to racing in Japan entitled *King of Sports* each year. Contact their International Department at the address or fax number listed below if you would like a copy. And make your request as early as possible—supplies do run out.

HORSE RACING

Horse racing is an extremely popular sport in Japan, as can be seen by the number of people who flock to the racecourses each weekend. Horses from other countries are often entered in the races, and Japan even has its own version of the "triple crown." It encompasses the Japan Derby in late May and two other races run in April and November. But you don't have to travel far to see these and other exciting races each weekend. You can watch them right in central Tokyo—at no charge. Here's how:

JAPAN RACING ASSOCIATION (Off-Track Facilities)
日本中央競馬会 （Nippon Chuo Keibakai）
Shiroyama JT Mori Building, 31F
4–3–1 Toranomon, Minato-ku, Tokyo 105–6231
☎ 3591–5251, fax: 5401–4157 (International Department)
3815–2725 (WINS Korakuen), 5600–1616 (WINS Kinshicho)
東京都港区虎ノ門4-3-1　城山JT森ビル31階　日本中央競馬会国際部
〒105-6231

The Japan Racing Association (JRA) operates a number of off-track betting facilities (OTB) that broadcast the races live at various locations throughout the city. The largest of these is WINS Korakuen, located next door to Tokyo Dome. Its seven floors have a capacity of 30,000 people at one time, but sometimes 150,000–200,000 people pass through the building in a single day. A visit here definitely gives one the impression that horse racing must be the nation's favorite pastime. There are small TV screens all over, but the 8F has a very large screen on which you can watch all the races from the eastern region of Japan (Tokyo and the surrounding areas), and also the main western region (the Kyoto-Osaka-Kobe axis) ones, too. About 12 races are televised per day. There are only a few chairs, so you can either stand, bring your own little portable seat, or spread out newspapers on the floor.

Other WINS buildings are located in Ginza, Shinjuku, Shibuya, Shinbashi, Asakusa, and Kinshicho. (There are quite a few chairs in front of WINS Kinshicho's 4F and 7F big screens.)

You can also see horse races on closed-circuit TV while sipping a beer (no, the beer is not free) at the outdoor Keyaki Beer Garden in the front of the WINS Korakuen Building. (Facilities for local government races are nearby too.) Afterward you might want to stroll over to the Korakuen Sports Club and watch people swimming in the Olympic-sized pool through large street-side windows—or enjoy a spectacular free view of the surrounding area from the 25F of the Bunkyo-ku Civic Center (see ch 16), located on the other side of Tokyo Dome.

NOTE: There are numerous non-free attractions in the Korakuen complex as well, such as the Baseball Hall of Fame and Museum (¥400), a very large ferris wheel, a steep roller coaster, and other amusements at the Korakuen Amusement Park.

Hours: Races are run between 10 AM and 4 PM on wknds.

Access: WINS Korakuen is 1 min from JR Suidobashi Stn, West Exit (Sobu Line). Go right from the ticket turnstile. Jog left, then right, and cross the bridge over Sotobori-dori. Make an immediate left into the first building on the other side and take the escalator up. The big screen is on the 8F. (WINS Kinshicho is also on the Sobu Line, 2 min from JR Kinshicho Stn, South Exit. Go straight out to the street, cross over and turn right. WINS is in Building A, on the next corner.)

PLAZA EQUUS
プラザ エクウス
Shibuya Beam Building, 2/3F
31–2 Udagawacho, Shibuya-ku, Tokyo 150–0042
☎ 5458–4331
東京都渋谷区宇田川町31-2　渋谷ビームビル2/3階　〒150-0042

Plaza Equus is the Japan Racing Association's showcase in central Tokyo. It was created to acquaint people with the culture of racing, its highlights, and its history. It features a large multisection screen displaying famous races (you can sit comfortably and watch them), an art gallery for horse-related shows, various other temporary and permanent exhibitions, and a library with about 200 English books on horses. (See ch 13.) The rooms on the 3F appear to be straight out of an English country estate and contain lots of little nooks and crannies to explore.

Hours: 11 AM–7:30 PM Wed–Mon. Clsd Tues (Wed if Tues is hol) and New Year hols.

Access: A 5-min walk from Shibuya Stn, Hachiko Exit (Yamanote and other lines). Walk left along Dogenzaka for about 1 min and turn right at the 109 Building (the big silver tower on the corner) onto Bunkamura-dori. Walk past three traffic lights. Then turn right at the next small street (across from Tokyu Department Store). Continue to the second corner and the Beam Building will be on the far right side. The inside escalator will take you up to the Plaza Equus Showroom and Library on the 2F and 3F.

HORSE RACING MUSEUM

JRA競馬博物館 （JRA Keiba Hakubutsukan）
Tokyo Racecourse (Tokyo Fuchu Keibajo)
1–1 Hiyoshicho, Fuchu-shi, Tokyo 183–0024
☎ 0423–63–3141
東京都府中市日吉町1-1　東京府中競馬場　〒183-0024

The Horse Racing Museum is located on the grounds of the Tokyo Racecourse at Fuchu, home of the Japanese Derby and Japan Cup. If you are planning a day at the races or are en route to a nearby destination such as Mt. Takao (see ch 3), you might want to stop by and experience their 360-degree multimedia "Circle Vision Theatre." Or you can sit astride a mechanical galloping horse as it races around the Tokyo Racecourse (seen on a screen in front of you) at the "Riding Vision" attraction. The machine simulates the change in a horse's strides as it takes the corners and speeds up over the final quarter of the race. Explanations are all in Japanese, but there is an English brochure, and graphic visuals such as oil paintings and statues of past champions, as well as special exhibitions, keep you interested.

Hours: 10 AM–4 PM (9:30 AM–4:30 PM on racing days). Clsd Mon and Tues.

Access:The museum is on the grounds of the Tokyo Racecourse, 10 min from Higashi Fuchu Stn, and 15 min from Fuchu Stn (both on the Keio Line). It is also a 5-min walk from Fuchukeiba Seimonmae, but you should check your train map for this station as it cuts off from the main Keio Line. On race days a walkway is open that leads directly to the track from the Fuchu Honmachi Stn (JR Nanbu or Musashino lines).

NOTE: Entrance to the museum is free. However, when an event is being held at the track there is a ¥200 fee to enter the grounds.

HORSE SHOWS

BAJI EQUESTRIAN PARK

馬事公苑 （Baji Koen）

2–1–1 Kami Yoga, Setagaya-ku, Tokyo 158–0098

☎ 3429–5101

東京都世田谷区上用賀2-1-1　〒158-0098

Baji Koen was the site of the 1964 Olympics equestrian events, and still holds horse-related events and shows. Conceived and owned by the Japan Racing Association (JRA), its horse theme is echoed in statues, horse-shaped water fountains, and shrubbery seen throughout the park. And it is the home to a number of real horses, too!

The park hosts two major events: one in May and the other in September. During the Golden Week holidays, a free three-day Spring Horse Show (May 3, 4, 5) includes a steeplechase and many other top-notch equestrian events. On the Sept 23 Autumn Equinox holiday, another big show called "Equestrian Day" celebrates the use of horses in the Japanese culture and in festivals. Some of its highlights are demonstrations of *yabusame* (archery on horseback) and *dakyu* (Japanese polo).

The 185,576-sq m (2 million-sq ft) park grounds also contain woods that you can stroll through and a small Japanese garden. Horses that are housed in the park can be visited in their paddocks daily between 10 AM and 2:30 PM. (Also see free rides for kids below.)

Hours: Open daily, 9 AM–5 PM *April–Oct*, and 9 AM–4 PM *Nov– March*.

Access:The easiest way to get to the park is to take the No. 24 bus (bound for Seijo Gakuen-mae) from the south bus terminal of

Shibuya Stn (Yamanote and other lines). It leaves from the curbside near the Tokyu Plaza Building and is a 30-min ride to the "Nodai-mae" bus stop. Then a 2-min walk straight ahead and left through the promenade at the far side of the Royal Host Restaurant brings you to the entrance to the park.

FREE RIDES FOR KIDS

BAJI EQUESTRIAN PARK

馬事公苑 （Baji Koen）

2–1–1 Kami Yoga, Setagaya-ku, Tokyo 158–0098

☎ 3429–5101

東京都世田谷区上用賀2-1-1　〒158-0098

One Sunday each month, "Get To Know Horses Day" features thoroughbred horse, pony, and carriage rides for kids four to ten years old. The tickets are free from the Information Booth at the entrance to the park, but they need to be picked up at noon for the 2 PM rides. (See above entry for more about the park and access.)

SHINOZAKI PONYLAND

篠崎ポニーランド

3–12–17 Shinozakicho, Edogawa-ku, Tokyo 133–0061

☎ 3678–7520

東京都江戸川区篠崎町3-12-17　〒133-0061

Free pony and stagecoach rides for elementary school kids and younger are available at Ponyland, as well as free carriage rides for everyone. All this at a great location right alongside the Edogawa River.

They also offer free horseback riding classes at their Riding Academy five times a year (January, March, May, September, and November) for females over twelve years of age who live in the area. Participants are chosen by lottery.

Hours: Pony and carriage rides are available 10 AM–11:30 AM and 1:30 PM–3 PM (except July 21–Aug 31 when only morning rides are given). Clsd Mon (Tues if Mon a hol), rainy days, and New Year hols.

Access: A 10- to 12-min walk from the South Exit of Shinozaki Stn (Toei Shinjuku Line). Turn left from the exit and right at the corner. When you reach the police box (koban) at the next corner, turn left and walk up that street for about 6–7 min until you reach a main street. Cross over and walk right, passing underneath the highway. Ponyland is about 2 min beyond that. You can't miss it—there is a big arched sign on the left that leads down to the riverbank. Or from the same exit, take a No. 71 or 72 bus (from bus stand No. 3) to the "Shinozaki Toshokan-mae/Ponyland" bus stop. It is probably a good idea to let the bus driver know you want "Ponyland," so he will call it out. It is a very short ride.

NAGISA PONYLAND

なぎさポニーランド

Nagisa Park, 7–3 Minami Kasai, Edogawa-ku, Tokyo 134–0085

☎ 5658–5720

東京都江戸川区南葛西7-3　なぎさ公園内　〒134-0085

Also in Edogawa Ward is Nagisa Ponyland, which offers the same features as above except for the carriage ride.

Hours: Same as above.

Access: At Kasai Stn (Tosei Line), take bus No. 24 heading for Nagisa New Town. It leaves from the No. 8 bus stand of the bus terminal just across the road from the station's only exit. Get off at the Nagisa New Town stop, about a 10-min ride. Nagisa Ponyland is inside Nagisa Park, which is next to the bus stop.

HIGASHI ITABASHI PARK

東板橋公園

3–50–1 Itabashi, Itabashi-ku, Tokyo 173–0004

☎ 3962–8419 (Zoo)

東京都板橋区板橋3-50-1　〒173-0004

Free pony rides are available for kids three years of age through elementary school (ages three to five should be accompanied by parents). Tickets are given out from 10:10 AM to 10:25 AM for the rides, which begin at 10:30. On weekdays thirty kids can ride, and on weekends the number is raised to fifty. There are lots of other animals and an aquarium here, too. (See ch 6 for more details.)

Hours: 10 AM–4:30 PM Tues–Sun. Clsd at 4 PM Dec–Feb. Clsd on Mon (Tues if Mon a hol) and New Year hols.

Access: An 8-min walk from Itabashi Kuyakusho-mae Stn, Exit A1 (Mita Line). Turn left from the exit and walk straight down the street. Turn left at the second traffic light (a large gray brick sports center is on the far left corner). Walk for another 3 min. The park entrance is on the left side—the critters are behind the baseball field and tennis courts.

5

FESTIVALS
AND OTHER
OUTDOOR
ENTERTAINMENT

FABULOUS JAPANESE FESTIVALS

NEIGHBORHOOD AND AREA FESTIVALS
- *Ueno Summer Festival*
- *Azabu Juban Summer Festival*
- *Shinjuku Grand Festival*
- *Ginza Grand Festival*

SOME OTHER CELEBRATIONS
- *St. Patrick's Day*
- *Earth Day*
- *Halloween*
- *Christmas in Tokyo*
- *New Year's Eve*
- *International School Carnivals and Fairs*

STREET ENTERTAINMENT

HORSE SHOWS

INTRODUCTION

*F*estivals are very much a part of Japanese life. Traditionally held at shrines and temples, they offer a delightful and meaningful insight into Japanese culture and customs. Celebrated with a glowing enthusiasm that is contagious and easy to get caught up in, Japanese festivals are an experience that is long-remembered.

In addition, numerous events and celebrations of foreign origin have been incorporated into the Japanese culture so neatly that they barely seem "foreign" at all.

All of these festivals and events are great, and they are plentiful. Interesting celebrations are going on just about year-round in Tokyo, so jump right in—these fascinating experiences are open to everyone.

FABULOUS JAPANESE FESTIVALS

Festivals, rites, and rituals have always been a very important part of the Japanese culture. Japan is historically a land of farmers, and even today the influence of the spring rice planting, the summer growing season, and the fall harvest can clearly be seen in the scheduling of the numerous festivals around the country.

Free exhibitions of many traditional performing arts (see ch 11) are among the offerings at these fabulous seasonal events, which generally last for several days each. Traditional martial arts (see ch 4)—including *kendo* (sword fighting), *yabusame* (archery on horseback), and sumo wrestling ceremonies and matches —are also featured, as are elegant court dancing, lion dances, magic shows, and concerts by traditional orchestras dressed in full regalia and playing ancient instruments.

The diverse aspects of nature are observed and celebrated as well. This can be seen most clearly in the colorful festivals that mark the blooming of the various flowers in Tokyo—the spring Cherry Blossom Festival being the biggest blowout of the year! Other examples are the mid-September moon-viewing (*Tsukimi*), the July 7 Star Festival (*Tanabata*), and the March 3 change of seasons from winter to spring (*Setsubun*).

People are not left out either, as can be seen in the May 5 Children's Day (*Kodomo-no-hi*), Jan 15 Coming of Age Day (*Seijin-no-hi*), and Sept 15 Respect for the Aged Day (*Keiro-no-hi*) hols. Buddha's birthday is observed every April 8 (*Hana Matsuri*), and the spectacular fireworks displays that light up the skies over Tokyo each summer have been going on for nearly 400 years—since 1613. (See the Fireworks Museum in ch 10.)

Festivals can also be great exercise. You are welcome to join the traditional Japanese *odori* dancing, following the lead of the dancers in front of you as they move slowly around in a circle. And how exciting it is to follow the route of the *mikoshi* (portable shrines) as they wind their way through the tiny back streets of Tokyo, hoisted on the sholders of the locals. You can even try your hand at carrying one if you like—I guarantee you will never forget the experience! Yes, Tokyo's many Japanese festivals and celebrations can serve as a comprehensive introduction to the cultural traditions of Japan—all for free.

Tokyo's major festivals and events are listed in the monthly *Calendar Events*, available at the Tourist Information Center. Pick up a copy toward the end of each month to preview the special events coming up. (Check their *Annual Events* pamphlet too.) Call the Teletourist Information Line (☎ 3201–2911) for twenty-four-hour information on festivals and other happenings, and read the monthly festival and events sections of the English-language publications as well.

NOTE: Those interested in learning more about Japan might want to pick up *Festivals of Japan*, an inexpensive little book packed with information about Japanese festivals and written in a very accessible style. It is part of the *Japan in Your Pocket* series published by Japan Travel Bureau (JTB).

Neighborhood and Area Festivals

Various areas of the city sponsor their own festivals. Often these are little neighborhood events centered around a local shrine or temple, but some—like the ones listed here—are staged on a grand scale.

■ **Ueno Summer Festival**—*Mid-July to mid-August*

The Ueno Summer Festival features a big pageant during which Ueno Park is lit up with hundreds of colorful lanterns, antique stalls are set up around Shinobazu Pond, and people from all over Japan perform their local dances in a big parade. There is also a nightly series of free concerts at the Waterside Music Hall (alongside the pond) that feature an eclectic variety of entertainment. One year there was even a Hawaiian music concert, complete with hula dancers!) ☎ 5685–1181 (Ueno Park Information Center.

■ Azabu Juban Summer Festival—*A three-day weekend in August*

This is one of the biggest three-day parties in town—and one of the most international as well. People stroll through the streets wearing *yukata*, Western clothes, and the national dress of many foreign lands. In addition to having all the ingredients of a great Japanese festival (delicious festival food, *bon odori* dancing, and such), there is a large international area where booths representing lands from around the globe display their country's wares and serve their national dishes and drinks. One year Holland's booth displayed a large windmill, the American area featured fossils and astronaut food, and the Russians sold *matryoshka* dolls (dolls inside of dolls) and flavored vodkas. There was even an area where you can play in snow at this summer event! This festival has something for everyone—and you never know what you are going to find here. ☎ 3451–5812 (Azabu Juban Shinko Kumiai)

■ Shinjuku Grand Festival—*October 1–November 3*

This festival offers a range of events: a bazaar, *awa odori* dancing, several concerts, a Sports Festa, stage performances, and a spectacular "Flower Fantasia" parade featuring over 1,000 people, marching bands, and twenty floats covered with beautiful flowers. This major event takes place in various locations around the Shinjuku area. ☎ 3209–1111 ext. 3261 (Shinjuku Ward Office)

■ Ginza Grand Festival—*The 2nd Sunday to 3rd Sunday of each October*

This is another winner that packs lots of things into one week. The Ginza stores compete to create the best window display, and the "Festival Promenade" presents a real carnival atmosphere. But the main event is definitely the evening of the "Sound and Illumination" (*Oto to Hikari*) parade. It features spectacular floats, bands, and hundreds of folk dancers from all around the country, who march along Ginza's main street after dark, to the delight of the many onlookers. About 2,000 people participate in this fun event every year. ☎ 3561–0919 (Ginza Grand Festival Office)

SOME OTHER CELEBRATIONS

In addition to the traditional festivals and the area-sponsored events, there are a number of other celebrations—many with international origins. Here are some of these free happenings:

■ **St. Patrick's Day**—*Sunday before March 17*

Although the Irish population in Tokyo is under 1,000, they put on quite a strong showing each year when Omotesando (Tokyo's Champs Elysées) is blocked off for a wing-ding of a St. Patrick's Day parade on the Sunday before March 17. The festivities are usually led by the Irish ambassador, and record stores, radio stations, and restaurants join in the spirit of the day by featuring Irish music, special menus, and big parties that often serve green beer! The parties are not free but they are fun. Call the Irish embassy at ☎ 3263–0695 for information and related activities.

■ **Earth Day**—*April 22*

Yes, Earth Day is celebrated in Tokyo, as it is in numerous places around the world each year. People gather in popular Yoyogi Park for an exciting two-day celebration consisting of international stage entertainment, ethnic food and handicrafts, and a number of special events, including a big Earth Day concert. Call Earth Day Headquarters at ☎ 3263–9022. Usually there is someone there who can speak English.

■ **Halloween**—*October 31*

Since 1980 people have been parading down Omotesando Avenue the last Sunday in October dressed in outrageous costumes that one can only get away with on Halloween. You are

NOTE: Halloween is also celebrated in amusement parks and in many restaurants and bars, particularly in the Roppongi area on Halloween night itself—Boo!

likely to see cute little fairies and elves marching next to macabre draculas dripping blood from their teeth. Feel free to join in and bring the kids along, too. There are free goodies for them afterward. If you don't see information about the event in the newspapers, call the Tourist Information Center (☎ 3201–3331) or the Harajuku Champs Elysées Association (☎ 3406–4303 in Japanese) for details.

■ Christmas in Tokyo

Although Japan is not a Christian country, no matter where you go in Tokyo during the Christmas season, there is never any question of what time of the year it is. Santa Claus is everywhere, and the whole city comes alive with twinkling lights, the smell of pine, and decorations that could hold their own against those of any major city in the West. In short, it's celebrated in a big way. The department stores are decked out in yuletide trappings (starting just after Halloween in some cases), Christmas carols can be heard in every building, and beautiful lighting displays suddenly appear on all the main shopping streets.

There are many free special events around the holiday season. A member of the imperial family generally oversees the lighting of the Christmas tree at Tokyo Stn, kicking off a week of bazaars, mini-concerts, and street performances there. Call Refugees International (☎ 5500–3093) for a schedule and information. The embassies often invite the public to join in and celebrate the traditions of their cultures—the Swedish Embassy's Santa Lucia performance featuring the Queen of Light is just one example.

The churches are particularly active during the Christmas season. Keep your eyes and ears open for wonderful free concerts of classical music, Gregorian chants, Christmas carols, brass bands, bell concerts, special pageants, and many other events that take place throughout the city at this special time of the year.

Christmas lights are everywhere, of course. But *the* show is on Omotesando, when the long rows of zelkova trees on either side of the wide avenue burst into twinkling masses of light at dusk each evening. The area fills with sightseers, and on some nights carolers move among the crowds, their songs enhancing the already wonderfully festive spirit of the season.

This spectacular yuletide light show dazzles spectators along Omotesando between Harajuku and Omotesando stations for the two weeks preceding Christmas each year. Then, on what should be the apex of all this—Christmas Day itself—the decorations all disappear, and everyone gets up and goes to work just like any other day. Call the Tourist Information Center (☎ 3201–3331) or the Harajuku Champs Elysées Association (☎ 3406–4303 in Japanese) for more information.

■ New Year's Eve

This is the day when the cultural differences of Japan and the West really stand out. Millions of Japanese visit shrines and temples at midnight (as well as during the first few days of the year) to purify themselves in preparation for a brand new year. Meiji shrine and Asakusa Kannon temple (Sensoji) draw the largest crowds. (See ch 8.) Meanwhile, Westerners are partying themselves crazy and doing everything possible to pollute their bodies so that they will have to start the new year in bed, recuperating from the night before. How did we get to be so different?

■ International School Carnivals and Fairs

The international schools in Japan put on wonderful carnivals, fairs, and festivals that bring together people from diverse cultures for a day of eating, drinking, playing, and fun. Many are held during the spring and summer seasons, and sometimes at other times of the year as well. The food is not free, of course, but the fun and entertainment are! And you don't need to be affiliated with the schools to attend.

ST. MARY'S INTERNATIONAL SCHOOL CARNIVAL

聖マリア学園スクール カーニバル

    1–6–19 Seta, Setagaya-ku, Tokyo 158–0095

    ☎ 3709–3411

    東京都世田谷区瀬田1-6-19 〒158-0095

Every year on the 2nd Saturday in May, St. Mary's International School pulls out all the stops and throws a huge outdoor party on its campus—rain or shine. Booth after booth of authentic and mouthwatering homemade food and drinks from twenty-five or more countries can be sampled at very reasonable prices. Live entertainment, games, handicrafts, and a fabulous raffle with major prizes such as cars and air tickets to faraway destinations are other highlights. Since over seventy nationalities attend the school, the day is always filled with a delightful mixture of music and entertainment of the cultures that they represent.

Hours: 10 AM–5 PM.

Access: Between Kaminoge Stn (Oimachi Line) and Futako Tamagawaen Stn (Shin Tamagawa Line). Call for specific directions.

Here are some other international schools. Call for festival dates and information.

THE AMERICAN SCHOOL IN JAPAN
アメリカン スクール イン ジャパン
1–1–1 Nomizu, Chofu-shi, Tokyo 182–0031
☎ 0422–34–5300
東京都調布市野水1-1-1　〒182-0031

AOBA INTERNATIONAL SCHOOL
青葉インターナショナル スクール
2–10–34 Aobadai, Meguro-ku, Tokyo 153–0042
☎ 3461–1442
東京都目黒区青葉台2-10-34　〒153-0042

THE BRITISH SCHOOL IN TOKYO
ブリティッシュ スクール イン 東京
1–21–18 Shibuya, Shibuya-ku, Tokyo 150–0002
☎ 3400–7353
東京都渋谷区渋谷1-21-18　〒150-0002

CHRISTIAN ACADEMY IN JAPAN

クリスチャン アカデミー イン ジャパン

    1–2–14 Shinkawacho, Higashi Kurume-shi, Tokyo 203–0013

    ☎ 0424–75–2200

    東京都東久留米市新川町1-2-14　〒203-0013

INTERNATIONAL SCHOOL OF THE SACRED HEART

聖心インターナショナル スクール

    4–3–1 Hiroo, Shibuya-ku, Tokyo 150–0012

    ☎ 3400–3951

    東京都渋谷区広尾4-3-1　〒150-0012

JAPAN INTERNATIONAL SCHOOL

ジャパン インターナショナル スクール

    2–10–7 Miyamae, Suginami-ku, Tokyo 168–0081

    ☎ 3335–6620

    東京都杉並区宮前2-10-7　〒168-0081

LYCEE-FRANCO-JAPONAIS DE TOKYO

リセ フランコ ジャポネ

    1–2–43 Fujimicho, Chiyoda-ku, Tokyo 102–0071

    ☎ 3261–0137

    東京都千代田区富士見町1-2-43　〒102-0071

NISHIMACHI INTERNATIONAL SCHOOL

西町インターナショナル スクール

    2–14–7, Moto Azabu, Minato-ku, Tokyo 106–0046

    ☎ 3451–5520

    東京都港区元麻布2-14-7　〒106-0046

SANTA MARIA SCHOOL

聖マリア学園

    2–2–4 Minami Tanaka, Nerima-ku, Tokyo 177–0035

    ☎ 3904–0517

    東京都練馬区南田中2-2-4　〒177-0035

SEISEN INTERNATIONAL SCHOOL

清泉インターナショナル学園

    1–12–15 Yoga, Setagaya-ku, Tokyo 158–0097

☎ 3704–2661
東京都世田谷区用賀1-12-15　〒158-0097

TEMPLE UNIVERSITY JAPAN
テンプル大学ジャパン

1–8–12 Minami Azabu, Minato-ku, Tokyo 106–0047
☎ 5441–9800
東京都港区南麻布1-8-12　〒106-0047

STREET ENTERTAINMENT

Yes, there is a lot of outdoor entertainment to be found in Tokyo—organized and otherwise. During the summer months, it is not unusual to come across free concerts and entertainment being staged in front of large buildings and inside parks. There are also outside venues like Shinjuku Station Square, the little stage at Shinjuku Station's East Exit where you can often see acts performing.

But things are not always so formal. In fact, impromptu acts can usually be found performing all over. Beatles and Elvis clones are commonly seen near major train stations such as Shibuya, Ikebukuro, and Shinjuku (particularly on weekend evenings). Streets that are closed to traffic on Sundays (such as Shinjuku-dori) generally draw a number of street performers in the warmer weather.

Among the acts I have seen are mimes twisting balloons into animal shapes for kids; rollerbladers performing gravity-defying feats; fire eaters swallowing hot flames; magicians amazing onlookers with their sleight-of-hand acts; and folk, rock, and Latin groups singing their hearts out for the passers-by.

And you never know when you will come across *chin-don-ya*—the traditional Japanese street musicians and entertainers hired to celebrate the opening of establishments or to promote new products. Dressed in bright, colorful clothes, and well made up, they crash cymbals, bang away on drums, and in general create a very noisy and festive atmosphere. There just seems to be no limit as to what you might find in the crazy and eclectic world of street entertainment in Tokyo.

Horse shows

Baji Equestrian Park holds two major horse events every year. Their three-day Spring Horse Show (May 3, 4, and 5) features a steeplechase and other equestrian events during the May Golden Week hols. The Sept 23 (Autumn Equinox Holiday) Equestrian Day demonstrates the use of horses in the Japanese culture and in festivals—including archery on horseback (*yabusame*) and Japanese polo (*dakyu*). And one Sunday each month, the park offers thoroughbred horse and pony rides for kids four-to-ten years of age. All events are free. (See the Horse section of ch 4 for details on the park and events.)

6

WONDERFUL
PARKS

PLACES TO HANG OUT

- *Arisugawa Park*—Streams, Ducks, and Oxygen Overload
- *Chidorigafuchi Waterfront Park*—Blossoms and Boats Alongside the Moat
- *Hibiya Park*—Tokyo's First Western Park
- *Inokashira Park*—A Walk in the Woods
- *Kasai Seaside Park*—Bliss by the Bay
- *Kitanomaru Park*—Shogun's Northern Citadel
- *Kodaira Furusato Park*—Stroll Through an Edo Village
- *Meiji Shrine Outer Gardens*—Stadiums, Sports, and Bicycling
- *Shiba Park*—Tokyo Tower, Zojoji Temple, and More
- *Shinjuku Central Park*—After the Descent Back to Earth
- *Tetsugakudo Park*—Philosophy Park
- *Ueno Park*—Japan's First City Park
- *Yoyogi Park*—Park with Many Incarnations

IF YOU LOVE ANIMALS . . .

- *Gyosen Park*—Nature Zoo and Japanese Garden
- *Higashi Itabashi Park*—Zoo, Aquarium, and Pony Rides
- *Baji Equestrian Park*—Tokyo's Horse Park
- *Shinozaki & Nagisa Ponylands*—More Fun for Kids

INTRODUCTION

*P*ublic parks are a fairly new concept to Japan. Ueno Park, the country's oldest city park, was established in 1873 on the grounds of the Kaneiji temple (formerly a powerful guardian temple of Edo Castle) following the overthrow of the Tokugawa shogunate.

Today the parks of Tokyo have become very popular places that serve a number of purposes. They can be casual, social spaces where people sit on the grass and relax, picnic and play frisbee, ride bikes, or jog. They can also be places where you go to see specific things—like animals and old farmhouses, or street entertainers and free concerts. There are even some where you can take a blissful walk in the woods or a peaceful stroll along the seashore.

Yes, Tokyo's green spaces are here for you to enjoy, and are one of the delightful ingredients that makes Tokyo what it is today—a place where you never know what interesting things may await you around the very next corner.

PLACES TO HANG OUT

ARISUGAWA PARK

有栖川宮記念公園（Arisugawa-no-miya Kinen Koen）
5–7–29 Minami Azabu, Minato-ku, Tokyo 106–0047
☎ 3441–9642
東京都港区南麻布5-7-29　〒106-0047

Located on a gently sloping hill and surrounded by an elegant residential area containing numerous embassies, this nature-filled park makes you forget that you are in the center of a major metropolis. Its bridges carry you over clear streams and waterfalls, and a tranquil stroll along one of its winding paths takes you past a pond with extremely friendly ducks that waddle right up to you.

On an upper level is an elegant wisteria trellis flanked by gnarled tree trunks with benches for resting underneath. And on the very top level is the Tokyo Metropolitan Central Library (see ch 13), across from which stands a statue of the man whose name the park bears—Arisugawa Taruhito (1835–95), a relative of the imperial family.

Hours: Open 24 hours.
Access: A 3-min walk from Hiroo Stn, Exit 1 (Hibiya Line). Turn left from exit, and left at the corner. Follow this street around and you will see the entrance to the park on the corner across from the National Azabu Supermarket.

CHIDORIGAFUCHI WATERFRONT PARK

千鳥ヶ淵公園（Chidorigafuchi Koen）
2 San-Bancho, Chiyoda-ku, Tokyo 102–0075
☎ 3261–6700
東京都千代田区三番町2　〒102-0075

This 800-m (730-yd) promenade running alongside the Imperial Palace moat is a beautiful place to take a stroll, for the branches of the numerous cherry trees that line the pathway dip down into the moat from both sides of the water. Each spring these trees burst into full bloom and the area becomes one of Tokyo's most popular places to celebrate the yearly *hanami* (cherry blossom viewing).

On the evening of July 13, hundreds of lanterns are lit and released into the moat to guide the spirits of ancestors who have come to visit earth—a Buddhist ritual known as *Toro Nagashi*. There is also a boathouse along the water from which rowboats can be rented and taken out onto the moat (see note). Across from the boathouse is the National Memorial Garden, a monument to unknown soldiers and civilians killed in World War II. It is a peaceful space with benches for quiet contemplation around the open-air shrine.

NOTE: Rowboats are available for rental 9:30 AM–4:30 PM (5:30 pm July/August) daily except Mon and Dec 25–March 1 (¥400/hr, ¥200/half hr).

Hours: The promenade is always open. The Memorial Garden is open daily, 9 AM–5 PM in summer, and 9 AM–4 PM in winter.

Access: A 4-min walk from Kudanshita Stn, Exit 2 (Hanzomon, Tozai, and Toei Shinjuku lines). Walk straight out from the exit and up the slope. The entrance to the park is on the left side where the moat curves to the left.

HIBIYA PARK

日比谷公園 (Hibiya Koen)

1 Hibiya Koen, Chiyoda-ku, Tokyo 100–0012

☎ 3501–6428

東京都千代田区日比谷公園1　〒100-0012

Hibiya Koen was Tokyo's first Western-style park (opened in 1903), and it still ranks up there among the best. It is located across the street from the Imperial Hotel and contains a 30-m- (100-ft-) wide fountain that spouts water 12 m (40 ft) into the air, refreshing you with a fine spray when the wind blows your way. This is reason enough to linger here in the heat of the summer months. But there's much more, including two exquisite Japanese gardens with ponds, and a beautiful, well-manicured Western garden with row after row of lovely flowers. The park's numerous benches are great places for relaxing or reading, which is what you see a lot of people doing here throughout the year.

It always smells so good in Hibiya Park. The trees are big and lush, and they make you forget that you are in the middle of a big city. On sunny days you can watch matches on the park's tennis courts, and on rainy ones you can read in the Hibiya Public Library. (See ch 13.) And if your timing is right, you might catch an open-air concert during lunchtime or even a free flower exhibition. The park spans 161,636 lovely sq m (405,432 sq ft).

Note: The several outdoor restaurants located within the park are great places to stop for a drink, a snack, or even a meal during the warmer months.

Hours: Open 24 hours.
Access: Hibiya Stn, Exit A10 or A14 (Chiyoda, Hibiya, and Mita lines). Also accessible via Kasumigaseki Stn (Marunouchi, Hibiya, and Chiyoda lines).

INOKASHIRA PARK

井の頭恩賜公園 （Inokashira Onshi Koen）
1–18–31 Gotenyama, Musashino-shi, Tokyo 180–0005
☎ 0422–47–6900 (Park Office),
　 0422–46–1100 (Zoo, Inokashira Shizen Bunkaen)
東京都武蔵野市御殿山1-18-31　〒180-0005

When you walk into Inokashira Park, it is as if you have just entered the deep woods. The long lake at its center is fed by natural spring water, and the bridges spanning it are made of natural wood. Everything has such an unpretentious feel to it that you cannot help but leave the outside world far behind you and start to absorb the tranquillity that the park offers. If you have a problem you are trying to work out, this might be just the place to take a stroll and gain a new perspective.

On weekends it is a hub-bub of activity. But even with all the dogs, bicyclers, boaters, artists, street entertainers, and strollers that can be found in its 363,773 sq m (912,452 sq ft), the peaceful feeling somehow remains.

Note: There are boats available for rental year-round (¥600 for either a 30-min paddleboat or a 1-hour rowboat ride). A zoo is also located in the park (¥400—open 9:30 AM–4:30 PM. Clsd on Mon, Tues if Mon is hol).

Hours: Open 24 hours.
Access: A 5-min walk through the small lanes leading out from the South Exit of Kichijoji Stn (Inokashira and Chuo lines) or next to Inokashira Koen Stn (Inokashira Line).

KASAI SEASIDE PARK

葛西臨海公園 （Kasai Rinkai Koen）

    6–2 Rinkaicho, Edogawa-ku, Tokyo 134–0086

    ☎ 5696–1331

東京都江戸川区臨海町6-2　〒134-0086

Also written up in ch 16, this park is a total escape from what has come to be known as "city life." Running alongside Tokyo Bay, it has one of the most romantic sunset views of shoreline, sky, and water to be found anywhere. You can stroll along the shore or enjoy the scenery from the Viewpoint Visitors Center, which contains illustrated information on the area and its wildlife in both English and Japanese.

Don't miss the large bird sanctuary (Choruien) in the far left-hand corner of the park. Here you can either watch the birds close-up from viewing stations situated around the two ponds, or observe them through the free telescopes and binoculars at the circular viewing house in the center.

The 783,000 sq-m (1.7 million sq-ft) park contains a number of other attractions too, such as two offshore beaches. One is for people and one is for critters. The people-beach can be reached by crossing over Nagisa Bridge, but the critters' beach is inaccessible to humans. You can pick up an English map and guide on your way into the park at the Administration Center—on the far right side of the entrance bridge.

NOTE: The famous Tokyo Sea Life Park, where you descend into the depths of the "ocean" and are surrounded by marine life, is also on the grounds (¥800 adults/ ¥300 students). It is clsd on Mon (Tues if Mon is a hol).

Hours: The park itself never closes, except Dec 29–Jan 3. **Bird Watching Center**—9:30 AM–4:30 PM daily. **Viewpoint Visitors Center**—9:30 AM–4:30 PM daily. **Beach (Nagisa Bridge)**— 9 AM–5 PM daily except the following: Open till 6 PM June 1–July 14 on wknds and Aug 16–31 daily, open till 7 PM July 20–Aug 15 daily.

Access: Park is across from JR Kasai Rinkai Koen Stn (Keiyo Line from Tokyo Stn). There is also a boat service between the park and Hinode Pier near JR Hamamatsucho Stn. See the posted schedule at the park to take one back or call Kasai Rinkai Koen Boatline at ☎ 5696–0287 or Hinode Pier at ☎ 3457–7830 (both in Japanese) for schedule.

KITANOMARU PARK

北ノ丸公園　(Kitanomaru Koen)

1–1 Kitanomaru Koen, Chiyoda-ku, Tokyo 102–0091

☎ 3211–7878

東京都千代田区北ノ丸公園1-1　〒102-0091

The name Kitanomaru means "northern citadel" in Japanese, for that is what this site was for the powerful Tokugawa shogun's castle during Edo (1600–1868) times. Nicely situated along the inner curve of the Imperial Palace moat, the park was officially part of the palace grounds until recently, and is still entered through the historic double Tayasumon Gate.

In 1969 it was turned into a park in honor of the Showa emperor's sixtieth birthday, and is now open to the public. Part of it is wooded, while another section is made up of a wide lawn that slopes down toward a peaceful pond. It all adds up to a very lovely setting.

NOTE: Several museums are located in the park: the National Museum of Modern Art, Craft Gallery, National Archives, and the Science and Technology Museum. All charge an entrance fee.

The Nippon Budokan hall located on the grounds holds many free sports events, and you can watch martial arts classes at their school as well (see ch 4).

Hours: Open 24 hours.

Access: 1 min from Kudanshita Stn, Exit 2 (Hanzomon, Tozai, or Toei Shinjuku lines). Walk straight out from the exit and you will see a bridge spanning the moat on your left side. This is the entrance to the park—through the double Tayasumon Gate.

KODAIRA FURUSATO PARK

小平ふるさと村　(Kodaira Furusato Mura)

2–57 Tenjincho, Kodaira-shi, Tokyo 187–0004

☎ 0423–45–8155

東京都小平市天神町2-57　〒187-0004

Take a stroll through a tiny Edo village at Kodaira Furusato Park. Authentic and beautifully preserved thatched-roof houses and a granary, an old post office and fire station, a watchtower, and a water mill run by a gurgling stream can all be seen and explored at this delightful little park with Edo-period (1600–1868) landscaping.

What isn't authentically historic has been painstakingly

re-created from official documents. Two examples are the water mill (with an exposed interior so you can see its inner workings) and the First Settlement Structure Building. The latter is a charming farmhouse with a thatched exterior. Located at the very back of the village, it looks like something out of a fairy tale. The entrance desk will provide you with an English pamphlet, and the plaques describing each structure are written in both English and Japanese.

Hours: 10 AM–4 PM Tues–Sun. Clsd on Mon and the 3rd Tues of each month (Wed if Tues is hol) and New Year hols.

Access: Kodaira Stn, South Exit (Seibu Shinjuku Line). It's a lovely 15-min walk along Sayama-Sakai, or the "Green Road" that runs parallel to the train tracks through parks, gardens, and small farms. Walk left from the front of the South Exit plaza and you will soon run into the "Green Road." Or take a bus headed for Musashi Koganei Stn (Chuo Line) from the front of the Seiyu Store to Yochien-mae stop and walk 3 min.

MEIJI SHRINE OUTER GARDENS
明治神宮外苑 （Meiji Jingu Gaien）
9 Kasumigaoka, Shinjuku-ku, Tokyo 160–0013
☎ 3401–0312
東京都新宿区霞岳町9　〒160-0013

This park was the primary site of the Summer Olympic Games held in Tokyo in 1964, and contains a number of sporting facilities on its 273,000 sq m (2.9 million sq ft). The main venue for the games was the National Stadium—Japan's largest, with a seating capacity of 75,000. The Jingu Baseball Stadium (home of the Yakult Swallows) is also located here, as is the Meiji Jingu Swimming Pool and the Prince Chichibu Rugby Stadium. Lest you get the wrong impression that the park is wall-to-wall stadiums and sports facilities, I should mention that it has no shortage of greenery.

Note: The park also contains the Meiji Memorial Picture Gallery (Meiji Jingu Seitoku Kinen Kaigakan), which portrays the life and times of the Meiji emperor and empress through both Japanese and Western art (¥300).

On Sundays and holidays the oval road circling the park is closed to traffic, and bicycles are loaned free of charge to people of all ages (see ch 4).

Hours: Open 24 hours.

Access: 5 min from Gaienmae Stn (Ginza Line). From the ticket turn-stile, turn right and go up the stairs. Walk left from the exit along Aoyama-dori until you see a big sign on the left that says "Meiji Jingu Shrine Outer Gardens." Turn left and walk up the lovely gingko tree–lined lane that leads into the park. It is also accessible from JR Sendagaya or Shinanomachi Stn (Chuo Line).

SHIBA PARK

芝公園 〔Shiba Koen〕

4–10–17 Shiba Koen, Minato-ku, Tokyo 105–0011

☎ 3431–4359

東京都港区芝公園4-10-17　〒105-0011

Shiba Park houses Tokyo Tower, the Tokyo Prince Hotel, a bowling center, a swimming pool, and a golf driving range. It also encloses Zojoji temple, the family temple and former burial grounds for the Tokugawa shoguns (see ch 8).

What is left of the park contains sections of pleasantly shaded areas with small streams running through them, and one hundred cherry trees that are the site of a big flower-viewing party each spring, when the area is lit up until quite late every evening.

Hours: Open 24 hours.

Access: Shiba Koen Stn, Exit A4 (Mita Line) is inside the park. Also accessible via Daimon Stn (Toei Asakusa Line) or Kamiyacho Stn (Hibiya Line).

SHINJUKU CENTRAL PARK

新宿中央公園 〔Shinjuku Chuo Koen〕

2–11 Nishi Shinjuku, Shinjuku-ku, Tokyo 160–0023

☎ 3342–4509

東京都新宿区西新宿2-11　〒160-0023

Shinjuku Central Park is located directly across from the Tokyo Metropolitan Government Building, one of several buildings in the area to offer dramatic vistas of Tokyo's skyline from observation platforms high in the sky (see ch 16). After taking in the awesome expanse of the city from above, you can literally come back down to earth and get grounded again in this green patch of nature set smack-dab in the middle of Nishi Shinjuku's towering skyscraper district.

The park is divided into three sections connected by bridges crossing over the busy streets below. The largest one contains a lawn area with shade trees and sculptures scattered about. There is also a wooded area known as "citizen's forest," where families sporting colorful yellow nets go butterfly hunting in summer. At the central entrance to the park is a 5-m- (16-ft-) high waterfall, and in one corner is a little branch of the Kii Peninsula's Kumano shrine where gold-laden portable shrines can be seen through a glass-walled storehouse. The park's other sections contain sports facilities and a children's playground.

Hours: Open 24 hours.

Access: A 10-min walk from the West Exit of Shinjuku Stn (Yamanote and other lines). Follow the signs through the underground passageway to the high-rise district. After emerging from the tunnel you will see the park on the left just beyond the Tokyo Metropolitan Government Building. Also accessible via Nishi Shinjuku Stn (Marunouchi Line).

TETSUGAKUDO PARK (Philosophy Park)

哲学堂公園 （Tetsugakudo Koen）

1–34–28 Matsugaoka, Nakano-ku, Tokyo 165–0024

☎ 3954–4881

東京都中野区松ヶ丘1-34-28　〒165-0024

As you cross the zigzagging wooden bridge at the entrance to this hands-on park, you can watch kids playing in the waterfall and climbing on the big rocks in the water during warm weather. But the real theme of the park is the study of philosophy. It was created by Meiji-period (1868–1912) philosopher Enryo Inoue (founder of Toyo University) as a "mind training park," where each section represents a different philosophical theory. There are seventy-seven spots in the park that symbolize various doctrines, such as *Yuishintei* (Mentalism), a belief which holds that the mind is the fundamental reality—or the contrasting *Yuibutsuen* (Materialism), the theory that only physical matter is real.

The park contains six old buildings from the Meiji period

that have been designated as "tangible cultural properties" of Nakano Ward. They are open twice a year for the public to explore—nine days in April during the cherry blossom season and again over weekends and hols in October. One is a lovely small pagoda with steep steps that lead up to the windows at the top where you can look out. Another is a hall of philosophy dedicated to Confucius, Buddha, Kant, and Socrates. It is known as Tetsugakudo—hence the name of the park.

Hours: 9 AM–5 PM (enter by 4:30) daily. Clsd New Year hols.

Access: A 12-min walk from Arai Yakushi-mae Stn, North Exit (Seibu Shinjuku Line, local train). Turn right from exit to the street, cross tracks to the right, and walk for about 12 min. The park is on the left side of Tetsugakudo-dori just after the river. Or you can take any bus from the bus stop on the left just beyond the tracks. Get off at Tetsugakudo stop, which is alongside the park.

UENO PARK

上野公園 （Ueno Koen）

　5–20 Ueno Koen, Taito-ku, Tokyo 110–0007

　☎ 3828–5644 (Park Office)

　　5685–1181 (Park Information Center)

東京都上野公園5-20　〒110-0007

Ueno Park was the nation's first city park, created in 1873 following the overthrow of the Tokugawa shogunate during the Meiji Restoration. It was founded on the grounds of the former Kaneiji temple—a powerful guardian temple of the shogun's Edo Castle. Some structures that were part of that huge complex were not destroyed during the fighting and can still be visited in the park today (see ch 8).

NOTE: There is a charge for some of the park's attractions, such as the National Museums and the National Zoo.

There is always a lot going on in Ueno Park. Each April it is the site of the biggest cherry blossom bash in Japan, and every summer it plays host to the month-long Ueno Summer Festival (see ch 5). There are also a number of free museums and a great music library. For more details on the many free attractions in Ueno Park, see ch 3.

Hours: 5 AM–11 PM daily.

Access:Across the street from JR Ueno Stn (Yamanote and other lines), Ueno Park Exit. Also accessible via Ueno Stn on the Ginza and Hibiya lines.

YOYOGI PARK

代々木公園 （Yoyogi Koen）

2–1 Yoyogi Kamizonocho, Shibuya-ku, Tokyo 151–0021

☎ 3469–6081

東京都渋谷区代々木神園町2-1　〒151-0021

Until recently, Yoyogi Park was synonymous with free Sunday afternoon entertainment. For it was here that rock bands would line the closed-to-traffic road alongside the park and play their hearts out, while kids dressed in Elvis gear, poodle skirts, pony tails, and some very outrageous attire, danced in the streets. That was one of its incarnations. In others it served as a training ground for the Japanese Imperial Army, the housing quarters for the American Occupation forces following World War II, and the Olympic Village for the athletes during the 1964 Tokyo Olympics. All this before it became a park in 1967.

Today the atmosphere is a little quieter in this 540,000-sq-m (1.4-million-sq ft) park, and it has become a favorite spot for people to relax on the grass and picnic on lazy weekend afternoons. There is also a bird sanctuary, a jogging path, and free bike riding for the kids. Some weekends you can find a flea market in the park—and a big Earth Day event is held here each April. (See ch 5.) You might want to pay a visit to the Meiji shrine, adjacent to the park. (See ch 8.)

Hours: Open 24 hours.

Access:Next to Meiji Jingumae Stn and Yoyogi Koen Stn (Chiyoda Line), or JR Harajuku Stn (Yamanote Line).

IF YOU LOVE ANIMALS

GYOSEN PARK
行船公園 （Gyosen Koen）
3–2–1 Kita Kasai, Edogawa-ku, Tokyo 134–0081
☎ 3687–3492 (Park Office), 3680–0777 (Zoo)
東京都江戸川区北葛西3-2-1　〒134-0081

This park is a real find. To begin with, the Edogawa Ward's free Nature Zoo (Edogawa-ku Shizen Dobutsuen) is located on the park grounds. Penguins, monkeys, sea lions, raccoons, iguanas, tortoises, and prairie dogs are some of the animals you can see here. You will even find wallabies donated by Gosford, the Australian sister-city of Edogawa Ward. Its aviaries contain over eighteen types of birds, including colorful parrots, toucans, pelicans, and beautifully-plumaged peacocks.

At the center of the zoo is a circular petting area where kids can mingle with the animals. Its sheep, goats, chickens, rabbits, guinea pigs, and other friendly animals enable folks to connect with nature in a way that's pretty hard to do when they spend every day in a big city. Petting hours are 10–11:45 AM and 1:15–3:00 PM (2 PM–4 PM in summer).

The park's round fountain provides a cooling-off mechanism in the summertime, as kids can swim in it and grown-ups are tempted to stick their feet in, too. A lovely 40,000-sq-m (432,000-sq-ft) Japanese garden, Heisei Teien (Peaceful Garden), is also part of the park, complete with its own teahouse, tiny waterfall, and carp-filled pond.

Hours: The **park and garden** are open 24 hours daily. **Zoo Hours**: *March–Oct*: 10 AM–4:30 PM wkdys, 9:30 AM–4:30 PM wknds and hols. *Nov–Feb*: 10 AM–4 PM wkdys, 9:30 AM–4 PM wknds and hols. During school summer hols, hours are slightly longer. Clsd Mon (Tue if Mon is hol).

Access: A 12-min walk from Nishi Kasai Stn, North Exit (Tozai Line). Turn left from the exit and go out to the street. Cross it and walk right. When the street ends, turn left and walk until you reach the five-street intersection (Jusco Dept Store will be on the left). Cross over the main street to the bicycle shop—the park is just to the left of it. Or from the South Exit of Nishi Kasai Stn, take the No. 21 bus (from No. 3 bus stand) bound for Shin-Koiwa Stn to Ukita bus stop. The park will be 1 min straight ahead on the right side.

HIGASHI ITABASHI PARK

東板橋公園 （Higashi Itabashi Koen）
   3–50–1 Itabashi, Itabashi-ku, Tokyo 173–0004
   ☎ 3963–8003 (Park), 3962–8419 (Zoo)
   東京都板橋区板橋3-50-1　〒173-0004

It is not that big of a park, but it sure packs a wallop, animal-wise. For within it is located the Itabashi Ward Children's Zoo (Itabashi Kuritsu Kodomo Dobutsuen).

In the petting section of the zoo, docile sheep and goats wander around freely and guinea pigs and rabbits can be held by children several times a day (10:45–11:15 AM, 1:30–2 PM, and 2:30–3 PM). Deer, flamingo, pheasants, peacocks, parakeets, chickens, ducks, and turtles can also be seen at the zoo, and free pony rides are available for kids three years of age through elementary school. (See ch 4 for details.)

The freshwater aquarium contains thirty tanks in a rock environment. Fish range from tiny guppies to giant catfish. Lobsters, salamanders, and small crabs can also be seen here, and kids can play with turtles in the turtle tank.

Hours: 10 AM–4:30 PM Tues–Sun (closes at 4 PM Dec–Feb). Clsd Mon (Tues if Mon is a hol) and New Year hols.

Access: An 8-min walk from Itabashi Kuyakusho-mae Stn, Exit A1 (Mita Line). Turn left from the exit and walk straight down the street. Turn left at the second light (a large gray brick sports center is on the far left corner), and walk about another 3 min. The park entrance is on the left side. The critters are behind the baseball field and tennis courts.

BAJI EQUESTRIAN PARK

馬事公苑（Baji Koen）

2–1–1 Kami Yoga, Setagaya-ku, Tokyo 158–0098

☎ 3429–5101

東京都世田谷区上用賀2-1-1　〒158-0098

Baji Park is Tokyo's "horse park." It was created by the Japan Racing Association (JRA) as a place for people to become more familiar with horses. Two main horse events are held here in the spring and autumn of each year and a monthly "get to know horses day" offers free horse, pony, and carriage rides for kids four-to-ten years of age. A number of horses are housed in the park and can be visited in the paddocks between 10 AM and 2:30 PM daily. (See the horse section of ch 4 for details on the park and events.)

Hours: Open daily, 9 AM–5 PM *April–Oct*, and 9 AM–4 PM *Nov– March*.

Access: The easiest way to get to the park is to take the No. 24 bus (bound for Seijo Gakuen-mae) from the south bus terminal of Shibuya Stn (Yamanote and other lines). It leaves from the curbside near the Tokyu Plaza Building and is a 30-min ride to the "Nodai-mae" bus stop. Then a 2-min walk straight ahead and left through the promenade at the far side of the Royal Host Restaurant brings you to the entrance to the park.

SHINOZAKI PONYLAND

篠崎ポニーランド

3–12–17 Shinozakicho, Edogawa-ku, Tokyo 133–0061

☎ 3678–7520

東京都江戸川区篠崎町3-12-17　〒133-0061

NAGISA PONYLAND

なぎさポニーランド

Nagisa Park, 7–3 Minami Kasai, Edogawa-ku, Tokyo 134– 0085

☎ 5658–5720

東京都江戸川区南葛西7-3　なぎさ公園内　〒134-0085

These two ponylands also offer free rides for elementary school kids and younger. (See the Horse section of ch 4 for details.)

7

EXQUISITE GARDENS

SOME LOVELY TOKYO GARDENS

- *Imperial Palace East Garden*
- *Akatsuka Botanical Garden and Manyo Medical Plant Garden*
- *Denpoin Temple Garden*
- *Horikiri Iris Garden*
- *Kyu Yasuda Garden*
- *Mejiro Garden*
- *Nanushi Waterfalls Garden*
- *Nezu Institute of Fine Arts Garden*
- *Otaguro Garden*
- *Roka Garden*
- *Shin Edogawa Garden*
- *Tokyo Metropolitan Medical Plant Garden*

HOTEL AND RESTAURANT GARDENS

- *Chinzanso Garden* (Chinzanso Restaurant/Events Center and Four Seasons Hotel)
- *Happoen* (Happoen Garden Restaurant)
- *Hotel New Otani Garden*
- *Takanawa Prince Hotels' Garden*

INTRODUCTION

*S*haped by a harmonious blend of Buddhist, Taoist, and Shinto traditions, Japanese gardens are mystical places with a long history. The natural forms of their rocks, plants, trees, and ponds create a peaceful haven for spiritual meditation and quiet contemplation, and their quiet beauty serves as a soothing refuge from the hectic pace of modern living.

Tokyo contains many beautiful gardens that can be visited any season of the year. They are generally more formal than parks, with pathways meandering through them from which you can view the lovely scenery. A large number of Tokyo's gardens were developed during the Edo period (1600–1868), when the country's center of activity shifted from the former capital of Kyoto to Edo (now Tokyo) under the rule of the Tokugawa shogunate.

Once part of the estates of wealthy daimyo (lords) and other high-ranking individuals, some of the gardens have been preserved on the grounds of the city's prestigious hotels and restaurants, wisely left intact when the property was purchased. Others can be found secluded behind the walls of temples, shrines, and former estates—and one very special garden can even be visited on the grounds of the Imperial Palace. Still others have been incorporated into the city's open and user-friendly parks. Many gardens charge admission, but all the ones listed here are free. Find your own personal favorite and visit it often.

SOME LOVELY TOKYO GARDENS

IMPERIAL PALACE EAST GARDEN
皇居東御苑 （Kokyo Higashi Gyoen）
1–1 Chiyoda, Chiyoda-ku, Tokyo 100–0001
☎ 3213–2050
東京都千代田区千代田1-1　〒100-0001

The Imperial Palace East Garden consists of 210,000 sq m (2.2 million sq ft) of Japanese- and Western-style gardens, making up about one-third of the palace grounds along its eastern edge. Although open to the public, it is still officially part of the residence of the emperor and empress of Japan.

Pink cherry blossoms and azaleas grace the Ninomaru section of the garden in the spring. Irises, dogwood, and magnolia are among the other flowers that can be enjoyed in this section of the larger garden. The Museum of the Imperial Collections (see ch 10) can be found on the grounds, as can the small wooden ceremonial structure in which part of the emperor's *daijosai* ceremony (one of the Shinto rituals required for ascending the throne) took place in 1990.

The site was also home to the Tokugawa shoguns for more than 200 years before the 1868 Meiji Restoration, at which time the shoguns were overthrown and the emperor restored to power. The East Garden occupied the center of what is said to have been the largest castle in the world at the time of the shogun's rule. Ruins of that castle can still be seen today, and the Honmaru Tenshukakuato—foundation for the central tower (*donjon*)—can be climbed and explored.

NOTE: Because of the garden's vastness and meandering paths, it is a good idea to have a guide. English maps are for sale at a nominal price in the gift shop just inside the Otemon Gate entrance.

Hours: 9 AM–4:30 PM (enter by 4 PM), *March–Oct*; 9 AM–4 PM (enter by 3:30 PM), *Nov–Feb*. Clsd Mon and Fri (open if a hol), and some irregular days.

Access: The East Garden can be entered through three palace gates: **Otemon Gate**—A 4-min walk straight ahead from Otemachi Stn, Exit C-13b (various subway lines). **Hirakawamon**

Gate—Takebashi Stn, Exit 1A (Tozai Line). Turn around and walk back for 2 min to reach the gate. **Kita-Hanebashimon Gate**—Also Takebashi Stn, Exit 1A (Tozai Line). Walk straight out from the exit and follow the road around (don't cross the street) for about 5 min until you reach the gate.

AKATSUKA BOTANICAL GARDEN and MANYO MEDICAL PLANT GARDEN

赤塚植物園及び万葉薬用園
（Akatsuka Shokubutsuen oyobi Manyo Yakuyoen）
5–17–14 Akatsuka, Itabashi-ku, Tokyo 175–0092
☎ 3975–9127
東京都板橋区赤塚5-17-14　〒175-0092

This hilly little garden contains over 600 kinds of trees, plants, flowers, and grasses—and a variety of terrains. Flowers and plants from every season can be found here, so there is always something to see. A number of mini-environments have been created at this 10,267-sq-m (110,000-sq-ft) botanical garden, among them a small bamboo forest, a swamp-land spanned by a wooden crisscross bridge, and a pond containing a variety of water plants. When the purple wisteria (*fuji*) blooms, it hangs from a trellis in the arbor that was created for it.

Since the garden is built on a hillside, it is navigated via straw mat–covered paths that wind up and down the hill. Across a small road is the Manyo Medical Plant Garden, named after the famous 8th-century writing, *Man'yoshu* (Collection of Ten Thousand Leaves), an anthology of poems in which 160 types of plants are mentioned. This is an area containing a number of plants, including those for medicinal use.

Hours: 9 AM–4:30 PM daily, *March–Nov*; 9 AM–4 PM daily, *Dec–Feb*. Clsd New Year hols. (Office closed Mon.)

Access: Narimasu Stn, North Exit (Tobu Tojo Line from Ikebukuro). The special express does not stop here, but it is just one stop from Ikebukuro on the other express trains. Outside, take Bus No. 2 heading for Akabane Stn (board at Bus Stand No. 1). It is a short bus ride to the Akatsuka 8-chome (Tokyo Daibutsu-mae) stop. Turn and walk back to the corner, where you will see a "Tokyo Daibutsu-dori" street sign. Go right and walk down the hill for about 3 min. Pass the next traffic signal and turn left into the second small street. The garden will be in front of you at the end of the short road, just beyond the Jorenji Daibutsu—Tokyo's own Big Buddha (see ch 3).

DENPOIN TEMPLE GARDEN

伝法院庭園　（Denpoin Teien）

2–3–1 Asakusa, Taito-ku, Tokyo 111–0032

☎ 3842–0181 (Ask for Denpoin Garden)

東京都台東区浅草2-3-1　〒111-0032

NOTE: You can obtain permission to visit the garden at the office of the five-storied pagoda, next to the Asakusa Kannon (Sensoji) temple. Enter through the black doorway to the left of the pagoda's main entrance (then go up the steps and to the third office on the left). It is best to call beforehand to make sure it will be open on the day you wish to visit. Upon arrival, they will ask you to sign a book, then issue you a ticket and an English map to the garden from the pagoda.

There is some debate about the origin of this garden. Some sources trace its beginnings back to the 7th century, while others place them in the 17th. It is the living quarters of the chief abbot of Asakusa Kannon (Sensoji) temple, and for most of its existence, has been closed to the public. Not until the mid-1980s was it finally opened for viewing, but permission from the temple is required (see note).

Visiting this garden is a unique experience. When you finally arrive at the entrance, you will find closed doors and "keep out" signs. Don't let them deter you, for you will have a ticket. Find your way in through the series of gates, surrender your ticket to the monk who slides open the door of the old wooden house at the end of the path, and duck through the passageway that burrows underneath the adjoining structure. You will then be in what has to be Tokyo's most secret garden—just steps away from the bustling Nakamise-dori shopping arcade. In the center of the garden is a large pond surrounded by paths similar in style to the famous Katsura Detached Palace of Kyoto. In one corner is a replica of the Fushin-an, a famous 18th-century Kyoto tea ceremony house that was destroyed by fire. The grounds also contain "The Old Bell of Shitoku," cast in 1387, one of the oldest in Tokyo. Also see ch 3, Shitamachi.

Hours: 9 AM–3 PM. Clsd Sun, hols, and when the premises are in use for special events.

Access: The five-storied pagoda (where you get permission to enter the garden) is about 5 min from Asakusa Stn, Exit 1 (Ginza Line).

Go straight out from the exit to the traffic light. Turn right and enter Nakamise-dori shopping street through the large Kaminarimon Gate. The pagoda is at the end, to the left of the Asakusa Kannon temple. Also accessible from Asakusa Stn (Asakusa Line).

HORIKIRI IRIS GARDEN

堀切菖蒲園 （Horikiri Shobuen）

2–19–1 Horikiri, Katsushika-ku, Tokyo 124–0006

☎ 3697–5237

東京都葛飾区堀切2-19-1　〒124-0006

The main attraction of this garden is the famous irises that bloom here each June (a whopping 200 varieties). The Horikiri area has been celebrated since Edo times (1600–1868) for its beautiful iris gardens, which can be traced in works of art and poetry from that time period.

Although a number of these gardens gave way to industrial development, fortunately the oldest one remains open for public viewing. Cherry blossoms, wisteria, water lilies, and other plants can also be enjoyed in this 7,700-sq m (83,000-sq ft) garden during the rest of the year. At one end is an elevated viewing platform where you can sit and view the entire garden.

Hours: Open 8 AM–6 PM every day during the month of June, when the irises are in bloom. At other times 9 AM–4:30 PM Wed–Sun. Clsd Mon, Tues (except 4th Tues), the 4th Sun of each month, and New Year hols.

Access: A 10-min walk from Horikiri Shobuen Stn (Keisei Line local stop). Turn left from the only exit. When the road forms a three-way fork at the second traffic light, go left down the small, winding shopping street in the middle. Follow this for about 5 min, then turn left at the last corner before the street ends at the river/overhead highway. You will see the garden straight ahead.

KYU YASUDA GARDEN

旧安田庭園 （Kyu Yasuda Teien）

1–12–10 Yokoami, Sumida-ku, Tokyo 130–0015

☎ 5608–1111 (Sumida Ward Office)

東京都墨田区横網1-12-10　〒130-0015

The water level of the pond that is the centerpiece of this lovely garden once rose and fell with the tides of the Sumida River, creating a constantly-changing scenario. A variety of bridges made of stone and brightly painted orange wood cross over the water at various spots, offering a number of interesting views. Although the water level is now controlled and kept constant, this small garden still feeds from the river and is considered one of the best examples of the charm of Tokyo's Edo-period (1600–1868) gardens. It was built by the feudal lord Honjo Inabanokami Munesuke and was the home to several different *daimyo* in the late Edo period.

Hours: 9 AM–5 PM daily (enter 4:30), except New Year hols.
Access: A 5-min walk from the West Exit of JR Ryogoku Stn (Sobu Line). It is just beyond the sumo stadium. However, the closest gate (south gate) is only open during sumo tournaments. At other times, walk around to the other side of the garden to enter.

MEJIRO GARDEN

目白庭園 〔Mejiro Teien〕
　　3–20–18 Mejiro, Toshima-ku, Tokyo 171–0031
　　☎ 5996–4810
　　東京都豊島区目白3-20-18　〒171-0031

Mejiro Teien is a small, neighborhood garden that has masterfully captured a variety of environments within a limited space. Near the entrance, a rest pavilion appears to float upon the water. As you progress around the central pond, you are greeted by a waterfall mountainside environment that can be navigated via stepping stones in the water. It is all laid out alongside a *sukiya*-style tea ceremony pavilion built entirely of Kyoto cedar (open for viewing by visitors free of charge on Thursdays).

Hours: 9 AM–5 PM (enter 4:30). 9 AM–7 PM *July and Aug*. Clsd 2nd and 4th Mon and New Year hols.
Access: A 5-min walk from JR Mejiro Stn (Yamanote Line). From the exit, cross the road and turn left. Make the first right at the Denmark Bakery and walk about 5 min until you come to the garden entrance on your left. (Jog to the left, then right around Hotel Seed.)

NANUSHI WATERFALLS GARDEN

名主の滝公園 (Nanushi-no-Taki Koen)
  1–15–25 Kishimachi, Kita-ku, Tokyo 114–0021
  ☎ 3908–3566
  東京都北区岸町1-15-25　〒114-0021

Famous gardens in Japan were usually built by wealthy samurai or belonged to temples or shrines, but this one is unique—it was created by the leader of the farmers in the Oji area in the mid-19th century to duplicate the scenic beauty of distant mountains. Its name translates into "Waterfall of the Leader of Local Farmers," and in fact the garden has four waterfalls. The largest one, Odaki (Man's Falls), is 8 m (26 ft) high. During the summer months children can play in the pond into which the falls spill, and enjoy the old tradition of catching goldfish that have been released into the water to take home as pets.

Note: The waterfall does not operate on Mon.

Hours: 9 AM–5 PM daily (enter by 4:30 PM). Clsd for New Year hols.
Access: A 10-min walk from North Exit of JR Oji Stn (Keihin Tohoku Line). Follow the small road that runs parallel to the train tracks across the street from Asukayama Park (away from central Tokyo). The entrance to the garden will be on your left.

NEZU INSTITUTE OF FINE ARTS GARDEN

根津美術館庭園 (Nezu Bijutsukan Teien)
  6–5–1 Minami Aoyama, Minato-ku, Tokyo 170–0062
  ☎ 3400–2536
  東京都港区南青山6-5-1　〒170-0062

This elegant and hilly garden is on the grounds of the famous Nezu Institute of Fine Arts. There is a charge to enter the museum, but none for the garden, which is generously endowed with beautifully carved stone and bronze statues, figures, lanterns, and pagodas throughout. There is much to see as you wander up and down its stone steps, including four teahouses that host private functions. The long, winding central pond is never far from view as you cross it a number of times on various bridges made of stone and wood.

The famous tea ceremony master Sen no Rikyu once

compared this garden to a beautiful Japanese haiku poem. The garden maintains a light, airy feeling, perhaps because so much of its lush foliage is of Japanese maple and other delicate varieties of trees and plants.

NOTE: The Nezu Institute of Fine Arts (¥800) owns a priceless collection of Oriental art, included in which is Ogata Korin's *Irises* from the *Tales of Ise*, an Edo-period (1600–1868) screen painting that has been designated as a National Treasure.

Hours: 9:30 AM–4:30 PM. Clsd Mon, New Year hols, and the day after hols.

Access: A 5-min walk from Omotesando Stn, Exit A5 (Ginza, Hanzomon, and Chiyoda lines). Turn right from the exit and walk away from Aoyama-dori. When you come to a big gray wall on the corner of Minami Aoyama 6-chome, turn right and walk alongside it. You will soon reach the entrance to the garden on your left.

OTAGURO GARDEN

杉並区立大田黒公園 （Suginami Kuritsu Otaguro Koen）
3–33–12 Ogikubo, Suginami-ku, Tokyo 167–0051
☎ 3398–5814
東京都杉並区荻窪3-33-12　〒167-0051

This garden is part of the former residence of Moto Otaguro, the musician who introduced Debussy and Stravinsky to Japan. After studying music at the University of London from the age of 19, he returned to Japan to become a well-known music critic. After his death in 1979 at the age of 86, his house was turned into the Moto Otaguro Memorial Museum. It still contains his belongings, including an old record player and the piano he used to play which you can see through the window. At the far end of the garden is a resting pavilion overlooking a small lake. The long entryway to the tranquil garden is lined with ginkgo trees that are over eighty years old.

Hours: 9 AM–5 PM (enter by 4:30 PM) daily. Clsd for New Year hols.

Access: An 8-min walk from Ogikubo Stn, South Exit (JR Chuo or Marunouchi lines). Go up the escalator and continue to follow the tracks in the same direction until you reach the first traffic light. Turn right. The garden will be on the 5th corner on your left.

ROKA GARDEN

芦花恒春園（Roka Koshunen）

    1–20–1 Kasuya, Setagaya-ku, Tokyo 157–0063

    ☎ 3302–5016

    東京都世田谷区糟谷1-20-1　〒157-0063

This garden stands as a memorial to a man of peace. For the thatched-roof cottage on the grounds was the former home of Roka Tokutomi, a famous Meiji-Taisho-period (1868–1926) author and peace advocate, and his wife Ai. The devout Christian couple moved to the countryside in order to live a life of simplicity, an endeavor in which they succeeded. Their lifestyle has been well preserved in their home—several small cottages connected by passageways.

    The couple was very active in matters of peace, and together they submitted a proposal to the Versailles Peace Conference in 1919. Roka rarely spoke in public, but after returning from a trip to Russia and a visit with author Leo Tolstoy, he began entertaining students in his home for philosophical discussions on universal peace.

    Everything here is just as they left it. Among their belongings are photos of Tolstoy and American President Abraham Lincoln. As you wander through the hallways, you almost expect to find them sitting in the next room. A memorial building near the entrance contains additional memorabilia, and the forest-like gardens surrounding the cottages support maples, oak trees, and bamboo. Their graves can be found in a grove of oak trees at the front of the house. Ask for an English pamphlet at the entrance that tells their story.

Hours: 9 AM–4:30 PM daily. Clsd for New Year hols.

Access: Take bus No. 23 from Chitose Karasuyama Stn (local and semi-express stop on the Keio Line). From the East Exit, go up the stairs on the right, walk toward the Fuji Bank and turn right. The bus stop is just beyond the next corner. Get off at Roka Koshunen-mae. Walk back toward the rear of the bus and make a right at the corner. It is about a 4-min walk down that street on the right side.

SHIN EDOGAWA GARDEN

新江戸川公園 (Shin Edogawa Koen)

 1–1–22 Mejirodai, Bunkyo-ku, Tokyo 112–0015

 ☎ 3941–9649

 東京都文京区目白台1-1-22　〒112-0015

As you walk through the gate of this garden, you are greeted by a large pond filled with Japanese carp and surrounded by thick foliage, weeping cherry trees, and stone lanterns. In the distance a stone bridge spans a narrow section of the water, which covers one-third of the total garden area.

 The building near the entrance originally served as a college for the Hosokawa clan that ruled the area during the Meiji and Taisho period (1868–1926). So if you stand and take in the overall view from the other side of the garden, you'll have a good sense of how these garden estates must have appeared when they were private domains—pretty impressive.

Hours: 9 AM–5 PM daily (enter by 4:30 PM) except for the New Year hols. Closes 30 min earlier *Nov–Jan*.

Access:A 12-min walk from Edogawabashi Stn, Exit 1A (Yurakucho Line). Cross the Edogawabashi Bridge, turn left and walk along the Kanda River, passing through Edogawa Park. The entrance to Shin Edogawa Koen is about 200 m (650 ft) past the end of the park.

TOKYO METROPOLITAN MEDICAL PLANT GARDEN

東京都薬用植物園 (Tokyo-to Yakuyo Shokubutsuen)

 21–1 Nakajimacho, Kodaira-shi, Tokyo 187–0033

 ☎ 0423–41–0344

 東京都小平市中島町21-1　〒187-0033

This is the only place in Tokyo authorized to grow poppy plants, from which morphine is extracted. It is done each summer with the permission of the Ministry of Health and Welfare. And that's not all. You can also find about 1,600 other varieties of plants used for medicinal purposes here, carefully cultivated in such varied environments as a tropical greenhouse, wooded area, aquatic plant pond, and rock garden.

 Since 1946 the garden has served as a "living classroom" for people studying medicinal plants, herbs, and trees. Its exhibition hall in the Reference Material Center at the entrance to the garden contains an interesting exhibition of ingredients that go into making medicines. In addition to the barks, seeds, roots, flowers, and resins, there are deer antlers, animal bones, giant mushrooms, a rhino horn, and even sloth scales on display. Also included are photos and samples of several poisonous plants grown in the garden every spring. Be careful, for they are among the prettiest specimens in the garden and look deceivingly harmless.

Plants are labeled in Latin and Japanese and free photos are given to visitors. Classes, observational gatherings, and other events are held here (in Japanese) once a month from April to October.

Hours: **Garden**: 9 AM–4 PM daily. **Reference Center**: same hours Mon–Fri, but clsd wknds. Both clsd for New Year hols.

Access: It is about a 30-min train ride from central Tokyo. Take the Haijima-bound express train on the Seibu Shinjuku Line to Higashi Yamato-shi Stn. The garden is on the right side of the station's only exit. To reach the entrance, make a right from the ticket wicket. Then turn left, go to the main street, and make an immediate right. The gate is about a 1-min walk down on the right side. The Reference Center is to the right as you enter.

HOTEL AND RESTAURANT GARDENS

CHINZANSO GARDEN (Chinzanso Restaurant/Events Center and Four Seasons Hotel)

椿山荘庭園 （Chinzanso Teien）

   2–10–8 Sekiguchi, Bunkyo-ku, Tokyo 112–8680

   ☎ 3943–1111

   東京都文京区関口2-10-8　〒112-8680

Encompassing one of the most popular gardens in Tokyo today, Chinzanso has had quite an interesting history. Famed for its

natural scenic beauty, the area was called Camellia Mountain after the numerous camellia flowers that blossomed here. Estate owner and well-known Meiji-period (1868–1912) statesman Prince Aritomo Yamagata hosted many important political meetings at his "Mansion on Camellia Mountain." Records show that these were not only attended by numerous high-ranking dignitaries, but also by the Meiji emperor himself.

When the property passed on to Baron Heitaro Fujita, he decorated the grounds with historical monuments to complement the natural beauty of the 70,000-sq-m (750,000-sq-ft) garden, and opened a restaurant. A thousand-year-old pagoda built without nails was transferred here from the wilderness of the Hiroshima mountains and now stands at the top of the hill as the symbol of Chinzanso. Other cultural treasures scattered throughout the site include carved Taoist and Buddhist images and over thirty stone lanterns. A large pond, waterfall, and natural spring are also part of the garden, as is a 500-year-old sacred tree that measures 4.5 m (14.5 ft) around its base.

NOTE: Chinzanso is a restaurant-and-event complex, hosting many weddings, conferences, and official celebrations. Guests will be dressed in more formal attire, so use discretion when visiting the garden here and at the other places listed in this section.

Hours: 9:30 AM–10 PM daily.

Access: A 10-min walk from Edogawabashi Stn, Exit 1A (Yurakucho Line). Cross over the bridge and walk straight until you reach Mejiro-dori. Go left and after about 8 min (uphill) you see a sign on your left for the hotel and garden. Enter the garden through the Chinzanso building complex, two levels down on the first floor. Or take the No. 61 bus from Edogawabashi Stn (board just after you cross the bridge) and get off at the Chinzanso-mae stop. It is about a 3-min ride.

HAPPOEN GARDEN (Happoen Garden Restaurant)

八芳園庭園 (Happoen Teien)

1–1–1 Shiroganedai, Minato-ku, Tokyo 108–0071

☎ 3443–3111

東京都港区白金台1-1-1　〒108-0071

This stunning traditional Japanese garden was once the estate of an Edo-period (1600–1868) *daimyo* (lord). It is beautiful every season of the year. In spring cherry blossoms bloom, and in summer azaleas cover the grounds. In autumn the maple trees turn brilliant shades of red and yellow, and in winter the garden resembles a Japanese ink painting (especially when covered with snow). In its center is a lake that houses colorful ducks and *koi* (Japanese carp). A quaint, traditional resting pavilion that can only be accessed by walking across stones in the water is a wonderful spot from which to view the entire scene.

Happoen contains a number of interesting historic items, including an 800-year-old stone lantern, a 12-story stone pagoda and a number of bonsai trees that date back over 200 years. A gnarled *sanshuyu* (Japanese cornerain cherry tree) near the main building (Nihonkan) survives from Edo times—and a chapel and shrine add to the serene atmosphere of this 50,000-sq-m (540,000-sq-ft) garden.

NOTE: Many parties and weddings are held on the grounds, including outdoor garden parties for over 1,000 people.

Hours: 11:30 AM–8 PM. Best to visit on wkdys, for it may be clsd on wknds for private functions.

Access: A 15-min walk from Meguro Stn East Exit (Yamanote Line), straight down Meguro-dori (the large avenue to your right). Or take buses No. 10, 93, or 98 from the station to the Hiyoshi Sakaue stop and walk straight ahead for 2 min. A Happoen shuttle operates irregularly from the station, so if you see it waiting outside the East Exit, discreetly hop on. Also accessible from Takanawadai Stn (Toei Asakusa Line).

HOTEL NEW OTANI GARDEN

ホテル ニュー オオタニ庭園

4–1 Kioicho, Chiyoda-ku, Tokyo 102–8578

☎ 3265–1111

東京都千代田区紀尾井町4-1　〒102-8578

This exquisite, 400-year-old garden delights visitors daily with its little bridges, ponds, waterfalls, and winding walkways. As you stroll through it, you can enjoy the numerous vistas it presents up and down the hillside. A number of its forty-two lanterns came from famous old temples, and some date back to the Kamakura period (1185–1333). A stone garden that runs along one side of it contains the largest red *akashaku* stone in Japan—which weighs in at twenty-two tons and comes from Sado Island.

EXQUISITE GARDENS

177

This 4-hectare (10-acre) garden was once part of the former residence of a famous Kumamoto samurai lord. When the land was purchased for the New Otani, the hotel's founder made the wise decision to leave the garden intact and preserve its extraordinary beauty. The grounds also house a charming little garden chapel, where you can attend services in the midst of this natural beauty (see ch 8).

Note: Umbrellas are available at the entrance of the garden if you would like to take a stroll in the rain.

Hours: 7 AM–10 PM daily.

Access: A 3-min walk from Akasaka-Mitsuke Stn, Akasaka-Mitsuke Crossing Exit (Marunouchi or Ginza lines). Cross Aoyama-dori and continue walking for about 2 min. The hotel entrance is on the left.

TAKANAWA PRINCE HOTELS' GARDEN
高輪プリンス ホテル庭園

3–13–1 Takanawa, Minato-ku, Tokyo 108–8612
☎ 3447–1111
東京都港区高輪3-13-1　〒108-8612

The two hotels on the property are joined by a lovely Japanese stroll garden that once belonged to Takedanomiya, cousin of the Showa emperor. His former Western-style villa is now an annex of the hotel (Kihinkan Guest House), and is used for important meetings and ceremonies such as *omiai* (pre-marriage introductions). The garden contains a carp-filled pond, streams, stone lanterns, and a Japanese teahouse. But the highlight is the architecturally stunning Kannondo, a small Buddhist temple brought from the ancient capital of Nara. It houses an exquisite Kannon (Goddess of Mercy) figure that dates from the Kamakura period (1185–1333) and very old wall drawings of Japanese, Chinese, and Indian Buddhist monks. The best time to view it is after dark, when the interior is lit up.

A covered walkway offers protection from the rain and sun for the less adventurous, but you can also explore the garden on your own via the stone paths that wind through it. Umbrellas are available on rainy days.

Hours: Open 24 hours a day.

Access: 5 min from JR Shinagawa Stn, Takanawa Exit (Yamanote and other lines). Turn right and walk to the first traffic light. Cross the street and walk up the road alongside the sign for the hotel. You will pass a restaurant and the Kihinkan Guest House on the way to the hotel. The garden entrance is through the hotel lobby. Also accessible from Takanawadai Stn (Toei Asakusa Line).

8

BUDDHIST TEMPLES, SHINTO SHRINES, AND OTHER RESTING PLACES FOR THE SPIRIT

BUDDHIST TEMPLES AND SHINTO SHRINES

Buddhist Temples

- *Asakusa Kannon Temple/Sensoji* (Tokyo's Oldest Temple)
- *Gokokuji Temple* (Beautiful Works of Buddhist Art)
- *Honmonji Temple* (Nichiren and Oldest Five-Storied Pagoda)
- *Jomyoin Temple* (48,900 Jizo Statues)
- *Jorenji Temple* (Tokyo's Own Big Buddha)
- *Reiyu-kai Shakaden Hall* (Pyramid-Shaped, Futuristic Architecture)
- *Rissho Kosei-kai* (Symbolism in Architecture)
- *Sengakuji Temple* (Graves of the 47 Ronin)
- *Takaozan Yakuoin Temple* (Keeper of the Eastern Peace from High on a Mountain Top)
- *Tennoji Temple* (Overseer of Yanaka Cemetery)
- *Tsukiji Honganji Temple* (Land Reclaimed from the Sea)
- *Zojoji Temple* (Protector of the Southern Gate and Shogun's Burial Grounds)
- *Ueno Park Temples* (Remains of Powerful Kaneiji)
  - *Kaneiji Temple* (Guardian of Vulnerable Northeastern Gate and Shogun's Burial Grounds)
  - *Bentendo Temple* (Longevity, Good Fortune, Happiness, and Prosperity)
  - *Kiyomizu Kannondo Temple* (View of Shinobazu Pond)

Shinto Shrines

- *Asakusa Shrine/Sanja Gongen* (Dedicated to Three Fishermen)
- *Ginza Hachikan Shrine* (Tiny Oasis in the Middle of Ginza)
- *Hanazono Shrine* (Pray for Commercial Success)
- *Hie Shrine/Sanno Gongen* (God of the Mountain)
- *Kameido Tenjin Shrine* (Wisteria and the Patron of Learning)
- *Kanda Myojin Shrine* (Legends and Festivals)
- *Meiji Shrine* (Dedicated to Emperor Meiji and Empress Shoken)
- *Nami-yoke Inari Shrine* (Tsukiji Fish Market Shrine)
- *Nezu Shrine* (Famous for its Azaleas)
- *Nogi Shrine* (Dedicated to a Faithful General)
- *Tomioka Hachimangu Shrine* (Monuments to Sumo Wrestlers)
- *Ueno Toshogu Shrine* (Dedicated to First Tokugawa Shogun)

- *Yasukuni Shrine* (Dedicated to Those Who Sacrificed Themselves for Their Country)
- *Yushima Tenjin Shrine* (Plum Blossoms and the Patron of Learning)

CHURCHES AND OTHER RESTING PLACES FOR THE SPIRIT

English/Japanese Speaking
- *Church of Jesus Christ of Latter-Day Saints* (Mormon)
- *First Church of Christ, Scientist Tokyo* (Christian Science)
- *Franciscan Chapel Center* (Roman Catholic)
- *International Christian Assembly/ICA* (Assemblies of God)
- *New Otani Garden Chapel/Shogetsu Tei* (Interdenominational)
- *St. Alban's Anglican-Episcopal Church*
- *St. Anselm's Benedictine Priory* (Roman Catholic)
- *St. Ignatius Church* (Roman Catholic)
- *St. Mary's Cathedral* (Roman Catholic)
- *St. Nikolai Cathedral/Nikolai-do* (Russian Orthodox)
- *St. Paul International Lutheran Church*
- *Tokyo Baptist Church*
- *Tokyo Central Church of Seventh-Day Adventists*
- *Tokyo Friends* Center and Meeting House (Quaker)
- *Tokyo Horizon Chapel* (Nondenominational)
- *Tokyo Union Church* (Interdenominational)
- *Tokyo Unitarian Fellowship*

French Speaking
- *Foyer de l'Aumonerie Catholique des Francophones* (Roman Catholic)

    Chappelle de l'Université du Sacre Cœur

    Maison Régionale des Missions Étrangères de Paris

German Speaking
- *Kreuzkirche* (German Protestant)
- *St. Michael* (Roman Catholic)

Spanish Speaking
- *St. Ignatius Church* (Roman Catholic)

Other Places of Worship
- *Yushima Seido Confucian Shrine*
- *The Arabic Islamic Institute*
- *Jewish Community Center*
- *Tokyo Baha'i Center*

INTRODUCTION

*H*umans were not made to go on and on indefinitely without stopping to rest and "refuel." This is just as true for our spirit as it is for our bodies and minds. For even the freest of spirits eventually seeks a place to alight— and gather the energy to continue its endeavor, whatever that may be.

And that is what this chapter is about—places of spiritual solace. For no matter what your religious orientation, Tokyo probably has a place to help you find your own personal peace before you are once again off to points unknown—rested and revitalized in mind, body, and spirit.

BUDDHIST TEMPLES AND SHINTO SHRINES

Shinto, Japan's "home-grown" religion, began with folk legends that explained the country's origins to the people. It is deeply connected with nature and contains many *kami*. These are divine spirits that can be found in natural forms such as the sun, the wind, and trees—or animals, people, and ancestral spirits.

Buddhism was introduced to Japan in the 6th century, and grew in popularity while coexisting harmoniously with Shinto. Since the two religions did not contradict each other, but rather dealt with different and compatible religious aspects, they were eventually united. This synthesis was known as *Shinbutsu-shugo,* and during the time that it was practiced took on characteristics of both religions. So when the two were later separated during the Meiji Restoration in 1868, it wasn't easy to undo this union in the minds and hearts of the people. Even today most Japanese profess to being both Shinto and Buddhist and take part in the rites of both. Weddings are usually Shinto ceremonies, and funerals Buddhist. The 108 worldly desires are rung out on Buddhist temple bells at midnight on New Year's Eve, and Shinto shrines are visited on New Year's Day.

In early times, shrines were simple structures of natural wood and thatched roofs, but eventually shrines and temples came to look very much alike. Today a shrine can be identified by its *torii* gate (the archway announcing the presence of a sacred space within) at its entrance. Shrines contain a representation of a deity, such as a mirror or a sword, rather than a specific image, while Buddhist temples prominently feature statues, carvings, and paintings of specific images of the Buddha and Buddhist deities. Buddhist temples are generally part of a compound containing a number of structures—such as a main hall, a pagoda, a residence for monks, a bell tower, and often a graveyard. Although there are some large Shinto shrines (Meiji and Yasukuni are two), most are of the charming neighborhood variety found in the nooks and crannies of the tiny back streets of Tokyo.

Today people go to temples and shrines to pray for good health, success in business ventures, and good luck in school examinations—to name a few reasons. Numerous festivals and events are held at them throughout the year. During the first few days of January, many people visit a series of seven temples and shrines dedicated to the Japanese "Seven Lucky Gods." Transitions and rites of passage are marked here, as well. Weddings, funerals, Seven-Five-Three Day (*Shichi-go-san*) for children, and Coming of Age Day (*Seijin-no-hi*) for twenty-year-olds are some of these. And it is not uncommon for a person to visit a shrine or temple simply in search of a peaceful respite from the frantic pace of daily living.

I have listed here just a few of Tokyo's many interesting temples and shrines. Some cover a vast expanse of land and are prominent on every map, while others are tiny and tucked away in the most unexpected of places. Each has its own unique quality—and each is its own experience.

NOTE: If you are interested in learning more about Shintoism or Buddhism in English, see ch 12—Japanese Religious Perspectives.

BUDDHIST TEMPLES

ASAKUSA KANNON TEMPLE (SENSOJI)

金龍山浅草寺 （Kinryuzan Sensoji）

　2–3–1 Asakusa, Taito-ku, Tokyo 111–0032

　☎ 3842–0181

　東京都台東区浅草2-3-1　〒111-0032

The Asakusa Kannon temple (*Sensoji*) was founded in the 7th century, when three local fishermen found a tiny statue of Kannon (Buddhist Goddess of Mercy) in their nets while fishing in the nearby Sumida River. The statue was enshrined, and the temple became a famous center for worship, which it remains to this day. It hosts many festivals and events—and each year over 30 million people visit the temple to pray and "bathe" in the healing smoke that billows out from the huge incense burner in front of the main hall.

It is the oldest and perhaps the best known of all the temples in Tokyo. The area still retains the feeling of old Edo, and is written up in greater depth in chapter 3—Shitamachi. The complex in which it rests has a lively, carnival atmosphere, and the colorful shops that line the road (Nakamise-dori) leading up to the main temple are great places to see all those hard-to-find traditional Japanese items. But be sure to allow yourself plenty of time, since it could take awhile to reach the temple—where, if you are lucky, you might catch a service in progress at the Kannondo (main hall). The Hozomon Gate that you pass through just before you reach the temple houses rare 14th-century sutras, and the five-storied pagoda to its left contains relics of the Buddha's bones in its uppermost level. To the right of the temple stands Asakusa shrine (Sanja Gongen), built to honor the fishermen who found the Kannon statue in the river (see the Shrine section below).

Hours: Asakusa Kannon (Sensoji) Temple is open 6 am–5 PM daily, grounds are open 24 hours. Nakamise-dori shops open about 9 am–9:30 AM and close about 7 PM–9 PM, depending on the individual shop.

Access: Asakusa Stn, Exit 1 (Ginza Line). Walk straight out from the exit. Very soon you will see a large vermilion gate (Kaminarimon) on your right side. Enter and walk through Nakamise shopping street to the Asakusa Kannon temple at the very end. It is also accessible via Asakusa Stn on the Asakusa Line.

GOKOKUJI TEMPLE
護国寺

5–40–1 Otsuka, Bunkyo-ku, Tokyo 112–0012
☎ 3941–0764
東京都文京区大塚5-40-1　〒112-0012

For people interested in Buddhist art, this is a must-see. The Gokokuji temple complex was founded in 1681 by the fifth Tokugawa shogun and was one of the biggest and best-known temples during Edo times (1600–1868). It survived earthquakes and war intact, and today a number of the buildings have been designated Important Cultural Properties. One of these is the

Main Hall (Hondo), which contains a magnificent collection of statues, paintings, carvings, and objects (I counted over seventy items) that rivals any exhibition of Buddhist art I have seen in museums. Even the ceiling is covered with beautiful paintings. And the best part is that it is all so accessible. You can walk around the side and behind the altar to view these precious objects close up.

Several leaders of the Meiji Restoration are buried in the temple's cemetery along with members of the imperial family. A number of old teahouses are on the grounds, and the 300-year-old Gekkoden Guest House (another Important Cultural Property) was moved to this location from Mii temple in Shiga Prefecture in 1928.

Many people visit Gokokuji temple during the *Hana Matsuri* (the Buddha's birthday) each April 8th. It is also a popular spot for *setsubun*, the February 3rd bean-throwing ceremony to drive out demons and bring in good luck as winter turns to spring.

Hours: The Main Hall is open 9 AM–12 PM and 1 PM–4:30 PM daily, but Sat, Sun, hols is often used for the tea ceremony, and permission may be required. Temple grounds are open 24 hours.

Access: Just outside of Gokokuji Stn, Exit 1 (Yurakucho Line). Turn left and walk into the entrance.

HONMONJI TEMPLE
本門寺

1–1–1 Ikegami, Ota-ku, Tokyo 146–0082

☎ 3752–2331

東京都大田区池上1-1-1　〒146-0082

After you pass through the main gate, which is over 300 years old, and ascend the ninety-six stone steps leading up to the Honmonji temple at the top of the hill, you are immediately struck with a sense of spaciousness and remoteness from the world below. It feels more like a Kyoto or Nara temple, rather than one in space-starved Tokyo.

Established in 1274 by Nichiren (founder of the large

Nichiren sect of Buddhism), it is also the place where he died in 1282. Each October 11–13 a huge festival (*Oeshiki*) is held here to commemorate his passing. The festival is highlighted by a big procession on the evening of the 12th, during which long poles with many lit lanterns hung from them (*manto*) are paraded to the accompaniment of flutes, drums, and gongs. Over a hundred groups march in this procession and thousands of people attend the event each year.

If you turn left along the road behind the main temple, you will come to a stairway that leads down to the room where Nichiren died and the place where he was cremated. Among the other buildings on the temple grounds is the oldest five-storied pagoda in the Kanto region (Important Cultural Property) and the mausoleum (Gobyo-sho) where Nichiren's ashes are enshrined. Ask for an English pamphlet (and Japanese map) inside the main hall and tour the area.

Hours: The buildings are open from 9 AM–4/5 PM, and the grounds remain open 24 hours.

Access: 10 min from Ikegami Stn, only exit (Tokyu Ikegami Line). The station is located two stops away from Kamata Stn on the JR Keihin Tohoku Line. Go straight out from the station exit. At a slight angle to the right is a shopping street (Honmonji Shotengai) with a big yellow sign over its entrance. Follow that street until it ends. Turn right, and then make an immediate left. You will see the old wooden main gate of the temple at the end of the street.

JOMYOIN TEMPLE
浄名院

2–6–4 Ueno Sakuragi, Taito-ku, Tokyo 110–0002
☎ 3828–2791
東京都台東区上野桜木2-6-4　〒110-0002

This temple is known for its thousands of statues of the benevolent Buddhist deity known as Jizo. When the temple won its independence in 1723 after having been one of the thirty-six subsidiaries of the all-powerful Kaneiji temple from 1666, the head priest made a vow to collect 84,000 of the figures. So far

48,900 have been accumulated. You can stroll through the temple grounds and see them neatly lined up row after row. Some wear red bibs around their neck, offerings from devotees.

One very large Jizo holds a sponge gourd, a traditional Chinese cure for respiratory ailments such as coughing and asthma. For the past hundred years a famous "Sponge Gourd Service" has been held at the temple on the 15th day of the 8th month of the old lunar calendar (September by today's calendar). The ceremony draws a great many people suffering from these ailments, as they come to offer their prayers and take part in a special service. Jizo is known as the guardian of children, mothers, travelers, health, and birth and death, so a wide variety of images are represented in the many statues that cover the temple grounds.

Hours: 7 AM–5 PM daily. Closes 4 PM in winter.

Access:A 5-min walk from JR Uguisudani Stn, North Exit (Yamanote Line or Keihin Tohoku Line). Go straight out to Kototoi-dori and turn left. You can either walk along at ground level and climb the stairs up to the Kaneijibashi bridge, or walk up the ramp the cars use. After you cross the bridge, the temple is on the right just past the second corner. Also accessible from Ueno Stn (Yamanote and other lines), Jomyoin is located across from Kaneiji temple in the far right corner of Ueno Park.

JORENJI TEMPLE

乗蓮寺

5–28–3 Akatsuka, Itabashi-ku, Tokyo 175–0092

☎ 3975–3325/6

東京都板橋区赤塚5-28-3　〒175-0092

This temple contains Tokyo's very own Daibutsu (Big Buddha). At 13 m (42.5 ft) the Daibutsu is only 1/2 m (19 in) shorter than its famous cousin in Kamakura. It sits in the open air on the grounds of this historic temple that was frequented by the Tokugawa shoguns on their hawk-hunting expeditions during Edo times (1600–1868). See chapter 3 for information about the temple, nearby attractions, and hours and access.

TEMPLES, SHRINES, AND OTHER RESTING PLACES FOR THE SPIRIT

REIYU-KAI SHAKADEN HALL

霊友会釈迦殿 （Reiyu-kai Shakaden）

1–7–8 Azabudai, Minato-ku, Tokyo 106–0041

☎ 5563–2507 (International Dept),

5563–2520 (Shakaden Hall, in Japanese)

東京都港区麻布台1-7-8　〒106-0041

If you stumble upon Shakaden without knowing what it is, you will swear that something from outer space has just landed. Yes, this huge and futuristic, pyramid-shaped structure tucked away on a side street definitely catches you off guard.

The building is open to the public, but you are asked to remain quiet and respectful and not to enter the front part of the Main Hall, since this is a place for self-reflection. The atmosphere within the hall is very hushed, with benches and floors of Brazilian red granite and walls of Iranian green onyx. An 8-m (26-ft) statue of Buddha (carved from a single piece of camphor wood that is a thousand years old) is only revealed during the twice-monthly gatherings for members on the 9th and 18th of every month. At other times it is enclosed in a climate-controlled chamber.

Reiyu-kai was founded in the 1920s as a lay Buddhist society that has no monks or priests, so the Shakaden is considered to be a meeting hall rather than a house of worship. Completed in 1975, the building was built to last. It contains more steel girders than Tokyo Tower and is based on a bed of granite 25 m (82 ft) below the ground. It contains 400,000 l (105,680 gal) of emergency drinking water in an underground tank and is meant to serve as a place of refuge in the event of a disaster.

Hours: Shakaden Hall is open 6 AM–8 PM daily. The International Department is open 9:30 AM–5:30 PM (clsd Sun and Wed) to answer your questions in English and other languages.

Access: 6 min from Kamiyacho Stn, Exit 2 (Hibiya Line). Turn right out of the station and walk up Sakurada-dori. Turn right again into the last small street before the big intersection at Gaien Higashi-dori. Shakaden will be on your right. English information is available on the first floor of the large square building you pass just before reaching the hall.

RISSHO KOSEI-KAI

立正佼成会

2–11–1 Wada, Suginami-ku, Tokyo 166–0012

☎ 5341–1124 (Overseas Mission Section)

東京都杉並区和田2-11-1　〒166-0012

The first time I drove past the Rissho Kosei-kai's Great Sacred Hall, my head swung around involuntarily, and I blurted out, "What was that?" For the building is like no other that I have ever seen. It is a huge, circular structure with eight large columns protruding from its exterior and an ornate spired roof modeled after the Mahabodhi temple in India, which was built on the spot where Buddha is said to have obtained enlightenment. Everything on the sacred hall is symbolic. The columns represent the eightfold path to enlightenment. The six pillars around the treasure tower on the top stand for the six perfections of Buddhism—and the four lions surrounding it represent the four noble truths.

The Great Sacred Hall of this Buddhist lay organization is open to the public. To enter, go up the ramp to the main entrance, which overlooks a lovely palm garden out front. Inside is a large circular room, rather reminiscent of a European-style opera house with three balconies winding around its upper reaches. I was lucky enough to be present for a service, which included gongs, drum, and a bell played from a stage that housed colorful red lanterns and a 7-m- (23-ft-) tall gold statue of the Eternal Buddha.

Rissho Kosei-kai was founded in 1938 and world peace is one of their main concerns. One of the founders, Nikkyo Niwano, was awarded the Templeton Prize (similar to the Nobel Prize for religious work) in 1979 for his efforts, and the temple's youth division also won the United Nations Peace Prize in 1985. English information is available, which they will send to you beforehand if you call. Or the temple receptionist can direct you to the Overseas Mission Office across the street. They also sponsor introductory seminars on Buddhism. Contact them for a schedule.

TEMPLES, SHRINES, AND OTHER RESTING PLACES FOR THE SPIRIT

Hours: The hall is open from about 5:30 AM–5 PM or so daily (no entry after 3 PM). Sutra services are held at 6 AM, morning ceremony at 9 AM, and shorter chanting services follow at 1 PM and 3 PM. Clsd on the 6th, 16th, and 26th day of each month. Overseas Mission Office hours are 8:30 AM–4:30 PM daily. Clsd national hols.

Access: It is a 5-min walk from Honancho Stn, Exit 1 (Marunouchi branch line). To transfer from the Marunouchi main line, switch to the train across the platform at Nakano Sakaue Stn (just beyond Shinjuku). At Honancho Stn, turn left and walk up Kan'nana-dori to the first crosswalk. As you cross the street to the right, you will see the Great Sacred Hall straight ahead of you.

SENGAKUJI TEMPLE

泉岳寺

2–11–1 Takanawa, Minato-ku, Tokyo 108–0074

☎ 3441–5560

東京都港区高輪2-11-1　〒108-0074

The forty-seven *ronin* (masterless samurai) who avenged the unjust death of their lord in 1703 are buried here alongside the grave of their master, Naganori Asano. The story of their loyalty has been spread far and wide via the popular tale of "Chushingura," and can be seen in Kabuki drama, Bunraku (puppet) plays, and a film of the same name. A memorial service is held at the temple each December 14 (the anniversary of the vendetta), and again on Feb 4, the day the *ronin* were forced to commit mass ritual suicide the following year.

The loyalty of the forty-seven *ronin* is still greatly admired today. During my visit to the temple, which was founded in 1612, there was a constant stream of visitors coming to pay their respects and pray at the grave of the *ronin*'s leader, Oishi Kura-nosuke. The grave site can be reached by taking the path and steps that veer off to the left side of the temple compound, just before the museum.

NOTE: The small museum on the grounds contains relics connected with the event, such as the ronin's special armor and weapons—and a receipt from the family for the shogunal bureaucrat's head that rolled when the ronin took their revenge. (¥200)

Hours: The temple gate and entrance to the graves are open 7 AM–5 PM daily (till 6 PM in summer). Museum is open 9 AM–4 PM daily (enter by 3:30).

Access: A 3-walk from Sengakuji Stn, Exit A2 (Toei Asakusa Line). Turn right and go up the hill. Cross the street when it curves to the right and continue in the same direction you were headed. The temple is directly in front of you. (The Toei Asakusa Line can get a little tricky here and some trains branch off, so make sure that the train you are boarding is going where you want to go—in both directions.)

TAKAOZAN YAKUOIN TEMPLE
高尾山薬王院

2177 Takao-machi, Hachioji-shi, Tokyo 193–0844
☎ 0426–61–1115
東京都八王子市高尾町2177　〒193-0844

Created by an edict of the emperor Shomu to be the official "guardian temple of peace for the Eastern part of Japan," this ancient temple was founded in 744 near the top of Mt. Takao, which is considered to be sacred. Its devotees worship nature and practice ascetic *yamabushi-do*, or "the way of the mountain dwellers." Some of these practices include bathing under a cold waterfall and walking across hot coals. Every second Sunday in March a "Fire Walking Festival" is held at the foot of the mountain, and visitors can walk across the hot coals—after the heat has waned some, of course. (See ch 3 for hours, access, and more information on the temple and the environs of Mt. Takao.)

TENNOJI TEMPLE
天王寺

7–14–8 Yanaka, Taito-ku, Tokyo 110–0001
☎ 3821–4474
東京都台東区谷中7-14-8　〒110-0001

This peaceful temple dates from the Kamakura period (1185–1333), and its monks served as caretakers for the many graves in the surrounding Yanaka Cemetery. A large bronze Buddha (Genroku Daibutsu) cast in 1690 overlooks the temple gate and greets visitors as they enter the well-manicured compound. This temple was one of the few places where people could buy

TEMPLES, SHRINES, AND OTHER RESTING PLACES FOR THE SPIRIT

lottery tickets in Edo times (1600–1868), which made it a very popular place, indeed.

Just outside the temple gate is the Yanaka Cemetery, one of the four largest in Tokyo. Its many trees and serene atmosphere create a lovely environment for a peaceful stroll, and for a number of people it is also a favorite spot to contemplate the cherry blossoms that bloom here in abundance each spring. Its atmosphere is far removed from the raucous activity that usually accompanies the yearly appearance of the beautiful flowers in other parts of the city.

NOTE: There are a number of other temples nearby. If you would like to explore the historic Yanaka area further, see ch 3—Shitamachi.

Hours: 5:30 AM–5 PM daily (6 AM–5 PM in winter). Grounds are open 24 hours.

Access: 2 min from JR Nippori Stn, South Exit (Yamanote and Keihin Tohoku lines). Walk left from the station exit until you reach the stairs on the left that lead up to the graveyard. Climb the stairs. Once inside the cemetery, follow the major road leading off to the left to the temple.

TSUKIJI HONGANJI TEMPLE
築地本願寺

3–15–1 Tsukiji, Chuo-ku, Tokyo 104–8435
☎ 3541–1131
東京都中央区築地3-15-1　〒104-8435

The name Tsukiji translates as "built-up/reclaimed land." When the original temple (located near Asakusa) burned down in 1657, another plot of land was granted on which to rebuild—but it was underwater! Thousands of local fishermen and other faithful followers took up the gigantic task of reclaiming the land from the sea by carrying gravel and earth to the site until it was stable enough to rebuild the temple. As a result, the new temple—and the district surrounding it—took on the name "Tsukiji."

The current building was designed by a professor of architecture at Tokyo University in a striking ancient Indian style, which is very unusual for Japan. To the far right of the ornately carved central altar in the Main Hall is a unique statue of Prince

Shotoku, who popularized Buddhism in Japan during his reign in the 6th and 7th centuries. Inner engravings show that the head of the statue was carved by the prince himself when he was only sixteen years old.

The temple, founded in 1617, is a branch of the Nishi Honganji temple of Kyoto. There is an English pamphlet available and sometimes an English-speaking guide stationed inside the main hall who can answer your questions. The temple is located next door to the popular Tsukiji Fish Market (see ch 3).

Hours: Temple hours are 6 AM–4 PM. Grounds are open 5:30 AM–midnight.

Access: In front of Tsukiji Stn, Exit 1 (Hibiya Line).

ZOJOJI TEMPLE
増上寺

4–7–35 Shiba Koen, Minato-ku, Tokyo 105–0011

☎ 3432–1431

東京都港区芝公園4-7-35　〒105-0011

Zojoji temple was moved here from another area in 1590 by Tokugawa Ieyasu, the first Tokugawa shogun. It served as the guardian of the South Gate of his Edo Castle, and along with Kaneiji temple made up the shogun's burial grounds. Although most of the buildings were destroyed during World War II and had to be rebuilt, Sanmon (the main gate, which dates from 1605) was left intact and today stands as a good example of how the architecture of the entire complex must have appeared. It has also been declared an Important Cultural Property by the Japanese government.

Two large mausoleums of the second and seventh shoguns once stood here. Their original gates can still be seen on either side of the temple, on property that was previously part of the vast temple grounds.

As you walk from the Sanmon Gate to the main temple, you will pass a large temple bell on your right that dates back to 1673. It was said to have been cast from the ornamental hairpins of the ladies at the shogun's castle.

The Buddha that was worshipped by the shoguns is placed on view three times a year—January 15, May 15, and September 15. It was originally gold, but the smoke from burning incense gradually turned it black, and it is now known as the Black Image of Amida Buddha.

Hours: Temple hours are 5:30 AM–5:30 PM daily. Grounds are open 24 hours.

Access: 3 min from Onarimon Stn, Exit A1 (Mita Line). Turn right from the exit and walk up Hibiya-dori toward the next traffic signal. When you reach it, enter the temple grounds through the large red Sanmon Gate. It is also accessible from Shiba Koen Stn (Mita Line).

Ueno Park Temples

KANEIJI TEMPLE

寛永寺

1–14–11 Ueno Sakuragi, Taito-ku, Tokyo 110–0002
☎ 3821–4440
東京都台東区上野桜木1-14-11　〒110-0002

There was once a powerful temple named Kaneiji. It was a favorite of the shogun for it kept evil spirits from entering through the vulnerable Northeastern Gate of Edo Castle. Founded in 1625 by the priest Tenkai (1536?–1643), its territory encompassed all of what is now Ueno Park (and more), and its main hall is said to have been the largest in all of Edo. In addition to the great number of buildings found in the main complex, it also controlled thirty-six subordinate temples.

When the shogun was overthrown during the Meiji Restoration of 1868, so went the shogun's temple. During the fighting, Kaneiji's grand main hall was burned to the ground along with all but a few of the temple buildings. About all that remains of the original structures today are Kiyomizu Kannon temple, the five-storied pagoda, and the Ueno Toshogu shrine—all located inside Ueno Park.

What is known as Kaneiji temple today is a smaller structure that sits along the outskirts of the original temple's vast domain.

It is the former temple of Kaneiji's founder, brought in from another area and settled on the grounds of a subordinate temple. Off to the side of the temple are the burial grounds of a number of the Tokugawa shoguns—surrounded by a thick stone wall. (Kaneiji and Zojoji temples together served as the official shogun burial grounds.) The story of Kaneiji is not well known today, for in the building of a modern Japan the entire area was soon designated as Japan's first city park—Ueno Park (see ch 3).

Hours: 5:30 AM–5 PM daily.

Access: JR Ueno Stn, Ueno Park Exit (Yamanote and other lines). The temple is at the far right corner of Ueno Park, just beyond Tokyo National University of Fine Arts and Music. A map is available from the Information Center at the entrance to the park. Or it is a 7-min walk from JR Uguisudani Stn, North Exit. Go straight out to Kototoi-dori and turn left. Cross the Kaneijibashi bridge, and turn left after you pass the Jomyoin temple on the right.

BENTENDO TEMPLE
弁天堂

2–1 Ueno Koen, Taito-ku, Tokyo 110–0007
☎ 3821–4638
東京都台東区上野公園2-1　〒110-0007

This temple is dedicated to Benzaiten, an Indian goddess who was the symbol of longevity, good fortune, happiness, and prosperity. So it is a good temple to remember.

Founded by the priest Tenkai shortly after the completion of the main Kaneiji temple in the mid 17th century, Bentendo was built on an island in Shinobazu Pond after a model found in Lake Biwa. Lotuses were planted in the pond and fish, turtles, and waterfowl were released into the water, for Tenkai taught that the way to purify your sins was to set creatures free. Consequently, Shinobazu became known as the "Pond of Release."

Originally Bentendo could only be reached by boat, but today worshippers can visit it by crossing over a bridge that connects it to the shore. The image of Benzaiten enshrined in the temple has eight arms—each holding a holy weapon to fight

TEMPLES, SHRINES, AND OTHER RESTING PLACES FOR THE SPIRIT

against evil. The ceiling of the main hall is decorated with the image of a dragon, painted by master artist Kibo Kodama.

Hours: 7 AM—sunset daily.

Access: JR Ueno Stn, Ueno Park Exit (Yamanote and other lines). The temple is in Ueno Park, in the middle of Shinobazu Pond. A map is available from the Information Center at the entrance to the park.

KIYOMIZU KANNONDO TEMPLE

清水観音堂 （Kiyomizu Kannondo）

1–29 Ueno Koen, Taito-ku, Tokyo 110–0007

☎ 3821–4749

東京都台東区上野公園1-29　〒110-0007

Modeled after the famous Kiyomizudera temple in Kyoto, this temple is built in the "*butai-zukuri*" (stage) architectural style. It sits on the side of a hill with a stage projecting out from the front. Founded in 1631, it is placed to give a view of Shinobazu Pond, and is one of the few buildings to have survived the destruction of the Kaneiji temple complex during the Meiji Restoration.

Its main image (Senju-Kannon, or thousand-handed Buddha) was originally enshrined in the Kiyomizudera temple in Kyoto, and was later moved here by the priest Tenkai (founder of Kaneiji) when it was awarded to him as a gift. Along with the Toshogu shrine and the five-storied pagoda, which also survived the 1868 razing of Kaneiji temple, Kiyomizu Kannondo has been declared an Important Cultural Property by the government of Japan.

Hours: 7 AM—5 PM daily.

Access: JR Ueno Stn (Yamanote and other lines), Ueno Park Exit. The temple is located inside the park. A map is available from the Information Center at the entrance to the park.

SHINTO SHRINES

ASAKUSA SHRINE/SANJA GONGEN

浅草神社／三社権現

2–3–1 Asakusa, Taito-ku, Tokyo 111–0032

☎ 3844–1575

東京都台東区浅草2-3-1　〒111-0032

The Asakusa shrine was founded in 1649 by the third Tokugawa shogun, and was built to honor the three fishermen who discovered the tiny Kannon statue enshrined in the Asakusa Kannon temple next door (see Asakusa Kannon temple above). Appropriately nicknamed "Sanja-sama," which means "Three Holy Shrines," the colorful building is decorated with vivid carvings and paintings of plants and animals, both real and imagined. It is possible to climb the red steps and enter the Outer Hall to study them up close—but please, please don't forget to leave your shoes outside!

The Asakusa shrine and the nearby Nitenmon—the East Gate through which the shogun entered the complex—managed to survive the fires and other disasters that destroyed most of the other buildings in the complex. Both have been designated as Important Cultural Properties by the government of Japan. The shrine's yearly *Sanja Matsuri* (festival) is one of the largest in Tokyo, when every mid-May about a hundred portable shrines (*mikoshi*) are carried through the streets by men and women sporting headbands and festival gear.

Nakamise-dori, the road leading up to the shrine, is lined with a myriad of tiny shops selling traditional Japanese items and makes for fun sightseeing. The temple complex and surrounding area are written up in greater depth in the Shitamachi section of chapter 3.

Hours: Asakusa shrine (Sanja Gongen) is open 6:30 AM–5 PM daily. The grounds are always open. The Nakamise-dori shops leading up to the shrine open about 9 AM–9:30 AM and close between 7–9 PM.

Access: Asakusa Stn, Exit 1 (Ginza Line). Walk straight out from the exit. Very soon you will see a large vermilion gate (Kaminarimon) on your right side. Enter and walk through the Nakamise shopping street to the very end. Asakusa shrine is on the right side of Asakusa Kannon temple (as you face it). It is also accessible via Asakusa Stn on the Toei Asakusa Line.

GINZA HACHIKAN SHRINE

銀座八官神社

Hachikan Building, 8–4–5 Ginza, Chuo-ku, Tokyo 104–0061

☎ 3571–2621

東京都中央区銀座8-4-5　八官ビル　〒104-0061

This is a delightful little shrine—located in the middle of all the shops, showrooms, restaurants, art galleries, and hustle and bustle of Ginza. Yes, in one of Tokyo's busiest areas, you suddenly come upon the serenity of the Ginza Hachikan shrine tucked away in the first floor of an eight-story building. An unlikely place for a shrine, you might say. But the truth is it was founded over 300 years ago when the idea of a city like Tokyo—let alone the glittering Ginza we know today—was far beyond the comprehension of those who visited the little shrine in old Edo times (1600–1868).

The tiny space has a bell you can ring, a fountain in which to purify yourself, and a mini cave complete with its own dragon. It even has a little art gallery with a display of two or three paintings on one wall. And there's a little machine from which you can buy your fortune. An annual festival associated with the shrine is held every June 15.

Hours: 9 AM–6 PM Mon–Fri. Clsd wknds and hols.

Access: 3 min from Ginza Stn, Exit 5 (Ginza or Asakusa lines). Turn right from the exit and walk down Sotobori-dori toward the tan overpass of the Shuto Expressway. The shrine is on the right side in the second block after the highway, a few doors beyond the Nikko Hotel. It is also accessible from JR Shinbashi Stn (Yamanote and other lines), Ginza Exit.

HANAZONO SHRINE

花園神社

5–17–3 Shinjuku, Shinjuku-ku, Tokyo 160–0022

☎ 3200–3093

東京都新宿区新宿5-17-3　〒160-0022

This bright orange shrine tucked away between tall buildings on the east side of Shinjuku Station was established even before the days of the Tokugawa shogunate (1600–1868). It is said to be lucky for those involved in commerce, and has long been a favorite of businessmen who come here to pray for success in their endeavors. (It is also said to promote good soil conditions, important to farmers and merchants back in the days when rice crops were the measure of wealth.)

It is a great place to come each November for the *Tori-no-Ichi* Festival when colorful *kumade* (brightly decorated rakes to be used for "raking in money") are sold from open-air stalls amidst the cheers and clapping of vendors and onlookers alike. Lots of food and drink stalls line the entrance to the shrine and spill out onto Yasukuni-dori during the festival.

A popular antique flea market is held on the grounds of the shrine every Sunday between dawn and dusk, and the fascinating mini-neighborhood Golden Gai (see ch 3) is just across the alleyway.

Hours: The shrine is open 7 AM–6 PM, but the grounds never close.

Access: A 3-min walk from Shinjuku-sanchome Stn, Exit B3 (Marunouchi or Toei Shinjuku lines). Turn left from the exit and walk along Meiji-dori to the next intersection. Cross Yasukuni-dori and the entrance to the shrine will be just to your left. Also 8 min from JR Shinjuku Stn, East Exit (Yamanote and various lines). Near the intersection of Meiji-dori and Yasukuni-dori.

HIE SHRINE/SANNO GONGEN

日枝神社／山王権現

2–10–5 Nagatacho, Chiyoda-ku, Tokyo 100–0014

☎ 3581–2471

東京都千代田区永田町2-10-5 〒100-0014

This shrine, nicknamed Sanno-sama (God of the Mountain), is a branch of the guardian shrine of sacred Mt. Hiei in Kyoto. It was originally built on the grounds of Edo Castle by the castle's founder in 1478, and in 1659 was moved to its present location on top of the hill. Although it was opened to public worship at that time, it still maintained its status as guardian deity for Edo Castle (now the Imperial Palace).

TEMPLES, SHRINES, AND OTHER RESTING PLACES FOR THE SPIRIT

During Edo times (1600–1868) the shrine's *Sanno Matsuri* was the biggest festival in Tokyo. In the festival procession, three divine palanquins (imperial carriages) were followed by forty-five festival cars and a large number of singers and dancers. Although smaller now, the festival is still one of Tokyo's largest. Today the palanquins are joined by about 400 people in Heian-period (794–1185) costume in a march to the Imperial Palace for the head priest to offer prayers for the emperor and his family. The festival takes place biennially for several days around June 15. On alternate years, a smaller festival is held.

The shrine's *torii* gate is characterized by the unusual triangular shape of its roof that can only be found at Hie (Sanno) shrines.

Hours: *April–Sept*—open 5 AM–6 PM. *Oct–March*—6 AM–5 PM.

Access: Kokkaigijido-mae Stn, Exit 5 (Chiyoda and Marunouchi lines). The exit lets you out in front of the Capital Tokyu Hotel. The shrine is behind the hotel. You can walk around to the back. (Or a shortcut would be to take the hotel elevator up to the lobby level, for the shrine is just outside the hotel's exit on that level. But please be discreet if you do this.)

KAMEIDO TENJIN SHRINE

亀戸天神

3–6–1 Kameido, Koto-ku, Tokyo 130–0071

☎ 3681–0010

東京都江東区亀戸3-6-1　〒130-0071

This shrine is (as are the other shrines with Tenjin in their name) dedicated to the noted Heian-period (794–1185) scholar Michizane Sugawara (845–903), more commonly known as Tenjin-sama. He is considered to be the deity of study and learning, so the shrine is very popular with students—particularly around exam time.

Founded in 1662, Kameido Tenjin is famous for its *Fuji* (Wisteria) Festival, which takes place in late April through early May each year. A multitude of people flock to the shrine at that time to walk over the traditional arched bridge and wander among the trellises that surround the pond with a breathtaking display of purple wisteria blossoms clustered on long, hanging vines swaying in the breeze. Other events, such as an open-air tea ceremony, take place during the festival.

Between mid-February and early March of each year, the red and white blossoms of some 300 plum trees can also be viewed here.

Hours: 6 AM–5 PM (shrine), grounds open 24 hours.

Access: 10 min from Kameido Stn, North Exit (JR Sobu Line). Walk north along Meiji-dori for about 5 min until you reach Kuramaebashi-dori. Turn left and walk about another 5 min. The shrine is on the right side, set back a little from the street.

KANDA MYOJIN SHRINE
神田明神

2–16–2 Sotokanda, Chiyoda-ku, Tokyo 101–0021

☎ 3254–0753

東京都千代田区外神田2-16-2 〒101-0021

Originally founded in the 8th century in Otemachi, Kanda Myojin was moved to Kanda at the start of the Edo period (1600–1868) in 1616, due to expansion plans for the shogun's castle. Frequented by the warrior class in Edo times, this shrine was equal in importance to the Hie shrine when the shoguns ruled. It sponsored one of Edo's three main yearly festivals—the *Kanda Matsuri*. Still held every two years in mid-May, this festival continues to be one of Tokyo's major events. A smaller event is held in alternate years.

There is a legend connected with the shrine regarding a rebel general named Taira-no-Masakado. Feeling that the farmers in his area were being unfairly and grossly overtaxed, he rose up against the emperor in the year 935. When he was captured and beheaded, his head was placed on a bridge for all to see. Then, as legend has it, the head suddenly rose up, flew through the air, and landed at the former location of Kanda Myojin. The people buried his head there and created a shrine for him on the site. When the Kanda shrine moved, his head and shrine stayed in their original spot, where they remain to this day.

TEMPLES, SHRINES, AND OTHER RESTING PLACES FOR THE SPIRIT

The Kanda Myojin was the first shrine to be built using the new ferroconcrete technology when it was restored following the devastating 1923 earthquake.

Hours: 9 AM–4 PM. Grounds are open 24 hours daily.
Access:3 min from JR Ochanomizu Stn, East Exit (Sobu or Chuo lines). From the exit, turn left and walk across the bridge, passing the Yushima Seido (Confucian shrine) on your right. At the next corner, turn and walk right. You will see the shrine's *torii* gate on the left side about 1 min down the street.

MEIJI SHRINE
明治神宮
1–1 Yoyogi Kamizonocho, Shibuya-ku, Tokyo 151–8557
☎ 3379–5511
東京都渋谷区代々木神園町1-1　〒151-8557

NOTE: The Meiji shrine Treasury Museum containing items used by the Meiji emperor and the empress during their lifetime, and a former imperial Japanese garden noted for the large variety of irises that bloom here every June, are also on the grounds. Both charge an admission fee.

The pathway leading to the Meiji shrine runs through a beautiful, thickly wooded area where the only sounds you hear are those of chirping birds and flowing streams—and perhaps the sound of your own footsteps on the gravel path. The walk serves to quiet your mind in preparation for your visit to the shrine.

Meiji shrine is the largest in Tokyo. It is dedicated to Emperor Meiji and Empress Shoken, who oversaw Japan's entry into the modern world following the Meiji Restoration of 1868. The shrine buildings are made of Japanese cypress and built in a classic Shinto architectural style that is simple but grand. The grounds cover an area of 72 hectares (178 acres) and contain foliage of nearly every kind of species to be found in Japan, from Hokkaido to Okinawa. It is a peaceful oasis in the midst of all the big-city madness that surrounds it.

This is a very popular place for New Year visits, and its famous spring and autumn festivals feature traditional performance arts such as Noh drama and ancient court music and dancing. Martial arts demonstrations and dedicatory sumo rituals are held here as well—as are the official sumo installation ceremonies for new grand champions, or *yokozuna* (see ch 4).

Hours: Varies according to sunrise and sunset times, but around 5 AM–
6 PM in summer and 6:30 AM–4 PM in winter.

Access: Next to Meiji Jingumae Stn on Chiyoda Subway Line or JR Harajuku Stn on the Yamanote Line.

NAMI-YOKE INARI SHRINE

波除稲荷

6–20–37 Tsukiji, Chuo-ku, Tokyo 104–0045

☎ 3541–8451

東京都中央区築地6-20-37　〒104-0045

When I happened upon this interesting little shrine at the Tsukiji Fish Market one day, I almost jumped out of my skin. For just
inside the gate is the largest animal head imaginable. It is dark
brown with huge golden teeth and a beard. Blonde locks of hair
fall over its large round eyes, which seem to follow one's every
move. I later learned that it is a lion's head (considered good
luck in Japan)—and a portable shrine carved from a 3,000-
year-old tree. The head measures 3.3 m (10.8 ft) across, is 2.4 m
(7.8 ft) high, and is paraded around the neighborhood at the
yearly festival held by this 330-year-old shrine in early June. It is
the biggest lion's head in Tokyo, and probably in the entire
country. This one is male, but a mate will join it in the future.
The wood for the female's head is currently drying.

This is the shrine of the local fishermen and fish sellers, and
offers them a place to come and pray for a good catch and protection from the waves. Monuments to the fish that have sacrificed themselves so that we humans might eat are lined up along
one wall of the grounds. There's even one for sushi!

Hours: The shrine is open 8 AM–5 PM daily. The grounds are open
24 hours.

Access: 5 min from Tsukiji Stn, Exit 1 (Hibiya Line). Turn left from the
station and walk to the corner (Harumi-dori). Cross the street
and turn left again. When you reach the second traffic light
(a large parking garage building will be on the corner), walk
right. The shrine is on the left side just before the bridge.

NEZU SHRINE

根津神社

1–28–9 Nezu, Bunkyo-ku, Tokyo 113–0031
☎ 3822–0753
東京都文京区根津1-28-9　〒113-0031

If it sounds as if the Tokugawa shoguns had a hand in just about everything during the Edo period (1600–1868)—well, they did. And flowers were no exception. For example, the first official cherry blossom festival was held when the 8th Tokugawa shogun opened up his private hawking grounds (in Tokyo's Asukayama Park) to the public in 1737. And the 3,000 azalea bushes (*tsutsuji*) that cover the hillside of Nezu shrine with a dramatic burst of color each springtime were planted by the 5th shogun on the grounds of this 2,000-year-old shrine. The shrine was rebuilt when the plantings were done (1706), during the time when Shinto and Buddhism were considered one religion. As you look around the buildings you can see many Buddhist signs and symbols incorporated into the shrine's architecture. A number of the structures have been deemed Important Cultural Properties.

The beautiful flowers are celebrated with a big *Tsutsuji Matsuri* (festival) each mid-April through May 5, which usually includes a flea market, *taiko* drumming, traditional dance, and other entertainment—as well as the carrying of the Nezu shrine's portable shrine (*mikoshi*) through the streets to bestow blessings upon the area.

NOTE: If you visit the shrine late in the day and have avoided going into typical Japanese eateries because of language difficulties, you might be interested in knowing about a couple of inexpensive little Japanese "pubs" located on the route between the station and the shrine. Both have English menus and welcome foreigners (although you will probably be the only non-Japanese there). They are Matsuyoshi (☎ 3821–4430, clsd Tues) and Tagosaku (☎ 3823–7146, clsd Sat). Both have signs out front in English and are open from 5/5:30 PM until about midnight.

Hours: Depends on sunrise and sunset times, but approximately 5:30 AM to 6 PM in summer and 6 AM to 5 PM in winter. The grounds are open 24 hours.

Access: 6 min from Nezu Stn, Exit 1 (Chiyoda Line). Turn left from the exit and walk along Shinobazu-dori. At the third traffic signal (a sign next to the signal will read "Nezujinja"), turn left. The shrine is about 2 min down that road on the right side.

NOGI SHRINE

乃木神社

8–11–27 Akasaka, Minato-ku, Tokyo 107–0052

☎ 3478–3001 (Nogi shrine), 5413–7011 (Ward Office)
東京都港区赤坂8-11-27 〒107-0052

Nogi shrine is dedicated to General Maresuke Nogi, who fought under the Meiji emperor during the Sino-Japanese (1894–95) and Russo-Japanese (1904–05) wars. He won many important battles for Japan, and at the end of the wars, tutored the young Prince Hirohito.

The shrine is located on the former grounds of the general's house, which has been preserved intact. The house is part Western and part Japanese-tatami rooms, and serves as an important example of how these two styles were combined in homes during the Meiji period (1868–1912) when Japan was opening up to the West. A simple wooden structure, it was designed by the general himself in the French army style with which he had become familiar during his schooling in Europe. An elevated walkway for visitors has been constructed around the house (although you can't really see much through the windows). Next door are the stables where you almost expect to see horses inside.

On the day of the demise of the emperor Meiji (September 13, 1912), General Nogi and his wife committed ritual suicide and joined him in death. The general's bravery and loyalty to the emperor were remembered. A shrine was dedicated to him on the grounds, and the area of the city was named in his honor. The house is open for public viewing every September 12 and 13. An English pamphlet describing General Nogi and his house is available at the shrine and a plaque in front of the house tells his story in English.

Every second Sunday of the month, an antique flea market is held at the shrine.

Hours: The grounds of the house are open daily (except hols) 9 AM–4 PM. (The house is open for viewing on Sept 12 and 13 only, 9:30 AM–4:30 PM.) The shrine's hours are 10 AM–5 PM daily.

Access: Next to Nogizaka Stn, Exit 1 (Chiyoda Line). As you enter the shrine, the house and grounds are through the brown wooden gate on your left.

TOMIOKA HACHIMANGU SHRINE
富岡八幡宮

1–20–3 Tomioka, Koto-ku, Tokyo 135–0047

☎ 3642–1315

東京都江東区富岡1-20-3　〒135-0047

Sumo became a professional sport in the 17th century, after having been banned by the shogun for a period of time to discourage gambling on unruly sumo wrestling in the streets. But once reinstated in 1684, regular tournaments were held here at the Tomioka Hachiman shrine for about the next hundred years. Today, stone monuments dedicated to the top-ranked wrestlers can be seen on the shrine grounds, engraved with the names of all the grand champions (*yokozuna*) of the sport. Included is the first non-Japanese ever to reach that rank—American-born Akebono, who achieved the status in 1993. The names of the first *yokozuna* (Akashi) through the forty-fifth (Wakanohana) can be found on the back of the monument's largest stone. The listing is carried over to an adjoining one, which begins with the forty-sixth champion (Asashio) and continues all the way up to the present. A smaller monument for *ozeki,* the second-highest sumo rank, is in front of the shrine.

The shrine, founded in 1627, holds a grand festival, the *Fukagawa Hachiman Matsuri,* once every three years for several days around mid-August. Over fifty portable shrines (*mikoshi*) are paraded through the streets while people throw buckets of water over them and the shrine carriers! There are a number of other events too, such as martial arts demonstrations, *taiko* drumming, and music and dance performances. The years of the festival will be 1999, 2002, 2005, and so on. An antique flea market is held at the shrine on the first, fifteenth, and twenty-eighth days of every month.

Hours: The shrine is open 9 AM–5 PM daily. The grounds are always open.

Access: 4 min from Monzen Nakacho Stn, Exit 1 (Tozai Line). Turn left from the exit and walk down Eitai-dori past the first traffic signal. You will soon see the shrine's large main torii gate on your left. About halfway down the shrine pathway on the right side is the monument to ozeki (Ozeki no Hi). When you reach the shrine, you will see an underpass to the right. The yokozuna monument (Yokozuna no Hi) is just on the other side of this.

UENO TOSHOGU SHRINE
上野東照宮

9–88 Ueno Park, Taito-ku, Tokyo 110–0007

☎ 3822–3455

東京都台東区上野公園9-88　〒110-0007

This shrine was founded in 1627 by the third Tokugawa shogun in honor of his famous grandfather, Ieyasu, first of the Tokugawa shoguns. It is one of a number of Toshogu shrines, the grandest one being located in Nikko, the final resting place of Ieyasu.

The building is quite elaborate. It is richly decorated with paintings and carvings and has been designated as a National Treasure. There is a ¥200 charge to enter the main hall, but the outside of the building and the grounds, which include a stage for musical performances and many large bronze and stone lanterns that line the walkway to the shrine (gifts from feudal lords to honor the shogun), can be enjoyed free of charge. The long approach to the shrine passes alongside the five-storied pagoda, one of the few structures that survived the destruction of Kaneiji temple during the Meiji Restoration (1868). The pagoda dates back to 1631 and has been designated as an Important Cultural Property by the Japanese government.

A little to the right of the shrine's main *torii* gate (as you exit) can be found the "Monster Lantern," or "Oishidoro." It is so-named because it stands 7 m (23 ft) high and measures 3.6 m (12 ft) around. It is one of three such lanterns in all of Japan.

Hours: 9 AM–sunset daily.

Access: JR Ueno Stn, Ueno Park Exit (Yamanote Line and other lines). The shrine is located in Ueno Park. A map is available from the Information Center at the entrance to the park.

YASUKUNI SHRINE

靖国神社

3–1–1 Kudan Kita, Chiyoda-ku, Tokyo 102–0073

☎ 3261–8326

東京都千代田区九段北3-1-1　〒102-0073

The name "Yasukuni" means "Peaceful Country," and this shrine was built in part to symbolize the peace that the country enjoys today. Founded in 1869, it is dedicated to those who died in internal and foreign wars, including those who died in the Meiji Restoration that led to the creation of a modern Japan.

One of the largest *torii* gates in Japan can be found at its entrance, and inside the grounds beautiful cherry trees bloom each spring. Its spring (April) and autumn (October) festivals are outstanding, and feature traditional Japanese performance arts and sporting events—as well as *taiko* drumming and join-in *odori* folk dancing. I even saw a magic show here once.

A permanent sumo ring is located around the side of the main hall where a dedicatory sumo ceremony and free matches are performed each April. College sumo tournaments are held here as well. (See ch 4 for details on all.)

NOTE: There is a museum on the grounds (Yushukan) that is dedicated to the memory of the 2.5 million military men who died serving their country. Aircraft, ships, and other wartime material and events are documented. It also contains poignant letters and poems written by young soldiers from the battlefield. (¥200)

Hours: The temple is open 9 AM–5 PM in summer and 9 AM–4 PM in winter. The gate hours are 5:30 AM–6 PM.

Access: Across from Kudanshita Stn, Exit 1 (Hanzomon, Tozai, and Toei Shinjuku lines).

YUSHIMA TENJIN SHRINE

湯島天神

3–30–1 Yushima, Bunkyo-ku, Tokyo 113–0034

☎ 3836–0753

東京都文京区湯島3-30-1　〒113-0034

This shrine was founded in the 14th century in honor of the great 9th-century scholar Michizane Sugawara. Given the name "Tenjin" following his death, he is considered to be the patron of learning. Consequently, many students flock here to pray for success around exam time. They buy small plaques (*ema*) from the shrine, write their wishes on them, and hang them on a board provided for this purpose—in hopes that these wishes will come true.

It is also known for its plum flowers (*ume*) that bloom from mid-February to mid-March each year. During this time, the shrine hosts the most famous plum blossom festival in Tokyo, when many people come to admire the 400 trees in full bloom throughout the garden and shrine grounds. This flower is greatly admired for its capacity to blossom in the bitter cold of February. A well-known and poignant love story from the Meiji period (1868–1912) entitled *Onna Keizu* was written against the backdrop of the plum blossom garden of Yushima Tenjin shrine. The shrine also hosts a big Chrysanthemum (*Kiku*) Festival each November, at which lifesize dolls created from chrysanthemums are generally on display.

Hours: 9 AM–7:30 PM daily.

Access: A 2-min walk from Yushima Stn, Exit 3 (Chiyoda Line). Turn left from the exit and left again at the corner. Walk up Kasuga-dori for about 2 min and you will see a stairway on the left side leading up to the shrine grounds.

Churches and other resting places for the spirit

In addition to Buddhist temples and Shinto shrines, there are many other houses of worship located throughout the city. They range from traditional to ultramodern, from simple to elaborate—and represent beliefs from around the globe. These various faiths and philosophies did not always have an easy time of it in Japan, but as a result of the country's internationalization, just about every spiritual path is represented in Tokyo today. So whatever your faith or leaning, you are just about guaranteed to find a place to fill your spiritual needs.

Introduced into Japan by Francis Xavier in 1549, Christianity has had its ups and downs, and was even banned for about 200 years between the 17th and 19th centuries. But as you can see from the listing below, there is a great variety of churches to be found in Tokyo today. They are particularly active during the Christmas season—which is celebrated in grand style in Tokyo. Keep your eyes and ears open for wonderful concerts of classical music, Gregorian chants, Christmas carols, brass bands, bell concerts, special pageants, and many other events that take place throughout the city at this very special time of the year.

NOTE: Although no admission is charged to enter these houses of worship, it is customary to leave a small offering if you attend a service. For an up-to-date listing of religious and spiritual centers in Tokyo and vicinity, check the monthly Church Guide in the *Japan Times*. (Offered the first Tues of every month at the time of this printing.)

ENGLISH/JAPANESE SPEAKING

CHURCH OF JESUS CHRIST OF LATTER-DAY SAINTS (Mormon)

末日聖徒イエス キリスト教会

（Matsujitsu Seito Iesu Kirisuto Kyokai）

5–8–8 Minami Azabu, Minato-ku, Tokyo 106–0047

☎ 3444–4834

東京都港区南麻布5-8-8　〒106-0047

Although only church members are allowed into the Mormon temple in Hiroo, the church's next-door chapel holds Sunday services open to all. In the organization of the Mormon Church there are no paid clergy—various members of the congregation are responsible for its leadership, teaching, and other church duties—such as speaking at the services where readings are from both the Bible and *The Book of Mormon*. Each first Sunday spontaneous testimony is given, where everyone is free to get up and share their feelings.

A number of activities are sponsored by the church, including Boy Scout units and young women's programs. It also maintains the world's largest family history (genealogy) research center (in Salt Lake City, Utah), accessible via local Mormon Church library branches. Church officials are currently working with the Japanese government to set up such a project for people of Japanese origin.

Hours: English services are 9 AM–noon and 1:30 PM–4:30 PM Sun. (In summer there is only one service, at 9 AM.) Sometimes they hold combination meetings with other chapels, so call to make sure there is a service that week.

Access: 5 min from Hiroo Stn, Exit 1 (Hibiya Line). Go left from the exit, and turn left at the corner. Follow this street as it winds around to the left of Arisugawa Park. The chapel is across from the park just beyond the Tokyo Mormon Temple.

FIRST CHURCH OF CHRIST, SCIENTIST TOKYO
(Christian Science)

東京第一科学者キリスト教会

（Tokyo Dai-ichi Kagakusha Kirisuto Kyokai）

5–6–3 Jingumae, Shibuya-ku, Tokyo 150–0001

☎ 3499–3951

東京都渋谷区神宮前5-6-3　〒150-0001

Beautiful in its simplicity, this church was designed by Dr. Yoshinobu Ashiwara, former chairman of the Japan Architects Association. The green Swedish marble behind the podium effectively sets off the central area of the interior, which is mostly of natural light wood. At the Sunday service, a different topic is covered each week, supplemented by readings from both the Bible and founder Mary Baker Eddy's *Science and Health*. At the Wednesday evening meetings, church members can get up and talk about their personal experiences in being healed. The church also offers periodic lectures and informal talks followed by question-and-answer periods.

Hours: English services are held at 11:30 AM Sun, and bilingual testimonial meetings at 7:30 PM Wed.

Access: A 4-min walk from Omotesando Stn, Exit A1 (Ginza, Hanzomon, and Chiyoda lines). Walk straight out from the exit and turn left into the small street alongside Tokyo Union Church, then take the first right. The church is on the left side.

FRANCISCAN CHAPEL CENTER (Roman Catholic)

フランシスカ チャペルセンター

4–2–37 Roppongi, Minato-ku, Tokyo 106–0032

☎ 3401–2141

東京都港区六本木4-2-37　〒160-0032

This very active church is the designated parish for English-speaking people in the Tokyo archdiocese. It is a kind of "church in the round," with benches that wrap around three sides of the altar. A large mosaic that takes up most of one wall depicts a famous poem written by St. Francis Assisi entitled "Canticle of the Sun." It was designed by an artist-priest and created by local art students in 1967—using broken potteryware from all the villages that the Christian martyrs passed through in their forced march from Kyoto to Nagasaki during the days of Christian persecution in Japan.

The church hosts a number of encounter and support groups, and other organizational meetings within its walls, and its central location near Roppongi Station makes it very accessible.

Hours: English masses are held Sat at 6 PM and Sun at 8 AM, 10 AM, noon, and 6 PM. Also wkdys at 8 AM and Wed at 6 PM.

Access: A 4-min walk from Roppongi Stn, Exit A4 (Hibiya Line). Go straight out from the exit, cross the street, and turn left. Turn right at the second small street, and walk until you come to a traffic light. The church is a short distance past the traffic light on the right side.

INTERNATIONAL CHRISTIAN ASSEMBLY (ICA)
(Member of the Assemblies of God, Fellowship of Independent Churches)

インターナショナル クリスチャン アセンブリー

Wing Building, 2F

5–25–18 Hongo, Bunkyo-ku, Tokyo 113–0033

☎ 3940–6691 (Church Office)

東京都文京区本郷5-25-18　ウィングビル2階　〒113-0033

If some Sunday morning you wake up feeling a little blue, the International Christian Assembly has a lively, uplifting service. Express your innermost feelings and sing your heart out at this upbeat gathering. African, Asian, and Western nations are all amply represented at this celebration of the Holy Spirit. Lots of other activities are held too, such as a mid-week service, water baptism class, and international coffee time with speakers.

Hours: English services Sun at 9:30 AM and 11 AM. Bring a box lunch (obento) and join the others for lunch at 1 PM following the service.

Access: 5 min from Hongo-sanchome Stn (Marunouchi Line). Turn left onto Hongo-dori and cross Hongo-sanchome intersection. Go straight past the police box (koban) and McDonald's. Turn left at the third street from the intersection and right at the first corner. About halfway down the block on your right you will see the gray brick Wing Building (written in English), with the large letters "ICA" in the 2F window.

NEW OTANI GARDEN CHAPEL (Shogetsu Tei)

ニューオオタニ ガーデン チャペル（招月亭）

> Hotel New Otani Tokyo
> 4–1 Kioicho, Chiyoda-ku, Tokyo 102–8578
> ☎ 3265–1111 ext. 3301 for chapel information
> 東京都千代田区紀尾井町4-1　ホテルニューオオタニ　〒102-8578

This tiny, six-sided, glass-enclosed chapel is located right in the middle of the sweeping 400-year-old New Otani Gardens (see ch 7). It has a friendly, intimate atmosphere and during services everyone stands up and introduces themselves. Chapel Director Reverend Dr. Lucius Butler says he never knows what nationalities are going to wander in through the door each week, but he is well-prepared with translations of the Bible in thirty different languages!

Other activities are a Tuesday Prayer Breakfast (in the Garden Lounge) followed by an hour of Bible study, and daily morning meditation and counseling.

Hours: Bilingual service held Sun 8:30 AM, followed by fellowship and coffee. Open 8:30–10 AM (wkdys).

Access: A 3-min walk from Akasaka Mitsuke Stn, Akasaka Mitsuke Crossing Exit (Marunouchi and Ginza lines). Located in the garden of the New Otani Hotel.

ST. ALBAN'S ANGLICAN-EPISCOPAL CHURCH

聖オルバン教会

3–6–25 Shiba Koen, Minato-ku, Tokyo 105–0011

☎ 3431–8534

東京都港区芝公園3-6-25　〒105-0011

This charming all-wooden church with brick trim was designed by Antonin Raymond, a protégé of Frank Lloyd Wright. Its criss-cross–beamed ceiling and inviting front porch radiate the feeling of the Japanese countryside, rather than that of the central Tokyo location on which it stands. Even the service books are covered with colorful, traditional *washi* paper. Members of the congregation hail from thirty different countries, and people from all religious faiths are very welcome to attend.

Hours: All services are in English. Eucharist services Sun at 8 AM (spoken) and 10 AM (sung), and Wed at noon.

Access: St. Alban's is located across the street from Tokyo Tower, a 7-min walk from Kamiyacho Stn, Exit 1 (Hibiya Line). Turn left from the exit and walk up Sakurada-dori to the major intersection at Gaien Higashi-dori. Turn left without crossing the street. The church will be 1 min up the hill on the left side.

ST. ANSELM'S BENEDICTINE PRIORY (Roman Catholic)

聖アンセルム教会

4–6–22 Kamiosaki, Shinagawa-ku, Tokyo 141–0021

☎ 3491–5461 Office (Japanese), 3491–6966 (Father Lawrence)

東京都品川区上大崎4-6-22　〒141-0021

Designed by the same architect as St. Alban's (see above), but worlds apart in style, this ultramodern church was built on the site of an old factory building that was used as a place of worship following World War II. Modern Western design was combined with traditional Japanese forms to create a building based on the concept of "noble simplicity." The natural concrete walls are angled to throw all light to the front of the church, where a large black-and-gold-lacquered cross hangs from the fluid form of the gilded canopy curving dramatically over the altar. To the left of the altar hangs a 13th-century Byzantine icon of the Madonna and Child.

All local materials were used to build this rectangular church that measures 15.2 m (50 ft) high and wide, and 30.5 m (100 ft) long. A number of activities for the international community are sponsored by the church, including St. Anselm's International Friendship Association.

Hours: English Mass is held Sun at noon. The church is open from 6 AM until 8/9 PM daily for prayer and meditation.

Access: A 3-min walk from JR Meguro Stn, West Exit (Yamanote Line). Turn left from the station, cross Meguro-dori, and enter the street located at an angle. Follow that around the Sakura Bank, then turn left down the first small street. The entrance to the church compound is on the left just beyond a modern, rectangular cement structure, a part of the church.

ST. IGNATIUS CHURCH (Roman Catholic)

聖イグナチオ教会

6–5 Kojimachi, Chiyoda-ku, Tokyo 102–0083

☎ 3263–4584

東京都千代田区麹町6-5　〒102-0083

Of the 3,000 people who attend masses here each weekend, about half are foreign. For over twenty years St. Ignatius has been offering a Sunday mass in English (there's also one in Spanish) to the foreign community. An International Folk Mass in which a pantomime is acted out replaces the sermon each first Sunday. It is created, directed, and performed by members of the international community.

A new building is presently under construction on the site to replace the existing structure, which was built shortly after World War II. The church's beautiful stained glass windows (seven large and twenty-two small ones) will be used in the new building.

NOTE: The church offers Japanese lessons following Sun Mass in both English and Spanish, and also Tues classes (which include cooking lessons) for foreign wives of Japanese.

Hours: English Mass is held at noon Sun, followed by Spanish Mass at 1:15 PM. The International Folk Mass is at noon each 1st Sun. Open daily from 6 AM–7 PM for prayer and meditation.

Access: Next to Yotsuya Stn. From subway Exit 1 (Marunouchi or Nanboku lines), bear right and cross over the bridge. From the JR Kojimachi Exit (Sobu or Chuo lines), cross the street to the right. The church is on the corner, next to the Sophia University Yotsuya campus.

ST. MARY'S CATHEDRAL (Roman Catholic)

東京カテドラル聖マリア大聖堂
(Tokyo Katedoraru Sei Maria Daiseido)
>3–16–15 Sekiguchi, Bunkyo-ku, Tokyo 112–0014
>☎ 3941–3029
>東京都文京区関口3-16-15　〒112-0014

This ultramodern cathedral with its sparkling stainless-steel exterior and pillarless gray concrete interior was designed by one of Tokyo's most famous architects, Kenzo Tange. Modern sculpture is scattered around the interior; the outside light shines through thin layers of marble instead of stained glass, and a spiral staircase with no visible means of support—except the concrete post it wraps around—leads up to the pipe organ (the largest one in use in any Japanese church). St. Mary's Cathedral is the seat (residence) of the city's archbishop—making it the central Catholic church in the Archdiocese of Tokyo.

Hours: There are no English masses, but Japanese masses are held Sun at 8 AM, 10 AM, and noon; Sat at 6 PM; and wkdys at 7 AM. St. Mary's is open for prayer and meditation every day from 9 AM–5 PM.

Access A 10-min walk from Edogawabashi Stn, Exit 1A (Yurakucho Line). Cross over the bridge and continue walking to Mejiro-dori. Turn left and walk for about 8 min (uphill) until you see the church on the right side. Or take No. 61 bus from Edogawabashi Stn. Board just after crossing over the bridge and get off at Chinzanso-mae stop (about a 3-min ride). The church is immediately across the street.

ST. NIKOLAI CATHEDRAL (Russian Orthodox)
(Holy Resurrection Cathedral)

日本ハリストス正教会教団東京復活大聖堂・ニコライ堂
(Nikorai-do)
>4–1 Kanda Surugadai, Chiyoda-ku, Tokyo 101–0062
>☎ 3295–6879 (Church Office in Japanese),
>3295–1294 (Father John's house in English)
>東京都千代田区神田駿河台4-1　〒101-0062

This beautiful cross-shaped Byzantine-style church, with a 38-m- (124-ft-) high dome at its center, is the headquarters of the Orthodox Church in Japan. Officially called the Holy Resurrection Cathedral, the more familiar name of St. Nikolai comes from its founding Russian missionary—Kassatkin Nikolai—who later became a saint. The original planning of the building took place in Russia, but the cathedral was constructed here in 1891. During its current renovation the cathedral is only open during services. But after completion of the work they expect to resume a full schedule and you will once again be able to visit the cathedral on weekdays. English- and Russian-speaking clergy are always in attendance at the cathedral.

Hours: There is no English liturgy, but a Japanese service is held each Sun 10 AM–12:30 PM. At the completion of renovation (scheduled for spring of 1998), weekday services will start again and the church may once again be visited Tues–Sat between 1 PM and 4 PM.

Access: A 2-min walk from JR Ochanomizu Stn, East Exit (Chuo and Sobu Lines). Make a left from the ticket turnstile. At the corner, cross the street to the right and continue down Hongo-dori away from the bridge. The church is on the following corner. Turn right and the entrance will be on the small street running alongside the church

ST. PAUL INTERNATIONAL LUTHERAN CHURCH

聖パウロ インターナショナル ルーテル教会

1–2–32 Fujimi, Chiyoda-ku, Tokyo 102–0071

☎ 3261–3740

東京都千代田区富士見1-2-32　〒102-0071

This cozy wood-and-brick chapel is housed on the 2F of the Tokyo Lutheran Center. The building was constructed in 1937—and its proximity to the Imperial Palace allowed it to survive the bombings of World War II, according to Pastor Karl Bachman.

St. Paul was established in 1965 as the only English-language Lutheran congregation in Japan. It is not a member of any large denomination, but rather is an officially recognized

TEMPLES, SHRINES, AND OTHER RESTING PLACES FOR THE SPIRIT

Independent Congregation that ministers to all Lutheran Christians. Bible-study courses are offered by the pastor on weekdays.

Hours: Sun worship service 9:30 AM in English. The chapel is open wkdys from 9 AM–9 PM and wknds 9 AM–7:30 PM for prayer and meditation (when not in use for a wedding or other event).

Access: 7 min from JR Iidabashi Stn, West Exit (Sobu Line), or Iidabashi Stn subway (Tozai, Yurakucho, and Nanboku lines), Exit B2a. Cross the bridge to the left and walk straight to the third main corner (Chez Daigo restaurant will be on the right side). Turn left and in 1 min you will see the church on the right side.

TOKYO BAPTIST CHURCH
東京バプティスト教会

9–2 Hachiyamacho, Shibuya-ku, Tokyo 150–0035
☎ 3461–8425
東京都渋谷区鉢山町9-2 〒150-0035

One of the friendliest churches around, the Tokyo Baptist Church is also involved in a great many activities. The Tokyo English Life Line (see ch 1) was originally housed here, and their church choir consists of fifteen to twenty different nationalities at any one time. In 1997 they inaugurated a Bachelor of Arts degree program in cooperation with the Tokyo Baptist Theological Seminary, through which you can earn an accredited BA degree.

The church also houses a lending library (open to all) that contains several thousand books on a great number of subjects, including a large children's section.

Hours: Sun worship services are at 8:30 AM, 11 AM, and 6 PM. All are in English.

Access: A 10-min walk from Daikanyama Stn, Main Exit (Toyoko Line). Walk straight out of the station and turn right at the end of the road. When you reach the main street, cross over, turn left, then make an immediate right and walk down Kyu Yamate-dori. Continue walking for 6 or 7 min and you will see the church on the right side. It's also about a 15-min walk from Shibuya Stn (Yamanote and other lines).

TOKYO CENTRAL CHURCH OF SEVENTH-DAY ADVENTISTS

S.D.A.東京中央教会 （SDA Tokyo Chuo Kyokai）

    1–11–1 Jingumae, Shibuya-ku, Tokyo 150–0001

    ☎ 3402–1517 or 045–921–1121 (Ask for Gemma Paloma or Mark Duarte)

    東京都渋谷区神宮前1-11-1　〒150-0001

Seventh-Day Adventists are a denomination of the Protestant Church with roots going back to the early 1800s. They observe the Sabbath on Saturday, recognizing it as the day following Good Friday (when Christ rested), instead of the more commonly practiced Sunday observance (when God rested following the creation of the world).

The church stresses health and education in their ministry, and sponsor hospitals and schools worldwide. Sometimes classes are offered in weight loss, vegetarian cooking, how-to-stop-smoking, and stress-reduction.

NOTE: After the service each Sat, a vegetarian lunch is available for a small donation.

Hours: English worship service is held Sat at 11 AM in the large meeting room on the main floor. There are several entrances at different levels, and there is a Japanese service at the same time in the upstairs church, so make sure you enter at the main floor.

Access: A 3-min walk from Meiji Jingumae Stn, Exit 5 (Chiyoda Line). After exiting, turn around and walk back to the corner (Meiji-dori). Make a left there, and another left at the first small street. The church is the second building on the left (immediately behind the LaForet Building).

TOKYO FRIENDS CENTER and MEETING HOUSE (Quaker)

キリスト友会東京月会 （Kirisuto Yukai Tokyo Gekkai）

    4–8–19 Mita, Minato-ku, Tokyo 108–0073

    ☎ 3451–0804 (Tokyo Friends Center),

    3451–7002 (Meeting House)

    東京都港区三田4-8-19　〒108-0073

The Tokyo Friends Center and Meeting House is the largest Quaker complex in Japan. Since Quakers believe that God is in each person, there is no minister. But individuals are free to

TEMPLES, SHRINES, AND OTHER RESTING PLACES FOR THE SPIRIT

stand and speak during the worship services, which are otherwise held in silence. The service takes place at the Friends Meeting House, during which translation is provided from both Japanese to English and English to Japanese. Periodic open houses are held at the adjoining Friends Center, where you will be met by such comforts as a large fireplace and a quilt display in the charming Western house that was built in 1923, one of the few buildings in the area to survive the Great Earthquake.

NOTE: A noon snack lunch is available for ¥300 following the meeting.

Hours: Bilingual services are held at 10:30 AM Sun.

Access: A 10-min walk from Mita Stn, Exit A3 (Asakusa and Mita lines). Enter the small alley behind the station and turn left. You will pass a post office on the right. When you come to the main street, go right, then make the first left. You will soon come to a fork in the road at the stoplight. Go left up the hill and pass the Kuwaiti Embassy on the right. At the top of the hill are a *koban* (police box) and two small parks. At the second park you will be at the center of a "V" in the road. The Friends Center is the second building to the right (an English sign will be in front). Also accessible from JR Tamachi Stn (Yamanote and Keihin Tohoku lines). Call for other directions.

TOKYO HORIZON CHAPEL (Nondenominational)
東京ホライゾン チャペル

☎ 0427–96–9484 (Church Office)
010–731–7327 (Pastor Wilson)

Guitars and keyboards provide the music for the main Sunday service at this youth-oriented church, which was founded as an offshoot of a California church known for reaching out to kids on the beach. It is meant to be "an oasis where people can come and feel refreshed," according to Pastor and founder Jonathan Wilson.

Bible study is emphasized, and the entire Bible is read from cover to cover over the course of a few years. The church also supports a Mission to Cambodia and a hotline that young pregnant Japanese and Filipino girls can call for counseling.

Hours: Two English services are held each Sun morning. A more traditional bilingual service (with organ music) is held at 8:30 AM at the 2F chapel of the Westin Hotel in Yebisu Garden Place. The 11 AM youth-oriented service is currently in temporary quarters. Call Pastor Wilson for information.

Access: For access to and more information about Yebisu Garden Place, see ch 3. Call for location and directions for the 11 AM service.

TOKYO UNION CHURCH (Interdenominational)

東京ユニオン チャーチ

5–7–7 Jingumae, Shibuya-ku, Tokyo 150–0001

☎ 3400–0047

東京都渋谷区神宮前5-7-7　〒150-0001

This church is among the most active in Tokyo today, supporting a women's shelter, prison ministry, feeding and clothing of the homeless, and numerous other domestic and international programs. They have a strong youth program, and their Women's Society offers interesting free talks each month (see ch 12).

The church was founded in 1872, and the present structure completed in 1980. The lovely stained glass window in the sanctuary was created by Christian designer Keiko Miura, and features crystal-colored representations of the tears of Jesus against a blue background.

Note: Tokyo Union Church also offers an extensive selection of culture classes and an Early Childhood Development Center for three-to-five-year-olds. Call for schedule and fees.

Hours: All services are in English. Worship services at 8:30 AM and 11 AM Sun (10 AM only mid-June through Aug) followed by a fellowship coffee hour. On the 1st Sun of each month, the church also holds an evening praise service—a contemporary informal worship service. The church is open for prayer and meditation weekdays 9:30 AM–5:30 PM.

Access: 2 min from Omotesando Stn, Exit A1 (Hanzomon, Ginza, and Chiyoda lines). It is straight down Omotesando avenue, on the left side.

TOKYO UNITARIAN FELLOWSHIP

東京ユニタリアン フェロウシップ

International House of Japan (Kokusai Bunka Kaikan)

5–11–16 Roppongi, Minato-ku, Tokyo 106–0032

☎ 3392–2227 (In English)

東京都港区六本木5-11-16　国際文化会館内　〒106-0032

These round-table, once-a-month English-langage gatherings with featured speakers are in the format of an informal meeting. They offer stimulating, participatory talks on a variety of subjects, such as *The Theology of Shinto, Work Songs through the Ages,* and *The Golden Age of China: Tang Dynasty.* The eclectic nature of the group is based on their belief in "the individual's free search for truth and of mutually sharing one's seeking and finding."

Note: Although there is no charge for the talks, it is requested that you help defray the cost of the room by leaving a contribution in a basket by the door.

Hours: 3 PM on the 2nd Sun of each month, *Oct–June* (no meetings July, Aug, or Sept).

Access: 7 min from Roppongi Stn, Exit 3 (Hibiya Line). Turn right from the station, and right again at the main street. When you reach the far end of the Roi Building, turn right and walk down the hill. The International House is about halfway down on the right side.

FRENCH SPEAKING

FOYER DE L'AUMONERIE CATHOLIQUE DES FRANCOPHONES
☎ 3944–1195 (for map). Fax 3941–0253

The French-speaking Catholic Chaplaincy offers a number of activities and services at two chapels for children and adults, including baptism, confirmation, Bible groups, retreats, and participation in programs to help the less fortunate. French masses are held at two locations:

CHAPPELLE DE L'UNIVERSITÉ DU SACRÉ CŒUR
(Chapel of the University of the Sacred Heart)
聖心女子大学聖堂 （Seishin Joshi Daigaku Seido）
4–3–1 Hiroo, Shibuya-ku, Tokyo 150–8938
☎ 3407–5811
東京都渋谷区広尾4-3-1　聖心女子大学内　〒150-8938

Hours: French mass at 10:30 AM Sun.

Access: 2 min from Hiroo Stn, Exit 3 (Hibiya Line). Cross the overpass next to the station. The church is on the campus of Sacred Heart University.

MAISON RÉGIONALE DES MISSIONS ÉTRANGÈRES DE PARIS (Paris Foreign Missions' Chapel)

パリ外国宣教会本部（Pari Gaikoku Senkyokai Honbu）

3–7–18 Meijirodai, Bunkyo-ku, Tokyo 112–0015

☎ 3944–1195 (for map). Fax 3941–0253

東京都文京区目白台3-7-18　〒112-0015

Hours: French mass at 6 PM Sat.

Access: 5 min from Gokokuji Stn, Exit 6 (Yurakucho Line).

GERMAN SPEAKING

The two German churches in Tokyo have a very close relationship. Once a year in April they hold a joint weekend seminar with a speaker outside of Tokyo. They also co-sponsor family services, youth groups, a Kris Krindl Market, hiking trips, etc.—and they even share a choir.

KREUZKIRCHE (German Protestant)

ドイツ プロテスタント教会

6–5–26 Kita Shinagawa, Shinagawa-ku, Tokyo 141–0001

☎ 3441–0673

東京都品川区北品川6-5-26　〒141-0001

Hours: German service at 10:30 AM Sun.

Access: A 15-min walk from Gotanda Stn. Near Sony headquarters and Toshiba. Call for directions or map.

ST. MICHAEL (Roman Catholic)

聖ミカエル教会

3–18–17 Nakameguro, Meguro-ku, Tokyo 153–0061

☎ 3712–0775

東京都目黒区中目黒3-18-17　〒153-0061

Hours: German mass at 10:30 AM Sun mornings.

Access: Near Nakameguro Stn (Toyoko Line). Call the church for a map.

SPANISH SPEAKING

See entry for St. Ignatius Church above.

OTHER PLACES OF WORSHIP

YUSHIMA SEIDO CONFUCIAN SHRINE
(Sacred Hall at Yushima)

湯島聖堂

    1–4–25 Yushima, Bunkyo-ku, Tokyo 113–0034

    ☎ 3251–4606

    東京都文京区湯島1-4-25　〒113-0034

Confucianism was introduced to Japan from China over twelve hundred years ago, and its influence has been a long and lasting one. This can clearly be seen in the emphasis placed on education, hierarchy, family values, and other prominent aspects of the Japanese culture. Yushima Seido, the sole remaining Confucian shrine in Tokyo today, has quite a history. Originally established in 1632 by order of the Tokugawa shogun as the Shohei Academy, it was a center for the study of Confucian classics. When it outgrew its original quarters in what is now Ueno Park, it was rebuilt at the present location in 1691—where it eventually evolved into an institution of higher learning—the prestigious Tokyo University.

    The shrine is depicted in many of Hiroshige's famous woodblock prints from the Edo period (1600–1868). A staircase leads down to its cool, low-lying gardens containing a large and impressive statue of the sage. Another set of steps leads up to the main hall—a stark, black building with just a touch of red trim. It has a very different feeling from the aged, natural-wood Shinto shrine buildings. Once a year on the fourth Sunday in April, a Festival of Confucius (*Koshisai*) is held at the shrine.

Hours: Open Fri–Wed, 9:30 AM–5 PM in summer, 9:30 AM–4 PM in winter. Clsd Thurs.

Access: The shrine compound lies just across the Hijiribashi (Sage's Bridge) from JR Ochanomizu Stn, East Exit (Sobu or Chuo lines). It is also accessible from Ochanomizu Stn (Marunouchi Line) or Shin Ochanomizu Stn (Chiyoda Line).

THE ARABIC ISLAMIC INSTITUTE

アラビック イスラミック インスティテュート

3–4–18 Moto Azabu, Minato-ku, Tokyo 106-0046

☎ 3404–6411 (after reopening)

東京都港区元麻布3-4-18　〒106-0046

This central-Tokyo mosque is close to Hiroo Station. Here, free classes are offered in the Arabic language and culture, and free prayer carpets are provided for those in need of them. The institute also conducts a food-for-the-needy program and supplies Japanese universities with Arabic-language texts. Construction of a new building that will be half-mosque and half-university is slated to finish in the spring or summer of 1998.

Note: For other places of worship, call the Islamic Center of Japan at ☎ 3460–6169.

Hours: Services are held every Fri at 12:30 PM. There are also prayers five times a day as well as a special program during Ramadan and holy days.

Access: 10 min from Hiroo Stn, Exit 1 (Hibiya Line). Turn left from the exit and left again at the corner. Follow this street as it winds around to the left of Arisugawa Park. Turn right at the second small street after the end of the park—just before the Chinese Embassy. (The YS Building will be on the corner.) The institute is a short distance down the road on the left.

JEWISH COMMUNITY CENTER

日本ユダヤ教団　(Nihon Yudaya Kyodan)

3–8–8 Hiroo, Shibuya-ku, Tokyo 150–0012

☎ 3400–2559　東京都渋谷区広尾3-8-8　〒150-0012

The Jewish Community Center is a very active place. In addition to the synagogue, the compound contains a library and religious school for children. It also offers a full religious program and free English adult education classes for people who want to learn more about Judaism. Services are held in Hebrew and announcements are made in English. Lots of social and youth activities are sponsored by the center, and the Japan-Israel Women's Welfare Association supports children's charities in both Israel and Japan. In addition, lectures by guest speakers and exhibitions are periodically held here at the center, which was founded in 1952.

Note: After each service a kosher meal is served—¥3,500 for Fri dinner and ¥2,000 for light lunch on Sat. Advance reservations are necessary.

Hours: Sabbath services are held each Fri at 6:30 PM (7 PM in summer) and Sat at 9:30 AM.

Access: The center is located behind the police box on Niseki-dori in Hiroo. It is a not-so-simple 15-min walk from Hiroo Subway Stn, Exit 3 (Hibiya Line). An easier route is to take the No. 3 bus from the East Exit of JR Shibuya Stn (Yamanote and other lines) and get off at Tokyo-Jogakan bus stop. Walk back to the police box (koban)—the center is behind it.

TOKYO BAHA'I CENTER
東京バハイ センター

7–2–13 Shinjuku, Shinjuku-ku, Tokyo 160–0022

☎ 3209–7521

東京都新宿区新宿7-2-13　〒160-0022

The Baha'i faith is concerned with the personal investigation of truth. There is no formal ministry or priests—individual responsibility is emphasized. The oneness of humanity, man's connection with nature, justice, and world-mindedness are stressed. Baha'i originated in Persia in the 19th century, and the headquarters of its International Community is based at the United Nations Plaza in New York.

At the monthly Fireside Meetings, topics of discussion might include such varied subjects as the environment or relationships between men and women. Those interested in learning more about the faith are invited to attend the meetings.

Hours: Bilingual Japanese/English Fireside Meetings are held 7:30–9 PM the 1st Sat of each month. Personal meetings are scheduled by individual request.

Access: Take bus No. 76 from Shinjuku Stn, West Exit (Yamanote and other lines), headed toward Iidabashi. Board alongside the corner Subaru Showroom Building just beyond the bus terminals. Get off at Nuke-benten stop (about a 10-min ride). The center is about 50 m (45 yd) away. Immediately in front of the bus stop you will see a row of vending machines alongside a liquor store. Go down that road and turn left at the end of the street. Look for a three-story white building on the left side a few doors down. There will be a sign in front in English and Japanese.

9

ANTIQUES, FOLKCRAFTS, AND FLEA MARKETS

ANTIQUES AND FOLKCRAFTS

- Halls, Arcades, and Shops

  HALLS   *Antique Gallery Meguro*
  Antique Market
  Tokyo Folkcraft and Antique Hall
  Tokyo Ochanomizu Antique Hall

  ARCADES   *International Arcade (Duty Free Shopping Mall)*
  Nakamise-dori
  Kotto-dori (Antique Road)

  SHOPS   *Art Plaza Magatani*
  Beniya Craft Shop
  Bingoya
  Edo-Tokyo Museum Shop
  Fuji Torii
  Harumi Antiques
  Isetatsu
  Oriental Bazaar
  Shoyeido
  Takumi
  Department Stores

CRAFT SPECIALISTS

- Craft Centers
  Japan Traditional Craft Center
  Prefectural Showrooms
- Visit local craftsmen in their homes and workshops
- Try your own hand at making some traditional crafts
  Sakura Horikiri

MOVEABLE TREASURES

- Antique Flea Markets
  Togo Shrine
  Nogi Shrine
  Hanazono Shrine
  Roppongi Antique and Flea Market
  Heiwajima Antiques Fair
- Regular Flea Markets and more . . .
  The Citizens Recycle Association
  Meiji Park Monthly Flea Market
  Salvation Army Bazaar
  Other Events

INTRODUCTION

In Tokyo, "things Japanese" are not always easy to find—you have to search them out. You will find lots of interesting offerings on the Tokyo antiques and crafts scene. Antique halls are filled with a mixture of Oriental and Western antiques, and the arcades and specialty shops offer traditional Japanese items not readily available in most stores.

And then there are the wonderful flea markets, a never-ending source of amazement and delight. You just never know what you are going to run across at one. Findings can range from the very old to the very new, and from elegant to kitsch. For those who like the traditional, there is everything from Buddhas to antique woodblocks for printmaking. And among the newer stuff—well, just about anything goes. My all-time favorite sighting: a wild pair of purple cowboy boots!

On many weekends, flea markets can be found at shrines and temples, on the steps and plazas of buildings, in parks and in parking lots—in short, any place that has the space and willingness to accommodate them. Some operate on a set schedule, while others are irregular. The Tourist Information Center publishes a leaflet entitled Antique and Flea Markets in Tokyo, *and some of the English-language publications carry a current listing of dates, times, and venues. Keep in mind, too, that they may be canceled in the event of rain.*

But enough talk about these things. Go and check them out for yourself. You'll have a great time doing it. And it goes without saying that you should get there early to see the good stuff.

ANTIQUES AND FOLKCRAFTS

HALLS

ANTIQUE GALLERY MEGURO (over 30 shops)

アンティーク ギャラリー目黒

Stork Mansion-Meguro, 2F

2–24–18–201 Kami Osaki, Shinagawa-ku, Tokyo 141–0021

☎ 3493–1971

東京都品川区上大崎2-24-18-201　ストークマンション目黒2階
〒141-0021

There is good stuff here. Chinese clay horses from the Han dynasty (206 BC–AD 220), very old Japanese dolls, meticulously beaded and embroidered Oriental and Western bags, and carved Indian pieces selling for over a million yen were some of the items on display. Strolling through this gallery complex of thirty-plus stores from around the country feels more like a walk through the corridors of a museum.

Hours: 11 AM–7 PM daily.

Access: 1 min from JR Meguro Stn, West Exit (Yamanote Line). Turn right out of the station. Go to the corner and cross the intersection in both directions to reach the diagonal corner, then walk left down the hill. It is the 3rd building on the right side, set back from the road.

ANTIQUE MARKET (about 35 shops)

アンティーク マーケット

Hanae Mori Building, B1

3–6–1 Kita Aoyama, Minato-ku, Tokyo 107–0061

☎ 3406–1021 (Hanae Mori Building—each shop has its own number)

東京都港区北青山3-6-1　ハナエモリビル地下1階　〒107-0061

These thirty-five shops sell old Western dolls, lamps, Oriental swords, chests, and other items. The offerings are about half Western and half Japanese. Yorozuya Antique Accessories (☎ 3499–4744) has jewelry that was made in occupied Japan between 1945 and 1950. This shop and Croa Antiques next to it are among the most interesting ones, since both have many little things to look at. However, there are proportionately too many expensive jewelry stores here and the atmosphere is not as inviting as in the other halls. But the location is central—and one shop even sells African goods.

Hours: Generally 11 AM–8 PM daily. Store hours vary slightly.
Access: Omotesando Stn, Exit A1 (Ginza, Hanzomon, and Chiyoda lines). Look for the neon sign just to the left of the exit.

TOKYO FOLKCRAFT AND ANTIQUE HALL (35 shops)

東京古民具こっとう館 (Tokyo Komingu Kotto-kan)

Satomi Building, 1F

3–9–5 Minami Ikebukuro, Toshima ku, Tokyo 171–0022

☎ 3982–3433

東京都豊島区南池袋3-9-5　サトミビル1階　〒171-0022

This place has a great atmosphere. An aura of mystery prevails, and you never know what you are going to come across around the next corner—perhaps an ancient Egyptian treasure or a Maltese falcon. Its thirty-five crowded little stalls carry artwork, jewelry, carvings, ceramics, pottery, dolls, clocks, chests, statuary, netsuke, and many more items of interest.

Hours: 11 AM–6:30 PM. Clsd on Thurs.
Access: A 5-min walk from Ikebukuro Stn, East Exit (Yamanote and other lines). Cross the street and walk right along Meiji-dori. Follow it around until you see the hall on the left side. The sign is in English.

TOKYO OCHANOMIZU ANTIQUE HALL (9 shops)

東京お茶の水アンティークホール

Kenkyu-sha Building, B1

2–9 Kanda Surugadai, Chiyoda-ku, Tokyo 101–0062

☎ 3295–7119

東京都千代田区神田駿河台2-9　研究社ビル地下1階　〒101-0062

Smaller version of the Tokyo Folkcraft and Antique Hall in Ikebukuro. Antiques and miscellany from China, Japan, and other

ANTIQUES,
FOLKCRAFTS, AND
FLEA MARKETS

Asian countries, as well as Western antiques—all mixed together. Nine shops make up this complex. Great stuff.

Hours: 11 AM–7 PM. Clsd Wed.

Access: A 5-min walk from JR Ochanomizu Stn, West Exit (Chuo and Sobu lines). Cross the intersection in front of the exit and walk down the small street alongside the police box that faces the station. It is the seven-story white building on the far left side of the second corner. The name is written in English on the awning leading down to the B1 shops.

ARCADES

INTERNATIONAL ARCADE (Duty Free Shopping Mall)
インターナショナル アーケード

Okay, so it's not exactly antiques, but a number of stores feature fans, dolls, mirrors, knickknacks, "Ichi-ban" (Number One) T-shirts, kimono for both children and adults, and all those "Japanese" items you never dreamed would be so hard to locate. All can be found here. It is a fun place to browse, and it could be a real lifesaver if you ever need to find these things quickly for a party, a gift, or whatever.

Hayashi Kimono (☎ 3591–9826) has a display of old kimono (between ten and fifty years old) and an informative (and free) English handout that explains the history of kimono, rules for wearing them, the appropriate colors for different age ranges, and the symbolism of the designs.

Hours: Basically 10 AM till about 6 PM or 7 PM daily. Store hours vary slightly.

Access: Hibiya Stn, Exit A4 (Hibiya, Chiyoda, or Mita lines). Go straight out and turn right into the small street alongside the train tracks. When you reach the next main street, you'll see the arcade to the left, underneath the tracks on both sides of the street. Also accessible via JR Yurakucho Stn (Yamanote and various lines) or Ginza Stn (various subway lines.)

NAKAMISE-DORI
仲見世通り

Nakamise-dori is a lively, 300-m- (360-yd-) long arcade that leads up to the Asakusa Kannon temple. It contains many small shops and stalls selling traditional Japanese items like oiled-paper umbrellas, Edo-style (1600–1868) straw sandals, kimono, dolls and toys, masks and fans, and traditional Japanese sweets. They even carry elaborate geisha and samurai wigs. You can watch rice crackers (and cakes stuffed with sweet bean paste) being made and sold hot off the grill. It is a fun, energetic atmosphere, and there is lots to see around the area. (See ch 3—Shitamachi/Asakusa.)

Hours: Shops generally open between 9 AM and 10 AM, and close between 7 PM and 9 PM. Each store has its own hours.

Access: 1 min from Asakusa Stn, Exit 1 (Ginza Line). Walk straight ahead and turn right into the large red Kaminarimon Gate—you will be on Nakamise-dori. Also accessible by Asakusa Line.

KOTTO-DORI (Antique Road)
骨董通り

Bigger than an arcade, Kotto-dori is a whole street of antique shops. On this stretch of road running between Aoyama-dori (across from Kinokuniya Supermarket) and Roppongi-dori, you can find about forty up-scale shops selling quality Oriental antiques. It would probably take less than 10 minutes to walk the entire length of the street, but with all the stops you will no doubt want to make along the way, be sure to give yourself plenty of time. The right side of the street (as you walk away from Kinokuniya) is lined with many shops at ground level, and some entire buildings specializing in antiques (such as the Jintsu Building) can be found near the end of the road.

There are art galleries and fashion boutiques here, too (see ch 14—Aoyama/Harajuku Art Galleries). So you might just want to make a day of it, stopping for lunch at one of the outdoor cafes found along Omotesando or nestled among the tiny streets of this very trendy section of town.

ANTIQUES, FOLKCRAFTS, AND FLEA MARKETS

Hours: Shops are generally open about 10 AM–6 PM and clsd on Sun,
but hours vary with each store.
Access: The beginning of the street is 1 min from Omotesando Stn, Exit
B1 (Ginza, Hanzomon, and Chiyoda lines). Walk straight to the
corner. There are more shops on the right side of the street, so it
is best to cross over before turning left down the street.

SHOPS

Here are just a few of the shops in Tokyo that sell antiques, crafts,
and traditional Japanese items.

ART PLAZA MAGATANI

アートプラザ マガタニ

> 5–10–13 Toranomon, Minato-ku, Tokyo 105–0001
>
> ☎ 3433–6321
>
> 東京都港区虎ノ門5-10-13　〒105-0001

The exterior of this shop is so intriguing—intricate wooden
carvings of flowers and mythological creatures—that you can't
help but wonder if the inside could ever measure up. But it does.
There are some great finds here. Japanese armor (both miniature and life-size), old dolls of samurai and other historical
characters, carved wooden fish meant to hang over traditional
sunken hearths, and woodblock prints are but a few. Some special items I spotted down in the basement level on a recent visit
were an old spinning wheel and a *koto* (a traditional Japanese
stringed instrument, sometimes called a "Japanese harp").
Wonderful browsing.

Hours: 10 AM–6 PM. Clsd Sun and hols.
Access: Kamiyacho Stn, Exit 2 (Hibiya Line). Turn right from the station exit and the shop will be about 2 min down the street on
your right.

BENIYA CRAFT SHOP

べにや民芸店 （Beniya Mingei-ten）

> 2–16–8 Shibuya, Shibuya-ku, Tokyo150–0002
>
> ☎ 3400–8084
>
> 東京都渋谷区渋谷2-16-8　〒150-0002

Many bamboo, straw, and other woven crafts can be found here including peasant hats, slippers, mats, baskets, and kitchen utensils. Traditional wood-and-paper umbrellas, fans, musical instruments, dishware, and textiles are also on display. The sign is in Japanese, but you can recognize the store by the baskets and pottery spilling out onto the street from the first of its five floors.

Hours: 10 AM–7 PM. Clsd Thurs.

Access: 5-min walk from Shibuya Stn, Hachiko Exit (Yamanote and other lines). Turn right on the street that runs in front of the station and walk under the train tracks. Cross Meiji-dori, and continue straight up the slope toward Aoyama-dori. It is on the corner of the second street on the far right side. Look for the handicrafts out front.

BINGOYA

備後屋

10–6 Wakamatsucho, Shinjuku-ku, Tokyo 162–0056

☎ 3202–8778

東京都新宿区若松町10-6　〒162-0056

This shop is a real treat. Everything here is hand-made. Folkcrafts from all over the country fill six delightful levels with goods which are a pleasure to behold—traditional paintings of animals, pottery, straw work, hand-dyed fabrics, hand-blown glassware, hand-painted Japanese kites, and a whole level of authentic folk toys, for openers. (The kid inside you will definitely want to spend a lot of time on the toy level.) There are many handmade objects for the home, too. Candles, placemats, and pillows are a few of these. They even have an art-crafts gallery on their top floor.

Mr. Okada, the owner, opened the original shop in a tiny wooden house at the same location in 1960. Although the shop is larger today, he somehow has managed to maintain that original homey feel.

Hours: 10 AM–7 PM. Clsd Mon.

Access: Take Bus No. 76 from Shinjuku Stn, West Exit (Yamanote and other lines), headed toward Iidabashi. Board alongside the

ANTIQUES,
FOLKCRAFTS, AND
FLEA MARKETS

corner Subaru Showroom Building, just beyond the bus terminals. Get off at the Yochomachi stop (about a 15-min ride). Continue walking in the same direction for about 2 min and you will see it on the left side. The shop's name is on the building in English.

EDO-TOKYO MUSEUM SHOP

江戸東京博物館ショップ

Edo-Tokyo Museum, 1F
1–4–1 Yokoami, Sumida-ku, Tokyo 130–0015
☎ 3626–9974
東京都墨田区横網1-4-1　江戸東京博物館1階　〒130-0015

The Edo-Tokyo Museum Shop carries its own line of products representative of Edo times (1600–1868) that is not to be found in other stores. Traditional crafts, games, toys, kites, woven slippers, maps of old Edo, and other special items can be seen here. On the shop's little balcony there is a display of rare and precious items, such as dolls and musical instruments. There is also an A/V library (B1) where you can watch videos on Japanese culture for free (see ch 13).

NOTE: There is an entrance fee for the museum's exhibitions of Edo times.

Hours: 10 AM–6 PM Tues, Wed, Sat, Sun. 10 AM–8 PM Thurs and Fri. Clsd Mon (Tues when Mon is a hol) and New Year hols.

Access: 3 min from Ryogoku Stn, West Exit (JR Sobu Line). Turn right from the exit and follow the signs for the museum. It is alongside the train tracks.

FUJI TORII

富士鳥居

6–1–10 Jingumae, Shibuya-ku, Tokyo 150–0001
☎ 3400–2777
東京都渋谷区神宮前6-1-10　〒150-0001

Fuji Tori has been selling antiques and Japanese works of art since 1948. The shop has a nice selection of paper goods—traditional stationery and cards with a Japanese motif. Scrolls, lacquer ware, ceramics, sculpture, and traditional and contemporary woodblock prints are carried as well, with older pieces and screens tucked away in the back section of the store.

CHAPTER 9

240

Hours: 11 AM–6 PM. Clsd Thurs.

Access: About 7 min from Omotesando Stn, Exit A1 (Ginza, Hanzomon, and Chiyoda lines). Walk out from the exit and go straight down the hill. It is on the left side of Omotesando Ave, a few doors past the Oriental Bazaar and next to the second pedestrian overpass.

HARUMI ANTIQUES

はるみ古美術 (Harumi Kobijutsu)

Roppongi Building, 2F

4–11–4 Roppongi, Minato-ku, Tokyo 106–0032

☎ 3403–1043

東京都港区六本木4-11-4　〒106-0032

Every surface is put to good use here, displaying many small, interesting items to look at. Oriental masks, dolls, statues, chests, paintings, and pottery are some of the things you will find at this convenient little antique shop close to Roppongi Station.

Hours: 10 AM–6:30 PM Mon–Sat, 11 AM–5:30 PM Sun.

Access: 2 min from Roppongi Stn, Exit 4A. Walk straight out from the exit, cross the street and continue down Roppongi-dori to the next small street. Turn left and go to the second small street. The Roppongi Building will be on the far left corner—go up the steps to the 2F.

ISETATSU

いせ辰

2–18–9 Yanaka, Taito-ku, Tokyo 110–0001

☎ 3823–1453

東京都台東区谷中2-18-9　〒110-0001

Founded in 1864, this shop is located in Yanaka, one of the oldest and best preserved neighborhoods of Tokyo (or perhaps I should say "Edo"). Traditional handmade *chiyogami* paper products made from original Edo period (1600–1868) woodblocks and earlier can be found here. Dolls, fans, papier-mâché animals, boxes, chests of drawers, hand-printed sheets of paper in numerous patterns, and (my favorite) note pads tied together with rope—the way it was done before the days of staples and

NOTE: You will probably want to walk around afterward and check out the charming old neighborhood. If you would like to do some research on the Yanaka area before your visit, see the Shitamachi section of ch 3 for possible sources. Or simply explore the area on your own

spiral wiring—fill the store. The shop carries over 2,000 designs of paper. There are two stores a few doors apart.

Hours: 10 AM–6 PM daily.

Access: A 4-min walk from Sendagi Stn, Dango-zaka Exit (Chiyoda Line). Cross Shinobazu-dori (directly in front of the exit) and continue walking straight. The first store is about 2 min down on your right and the main store about 2 min further along, also on the right.

ORIENTAL BAZAAR

オリエンタル バザール

5–9–13 Jingumae, Shibuya-ku, Tokyo 150–0001

☎ 3400–3933

東京都渋谷区神宮前5-9-13　〒150-0001

This is the biggest art and antique store in Tokyo—four stories of Japanese items that range from antiques, reproductions, and interior furnishings to small souvenirs and knickknacks. There are also ample supplies of T-shirts, *yukata* (cotton kimono), beach towels with Japanese designs, and the like. B1 has a corner with smaller Japanese items, such as fans, coin purses, and silk wallets.

Hours: 9:30 AM–6:30 PM. Clsd Thurs.

Access: About 7 min from Omotesando Stn, Exit A1 (Ginza, Hanzomon, and Chiyoda lines). Walk straight out from the exit and continue down the hill. The store is on the left. You can't miss the bright red Oriental exterior.

SHOYEIDO

松栄堂

Kyoto Shinbun Building, 1F

8–2–8 Ginza, Chuo-ku, Tokyo 104–0061

☎ 3572–6484

東京都中央区銀座8-2-8　京都新聞ビル1階　〒104-0061

If you like incense, this store is a must-see. It was founded in 1705 by a man who hand-created incense for the Imperial Palace in Kyoto, Japan's former capital. These same methods were carried on by his family, and eleven generations later you can still enjoy this olfactory delight that was once used exclusively by the imperial family. The materials and methods that go into making the incense are on display in the shop and illustrated in a free English booklet, which also includes the *Ten Virtues of Koh* (incense) as proclaimed in the 16th century.

Aromatic wood, joss sticks, cones, sachets, and kneaded and powdered incense (for rubbing on the body) bearing such names as Kyoto Autumn Leaves are on display, as are a beautiful array of burners. One decorative burner is in the form of a fan in which little flower-shaped pieces of incense are set in it as part of the design. In one corner of the shop you can sometimes watch a woman hand-sew the little figures of animals and dolls into which she places tiny sachets of incense made from sweet-smelling woods and spices.

Hours: 10 AM–7 PM Mon–Fri. Clsd wknds and hols.

Access: 5 min from Ginza Stn, Exit C2 (Marunouchi, Ginza, and Hibiya lines). Walk to the corner and turn right on Sotobori-dori. The shop is in the 4th block on the right side, across from the Nikko Hotel. Also accessible from Shinbashi Stn. (Yamanote and other lines).

TAKUMI

たくみ

8–4–2 Ginza, Chuo-ku, Tokyo 104–0061

☎ 3571–2017

東京都中央区銀座8-4-2　〒104-0061

The word *takumi* means skill or dexterity, and that is what went into the making of these high-quality, handcrafted goods from various parts of Japan. Pottery, textiles, lacquer ware, furniture, handmade paper, and glass, metal, and bamboo work are some of the offerings in this elegant little Ginza shop. There are often nice folk toys hanging from the ceiling, too.

Hours: 11 AM–7 PM (5:30 PM on hols). Clsd Sun.

Access: 5 min from Ginza Stn, Exit C2 (Marunouchi, Ginza, and Hibiya lines). Walk to the corner and turn right on Sotobori-dori. The shop is near the beginning of the 4th block on the left side, in

ANTIQUES,
FOLKCRAFTS, AND
FLEA MARKETS

the same block as the Nikko Hotel. Also accessible from Shin-bashi Stn (Yamanote and other lines).

DEPARTMENT STORES

Amongst all the Western wear, cosmetics, restaurants, modern appliances, furniture, art, accessories, and various goods found in Japanese department stores these days, you can generally find a tiny little corner that has been designated as the "Japanese Section." A combination of elegant handmade items and inexpensive, smaller items of souvenir quality are usually sold here.

CRAFT SPECIALISTS

CRAFT CENTERS

JAPAN TRADITIONAL CRAFT CENTER
全国伝統的工芸品センター
（Zenkoku Dentoteki Kogeihin Senta）
> Plaza 246 Building, 2F
> 3–1–1 Minami Aoyama, Minato-ku, Tokyo 107–0062
> ☎ 3403–2460
> 東京都港区南青山3-1-1　プラザ246ビル2階　〒107-0062

If you are a fan of Japanese handicrafts, you should visit this place. It was established to promote the traditional crafts of Japan, and to help preserve the techniques and skills needed to create them.

Lovely handmade crafts from around the country with a tradition of at least 100 years are exhibited here. Some of the many items recently on display were pottery, dolls, lacquer ware, carved wood, stone lanterns, fans, ceramics, Japanese knives, kimono, paper goods, incense burners—and even a gold-and-lacquer portable shrine worth ¥5 million! One section of the room has special exhibitions that change every two weeks—and sometimes include demonstrations by the craftsmen.

A library with 1,700 books (over 80 in English) and a video

corner with over 270 videos (24 in English) on Japanese crafts is open to the public. Free craft classes, a consultation clinic, and a kimono-wearing class are offered (in Japanese) at no charge.

Each March, in cooperation with the Ministry of Trade and Industry and Japan's forty-seven prefectures, the center organizes a large show next to Tokyo Dome. Here you can see traditional crafts from all over Japan as well as demonstrations on how they are made—and you may even have the chance to make something yourself.

Hours: 10 AM–6 PM (4 PM on final day of exhibition). Clsd Thurs, summer *Obon* hol, and New Year hols.

Access: A 3-min walk from Gaienmae Stn (Ginza Line). Go left from the ticket turnstile at the station's only exit. Go up the stairway on the right side at the end of the passage and walk straight out. The center is at the first traffic signal (upstairs from Haagen-Dazs Ice Cream in the Plaza 246 building).

PREFECTURAL SHOWROOMS

Another great place to see the authentic handicrafts of Japan is at the showrooms of the country's forty-seven prefectures. Most are conveniently located together in two buildings at Tokyo Station, where you can wander from showroom to showroom, seeing and comparing the handiwork from the various areas of the country. (See ch 15 for details.)

VISIT LOCAL CRAFTSMEN IN THEIR HOMES AND WORKSHOPS

It is now possible to visit the homes and workshops of master craftsmen who are doing their part to keep the traditional arts and crafts alive here in the Tokyo area. Thanks to a recently initiated program by Sumida Ward, you are able to see first-hand how such items as Noh masks, Japanese dolls, and *tabi* (traditional Japanese socks) are still being made in the same manner as they have been for many generations—and see samples of the finished products in the accompanying tiny museums. (See Little Museums of Sumida-ku in ch 3 for details.)

ANTIQUES,
FOLKCRAFTS, AND
FLEA MARKETS

TRY YOUR OWN HAND AT MAKING SOME TRADITIONAL CRAFTS

SAKURA HORIKIRI

さくら・ほりきり

1–26–2 Yanagibashi, Taito-ku, Tokyo 111–0052

☎ 3864–1773

東京都台東区柳橋1-26-2　〒111-0052

NOTE: If you should decide to tackle a bigger project, they stock a large variety of items that are not only lovely to look at, but also very practical. There is a charge for these kits of course, but instruction is always free and available every day the store is open. Reservations are not needed. Chests, *washi*-paper pictures and boxes, dishes and coasters, picture frames, sewing kits, and jewelry and jewelry boxes are just a few of the many items you can make here.

There is a place in Tokyo where you can learn how to make crafts for free. Your creative urge can be satisfied at this do-it-yourself craft store called Sakura Horikiri. The shop does not carry any finished products—only the makings—and their motto is "Make it and take it." They will supply you (at no charge) with one of their beginner kits that takes about 15 minutes to assemble. The instructions and all the materials needed to put it together are also included.

Hours: 9:30 AM–5:30 PM Mon–Sat. Clsd Sun and hols.

Access: 3 min from Asakusabashi Stn, East Exit (JR Sobu or Toei Asakusa Line). Cross the street (Edo-dori) in front of the station and walk straight alongside the railway tracks for two blocks. Turn left, and it will be on the following far right corner.

MOVEABLE TREASURES

ANTIQUE FLEA MARKETS

Beautiful pieces from around Japan and other parts of Asia and the world can be seen at Tokyo's popular antique flea markets. Ornate Tibetan prayer wheels, antique wedding kimonos, Buddhist statuary, and traditional Japanese dolls are only some of the infinite variety of items on display.

Many exhibitors have antique shops and bring a sampling of their wares to these weekend flea markets. If you like what you see, you can visit their shops during the week for more. But other vendors, including one who specializes in exotic statuary from the Himalayas, display their goods only at these markets.

Most of them open extremely early and close early, too. So go early if you want to see the best items. A lot of careful packing is needed at the end of the day, and everything is usually put away by mid-afternoon, even though the official closing time may be dusk.

TOGO SHRINE

東郷神社（Togo Jinja）

1–5–3 Jingumae, Shibuya-ku, Tokyo 150–0001

☎ 3403–3591

東京都渋谷区神宮前1-5-3　〒150-0001

This is the largest of the shrine antique flea markets. Chests and other interior furnishings, kimono, statuary, toys, and much more can be found along the path that meanders through the grounds of the shrine. It passes over bridges and alongside a lovely Japanese garden where you can sit and watch the carp swimming in a pond while you rest and gather energy to continue your antique explorations.

Hours: Dawn till dusk, the 1st, 4th, and 5th Sun of each month.

Access:A 5-min walk from Meiji Jingumae Stn, Exit 5 (Chiyoda Line). Turn around after surfacing and walk back to the corner. Make a left and walk straight up Meiji-dori. It will be on your left near Takeshita-dori. Also accessible from JR Harajuku Stn (Yamanote Line).

NOGI SHRINE

乃木神社（Nogi Jinja）

8–11–27 Akasaka, Minato-ku, Tokyo 107–0052

☎ 0426–91–4687 (Mr. Takiguchi), 3478–3001 (Nogi Shrine)

東京都港区赤坂8-11-27　〒107-0052

Apart from the monthly flea market, Nogi shrine is a worthwhile historical site (see ch 8).

Hours: Dawn till dusk, the 2nd Sun of each month.

Access:Next to Nogizaka Stn, Exit 1 (Chiyoda Line).

ANTIQUES,
FOLKCRAFTS, AND
FLEA MARKETS

HANAZONO SHRINE

花園神社 （Hanazono Jinja）

> 5–17–3 Shinjuku, Shinjuku-ku, Tokyo 160–0022
> ☎ 3200–3093
> 東京都新宿区新宿5-17-3　〒160-0022

For a detailed description of the shrine, see ch. 8.

Hours: Dawn to dusk, every Sun.

Access: Near the intersection of Meiji-dori and Yasukuni-dori. A 3-min walk from Shinjuku-sanchome Stn (Marunouchi or Toei Shinjuku lines). Take Exit B3 up to street level. Turn left and walk along Meiji-dori to the next intersection. Cross Yasukuni-dori and the entrance to the shrine will be a short distance up on your left. Or 8 min from JR Shinjuku Stn, East Exit (Yamanote and other lines).

ROPPONGI ANTIQUE AND FLEA MARKET

六本木アンティーク フリーマーケット

> On the steps of the Roi Building.
> 5–5–1 Roppongi, Minato-ku, Tokyo 106–0032
> ☎ 3583–2081
> 東京都港区六本木5-5-1　ロアビル　〒106-0032

For two days each month, antiques and lots of interesting goods are sprawled out along the steps of the well-known Roi Building, located in the heart of Roppongi—one of Tokyo's main entertainment areas.

Hours: Dawn till dusk the 4th Thurs and Fri of each month.

Access: 3 min from Roppongi Stn, Exit 3 (Hibiya Line). Turn right from the station, and right again along the main street. The Roi Building is on the right side with wide steps leading up from the street.

HEIWAJIMA ANTIQUES FAIR

平和島アンティーク フェアー

> Tokyo Ryutsu Center, 2F
> 6–1–1 Heiwajima, Ota-ku, Tokyo 143–0006
> ☎ 3980–8228 (Antique Fair Co) or 3767–2141 (Ryutsu Center)
> 東京都太田区平和島6-1-1　東京流通センター2階　〒143-0006

This major event hosts over 200 antique dealers from around the country. Old artwork such as paintings, calligraphy, and ceramics as well as statuary, furniture, and other items are all on display. Since it is an indoor location, things are also hung from the ceiling, too, which makes for a great atmosphere.

Hours: 10 AM–6 PM. Held quarterly for 3 days each March, June, Sept, and Dec. (Additional fairs are sometimes scheduled—be sure to check local monthly listings.)

Access:Across the street from Ryutsu Center Stn on the Tokyo Monorail Line (a 15-min ride from JR Hamamatsucho Stn).

REGULAR FLEA MARKETS AND MORE ...

A number of just plain old down-home flea markets are held regularly in Tokyo as well. These contain—shall we say—old, but not quite antique goods. While these events may not offer expensive treasures, they still make for a fun outing. Here are a couple of suggestions to get you started. Check the English-language publications for up-to-date information on others. You can also call the following organizations (in Japanese) for a schedule of their upcoming flea markets:

THE CITIZENS RECYCLE ASSOCIATION
リサイクル運動市民の会 （Recycle Undo Shimin no Kai）
☎ 3226–6800, 0180–99–3355 (Tape)

This organization sponsors a number of flea markets. Call for information (in Japanese).

MEIJI PARK MONTHLY FLEA MARKET
明治公園フリーマーケット
☎ 5228–3320, 5228–3307 (Tape)

Sponsored by the Japan Ecology Center, this is probably the biggest monthly flea market in Tokyo. About 650 vendors draw a crowd of approximately 50,000 people for the event. It is held once a month in an open area in Meiji Park, where people in vans loaded with goods display their wares from blankets spread out at the backs of their vehicles. There are food stalls too, and

ANTIQUES,
FOLKCRAFTS, AND
FLEA MARKETS

an invigorating sense of excitement in the air. During the summer, large colorful umbrellas provide shade for the vendors and their offerings, adding to the festive feeling of the event.

Although you probably won't find many antiques, just about anything else you could ever imagine can be seen here. Make a day of it. Check listings or call for the date of the next one, or other flea markets that they sponsor.

Hours: 10 AM–4 PM (until 3 PM in winter). The date varies each month, but it is always on a weekend.

Access: A 5-min walk from JR Sendagaya Stn (Sobu Line). Walk straight out from the station's only exit until you reach the next traffic signal (Mos Burger is on the corner), and turn left. When the road ends at Gaien Nishi-dori, cross the street, turn right, and walk to the next traffic signal. The flea market will be directly in front of you. Also accessible from Gaienmae Stn (Ginza Line).

NOTE: For more information on the Japan Ecology Center, see ch 13.

SALVATION ARMY BAZAAR
救世軍男子社会奉仕センター
(Kyuseiugun Danshi Shakai Hoshi Center)
2–21–2 Wada, Suginami-ku, Tokyo 166–0012
☎ 3384–3769
東京都新宿区和田2-21-2　〒166-0012

A warehouse full of stuff—kind of like a second-hand department store with everything organized into neat little departments. Housewares, clothes, furniture, musical instruments, toys, books, appliances, and all kinds of odds and ends. I saw a large collection of 78 rpm classical records, a big basket full of bicycle pumps, some curious wall clocks, and an entire shelf filled with pencil sharpeners.

Hours: 9 AM–1 PM every Sat.

Access: A 12-min walk from Nakano Fujimicho Stn (Marunouchi Line). The station attendant usually has a map with directions he will show you. Turn left from the exit and walk four traffic lights to Wada 2-chome. Then walk right until you reach the Salvation Army Booth Hospital at the end of the road. Turn left and the Salvation Army Bazaar will be on the right side of the street just beyond the hospital.

OTHER EVENTS

In addition to flea markets, a number of bazaars, garage sales, and fairs are held by women's organizations, churches, and international schools. These are lively events and provide a chance to mingle with people, too. The *Tokyo Weekender, City Life News*, and other English-language publications carry information on upcoming events.

10

A MYRIAD OF MUSEUMS

UNIVERSITY MUSEUMS

- International Christian University (ICU)
  Hachiro Yuasa Memorial Museum (Archaeological and Folk Art Collection)
- Kokugakuin University
  Archaeological Museum
  Shinto Museum
- Meiji University
  Archaeological Museum
  Commodity Museum
  Criminal Museum
- Musashino Academia Musicae
  Museum of Musical Instruments
- Tokyo National University of Fine Arts and Music
  Art Museum
- Tokyo University
  University Museum
- Waseda University
  Tsubouchi Memorial Theater Museum

PRIVATE AND GOVERNMENT MUSEUMS

- *Ace World Bags and Luggage Museum*
- *Azabu Museum of Arts and Crafts*
- *Beer Museum Yebisu*
- *Bicycle Culture Center*
- *Cigarette Lighter Museum*
- *Currency Museum*
- *Eyeglass Museum*
- *Fire Museum*
- *Fireworks Museum*
- *Horse Racing Museum*
- *Isetan Museum of Art*
- *Japan Art Academy*
- *Kobayashi Doll Museum*
- *Konica Camera Museum*
- *Little Museums of Sumida-ku*
- *Meguro Parasitological Museum*
- *Museum of Contemporary Sculpture*
- *Museum of Dry Cleaning and Laundering*

- *Museum of the Imperial Collection*
- *NHK Broadcast Museum*
- *Noh Mask Museum*
- *Parliamentary Museum*
- *Printing Bureau Museum*
- *Stationery Museum*
- *Stock Market Museum*
- *Striped House Museum*
- *Sumo Museum*
- *Tabi Museum*
- *Takao Natural Science Museum*
- *Takinami Glass Museum*
- *Tokyo Central Museum*
- *Tokyo Metropolitan Art Museum*
- *Tokyo Metropolitan Children's Hall*
- *Tsukiji Fish Information Center and Museum*
- *Ward Municipal Museums*
- *Waterworks Museum*

INTRODUCTION

*T*okyo has museums in abundance, many of which are totally free. Their offerings are eclectic, and range from the sublime to the ridiculous. You may encounter a calligraphy brush made from the tails of 50 horses, a bicycle built for three, the largest gold coin in the world, and an 8.8-m (29-ft) tapeworm extracted from a human body. (Now you have to agree—that's ridiculous!) On the sublime side, you can watch elegant Noh masks and beautiful Japanese dolls being hand-crafted inside the small workshops of some of Tokyo's oldest and most traditional neighborhoods.

Japanese universities are another fertile (and often untapped) source of interesting museums. A great many archaeological excavations are being carried on by the universities, and their campus museums are the places to go to view the unearthed treasures. Sometimes unexpected offerings can be found on college campuses too—like Meiji University's Criminal Museum and Musashino Academia Musicae's incredible Museum of Musical Instruments.

There seems to be no limit to what you might find in the wonderful free museums of Tokyo. But whatever the subject matter, it is sure to be carried out in the typical Japanese manner. That is, with a great deal of pride and attention to detail. So take in some of Tokyo's museums soon. They are ready and waiting for your visit.

A Few Important Rules
Keep in mind that entrance to museums and exhibitions in Japan often concludes one half hour before the posted closing time—and that on the final day of temporary shows, closing time is generally several hours earlier still. Often they remain open on holidays, and close the following day instead. Other closing days might include the spring Golden Week holidays, mid-August summer holidays, and New Year holidays. It is best to phone ahead if you have any questions.

UNIVERSITY MUSEUMS

■ International Christian University (ICU)

HACHIRO YUASA MEMORIAL MUSEUM
(Archaeological and Folk Art Collection)

ICU 湯浅記念館 （ICU Yuasa Kinenkan）

    3–10–2 Osawa, Mitaka-shi, Tokyo 181–8585

    ☎ 0422–33–3340

    東京都三鷹市大沢3-10-2　〒181-8585

Located on a 630,000-sq-m (6.8-million-sq-ft) college campus that looks and feels more like a forest than a campus, this museum is far removed from the hustle and bustle of the city center. Amidst this rustic setting you can see a display of folk arts and a collection of important prehistoric artifacts—most of which were excavated right here on the campus grounds.

The land on which the school stands was once terraced earth and natural springs, and is known to have been inhabited by people nearly 30,000 years ago. Needless to say, it has been a fertile site for archaeological excavations, which the school has been carrying out since 1957. Among the unearthed objects in the museum is a stone floor that is thought to have been a spiritual ceremonial center. A real stratigraphic cross-section of the Kanto loam hangs on one wall, and numerous ritual objects, tools, pots, and costume ornaments encompass two levels of the building.

The museum was established in 1982 in honor of Dr. Hachiro Yuasa, the university's first president—a founder of the school and curator of the museum's vast folk art collection. Chests, hearth hangers, fishermen's festive coats, and utensils used in everyday life are some of the items you can see in the folk art section of the museum. In addition, special exhibitions on some aspect of Japanese culture are offered three times a year, accompanied by a lecture. English translations of this lecture are available with an advance reservation. All written descriptions at the museum and in their brochure are in English and Japanese.

NOTE: If you want to remain in the area afterward, the campus skirts the free Nogawa Nature Park (☎ 0422–31–6457) to the south, and the Middle Eastern Culture Center (¥300) a few minutes to the north (☎ 0422– 32– 7111). The latter contains a fine collection of art from ancient Egypt, Syria, Mesopotamia, and other countries.

Hours: 10 AM–5 PM Tues–Fri, 10 AM–4:30 PM Sat. Clsd Sun, Mon, between
special exhibitions, and national, New Year, and summer hols.
During July and Aug the museum is clsd on Sat as well.

Access: From JR Mitaka Stn, South Exit (Chuo Line), board the Odakyu
Bus No. 51 bound for ICU (from bus stand No. 3). The bus will
take you right onto the campus. Continue walking along the
same road to the next circle and turn right. The Museum is a
red brick building a few minutes down this road on the left side.

■ Kokugakuin University

ARCHAEOLOGICAL MUSEUM

国学院大学考古学資料館

(Kokugakuin Daigaku Kokogaku Shiryokan)

Tokiwamatsu No. 2 Building, 1F

4–10–28 Higashi, Shibuya-ku, Tokyo 150–8440

☎ 5466–0249/50

東京都渋谷区東4-410-28　常盤松2号館1階　〒150-8440

I guarantee that when you walk into this room you will be
stunned. For it is absolutely chock-full of artifacts, and quite a
sight to see. Wander among the findings from the ancient Jomon
(ca 10,000 BC–ca 300 BC), Yayoi (ca 300 BC–ca AD 300) and
Kofun (ca AD 300–ca AD 710) periods and let your imagination
soar. Approximately 4,000 items, many excavated by teachers,
archaeologists, and students of the university since 1928, are on
display, including a rare stone pillow that dates back 1,500 years.

If you are a fan of *haniwa* (ancient clay figures), you will
love the interesting variety seen here—deer, pigs, people, horses,
and a number of interesting and intricately carved houses. There
are old stone ovens, vases, jewelry, dishes, skulls, and skeletons,
too. One complete skeleton from the Jomon period is displayed in
a glass case, partially covered by sand.

NOTE: If you visit on a Mon, Wed,
or Fri, you can see the Shinto
museum next door (see below)

Items from more recent times are presented too, and some
Chinese and Korean objects are shown for comparative purposes.
Many many more things too numerous to mention are on
display here. Check them out for yourself.

Hours: 9 AM–5 PM Mon–Fri. Clsd wknds, hols, and university hols
(sometimes open Sat).

Access: From JR Shibuya Stn, East Exit, take bus No. 3 (from alongside the curb near Hobson's Ice Cream) bound for Nisseki Iryo Center. It is just a short ride to the Kokugakuin-mae stop. Walk to the next corner and turn left. The entrance is half a block down on the left side, just to the left of the security guard's box.

SHINTO MUSEUM

国学院大学神道資料館
（Kokugakuin Daigaku Shinto Shiryokan）
Tokiwamatsu No. 3 Building, 1F
4–10–28 Higashi, Shibuya-ku, Tokyo 150–8440
☎ 5466–0210
東京都渋谷区東4-10-28　常盤松3号館ビ1階　〒150-8440

Shinto, the original folk religion of Japan, is closely connected with nature, and contains many *kami,* or gods, which are thought to live everywhere. It is still very much a part of the Japanese culture, and coexists harmoniously with Buddhism in modern Japan—for today most Japanese follow both Shinto and Buddhist religious practices.

This museum contains items connected with Shinto and its rites, rituals, and history. Figures of folk deities, garments worn by Shinto priests, and scrolls and screens of Shinto festivals are among the items on display. You can also see models and drawings of the various types of shrines, ceremonial musical instruments, and displays of food offerings.

The descriptions are all in Japanese, as is the museum's pamphlet, but many of the objects can be easily identified and should be educational for those interested in Japanese religions. It is located in the building just behind the university's fabulous archaeological museum, so see both while you are there—keeping in mind that this one closes earlier on Mondays and Fridays.

Hours: 10:30 AM–3 PM Mon and Fri, 10:30 AM–6 PM Wed. Clsd other days, national and university hols.

Access: See access instructions for the architectural museum above. Then walk along the right side of the security guard's box. It will be in the next building back to the left.

A MYRIAD OF MUSEUMS

■ Meiji University

ARCHAEOLOGICAL MUSEUM

明治大学考古学博物館

（Meiji Daigaku Kokogaku Hakubutsukan）

Daigaku Kaikan, 4F

1–1 Kanda Surugadai, Chiyoda-ku, Tokyo 101–8301

☎ 3296–4432

東京都千代田区神田駿河台1-1　大学会館4階　〒101-8301

At the entrance to this museum is a little setting that contains items commonly used on archaeological digs—excavation tools, photographic equipment, and the like.

Inside, a display of *haniwa* (ancient clay figures) of many shapes and sizes lines one wall—and includes a house with a gabled roof. An exquisite *haniwa* horsehead can be seen in a nearby display case, too. Other very old pieces dating from the pre-Jomon (pre-10,000 BC) through the Kofun (ca AD 300–AD 710) periods have been brought back from the university's numerous excavations around the country and painstakingly restored by the school's Archaeological Institute, which has been very active since its founding in 1950. Old armor, figures, pots, and flints—including pieces from Japan's earliest known period of tool-making—are among the university's collection. Chinese and Japanese objects are shown together for the sake of comparison in a small room near the entrance.

The descriptions are written in both English and Japanese, and the brochure includes some English. Don't miss the other two university museums located in the same building (see below).

Hours: *Regular hours for all three museums*:10 AM–4:30 PM. (Closes at 6:30 PM Tues and 12:30 PM Sat.) Clsd Sun, and national and school hols. *Summer hours*: Mon–Fri only, 10 AM–4 PM, **Archaeological Museum**; 10 AM–3 PM, **Commodity Museum**; 10 AM–3:30 PM, **Criminal Museum**.

Access: A 5-min walk from JR Ochanomizu Stn, West Exit (Chuo and Sobu lines). Turn left from the exit and walk down the main street away from the bridge. All three Meiji University museums are in the tan building on the right corner just before the second traffic light.

COMMODITY MUSEUM

明治大学商品陳列館 （Meiji Daigaku Shohin Chinretsukan）

　Daigaku Kaikan, 3F

　1–1 Kanda Surugadai, Chiyoda-ku, Tokyo 101–8301

　☎ 3296–4433

　東京都千代田区神田駿河台1-1　大学会館3階　〒101-8301

This museum contains a vast array of products gathered from local factories, large manufacturers, and distributors all around Japan. Along with the finished items this museum often displays the step-by-step processes and the raw materials used in their production. The various paraphernalia are laid out and actual samples from every stage are displayed, promoting a greater appreciation for the finished product. One of the functions of the museum is to research and document the development of traditional items that have been in use from early times to the present day, so one section has been set aside for objects that fit this category, such as tea-service utensils and square serving dishes. Two such examples I spotted during my visit were the manufacture of candles and Japanese traditional *washi* paper, which is still made with techniques initially devised 1,200 years ago.

Exhibitions change yearly, but among the offerings that you might find are metal and wooden goods, pottery, ceramics, lacquer ware, candles, calligraphy brushes, and textiles. There's also a collection of dolls and toys from around the country. The descriptive pamphlet carries information in English, German, French, Chinese, and Korean. And don't miss the other two university museums located in the same building. See the preceding entry (Meiji University Archaeological Museum) for the Commodity Museum's hours and access. Displays are rotated periodically.

CRIMINAL MUSEUM

明治大学刑事博物館 （Meiji Daigaku Keiji Hakubutsukan）

　Daigaku Kaikan, 3F

　1–1 Kanda Surugadai, Chiyoda-ku, Tokyo 101–8301

　☎ 3296–4431

　東京都千代田区神田駿河台1-1　大学会館3階　〒101-8301

This museum is not full of blood and gore, nor does it give insight into the criminal mind. This is a little more conservative version of the criminal world. Don't be put off by all the maps and documentation in the first section of the museum. There are many interesting items ahead, such as old wooden signboards that were posted outside towns during Edo (1600–1868) times, warning people about various prohibitions: fires, poison, killing, and sometimes even Christians! An old woodblock print documents the location of these signs at the famous Nihonbashi Bridge in what is now central Tokyo.

Those in search of the macabre will be rewarded in the very last aisle, where grim instruments of torture and punishment await them. Chopping blocks, hanging devices, a stake, iron balls and chains, and even an old guillotine and "iron maiden" are on display. Methods of capturing and punishing Japanese criminals are depicted in drawings, too.

There is no information in English, but it is pretty clear what the above items are. And you can combine the visit with seeing the two other university museums in the same building (see above). See Meiji University's Archaeological Museum for hours and access.

■ **Musashino Academia Musicae**

MUSEUM OF MUSICAL INSTRUMENTS

武蔵野音楽大学楽器博物館
（Musashino Ongaku Daigaku Gakki Hakubutsukan）
　　1–13–1 Hazawa, Nerima-ku, Tokyo 176–8521
　　☎ 3992–1410 (Direct), 3992–1121 ext. 243 (School)
　　東京都練馬区羽沢1-13-1　〒176-8521

The love of music seems to have permeated this entire area. Immediately upon stepping out of the train station, you are greeted by classical music playing in the streets—an uplifting experience which continues as you wander among the tiny lanes that make up the neighborhood.

Once at the museum, another treat awaits you in the form of a mind-boggling collection of musical instruments that seems to cover the musical history of the world. I began to wonder if there was a musical instrument created that wasn't represented in this museum. Expect the unexpected: in the Japan room, musical conch shells, native Ainu instruments, and a *kei-seki* (mounted series of rocks of various shapes for striking) are shown along with a unique version of a *taiko* drum—a large square one!

A delicately carved and inlaid peacock-shaped stringed instrument decorated with real peacock feathers is one of the offerings from India. An armadillo-shell stringed instrument, a musical bracelet and necklace made of boar's teeth, and a brightly painted Aboriginal *didjerido* from Australia are part of the Oceania section. In the folk room, you will find an *organillo* from Madrid (minus the monkey) and beautiful music boxes of unusual shapes and sizes, among other things. A colorful display of gongs, bells, and whistles from Asia and wooden rattles and drums from Africa are in other rooms. Long horns from the Swiss Alps and a large brass instrument with the open, gaping mouth of a snake, appropriately named "Serpent," round out the wind section.

The keyboard room takes up the entire 1F. I went in expecting to take a quick look around and ended up spending nearly an hour. The star attraction is an incredible "Napoleon Hat Piano" that has to be seen to be believed. Some of the other pianos on display are harp-shaped and "giraffe-necked" pianos, a French piano with gold and cloisonne and an Oriental motif, and models from the 1800s with built-in candlesticks over the keys that enabled people to play at night before the days of electricity.

The school was founded in 1920 to promote Western music culture in Japan. Statues of the great composers—mostly gifts from foreign governments—dot the campus. As you wander through the grounds, the sound of students playing various instruments serves as a backdrop. It is a very special place.

Hours: Open 10 AM–3 PM Wed, other times by appointment. Clsd university hols and during school examinations.

Access: A 5-min walk from Ekoda Stn, North Exit (Seibu Ikebukuro Line). Exit via the steps on the left and turn right at the first corner (at the shrine). In a few minutes you will see a big white building with unusual geometric-shaped windows on a far left corner. Turn left to reach the entrance to the campus. The people at the front information window will direct you to the museum.

■ Tokyo National University of Fine Arts and Music

ART MUSEUM

東京芸術大学芸術資料館
（Tokyo Geijutsu Daigaku Geijutsu Shiryokan）
12–8 Ueno Koen, Taito-ku, Tokyo 110–0007
☎ 5685–7744 (Direct), 5685–7700 (School Office)
東京都台東区上野公園12-8　〒110-0007

This museum sits in a far corner of Ueno Park, on the campus of the highly respected Tokyo National University of Fine Arts and Music. The exhibitions here are mainly presented for the benefit of the students, but are also open to the general public at no charge.

The school's archives contain 44,000 items, including Important Cultural Assets and National Treasures. Exhibitions change monthly and run concurrently with the school's curriculum. Works of former students (some of whom have gone on to become very well known) can sometimes be seen here, and each April a teacher's memorial exhibition is held. At one show I saw some very old sketchbooks in which former students had casually scrawled what turned out to be incredibly beautiful works of art. It was a rare treat, indeed.

Free concerts (see ch 11) are also offered by the school's music department, which has nurtured some of the most creative musical talents of Japan, including the popular Ryuichi Sakamoto, probably best known for composing the music for the film *The Last Emperor*. Ueno Park itself contains numerous other free attractions (see ch 3).

Hours: 10 AM–4 PM Mon–Fri. Open some wknds, but usually clsd on

Sat, Sun, Jan–March, and national and school hols (which can
be long). Best to call and check first.

Access:A 10-min walk from JR Ueno Stn, Ueno Park Exit (Yamanote
and other lines). Turn right from the exit and walk to the traffic
light. Turn left and walk past the National Museum to the
second light. Enter the campus gate on the left and make an
immediate left. It is the orange brick building alongside the
street. In 1999, the collection will move to a new building.

■ Tokyo University

UNIVERSITY MUSEUM
東京大学総合研究博物館
（Tokyo Daigaku Sogo Kenkyu Hakubutsukan）
   7–3–1 Hongo, Bunkyo-ku, Tokyo 113–0033
   ☎ 3812–2111 ext. 2802/3
   東京都文京区本郷7-3-1　〒113-0033

This museum is located on the campus of prestigious Tokyo
University. (See ch 8—Yushima Seido Confucian Shrine for
its origins.) The museum offers periodic exhibitions based on
themes from various departments of the university (i.e., art,
architecture, archaeology, culture, history, natural history, and
others).

During their "Digital Museum" series of exhibitions, visitors
could wander through a virtual museum of dinosaurs and large
fossils with the use of a computer joy stick. The "Virtual Architecture" portion featured interactive displays where you could
manipulate the computer-generated architectural images to
view them from any angle.

Another show was entitled "Letters of History" and explored
the various forms of letters and characters used in writing systems from ancient times to the present day. Still another display
consisted of photos showing ordinary Japanese people caught up
in the transition from the Edo to Meiji periods in the latter 19th
century. It showed how the change affected their lives and manner of dress, which often turned out to be a strange combination
of traditional Japanese and new Western styles.

The university sponsors two or three shows a year. If you are interested in visiting the museum, call (in Japanese) for information on their next exhibition. Groups of twenty or more are requested to make a reservation.

Hours: 10 AM–5 PM when exhibitions are on. Clsd Mon, New Year, and university hols. Times may change, so check before going.

Access: A 10-min walk from Hongo-sanchome Stn's only exit (Marunouchi Line). Go out to Hongo-dori and turn left. Walk until you see a big red gate on the right. This is Akamon (Red Gate), the main entrance to the campus. Enter here and make an immediate right. Walk all the way down to the end of the road. It ends at the door to the museum.

■ Waseda University

Tsubouchi Memorial Theater Museum

早稲田大学演劇博物館

（Waseda Daigaku Engeki Hakubutsukan）

1–6–1 Nishi Waseda, Shinjuku-ku, Tokyo 169–0051

☎ 3203–4141 ext. 5214 (Reopening October 1998)

東京都新宿区西早稲田1-6-1　〒169-0051

A theater buff's delight, this is the only museum of its kind in the country. Modeled after Elizabethan England's Fortune Theatre, the building has been wonderfully recreated, with a stage built into the front where performances of Shakespeare and other plays are presented periodically.

The Waseda University Theater Museum serves as the center of theatrical information in Japan, and houses three floors of material from both Western and Oriental theater. The permanent collection covers a wide range of subject matter. Among the things you can see here are theatrical masks, props, and costumes; one-third life-size Bunraku puppets that you can study close-up; Japanese folkloric materials used in religious rituals as far back as 1,200 years ago; and musical instruments played in various types of theatrical productions. There are also detailed models of Noh and Kabuki stages, Shakespeare's Globe Theatre, and the intricate inner workings of a revolving stage.

The subject of one of their recent special exhibitions was old Japanese movies. Projectors and editing machines from the late Meiji period (1868–1912) were on display—as were old movie magazines, postcards of actors, and posters of films that starred famous actors like Toshiro Mifune and creations like Godzilla.

The museum is named in honor of Tsubouchi Shoyo, translator of the complete works of Shakespeare into Japanese and one of the founders of Waseda University. The excellent English pamphlet contains information about theater in Japan in general, as well as about the collection. The museum building also houses a theatrical library. Closed until October 1998.

Access: A 7-min walk from Waseda Stn, Exit 3A (Tozai Line). Turn left from the exit and left again when you reach the major street. It will run right into an entrance to the university. Enter the campus and follow the wide center road to the second small crosswalk. Look right and you will see the museum (Building No. 5) at the end of the lane. There will be no doubt about which building it is.

Pʀɪᴠᴀᴛᴇ AND GOVERNMENT MUSEUMS

ACE WORLD BAGS AND LUGGAGE MUSEUM
エース世界の鞄館（Esu Sekai no Kabankan）
　　1–8–10 Komagata, Taito-ku, Tokyo 111–0043
　　☎ 3847–5515
　　東京都台東区駒形1-8-10　〒111-0043

Now who would ever think that a few rooms full of old suitcases and bags would be interesting enough to go and see? Well, guess what—they are. Each bag has its own story to tell—about a trend, a culture, or the person whose life it was part of. This museum brings together travel and carrying gear made around the world over the last 200 years, resulting in an eye-opening tour of travel history that takes you back to a time when any transportation other than a horse-and-buggy existed only in the minds of dreamers.

There are exquisite bags from Italy and France, Dunhill bags from England, and a stunning quilted, black leather item from Germany. The American examples provide a sharp contrast with their streamlined shapes and glass fiber and aluminum bodies. A surprising entry is an artificial leather case from Portugal that dates back to 1892.

Mexican leather suitcases intricately carved in the manner of the country's handicrafts are matched only by the Chinese versions carved with the same painstaking detail from camphor wood—said to "protect clothing from vermin." Woven bamboo bags from Thailand and China, and Japanese wallets and coin purses fashioned out of salmon skin (an old Ainu custom), are also on display. A long, narrow 1834 handbox for holding valuables served double-duty as a pillow for its owner, and a 1936 suitcase that once belonged to a Japanese Olympic diver is smothered with stickers from his world travels.

But the centerpieces are the big cabin trunks and wardrobes used for ocean voyages. An 1874 German waterproof cloth trunk won a gold prize from that country's government for its innovation that year, and a 1914 American version actually devoted one-quarter of its total space to stow a man's top hat!

There are no English pamphlets, but English labels and plaques are found throughout the museum.

Hours: 10 AM–4:30 Mon–Fri. Clsd wknds and national, New Year, and summer hols.

Access: 1 min from Asakusa Stn, Exit A1 (Toei Asakusa Line). Go straight out from the exit. It is the big brown building just ahead on the right side. Sign the visitor's book and get your badge at the desk, then take the elevator to the 8F.

AZABU MUSEUM OF ARTS AND CRAFTS
麻布美術工芸館 （Azabu Bijutsu Kogeikan）
4–6–9 Roppongi, Minato-ku, Tokyo 106–0032

☎ 5474–1371
東京都港区六本木4-6-9　〒106-0032

This attractive museum, located a few minutes from Roppongi Crossing, is a showcase for a wide range of arts and crafts. About half of its exhibits are free. Ceramics, carvings, cultural art, design, illustration, and architectural-related events are just a few of the shows that you might find on the various floors of this building. Traditional, contemporary, and practical crafts can all be seen here, and there are usually several exhibitions going on at the same time. Previously, an international art forum on leather art showcased a stunning variety of leather works with surface textures resembling those of wood, cloth, metal, feathers, fur, velvet, glass, or ceramics.

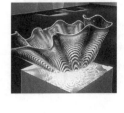

Two or three times a year *ukiyo-e* prints are exhibited from the museum's collection of 3,000. Special international shows are also held several times each year. Sometimes graduation exhibitions from art universities are held at the museum, which is affiliated with the Crafts Association Foundation.

Note: About half of the exhibitions at the museum are free.

Hours: 10 AM–6 PM (enter by 5:30 PM). Clsd Mon and New Year and summer hols.

Access:4 min from Roppongi Stn, Exit 4A (Hibiya Line). Walk straight out from the station, cross the street, and turn left. Turn right at the second small street. Take the next left and you will be at the museum's door. It is a gray building with large floor-to-ceiling windows.

BEER MUSEUM YEBISU

エビス ビール記念館　（Yebisu Biru Kinenkan）

Yebisu Garden Place, B1

4–20–1 Ebisu, Shibuya-ku, Tokyo 150–6090

☎ 5423–7255

東京都渋谷区恵比寿4-20-1　恵比寿ガーデン プレース地下1階
〒150-6090

This museum takes you on a trip through a beer factory that no longer exists! It's a kind of multimedia re-creation of the old Sapporo Brewery (parent company of Yebisu Beer) that operated

on the site for over a hundred years, between 1887 and 1988.

The **Virtual Brewery Adventure** takes you on a virtual reality journey through one of the four beer-making processes—brewing, fermentation, filtration, or bottling. Starting from a broad landscape of Japan, you begin to zoom in closer and closer until you are actually inside one of the processes, flying over the "mountain peaks" of fermentation or entering the tiny bubbles of the brewing process.

World Beer History is traced through milestones such as European monastery brewing, Mesopotamian stone carvings that actually documented beer-drinking way back then, Dutch engravings, German quilts, and beer festivals around the world.

The Gallery presents the advertising history of Sapporo Beer. A display of old beer print ads and posters is featured alongside more modern media such as TV commercials. It is interesting to note that in the years between two adjoining posters (1930s and 1950s), the direction in which Japanese *kana* characters were written was reversed! The earlier poster spells out words from right to left instead of in the present left-to-right direction. This is easy to spot by looking for the word "Sapporo," which is sure to be on every piece of advertising. The gallery sometimes holds other beer-related special exhibitions as well. The museum is located inside a lively complex known as Yebisu Garden Place (see ch 3).

Note: At the end of the museum is a tasting room where you can sample Yebisu beer for ¥200.

Hours: 10 AM–6 PM Tues–Sun. Clsd Mon and New Year hols.

Access: 7 min from JR Ebisu Stn (Yamanote Line) via the Skywalk from the East Exit, which takes you directly to Yebisu Garden Place. The museum is located behind Mitsukoshi Department Store. It is also accessible from the Hibiya Line's Ebisu Stn.

BICYCLE CULTURE CENTER

自転車文化センター （Jitensha Bunka Center）
　Jitensha Kaikan No. 3 Building, 2/3F
　1–9–3 Akasaka, Minato-ku, Tokyo 107–0052
　☎ 3584–4530
　東京都港区赤坂1-9-3　自転車会館3号館2/3階　〒107-0052

Sixty-three interesting and unusual bicycles are on display at the museum on the 2F of the Bicycle Culture Center. You can see the 1908 wooden-wheeled "royal tricycle" that belonged to the emperor Showa when he was a child, as well as the very first bicycle (a French Michaux) brought to Japan over a hundred years ago. Also on display are Olympic cycles, a bicycle-built-for-three, and the horse-shaped, wooden tricycle familiar to many people from the paintings of French artist Claude Monet.

Upstairs on the 3F is a bicycling information center with a comprehensive library. You can learn about the history of bicycles here, or just relax and browse through cycling magazines and books in English, French, Italian, German, Spanish, and Japanese (see ch 13).

Hours: 10 AM–4 PM Mon–Fri. Clsd wknds and hols.

Access: 7 min from Toranomon Stn, Exit 3 (Ginza Line). Walk straight out of the exit and follow the sidewalk as it curves to the left. (Don't cross the street here.) Continue walking for about 5 min until the road ends at a T-crossing at the Shin Nikko Building. Turn right. When you reach the main intersection, continue across the street. The entrance is on the right, directly across from the main entrance to the American Embassy. Enter under the English "Bicycle Culture Center" sign on the building and walk back to Building No. 3.

CIGARETTE LIGHTER MUSEUM

ライター博物館 （Raita Hakubutsukan）
   Ivy Antique Gallery, 3F
   1–27–6 Mukojima, Sumida-ku, Tokyo 131–0033
   ☎ 3622–1649
   東京都墨田区向島1-27-6　アイビー アンティーク ギャラリー3階
   〒131-0033

The Cigarette Lighter Museum is found on the third floor of a spacious five-story western antique store. This mind-boggling collection of lighters was painstakingly gathered by the store's owner over a twenty-year period, mostly during her travels to London, Paris, and New York. The 400-plus items in the collection are periodically rotated, and about 200 of them can be seen at any one time. You are sure to find a fascinating assortment whenever you go—for the range is extremely broad. Some of the forms I observed during my visit were a tiny typewriter, a camera, guns, grenades, bells, boots, clocks, keys, knives, boats, trains, planes, rocket ships, cars, spark plugs, outboard motors, a dart board, and numerous animal figures. There were lighters in human form, too: an English Beefeater guard, a Middle-Eastern rug seller on camel-back, a German man in *liederhosen*, a bartender with a fully stocked bar, a woman in a hoop skirt, and a knight in shining armor were among them. Many dated to the 1930s, when table-top lighters were very popular.

NOTE: This is one of the "Little Museums of Sumida-ku." (See ch 3.)

Hours: 10 AM–6:30 PM daily except national and New year hols.

Access: An 8-min walk from the Honjo Azumabashi Stn on the Asakusa Line, Exit A4. When you come out the exit, turn and go back to the corner and veer right. At the next main intersection, Kototoi-dori (about a 5-min walk), go right again and walk to the next traffic light. The building will be on the right side just beyond the light. It is also accessible from the Narihirabash Stn on the Tobu Isezaki Line.

CURRENCY MUSEUM

貨幣博物館 （Kahei Hakubutsukan）

Bank of Japan Annex (Nihon Ginko Minami Bunkan), 2F

2–1–1 Nihonbashi Hongokucho, Chuo-ku, Tokyo 103–8660

☎ 3279–1111

東京都中央区日本橋本国町　日本銀行南分館2階　〒103-8660

As you walk through the slow-opening vaultlike doors of this building, it feels as if you are entering a huge depository of treasures—and you are. For among the historical items housed here in the Bank of Japan's Currency Museum is the biggest gold coin in the world: a 17 x 10 cm (7 x 4 in), 165 gm (5.8 oz) oval-shaped beauty that dates back to 1588 and is considered a work of fine art today. Also in the museum's collection are items that served as secret hiding places for money during Edo times (1600–1868), including sword handles, scabbards, inkpots, brushes, and other calligraphy materials.

The history of the Japanese currency system is traced from its pre-money days, when rice and arrowheads were bartered, up to the country's current monetary system, with paper money that is one of the most difficult in the world to counterfeit (see Printing Bureau Museum below). Money from many other parts of the world can also be seen.

A detailed guide to the museum and a nicely illustrated booklet that describes the history of money are available in English at no charge from the entrance desk, and an English video in which "Mr. Bank" explains in simple terms the financial system and mission of the Bank of Japan can be viewed before or after your visit.

Hours: 9:30 AM–4:30 PM (enter by 4 PM) Mon–Fri. Open 2nd and 4th Sun, but otherwise clsd wknds, and national and New Year hols.

Access:Across the street from Mitsukoshimae Stn, Exit B1 (Hanzomon or Ginza lines). When you come out of the exit, you will see a building with green trim diagonally across the road. Cross the main street to your left and then the smaller street to your right. The building's entrance is to the left near the corner.

EYEGLASS MUSEUM

めがねの博物館 （Megane no Hakubutsukan）

 Iris Optical Building, 6/7F

 2–29–18 Dogenzaka, Shibuya-ku, Tokyo 150–0043

 ☎ 3496–3315

東京都渋谷区道玄坂2-29-18　アイリスめがねビル6/7階　〒150-0043

So you thought eyeglasses were boring? Well, you may just change your mind after visiting this little gem of a museum. Goggles used when flying in an open-cockpit airplane, the world's first frameless eyeglasses (made from crystal by the Chinese about 200 years ago), a stereoscope, a 250-year-old English microscope, bejeweled monocles, and even a gas mask—these are just a few of the curiosities you can see at this museum dedicated to the art of making instruments to improve vision. It was founded by the president of Iris Optical, whose family has been collecting items for three generations (over ninety years). In 1990 he decided to share the fruits of their efforts.

A MYRIAD OF MUSEUMS

The evolution of eyeglasses is traced from its beginnings in 13th-century Italy. Glasses and related items from Europe, the United States, China, and Japan are all on display, and examples of the real thing are supplemented by artwork of people wearing glasses of various styles. There is also a large statue of Jesuit priest Francis Xavier, who brought the first pair of eyeglasses to Japan in the 1500s. But the highlight is an authentic French eyeglass workshop that dates from 1800. It was shipped over from a small town in the French Alps and reassembled at the museum, where it takes up most of the 6F. Here you can see the old water-powered and treadle-type machinery used to make eyeglasses in those days.

The museum's collection totals 6,000 items, with 250 displayed at a time. One of my favorites was a French magazine advertising eyeglasses for dogs! Although the captions are all in Japanese, it's a very visual museum (no pun intended). And Mr. Yamakawa, the museum's administrator (who is there on Sundays and Thursdays and speaks a little English) is always happy to welcome visitors of all nationalities.

Hours: 11 AM–5 PM (enter by 4:30 PM) Tues–Sun. Clsd Mon and New Year hols.

Access:A 5-min walk from JR Shibuya Stn, Hachiko Exit (Yamanote and other lines). Walk left along Dogenzaka for about 1 min, and turn right at the 109 Building (the big silver tower on the corner) onto Bunkamura-dori. The museum is in the Iris Optical Building on the left side of the street at the 2nd light. Take the elevator up to the 7F to begin your tour.

FIRE MUSEUM

消防博物館 （Shobo Hakubutsukan）

3–10 Yotsuya, Shinjuku-ku, Tokyo 160–0004

☎ 3353–9119

東京都新宿区四ッ谷3-10　〒160-0004

The Fire Museum's 1F entrance hall contains a horse-drawn, steam fire engine that was used at the beginning of the 20th century to fight fires. On the roof of another floor you can climb into a real firefighting helicopter, sit behind the controls, and fantasize away. An array of real firefighting equipment and numerous models, dioramas, and other visuals document the history of firefighting from the Edo period (1600–1868) to modern times in such an interesting way that even kids will be entertained.

In Edo times, for example, the lack of water facilities made it necessary to tear down nearby buildings to keep fires from spreading. This was known as "demolition firefighting," and a huge diorama on the 5F vividly depicts the process. The museum owns about 3,000 fire-related items, including some very old and valuable works of art that depict fires and firefighting.

Special exhibitions are held twice a year, one in winter and the other during the summer. One of these was a display of 2,000 miniature fire vehicles (trucks, cars, buses, ambulances, helicopters, and boats) from around the world. Besides the easy-to-understand visual nature of the museum, some of the captions are in English, and an English pamphlet gives the specifics of what is on each floor.

Hours: 9:30 AM–5 PM Tues–Sun (enter by 4:30 PM). Clsd hols, Mon (Tues if Mon is a hol), and New Year hols.

Access: Upstairs from Yotsuya-sanchome Stn, Exit 2 (Marunouchi Line).

FIREWORKS MUSEUM
両国花火資料館 （Ryogoku Hanabi Shiryokan）
　　Sumitomo-Fudosan Ryogoku Building, 1F
　　2–10–8 Ryogoku, Sumida-ku, Tokyo 130–0026
　　☎ 5608–1111 (Sumida Ward Office) ext 3406
　　東京都墨田区両国2-10-8　住友不動産両国ビル1階　〒130-0026

Japanese fireworks are world famous. Why? Because they explode evenly in all directions—a feat not quite duplicated by their counterparts in other countries.

Here at Japan's only fireworks museum you can see the big round balls that house such spectacular effects and have been lighting up the summer skies over Tokyo for almost 400 years. Yes, as far back as 1613, people lined the banks of the Sumida River and went out on pleasure boats to watch Tokyo's most

famous fireworks display each July (see ch 5). This popular summertime tradition was depicted in woodblock prints dating back to the Edo (1600–1868) and Meiji (1868–1912) period.

On the floor of the museum is a fireworks ball that measures 60 cm (2 ft) across, weighs a whopping 80 kg (176 lb), and explodes into a 400-m (365-yd) sparkling burst of color. (The largest one in Japan is 90 cm [35 in] across, and explodes to 550 m [500 yd] across.) Some of the big balls have been cross-sectioned so you can study their inner workings. There are some elongated fireworks too, but the round ones are much more interesting. The video, display captions, and printed information are all in Japanese, but the museum makes it quite clear what you are looking at—fireworks!

Hours: Noon–4 PM Thurs, Fri, Sat. Open daily noon–4 PM during July and Aug.

Access: A 2-min walk from Ryogoku Stn, West Exit (Sobu Line). Go left at the exit and walk down the main street until it ends at the Sumitomo Fudosan Ryogoku Building (a little to the right). A sign showing a fireworks display is usually set out in front of the building, and the entrance to the museum is around the right side.

HORSE RACING MUSEUM

JRA 競馬博物館

(Japan Racing Association [JRA] Keiba Hakubutsukan)

　　Tokyo Racecourse (Tokyo Fuchu Keibajo)

　　1–1 Hiyoshicho, Fuchu-shi, Tokyo 183–0024

　　☎ 0423–63–3141

　　東京都府中市日吉町1-1　東京府中競馬場　〒183-0024

The Horse Racing Museum is located at the Tokyo Racecourse in Fuchu. (See the Horse section in ch 4 for details.)

ISETAN MUSEUM OF ART

伊勢丹美術館　(Isetan Bijutsukan)

　　Isetan Department Store, Annex Building, 8F

　　3–14–1 Shinjuku, Shinjuku-ku, Tokyo 160–8011

☎ 3225–2514 (Foreign Customer Service), 3225–2490 (Museum)
東京都新宿区新宿3-14-1　イセタン新館8階　〒160-8011

Isetan Foreign Customer Service offers free membership in their "I Club" to the foreign community in Japan. Benefits include complimentary tickets for members and their families to their high-quality art museum, which often features the works of internationally acclaimed artists. A recent offering from the West was "Miró on Stage," which traced the famous Spanish artist's venture into the theater, where he was able to bring his fantastic creations to life. The giant biomorphic costumes he designed and built for a stage production brought a big smile to everyone's face and completely stole the show.

Isetan's exhibitions of Oriental art are just as stunning: two recent ones featured beautiful kimono throughout history and a display of sliding doors from Kyoto's renowned Golden Pavilion temple. The doors were covered with exquisite black-and-white ink paintings. After seeing the exhibition in the museum, be sure to check out the fine arts and crafts salons on the same floor.

For membership in the "I Club," contact Isetan Foreign Customer Service on the 7F of the main building or call the above number.

Hours: 10 AM–7:30 PM (enter by 7 PM). Clsd some Wed.

Access: Above Shinjuku-sanchome Stn, Exit B5 (Marunouchi or Shinjuku lines), or a 5-min walk from JR Shinjuku Stn, East Exit (Yamanote and other lines).

JAPAN ART ACADEMY
日本芸術院 （Nihon Geijutsuin）
　1–30 Ueno Park, Taito-ku, Tokyo 110–0007
　☎ 3821–7191
　東京都台東区上野公園1-30　〒110-0007

This national honorary institute holds exhibitions between July and February each year of the works of people who have been given special awards in various fields of the arts. Paintings, sculpture, books, and various other works are placed on display at this long, low building built in the Heian (794–1185) style of

A MYRIAD OF MUSEUMS

architecture and located close to the entrance to Ueno Park. There are many other free attractions in the park, also. (See ch 3—Ueno Park.)

Hours: 10 AM–noon, 1 PM–4 PM when shows are on. Call for days open.
Access: Across from JR Ueno Stn, Ueno Park Exit (Yamanote and other lines). The building is inside the park and a little to the left of the main entrance, just beyond the Tokyo Metropolitan Festival Hall (Tokyo Bunka Kaikan).

KOBAYASHI DOLL MUSEUM
小林人形資料館 （Kobayashi Ningyo Shiryokan）
6–31–2 Yahiro, Sumida-ku, Tokyo 131–0041
☎ 3612–1644
東京都墨田区八広6-31-2　〒131-0041

This is one of the "Little Museums of Sumida-ku." (See ch 3.)

KONICA CAMERA MUSEUM
コニカ カメラ ミュージアム
Konica Plaza, Shinjuku Takano Building, 4F
3–26–11 Shinjuku, Shinjuku-ku, Tokyo 160–0021
☎ 3225–5001
東京都新宿区新宿3-26-11　新宿高野ビル4階コニカプラザ
〒160-0021

The Konica Photo Plaza covers the entire 4F of the Shinjuku Takano Building, and includes a comprehensive camera museum along with its two photo galleries. (See ch 14.)

LITTLE MUSEUMS OF SUMIDA-KU
In addition to all the museums listed in this chapter, be sure to check out the wonderful "Little Museums of Sumida-ku" in chapter 3. A visit may include entrance to the homes and workshops of traditional craftsmen, where oftentimes you can watch them practicing their crafts. The following Sumida-ku museums are written up here: the Cigarette Lighter Museum, Fireworks Museum, Sumo Museum, and Takinami Glass Museum.

MEGURO PARASITOLOGICAL MUSEUM

目黒寄生虫館 （Meguro Kiseichukan）

4–1–1 Shimo Meguro, Meguro-ku, Tokyo 153–0064

☎ 3716–1264 (Tape), 3716–7144 (Museum)

東京都目黒区下目黒4-1-1　〒153-0064

This museum is just what you dreaded it would be—a documentation of all the creepy, crawly things that could possibly invade your body. One diagram shows all the ways and places humans and animals can be attacked by parasites—and they seem endless.

Everyone's favorite will no doubt be the 8.8-m- (29-ft-) long tapeworm that was removed from a human intestine. It was ingested as a result of eating a kind of countrified sushi. Once inside, it grew to outlandish proportions before being removed and finding its posthumous place in history at this one-of-a-kind museum in Meguro Ward.

The museum is located on the premises of a parasitological laboratory, founded in 1953 by Dr. Satoru Kamegai. In the years after World War II, about 70 percent of the population of Tokyo suffered from parasites, so Dr. Kamegai built the museum to educate people about these medical pests. Many of the displays are pretty scientific, but there are enough things to see to keep you interested (over and above the aforementioned tapeworm), including a couple of display cases of cockroaches and the large rubber replicas of a mosquito, mite, and lice.

NOTE: After you have seen everything, you can buy T-shirts with "Meguro Parasitological Museum" emblazoned across them as presents for all your friends!

Hours: 10 AM–5 PM Tues–Sun. Clsd Mon.

Access: Take Tokyu Bus No. 1, 2, 6, or 7 from the West Exit of Meguro Stn (Yamanote Line). Go two stops to Otori Jinja-mae. Continue walking in the same direction—the museum is the pinkish-brown building on the next corner.

MUSEUM OF CONTEMPORARY SCULPTURE

現代彫刻美術館 （Gendai Chokoku Bijutsukan）

Chosenin Temple

4–12–18 Naka Meguro, Meguro-ku, Tokyo 153–0061

☎ 3792–5858

東京都目黒区中目黒4-12-18　長泉院　〒153-0061

This lovely sculpture garden and museum is a real find. Located on the grounds of a Buddhist temple, it is a little out of the way, but worth the trip. The museum's collection of works in stone and metal by forty modern Japanese sculptors are beautifully and tastefully displayed. The modern, two-story building that houses the smaller pieces is filled with special little touches—such as antique furniture set amidst the sculptures, and figurine door handles that are works of art themselves.

The larger, more substantial pieces are displayed in the garden, which is located on several levels and enclosed by ivy and trees. The atmosphere is very calming and it has been compared with the Milles Garden in Stockholm, Sweden. It's a place you won't want to leave.

Hours: 10 AM–5 PM Tue–Sun (till 8 PM on Sat in July–Aug). Clsd on Mon and Dec 20–Jan 14.

Access: Take Tokyu Bus No. 6 from the West Exit of Meguro Stn (Yamanote Line) to Shizen-en-shita. It's about 3 min from there. Walk forward to where the street ends directly in front of the bus, turn right and follow the larger street to the end of the graveyard. Turn left and you will immediately see the museum on the right side.

MUSEUM OF DRY CLEANING AND LAUNDERING
(Kenji Igarashi Memorial Museum)

五十嵐健治記念洗濯資料館
（Igarashi Kenji Kinen Sentaku Shiryokan）
　　Hakuyosha, 3F
　　2–11–1 Shimomaruko, Ota-ku, Tokyo 146–0092
　　☎ 3759–1336
　　東京都大田区下丸子2-11-1　白洋舎3階白洋舎研究所　〒146-0092

Each year—believe it or not—2,500 people visit this museum, opened as a memorial to laundry pioneer Kenji Igarashi, founder of the Clean Living stores. It may not be for everyone, but it's of the little, off-beat variety that affords you the opportunity to visit a very pleasant neighborhood of Tokyo that you would ordinarily never get to see.

Old items from the laundry business, such as a hand-drawn

delivery cart and *happi*-coat uniform, have been preserved in this unique museum. Other pieces that greet you as you enter the room include a delivery sled and a "boiler," in which clothes were boiled with soap and soda while being stirred with a rod to get them clean. A large blow-up of an *ukiyo-e* print from the Edo period (1600–1868) shows women washing clothes in the nearby Tamagawa River, and copies of artworks by Renoir, Pissaro, Chardon, and Degas also depict laundry scenes.

A fairly large collection of old irons, which were heated by placing hot coals inside them, includes a rounded iron for ironing cuffs and collars. A reference library of 8,000 volumes is available for use, among then a number of industry-related journals from England and the United States. If you happen to be a cleaning freak, you have found a home.

Hours: 10 AM–4 PM Mon–Fri. Clsd wknds and hols.

Access: An 8-min walk from Shimomaruko Stn's only exit (Mekama Line). The station is three stops from Kamata Stn on the JR Keihin Tohoku Line. From the front of the station, walk down the street across from the exit alongside McDonald's. Turn right at the flower shop and follow this road to the end. Turn right on the main street and walk to the next traffic signal. The museum will be on the far left corner, on the 3F of the dry-cleaning store next to the factory.

MUSEUM OF THE IMPERIAL COLLECTION

宮内庁三の丸所蔵館 （Kunaicho Sannomaru Shozokan）

1–1 Chiyoda, Chiyoda-ku, Tokyo 100–8111

☎ 3213–1177

東京都千代田区千代田1-1　〒100-8111

This museum is located on the grounds of the Imperial Palace East Garden and showcases the Imperial Art Collection. Once the property of the imperial family, the collection was donated to the general public in 1989 and the museum was created in 1993 to enable people to come and view the works. The 6,000 items in the collection are rotated four times a year.

The wide range of art represented here includes gifts to the imperial family from foreign governments. Needless to say, there are some very valuable pieces in the collection. (See also the Imperial Palace East Garden entry in ch 7.)

Hours: The museum closes 15 min before the garden. Open 9:15 AM–4:15 PM *March–Oct* (9:15 AM–3:45 PM *Nov–Feb*). Clsd Mon, Fri, New Year hols, two weeks between exhibitions, and some irregular days.

Access: Located in the Imperial Palace East Garden, just inside the Otemon Gate entrance. It is a 4-min walk straight ahead from Exit C-13b of Otemachi Stn (various subway lines).

NHK BROADCAST MUSEUM

NHK 放送博物館 （NHK Hoso Hakubutsukan）
2–1–1 Atago, Minato-ku, Tokyo 105–0002
☎ 5400–6900
東京都港区愛宕2-1-1　〒105-0002

This museum sits high atop Atagoyama Hill, where Japanese broadcasting was born in 1925. The original building has been replaced but the museum marks the location, and thoughtful displays trace the development of Japanese radio and TV broadcasting from its beginnings through the present day. Old newsreels and documentaries are on view throughout the museum, which also contains many old radios, televisions, cameras, and other equipment.

There are some very important historical items here, including the original recording of the Showa emperor's 1945 address to the people announcing the end of World War II—the first time an emperor's voice was heard in public. In one room it is possible to sit back in a comfortable Shinkansen train seat, push a start button, and watch the world whiz by through a "train window." The window is really a TV screen, and the seat part of a TV studio set

A pamphlet identifies some of the exhibits in English, but it's a little hard to match up the pictures with the items, and there is no trace of English in the exhibition itself—a little surprising since so many of Tokyo's museums pride themselves on being accessible to international visitors.

Hours: 9:30 AM–4:30 PM (enter by 4 PM). Clsd Mon (except hols) and New Year hols.

Access: An 8-min walk from Onarimon Stn, Exit A5 (Mita Line). Go left from the station exit and walk along Hibiya-dori to the first traffic light. Turn left. When you reach the next traffic light, continue across the street and turn right. You will soon see eighty-six stone steps on your left that lead up to the 200-year-old Atago shrine. This is the scenic route. You can go up these steps and walk through the lovely grounds of the shrine to the next-door museum, or continue along at street level to the next road on the left, which leads to the top of the hill and the museum. It is also accessible from Kamiyacho Stn (Hibiya Line).

NOH MASK MUSEUM

能面博物館 （Nomen Hakubutsukan）

15–10–5 Narihira, Sumida-ku, Tokyo 130–0002

☎ 3623–3055

東京都墨田区業平15-10-5　〒130-0002

One of the "Little Museums of Sumida-ku" (see ch 3).

PARLIAMENTARY MUSEUM

憲政記念館 （Kensei Kinenkan）

1–1–1 Nagatacho, Chiyoda-ku, Tokyo 100–0014

☎ 3581–1651

東京都千代田区永田町1-1-1　〒100-0014

This museum supplements a tour of the National Diet/Parliament Building across the street (see ch 3), or can be a substitute for a visit to the Diet if you are not able to take the tour. Although the written descriptions are in Japanese, the exhibit contains many photographs, paintings, and other visual material. There are beautifully detailed models of the Diet Building and Parliamentary Museum, the interior Chamber of the House of Representatives, and the London Parliament Building. And you can sit in a simulated House of Representatives chamber and imagine how it must feel to be a member of the Japanese Diet (Parliament). The museum is located in the Western-style North Garden

of the Diet Front Park, where the designated spot for measuring distances from Tokyo to the provinces is housed. The lovely Japanese-style South Garden across the street is also open to the public, and the National Diet Library (similar to the Library of Congress in the United States) is located between the museum and the subway station (see ch 13).

Hours: 9:30 AM–4:30 PM Mon–Fri. Clsd wknds.

Access: A 4-min walk from Nagatacho Stn, Exit 2 (Yurakucho or Hanzomon lines). If traveling by the Hanzomon Line, access Exit 2 through the Yurakucho Line. From the station exit, cross the street to your left and continue straight past the Diet Library to the next corner. The museum is directly across the street. It is in the section of the building to the left of the center courtyard.

PRINTING BUREAU MUSEUM

大蔵省印刷局記念館 （Okurasho Insatsukyoku Kinenkan）

9–5 Ichigaya Honmuracho, Shinjuku-ku, Tokyo 162–0845

☎ 3268–3271

東京都新宿区市ヶ谷本村町9-5　〒162-0845

Japanese money is considered to be one of the most difficult in the world to counterfeit, and the precautions taken to insure that this remains the case is one of the topics explored at this museum. You can observe the currency's luminescent ink mark under ultraviolet lighting and read the microlettering (too small for the human eye to read) under a magnifying glass. Nearby is a bundle of notes totaling ¥100 million (U.S. $1 million)—and a sign challenging you to lift it. Two armholes are provided for you to reach in and try.

On the 2F, maps of the world are shown with currencies from 122 countries posted underneath. Interesting and unusual banknotes are also on display. "Animals on Bills" features Zairian gorillas, Singapore lions, Indonesian rhinos, and Thai elephants, among others. Anticounterfeiting techniques used by France, Italy, Germany, England, Canada, the United States, and Japan can be seen through back lighting and other special lighting effects. An image of the new (1996) U.S. $100 bill is studied from a number of angles and perspectives (enlarged, sectioned off, dissected, etc.). Among the postage stamps in the museum's collection are the world's very first stamp (of British issue dating from 1840), and also Japan's first effort, from 1871.

In addition to the permanent collection, special exhibitions are held in the lobby area of the building. "Techniques of Watermarking" was one of these. There are also a number of English and Japanese videos to watch that deal with various aspects of printing, currency, and stamps.

Hours: 9:30 AM–4:30 PM (enter by 4 PM) Tues–Sun. Clsd Mon.

Access: 10 min from Ichigaya Stn (Sobu Line). From the (only) JR Exit, turn left and walk across the bridge to Sotobori-dori. Cross and walk right, then go up the hill alongside McDonald's. After the road jogs right at the tennis courts, make the next left. Walk about 5 min and the Printing Bureau will be on your left side, just before the brown building with the 10-story white tower.

STATIONERY MUSEUM

文具資料館 （Bungu Shiryokan）

    Bungu Hanbai Kenpo Kaikan, 1F

    1–1–15 Yanagibashi, Taito-ku, Tokyo 111–0052

    ☎ 3861–4905

    東京都台東区柳橋1-1-15　文具販売健保会館1階　〒111-0052

As you step into the Stationery Museum, a giant pen standing on end greets you. This is the first indication that this museum is going to offer a lot more than just stationery. It starts off with ancient writing materials—flints and a tablet from Mesopotamia—and works its way through utensils made from bone and horn, Egyptian papyrus, and other early writing materials and methods. A giant Chinese *suzuri* (stone for grinding inksticks to make ink) is sure to catch your eye with its spectacular carvings of plants and animals. Nearby, smaller stones in the shapes of animals date back about 500 years.

There are 850 items in this "history of world writing." Both East and West are well represented, with a collection of old posters, ink bottles, and pens from Europe and the United States

given equal billing with Japanese writing boxes from the Edo period (1600–1868) and *kanji* typewriters—those awkward machines with a keyboard of several thousand individual characters that were used before the advent of the desktop computer.

The evolution of the abacus is traced, as is the more recent history of the calculator from the big, bulky machines to the pocket-sized versions so familiar to us today. An oversized calligraphy brush (170 cm/66 in) made from the tails of fifty horses, and a writing implement belonging to the first Tokugawa shogun are also among the museum's collection. The final entry is a robot writer that receives its instructions from a computer. It is a pretty long span from a Mesopotamian tablet to a robot writer—and a good concept for a museum.

Although there are no English pamphlets and the written descriptions are all in Japanese, there are many objects of interest that can be appreciated for their beauty and/or age alone. And the area around the train station is Tokyo's center for dolls, toys, stationery goods, and craft supplies, so you might want to explore a little.

NOTE: You can try your hand at making a craft to take home for free at the nearby Sakura Horikiri (see ch 9).

Hours: 10 AM–4 PM Mon–Fri. Clsd wknds and national, New Year, and summer hols.

Access: A 4-min walk from Asakusabashi Stn, East Exit (JR Sobu or Toei Asakusa lines). Turn right from the exit and go under the train tracks, then immediately turn left and walk along the other side of the tracks toward the Sumida River. It is in a white corner building on the right side just before the river. Please call first as they were considering a move to a new location.

STOCK MARKET MUSEUM

証券資料館 （Shoken Shiryokan）

Tokyo Stock Exchange, 1F

2–1 Nihonbashi Kabutocho, Chuo-ku, Tokyo 103–0026

☎ 3666–0141 (Tokyo Stock Exchange)

東京都中央区日本橋兜町2-1　東京証券取引所1階　〒103-0026

The Tokyo Stock Exchange was established in 1878, but has operated in its present form only since 1949. Since then, it has miraculously grown to become one of the top three exchanges in the world today, ranking beside those of London and New York. In 1978, on the 100th anniversary of its founding, material was collected from many dealers and investors for an exhibition, which later led to establishing the Stock Market Museum.

The history of the exchange from its beginnings is covered here, and nearly everything is explained in both English and Japanese. This includes telephone guides and information on computers, as well as written descriptions. It's a nice supplement to your visit to the Stock Exchange upstairs (see ch 3 for details). And you can end the day by taking their bilingual computer quiz to test and reinforce what you've learned from your visit.

NOTE: Flash photography, smoking, and eating is not allowed.

Hours: 9 AM–4 PM Mon–Fri. Clsd wknds and hols.

Access: 4 min from Kayabacho Stn, Exit 11 (Tozai and Hibiya lines). Turn right from the exit and walk to the street just before the highway. Turn right again and walk straight until you reach the Stock Exchange, the last building on the right side. Enter through the visitor's entrance.

STRIPED HOUSE MUSEUM

ストライプドハウス美術館
5–10–33 Roppongi, Minato-ku, Tokyo 106–0032
☎ 3405–8108
東京都港区六本木5-10-33　〒106-0032

Noted for its originality, the Striped House Museum features contemporary works by both established and new artists in every field of art. In the past they have held exhibitions ranging from painting and sculpture to performance art and poetry readings. The display area is an airy four-level open space and the interesting yellow-and-brown-striped building (hence its name) was inspired by the architecture of a Byzantine church

Hours: 11 AM–6:30 PM. Clsd Sun, hols, and for changes of exhibitions.

Access: A 5-min walk from Roppongi Stn, Exit 3 (Hibiya Line). Turn right from the station and right again down Imoarai-zaka, the small street that runs alongside the Almond Coffee Shop. You will see the striped building on the left-hand side about 5 min down the road.

SUMO MUSEUM

相撲博物館 （Sumo Hakubutsukan）

Kokugikan (Sumo Association Headquarters and Hall), 1F

1–3–28 Yokoami, Sumida-ku, Tokyo 130–0015

☎ 3622–0366

東京都墨田区横網1-3-28　国技館1階　〒130-0015

The Kokugikan is the headquarters of the Japan Sumo Association and the main hall for sumo tournaments. The huge structure is very impressive—built on a grand scale that instills a sense of awe as you approach. It also houses the Sumo Museum.

The museum documents the history of sumo, which originated in early times as a Shinto ritual connected with the outcome of the year's rice crop. Although the museum's contents change frequently, it is always very visual and offers insight into the sport. Memorabilia of famous wrestlers—such as *kesho mawashi* (ornamental aprons), handprints, and fans decorated with the calligraphy of sumo champions—are some of the items you may find here. Sumo dolls and artwork depicting sumo in screens, scrolls, woodblock prints, and old instruction books are others. One exhibition documented the making of a wrestler's "topknot" before each match with step-by-step photographs.

NOTE: This is one of the "Little Museums of Sumida-ku." (See ch 3 for details.)

Hours: 9:30 AM–4:30 PM wkdys (except during tournaments, when only ticket holders may enter the grounds). Clsd Sat, Sun, and hols.

Access: A 1-min walk from JR Ryogoku Stn, West Exit (Sobu Line). Turn right from the exit and you will see the building in front of you.

TABI MUSEUM

足袋資料館 （Tabi Shiryokan）

Kikuya Tabi Shop

1–9–3 Midori, Sumida-ku, Tokyo 130–0021

☎ 3631–0092

東京都墨田区緑1-9-3　喜久や足袋本舗　〒130-0021

One of the "Little Museums of Sumida-ku" (see ch 3).

TAKAO NATURAL SCIENCE MUSEUM

東京都高尾自然科学博物館

（Tokyo-to Takao Shizen Kagaku Hakubutsukan）

2436 Takao-machi, Hachioji-shi, Tokyo 193–0844

☎ 0426–61–0305

東京都八王子市高尾町2436　〒193-0844

Looking for an excuse to get away from the city and breathe some fresh air? Well, here's a museum just for you. Located at the foot of Tokyo's sacred Mt. Takao, it is the place to visit for an introduction to the flora and fauna of the area. It also offers a visual orientation to the topography and various hiking trails. The captions are in Japanese, but the displays are self-explanatory in many cases.

Hours: The Takao Natural Science Museum is open 9 AM–5 PM daily (9 AM–4 PM Dec–March). Clsd 1st and 3rd Mon (Tues if Mon is a hol), Christmas, and New Year hols.

Access: A 3-min walk from Takaosan-guchi Stn (Keio Line). Walk along the road that runs off to the right alongside the station and you will soon see a sign (in English) on the left side directing you across a small bridge to the museum. For directions from Tokyo, see ch 3—Mt. Takao.

TAKINAMI GLASS MUSEUM

タキナミ ガラス博物館

Takinami Glass Factory

1–18–19 Taihei, Sumida-ku, Tokyo 130–0012

☎ 3622–4141

東京都墨田区大平1-18-19　瀧波硝子(株)　〒130-0012

This little museum is part of the Takinami glass factory, and exhibits glass items made by a number of different techniques. Each is labeled in English and Japanese, and accompanying photos demonstrate the steps used in the various processes. Some samples of glasswork at various stages are also on display. In addition to the core glass method (the technique of making glass by hand that was used from the 15th century BC to Roman times), some other processes explored are glass-blowing, fusing, slumping, casting, *pâte de verre,* enameling, engraving, sand-blasting, mosaic-glass making, and crystal-cutting.

But the museum is just one of the features of the Takinami glass factory. It also contains a showroom, a factory, and a glass-making school. The glass factory can be viewed at no charge, and glass-making classes can also be observed (or taken for a fee). The adjacent showroom contains many interesting glass items too (see ch 15).

NOTE: This is one of the "Little Museums of Sumida-ku." (See ch 3 for details.)

Hours: 10 AM–6:30 PM daily. Clsd on 2nd Mon of each month and New Year hols. The glass factory closes at 5 PM and classes (for a fee) are offered 10 AM–4 PM.

Access: A 12–15 min walk from Kinshicho Stn, North Exit (JR Sobu Line). Turn right from the exit and left at the main street (Yotsume-dori). Walk north for 5–6 min, passing Kinshi Park on your right. When you reach the Taihei 4-chome intersection (police box on corner), turn left and walk down Kuramae-bashi-dori for about another 6–7 min to the Taihei 1-chome intersection (gas station on corner). Turn right—the factory will be a few doors down on the left side.

TOKYO CENTRAL MUSEUM
東京セントラル美術館
Ginza Boeki Building, 5F
2–7–18 Ginza, Chuo-ku, Tokyo 104–0061
☎ 3564–4600
東京都中央区銀座2-7-18　銀座貿易ビル5階　〒104-0061

I have never been able to figure out this museum. It is a very large art space with a personality all of its own tucked away in an office building above Galleries Lafayette Department Store. About half the time it hosts exhibitions of calligraphy. The rest of the shows are an eclectic mix of painting, sculpture, and other media. On one occasion I saw an impressive display of large rubbings taken from old temples and tombstones. Generally there is no fee for admission, but once in a while there is a charge for a special exhibition.

Hours: 10 AM–6 PM Tues–Sun. Clsd Mon.
Access: It is located directly above Ginza Itchome Stn, Exit 9 (Yuraku-cho Line). Take the elevator from the lobby of the building to the 5F.

TOKYO METROPOLITAN ART MUSEUM

東京都美術館 （Tokyo-to Bijutsukan）

8–36 Ueno Koen, Taito-ku, Tokyo 110–0007

☎ 3823–6921

東京都台東区上野公園8-36　〒110-0007

This multilevel building hosts a myriad of exhibitions by art groups of various kinds. Contemporary paintings, prints, calligraphy, sculpture, crafts, and other media can all be seen here. Often entry is free, but sometimes there is an admission charge. You can easily see which ones are free by going to the ticket windows, where the name, room number, and price are listed for each show. Since there are always a number of events taking place, chances are a certain percentage will be free at any one time. Periodically the museum sponsors free showings of its own collection of about 3,000 modern Japanese works.

In the museum's library, you can relax and browse through beautiful art books, some of which illustrate the entire collections of such famous museums as the Hermitage in St. Petersburg, Russia, or the Louvre in Paris. (See ch 13.)

Free sculpture exhibitions are often held in the open-air sculpture garden at the back of the museum. Some of the installed pieces are so substantial that it is hard to imagine they are only temporary. And there are always many free activities in the surrounding Ueno Park. (See ch 3—Ueno Park.)

NOTE: Special "blockbuster"-type exhibitions are held in the Museum Gallery, for which there is a charge. It is closed on Mon.

Hours: 10 AM–5 PM daily. Clsd 3rd Mon (Tues if Mon is a hol), and New Year and museum hols.

Access: A 3-min walk from JR Ueno Stn, Ueno Park Exit (Yamanote and other lines). Walk straight through the park from the main entrance just across from Ueno Stn. It is to the right of the zoo.

TOKYO METROPOLITAN CHILDREN'S HALL

東京都児童会館 （Tokyo-to Jidokaikan）

1–18–24 Shibuya, Shibuya-ku, Tokyo 150–0002

☎ 3409–6361

東京都渋谷区渋谷1-18-24　〒150-0002

This is Tokyo's largest public facility for kids and young people (up to eighteen years)—created to provide a place where

youngsters can learn about science, music, and crafts in a stimulating environment. Children and teenagers can play pianos and other instruments in the music section, and there is an international library where they can read or check out books. There is also an audio-visual room; a space corner; techno-craft, handicraft, and drawing areas; computers to learn on; and even an old Japanese farmhouse to play inside. Special events are offered periodically.

Hours: 9 AM–5 PM (enter by 4:30 PM). 9 AM–6 PM July and Aug (enter by 5:30 PM). Clsd two Mon a month and some irregular days. It is best to call first.

NOTE: Once in a while there may be a very small charge for special materials to make something, but otherwise this place is free.

Access: 3 min from Shibuya Stn, Exit 11 (Hanzomon Line). Walk straight up Meiji-dori from the exit and make a right at the 3rd corner. You will see the hall on the left side of the street at the first traffic light. It is also a 7-min walk from JR Shibuya Stn, East Exit (Yamanote and other lines).

TSUKIJI FISH INFORMATION CENTER AND MUSEUM

おさかな普及センター資料館

（Osakana Fukyu Senta Shiryokan）

6–20–5 Tsukiji, Chuo-ku, Tokyo 104–0045

☎ 3547–8824 (Direct)

東京都中央区築地6-20-5　〒104-0045

This little gray building is almost invisible from the outside, but when you step inside it is a whole different story. Three large tanks in the middle of the room house edible saltwater fish from Japan, and other tanks display tropical fish from various parts of the world. The special temporary exhibitions change every three months and are built around piscine specimens from other countries or around a specific theme. Some past exhibitions have been the fish of Australia (complete with maps and a very rare example of the Queensland Lungfish—a holdover from primitive times), deep-sea fish, flatfish, and fish of the Antarctic.

If you would like to watch a video (there are several by *National Geographic*), someone from the office upstairs can help you. For those seriously interested in studying fish, there is an excellent library on the premises that includes scientific journals in English. If you are planning a trip to the Tsukiji Fish

Market, drop by this nondescript building that proves just how deceiving looks can be. (See ch 3—Tsukiji Fish Market.)

Hours: 10 AM–4 PM Mon–Sat. Clsd Sun, hols, and every 2nd and 4th Wed.

Access:A 7-min walk from Tsukiji Stn, Exit 1 (Hibiya Line). Turn left from the exit and walk to the next corner. Cross the street and walk left down Harumi-dori. At the last small street before the bridge, turn right. This will be a road leading back into the inner market, and the Fish Center is the second building on the left.

WARD MUNICIPAL MUSEUMS

A great number of local ward (*ku*) and city governments have opened historical museums that introduce the history and culture of the area to the public. Check with the nearest ward office to see what it offers.

WATERWORKS MUSEUM

東京都水道歴史館 （Tokyo-to Suido Rekishikan）
    Tokyo-to Suido-Kyoku, 1/2F,
    2–7–1 Hongo, Bunkyo-ku, Tokyo 113–0033
    ☎ 5802–9040 (Office, 3F)
    東京都文京区本郷2-7-1　東京都水道局1/2階　〒113-0033

The history of the Tokyo waterworks from its beginnings in the 1600s under the first Tokugawa shogun is traced at this museum. A small but well-done re-creation of an Edo neighborhood is brought to life by the recorded sounds of vendors shouting, babies crying, and women gossiping around the community washtubs at the end of the street as they wash their clothes in swirling waters. You can stroll through and peek into the model homes for a glimpse of how people lived and worked in Edo times (1600–1868).

A replica of an Edo-period "pipe" used to transport the area's water supply can be seen out back—a 20-m- (65-ft-) long trench dug out of the ground and lined with stones. By stark contrast, a cross-section of a huge, modern 2.9-m- (9.4-ft-) diameter metal pipe illustrates clearly the vast amount of water

A MYRIAD OF MUSEUMS

needed to supply the population of the Tokyo area today. Also on display is a large, elegantly carved lion's head stone fountain (a gift from the City of London in 1906) that was for many years a source of drinking water for the people in the Marunouchi business district of Tokyo. Its twin can still be found in the small park outside of Shinjuku Station's East Exit.

Although the information on all the exhibits in the museum is in Japanese, an English handout covers the main points. An illustrated booklet entitled *Waterworks in Tokyo* explains the Tokyo water system and contains lots of important general information about the city and its environs as well.

Hours: 9:30 AM–4:30 PM Mon–Sun. Clsd New Year hols.

Access: 5 min from JR Ochanomizu Stn, West Exit (Chuo and Sobu lines). Turn right and cross the bridge, then walk left alongside the river to the next light. At the far side of that crossing, cross the street to the right and turn left. Go to the first small street and turn right—the museum is in the second block on the left in the tallest tan building. Also accessible from Ochanomizu Stn, Marunouchi Line.

11

PERFORMANCES
AND
THE ARTS

GAGAKU—ANCIENT IMPERIAL COURT MUSIC AND DANCE
- *Imperial Household Musicians*

NOH, KYOGEN, AND KABUKI
- *National Theater Training Program Performances*

CLASSICAL JAPANESE DANCE
- *Hana no Kai Classical Japanese Dance Group*
- *Nishikawa School of Classical Dance*
- *Nihonbuyo Association*

FOLKLORIC ARTS
- *Japanese Folk Preservation Society Performances*
- *Festa de Nippon*

FLOWER ARRANGING
- *Sogetsu School of Flower Arranging*

WESTERN CLASSICAL MUSIC CONCERTS
- *Hotel Okura Lobby Concerts*
- *Musashino Academia Musicae*
- *Tokyo National University of Fine Arts and Music*

INTRODUCTION

*T*okyo *certainly does not lack for things to do. But ticket prices and attendance fees can put a serious dent in your wallet, limiting the number of events you are able to attend. Yet this doesn't necessarily have to be the case. There are many worthwhile activities that can enliven your intellectual and social calendars—without draining your pocketbook.*

You will no doubt still want to take in your favorite singer or group when they come to town, but if you follow some of the suggestions in this chapter you won't have to stay home for a week or so afterward just to make up for what you spent on the ticket. If you've just laid out some of your hard-earned cash for a pricey Tokyo event, you can balance your budget with a few suggestions from this chapter.

Most of the traditional performing arts listed here can also be seen at Tokyo's shrines and temples during festivals and events. Check the Tourist Information Center's monthly Calendar Events *handout as well as the listings in the English-language publications for details of what each festival offers.*

GAGAKU—ANCIENT IMPERIAL COURT MUSIC AND DANCE

THE IMPERIAL HOUSEHOLD MUSICIANS

宮内庁楽部 (Kunaicho Gakubu)

    c/o Imperial Household Agency (Kunaicho), Music Dept

    1–1 Chiyoda, Chiyoda-ku, Tokyo 100–8111

    ☎ 3213–1111 (In Japanese) or 3201–3331 (Tourist Information Center, for information in English)

    東京都千代田区千代田1-1　宮内庁楽部　〒100-8111

Gagaku, or "Gracious Music Played at the Imperial Court," dates back about one thousand years. It is performed for the public by the emperor's own Imperial Household Musicians each October at the Imperial Court Music Building on the grounds of the palace. The dates are announced in the newspapers (usually in July), and you are asked to send a return postcard (*ofuku-hagaki*) requesting a ticket to the performance. If you don't see the notice and are interested in attending the event, contact the Tourist Information Center in July for details on how to apply. Make sure you get your request in on time (usually by the end of July), for there is a strict deadline. A lottery will be held for ticket distribution and only one ticket per postcard will be issued.

Hours: Performances are held at 10:30 AM and 2 PM on the scheduled days.

Access: Directions will be given with your ticket.

NOH, KYOGEN, AND KABUKI

■ National Theatre Training Program Performances

The National Theatre (Kokuritsu Gekijo) was founded in 1966 for the purpose of preserving and showcasing Japan's traditional performing arts. The theater offers training programs for those interested in becoming professional performers—after they pass an entrance examination. The program's graduation performances of Kabuki, Noh, and Kyogen (traditional comedy) may be attended by the public at no charge at the two locations below.

NATIONAL NOH THEATRE

国立能楽堂 (Kokuritsu Noh Gakudo)

4–18–1 Sendagaya, Shibuya-ku, Tokyo 151–0051

☎ 3423–1331

東京都渋谷区千駄ヶ谷4-18-1　〒151-0051

Noh is Japan's oldest musical-theater form, having originated in the 14th century. The slow-measured, serious drama is sometimes compared to classical Greek theater because of its use of masks, chorus, and classical literature. Elegant brocade costumes are worn, and the lines are chanted in an archaic language no longer used. Kyogen is traditional slapstick comedy-drama that originated about the same time as Noh, and was performed between the scenes of Noh plays. Masks and make-up are not generally used, and everyday clothes from that period are worn at performances, as they were then.

Graduation performances for both are held at the National Noh Theatre in February or March every three years. Actors, musicians, and singers appear. Seating for 600 is available, and no tickets are necessary to attend. (Also see ch 3—Noh Mask Museum, under Little Museums of Sumida-ku.)

Access: A 4-min walk from JR Sendagaya Stn (Sobu Line). From the station's only exit, cross the street, turn to the right and walk until you reach the first traffic signal. Walk left and you will immediately see the theater in front of you.

NATIONAL THEATRE OF JAPAN

国立劇場 (Kokuritsu Gekijo)

4–1 Hayabusacho, Chiyoda-ku, Tokyo 102–8656

☎ 3265–7411

東京都千代田区隼町4-1　〒102-8656

Kabuki is a popular theater form created by and for the common man in 17th-century Edo (Tokyo). The pace is faster than in Noh and plots are more melodramatic. Brightly colored makeup is worn instead of masks, and colorful costumes are donned. Stage mechanisms not found in Noh are used as well, such as trap doors, a revolving stage, and an elevated runway through the audience.

New graduates perform at the Shogekijo (small theater) at the National Theatre in March of every year and in October of every other year. Actors, musicians, and accompanying singers take part. About 550 seats are available, but since Kabuki is very popular, tickets are issued by request. Contact the National Theatre and you will be sent a postcard for admission.

Access: A 5-min walk from Hanzomon Stn, Exit 1 (Hanzomon Line). Turn right from the exit, then make a left at the corner. (There will be arrows on Japanese signs pointing you in the right direction.) When the street ends at the moat (Uchibori-dori) turn right. It is about 1 min down on the right side—a long, dark brown building.

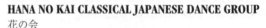

CLASSICAL JAPANESE DANCE

HANA NO KAI CLASSICAL JAPANESE DANCE GROUP
花の会
    1–24–8 Nakacho, Meguro-ku, Tokyo 153–0065
    ☎ 3719–2868 (Leave a message in English and your call will be returned, or send a fax)
    東京都目黒区中町1-24-8　〒153-0065

Fukagawa Edo Museum Auditorium
    深川江戸資料館 （Fukagawa Edo Shiryokan）
    1–3–28 Shirakawa, Koto-ku, Tokyo 135–0021
    ☎ 3630–8625
    東京都江東区白河1-3-28　〒135-0021

Hana no Kai's elegant *kamigata-mai* style of dance is derived from the ancient court dances of Imperial Japan. The members of the group perform in beautiful traditional costume to a variety of music, ranging from slow (*jiuta*) to lively (*nagauta*). Horizontal rather than vertical movement is emphasized in these graceful dances that can be seen twice a year without charge at the Fukagawa Edo Museum Auditorium.

Founded in the mid-18th century by Fuku Yamanouchi, a choreographer for the Kyoto imperial household, the school now has bases in both Kyoto and Tokyo. Its fourth and present headmaster, Yuki Yoshimura, was named an "Intangible Cultural Asset" by the Japanese government in 1985. The group has given a number of performances overseas, including one in the Japanese Tea Garden in San Francisco's Golden Gate Park for its 1994 centennial celebration. They also offer free dance classes (see ch 12).

NOTE: The Fukagawa Edo Museum is a realistic, life-size recreation of an Edo neighborhood that you can wander through and explore. If you wish to visit the museum in conjunction with the free performance, entrance is ¥300 and hours are 10 AM–5 PM daily.

Hours: April performances are noon–4:30 PM (with a shorter version offered in Aug or Sept of each year). An English program is provided.

Access: The Fukagawa Edo Museum Auditorium is a 15-min walk from Monzen Nakacho Stn Exit 3 (Tozai Line). Turn left from the exit, cross the street at the corner and walk left along Kiyosumi-dori for about 15 min. You will walk under a highway and then cross a bridge. At the third traffic light after the bridge, you will see two Edo-style gas lamps at the entrance to a small street on the right. Enter this street—the museum is on the left side at the end of the second block. It is also accessible from Morishita Stn on the Toei Shinjuku Line.

NISHIKAWA SCHOOL OF JAPANESE CLASSICAL DANCE

西川流十世宗家西川扇蔵

(Nishikawa-ryu Jyussei Soke Nishikawa Senzo)

2F, 8 Ichigayadai-machi, Shinjuku-ku, Tokyo 162–0066

☎ 3355–2227

東京都新宿区市ヶ谷台町8　〒162-0066

The Nihonbuyo style of dance is based on kabuki, giving it a totally different flavor from the Kyoto imperial court–style dances. The 300-year-old Nishikawa School is one of the oldest schools of classical dance. Assistant Headmaster Minosuke Nishikawa began studying with his headmaster father, Senzo Nishikawa, when he was just three years old. Fluent in English, he teaches dance to both Japanese and foreign students, and travels to the United States twice a year to give classes at the Japanese-American Cultural Society in San Francisco.

Note: Call the school for the time and location of upcoming performances and recitals. Assistant Headmaster Minosuke Nishikawa will be happy to answer your questions in English. If he is not in, leave your number and he will return your call.

Twenty recitals/performances are held throughout Japan by the students of the school each year—about half of these in Tokyo. Each November they perform at the Shinjuku Bunka Center. Although tickets are sold for this event, Nishikawa (who also dances at the shows and recitals) invites foreign guests to attend for free. Recitals may also be attended at no charge.

NIHONBUYO ASSOCIATION
日本舞踊協会

> Reimei Sky Resitel #210
> 2–18–1 Kachidoki, Chuo-ku, Tokyo 104–0054
> ☎ 3533–6455
> 東京都中央区勝どき2-18-1　レイメイスカイレジテル210号
> 〒104-0054

Fukagawa Edo Museum Auditorium
深川江戸資料館　(Fukagawa Edo Shiryokan)

> 1–3–28 Shirakawa, Koto-ku, Tokyo 135–0021
> ☎ 3630–8625
> 東京都江東区白河1-3-28　〒135-0021

Note: The Fukagawa Edo Museum is a realistic, life-size re-creation of an Edo neighborhood that you can wander through and explore. If you wish to visit the museum in conjunction with the free performance, entrance is ¥300 and hours are 10 AM–5 PM daily.

Since 1992, the Nihonbuyo Association has been inviting non-Japanese to attend their early-November performance at the Fukagawa Edo Museum free of charge. The association prepares a special English lecture and demonstration to accompany this special show each year. Tickets are unnecessary for foreigners—just go. For more information on Nihonbuyo dance, see the earlier entry on the Nishikawa School of Japanese Classical Dance.

Hours: The special performances are held 6:30 PM–8:30 PM the 1st Mon in Nov.

Access: For directions to the Fukagawa Edo Museum Auditorium, see the entry for the Hana no Kai dance group above.

FOLKLORIC ARTS

At the Nihon Seinenkan Hall
JAPANESE FOLK PRESERVATION SOCIETY PERFORMANCES
全国民族芸能大会 （Zenkoku Minzoku Geino Taikai）
FESTA DE NIPPON
全国青年文化祭 （Zenkoku Seinen Bunka-sai）

Nihon Seinenkan Hall
15 Kasumigaoka, Shinjuku-ku, Tokyo 160–0013
☎ 3475–2570 (Mr. Kakeya in simple English)
東京都新宿区霞岳町15　日本青年館ホール　〒160-0013

For those who want a taste of the traditional Japan of the common man, performances of songs, dances, and other folkloric traditions rooted in the various prefectures of the country can be enjoyed at these folk festivals, which can each last from one to three days. Sometimes children and adults are invited to come and participate in the activities taking place on stage, much to the delight of the rest of the audience.

The Japanese Folk Preservation Society was formed to bring together the many small folkloric groups throughout the country. It has been helping to preserve Japan's folk traditions by presenting original folk shows annually for the past forty-five years.

An arts and culture exhibition and open-air stalls selling local products from around Japan accompany the Festa de Nippon, a newly created festival that began in 1995. It is part folk arts and part modern—with the latter featuring well-known singers performing a variety of musical styles. No tickets are needed for either festival. You can just go.

NOTE: For information on the forty-seven prefectures around the country, see ch 15.

Hours: These all-day events are held over a 1–3 day period in Nov of each year. Watch the listings or call the above number (in Japanese) for festival dates.

Access: The Nihon Seinenkan Hall is in Meiji Shrine's Outer Garden, a 7-min walk from Gaienmae Stn Exit 2 (Ginza Line). Turn right from the ticket wicket and go up the stairs. Turn right from the exit, and right again at the corner. Pass the Prince Chichibu Memorial Rugby Ground and the TEPIA Building on the right side. In 3–4 min you will reach a major T-intersection. The hall is on the far left corner and the theater is up the steps along the left side of the building. It is also accessible from JR Sendagaya or Shinanomachi Stn (Sobu Line).

FLOWER ARRANGING (Ikebana)

SOGETSU SCHOOL OF FLOWER ARRANGING

草月会 （Sogetsu-kai）

Sogetsu Kaikan Building

7–2–21 Akasaka, Minato-ku, Tokyo 107–0052

☎ 3408–1126 (Ask for Overseas Affairs Dept)

東京都港区赤坂7-2-21　草月会館ビル　〒107-0052

The world-famous Sogetsu School of Flower Arranging will allow you to observe a class (in English or Japanese) at no charge. Call one day in advance to make a reservation. If you go, take a few moments to enjoy the stone garden (*sekitei*) in the lobby of the building. It was designed by the renowned artist Isamu Noguchi.

NOTE: If you would like to try your hand at making an arrangement, Sogetsu also offers a one-time lesson for a fee (about ¥5,000).

Hours: Classes are given in English 10 AM–noon the first four Mon of each month, and in Japanese three times a day (10 AM, 1:30 PM, and 6 PM) the first three Tues and Thurs of each month. No classes on hols and no English classes offered in Aug.

Access: A 5-min walk from Aoyama-itchome Stn (Ginza or Hanzomon lines). Take Exit 3 for Minami Aoyama. Turn right from the exit and right again at the corner. Walk along Aoyama-dori until you reach a big mirrored building just past the Canadian Embassy. This is the Sogetsu Kaikan Building.

WESTERN CLASSICAL MUSIC CONCERTS

HOTEL OKURA LOBBY CONCERTS

ホテル オオクラ ロビー コンサート

Main Building, 5F

2–10–4 Toranomon, Minato-ku, Tokyo 105–8416

☎ 3582–0111

東京都港区虎ノ門2-10-4　〒105-8416

Hotel Okura presents a free chamber music concert in the lobby of its main building on the twenty-fifth day of each month. The music of such composers as Wolfgang Mozart and Franz Haydn is performed by musicians from the New Japan Philharmonic Orchestra and the Japan Chamber Orchestra at these monthly mini-concerts. English programs are available, and free champagne is served to attendees.

The concerts were started in 1987 to commemorate the hotel's twenty-fifth anniversary, and have since become a tradition.

Hours: The concerts begin at 6 PM and last for about 30 min.

Access: A 6-min walk from Toranomon Stn, Exit 3 (Ginza Line). Walk straight out from the exit and follow the sidewalk as it curves to the left. (Don't cross the street here.) Continue walking for about 5 min until the road ends at a T-crossing at the Shin Nikko Building. Turn right and the next building on the left side will be the Hotel Okura. Take the elevator up to the lobby on the 5F.

MUSASHINO ACADEMIA MUSICAE

武蔵野音楽大学 （Musashino Ongaku Daigaku）

1–13–1 Hazawa, Nerima-ku, Tokyo 176–8521

☎ 3992–1120—Performance Department (English speaker usually available)

東京都練馬区羽沢1-13-1　〒176-8521

The Musashino Academia Musicae sponsors about twenty free classical music concerts, recitals, and talks each year. They are presented by both Japanese and international musicians as a public service. Performances are given by individuals and string quartets, and sometimes chamber music is played. Call for information regarding upcoming events and/or a Japanese schedule.

NOTE: The school also houses a fantastic museum of musical instruments from around the world. If you are a music lover and can possibly see it—by all means, do! (See ch 10 for details.)

Access: A 5-min walk from Ekoda Stn, North Exit (Seibu Ikebukuro Line). Exit the station via the steps on the left side. Walk to the corner and turn right (at the shrine). In a few minutes you will see a big white building with unusual geometric-shaped windows on the far left corner. Turn left here to reach the entrance to the campus. The staff at the front information window will direct you to the museum.

TOKYO NATIONAL UNIVERSITY OF FINE ARTS AND MUSIC

東京芸術大学 （Tokyo Geijutsu Daigaku）

12–8 Ueno Koen, Taito-ku, Tokyo 110–0007

☎ 5685–7673/7700 (Music Department)

東京都台東区上野公園1-2-8　〒110-0007

Free concerts are also offered by the Tokyo National University of Fine Arts and Music. This highly ranked school has turned out some of the most creative musical talents of Japan, including the popular Ryuichi Sakamoto, who is perhaps most well-known for his musical scores for the films *The Last Emperor* and *Little Buddha*.

NOTE: Ueno Park itself contains numerous other free attractions (see ch 3), and the school has its own art museum on the campus (see University Museums in ch 10).

Between mid-May and mid-July each year the school presents free Thursday morning classical music concerts performed by the Geidai Philharmonic Orchestra, which is made up of the school's top students. No tickets are needed. You can just go. In addition, student concerts are performed in May/June and again in October/November, and graduation performances are held in December and January of each year.

Hours: The Thurs morning concerts are held at 11 AM in Dairoku Hall in Building No. 4. Call (in Japanese) for dates and location of other events.

Access: A 10-min walk from JR Ueno Stn, Ueno Park Exit (Yamanote and other lines). Turn right from the exit and walk to the traffic light. Turn left and walk past the National Museum to the second light. Enter the campus gate on the right. The guard at the gate can help you to find the building.

12

LECTURES, MEETINGS, CLASSES, AND EDUCATIONAL EVENTS

TALKS ON ASIA AND RELATED INTERNATIONAL MATTERS

- *Asiatic Society of Japan*
- *Temple University Japan (Institute for Pacific Rim Studies)*
- *United Nations University—Public Forums and Meetings*
- *The* Nikkei Weekly *Special Forums*
- *Tokyo Union Church Women's Society*
- *Tokyo Unitarian Fellowship Meetings*

JAPANESE RELIGIOUS PERSPECTIVES

- Buddhism
- Shinto

LEARNING TO MEDITATE

- *Brahma Kumaris Raja Yoga Center*

JAPANESE CLASSICAL DANCE LESSONS

- *Hana no Kai*

ACTING CLASSES

- *The Light Company*

POETRY WORKSHOPS

- *Eri Hara's Poetry Workshops*

INSTRUCTION IN THE JAPANESE LANGUAGE

- *Language Exchange Opportunities*
- *Ward Offices and International Friendship Associations*
- *Tokyo Volunteer Center*

VARIOUS CLASSES AND EVENTS

- *International Friendship Associations*
- *Tokyo Metropolitan Foundation for History and Culture*

INTRODUCTION

A number of organizations in Tokyo host free talks on Japan and Asia-related topics—good news for those interested in learning more about Japan (and Asia in general). Subject matter ranges from folklore and religion to politics and business.

Free classes and workshops are offered, too. You can learn how to write poetry, attain harmony through meditation, and execute the graceful steps of classical Japanese dance. You can even take basic Japanese lessons! Yes, Tokyo offers many free opportunities to learn about Japan, its traditions, and its position in the world today. All you have to do is attend what is already out there waiting for you.

TALKS ON ASIA AND RELATED INTERNATIONAL MATTERS

ASIATIC SOCIETY OF JAPAN

アジアティック ソサエティ オブ ジャパン

OAG Haus Auditorium, 1F
7–5–56 Akasaka, Minato-ku, Tokyo 107–0052
☎ 3586–1548. Fax: 5572–6269
東京都港区赤坂7-5-56　OAGハウス1階　〒107-0052

Established in 1872, the Asiatic Society of Japan offers monthly lectures by distinguished speakers. HIH the Crown Prince, ambassadors from various countries, and college professors are among those who have made presentations at these meetings. Afterward the talks are published by the society and distributed to libraries around the world. Some recent topics have been the influence of Japanese kabuki theater on the films of Russian film director Sergei M. Eisenstein and a talk on "Hannah Riddell, an Englishwoman in Japan," by Lady Boyd, wife of the British ambassador to Japan.

Note: The society assures us that there is no compulsory fee for the meeting, but a ¥1,000 contribution to the Asiatic Society may be left at the door if you wish.

Hours: Meetings are generally held at 6:30 PM the 2nd Mon of each month (except during July and Aug) and are open to the public. Sometimes they are held at other locations, so it is best to check first if you have not seen an announcement.

Access: A 5-min walk from Aoyama-ichome Stn, Exit 3 (Ginza and Hanzomon lines). Turn right from the exit, and right again at the corner. Walk straight down Aoyama-dori until you reach the big mirrored Sogetsu Kaikan Building. The OAG Haus is behind it and can be reached via the small street alongside it.

TEMPLE UNIVERSITY JAPAN

テンプル大学ジャパン

Institute for Pacific Rim Studies (IPRS)
2–8–12 Minami Azabu, Minato-ku, Tokyo 106–0047
☎ 5441–9840. Fax: 5441–9822
東京都港区南麻布2-8-12　〒106-0047

Temple University Japan (TUJ) offers a Wednesday Evening Lecture Series in English—free of charge to the public. A wide range of subjects dealing with Asia and the Pacific Rim are covered at the talks, which take place about twelve times each year. Past topics have included art, technology, the environment, politics, security matters, and health issues. Contact Jon Dalrymple at the above numbers for information on current lectures, reservations, and directions to the campus. TUJ is the largest branch of an American university represented in Japan, with approximately 1,700 students.

Hours: Lectures generally begin at 6:30 PM.

Access: Maps and directions to Temple University Japan's Minami Azabu campus are available from the numbers listed above.

UNITED NATIONS UNIVERSITY

国連大学 （Kokuren Daigaku）

United Nations University Headquarters Building
5–53–70 Jingumae, Shibuya-ku, Tokyo 150–0001
☎ 5467–1243/1246 (Public Affairs Section)
東京都渋谷区神宮前5-53-70　国連大学本部ビル　〒150-0001

The United Nations University sponsors a number of open forums, symposia, and meetings each year to which the public is invited free of charge. They are either conducted in English or simultaneous English interpretation is provided. Topics generally deal with matters of international significance such as "Human Rights and NGO's," "Symposium on the United Nations: Its Past and Future," and "Fifty Years Later: The Second World War and Japanese Historical Memory in a Comparative Perspective." Watch listings in the foreign-language publications for upcoming events.

Hours: Hours and dates vary according to the event.

Access: 5 min from Omotesando Stn, Exit B2 (Ginza, Hanzomon, and Chiyoda lines). Walk straight down Aoyama-dori past Kinokuniya Supermarket and Citibank. The United Nations University is on the right side of the street across from Aoyama Gakuen University.

THE *NIKKEI WEEKLY* SPECIAL FORUMS
日経ウィークリー スペシャル フォーラム

> Nikkei Hall, Nihon Keizai Shinbun Headquarters Building, 8F
> 1–9–5 Otemachi, Chiyoda-ku, Tokyo 100–8066
> ☎ 5255–2164. Fax: 5255–2678 (International Sales Department)
> 東京都千代田区大手町1-9-5　日本経済新聞本社ビル8階
> 日経ホール　〒100-8066

The *Nikkei Weekly* English-language business newspaper sponsors special forums once or twice a year in May/June and October/November, either in English or with simultaneous English interpretation. Japanese and international business/politics are explored, as in two recent offerings, "Business Opportunities in Asia: How to Deal with China" and "Japan's Politics and Diplomacy." The forums are free, but reservations are needed to guarantee a seat. So if you don't see an announcement in the English-language newspapers, contact the *Nikkei Weekly* at the above numbers (in English or Japanese) for information on upcoming forums.

Hours: Approximately 1:30 PM–3:30 PM.

Access: The forums are usually held in the Nikkei Hall at the newspaper's headquarters, which is located in front of Otemachi Stn, Exit A1 (various subway lines).

TOKYO UNION CHURCH WOMEN'S SOCIETY
東京ユニオン チャーチ ウィメンズ ソサエティ

> Tokyo Union Church
> 5–7–7 Jingumae, Shibuya-ku, Tokyo 150–0001
> ☎ 3400–0942 (10 am–2 pm Mon–Fri)
> 東京都渋谷区神宮前5-7-7　東京ユニオン チャーチ内　〒150-0001

The Tokyo Union Church Women's Society offers free monthly talks on subjects of cross-cultural interest. Past programs have included the "Japanese Mass Media" by Hisanori Isomura, journalist and former general managing director of NHK (the Japan Broadcasting Company); "Sumo Wrestling" by Doreen Simmons, sumo TV commentator and columnist; and "Women in

Crisis," a forum of counselors from three charities that offer aid to abused women (and which are also supported by the Women's Society).

Hours: 10:30 AM–noon the 1st Thurs of each month Sept–June.

Access: 2 min from Omotesando Stn, Exit A1 (Hanzomon, Ginza, and Chiyoda lines). The church is straight out the exit on the left side of Omotesando.

TOKYO UNITARIAN FELLOWSHIP

東京ユニタリアン フェロウシップ

International House of Japan (Kokusai Bunka Kaikan)
5–11–16 Roppongi, Minato-ku, Tokyo 106–0032
☎ 3392–2227 Mary Louise Robbins
東京都港区六本木5-11-16　国際文化会館内　〒106-0032

These once-a-month informal gatherings consist of stimulating round-table talks by university professors and other experts. An interesting variety of subjects are covered, some past ones being "The Theology of Shinto," "The Golden Age of China: Tang Dynasty," and "Work Songs through the Ages." The eclectic nature of the group is based on their belief in "the individual's free search for truth and of mutually sharing one's seeking and finding." (Also see ch 8.)

NOTE: Although there is no charge for the meeting, it is requested that you help defray the cost of the room by leaving a contribution in the basket by the door.

Hours: 3 PM on the 2nd Sun of each month, Oct–June (no meetings July, Aug, or Sept).

Access: 7 min from Roppongi Stn, Exit 3 (Hibiya Line). Make a right from the station, and another right along the main street. At the far end of the Roi Building, turn right and walk down the hill. International House is about halfway down on the right side.

JAPANESE RELIGIOUS PERSPECTIVES

■ Buddhism

INTERNATIONAL BUDDHIST ASSOCIATION (IBA)

IBA 英語法座 （IBA Eigo Hoza）

Tsukiji Honganji Temple

3–15–1 Tsukiji, Chuo-ku, Tokyo 104–8435

☎ 3541–1131 (Tsukiji Honganji Temple, IBA Section, in Japanese). Fax: 3541–7071 (IBA, in English)

東京都中央区築地3-15-1　築地本願寺　〒104-8435

Yes, you can attend a real Buddhist service conducted in English, complete with chants, songs, and talks on various aspects of Buddhism—followed by a question-and-answer period. The International Buddhist Association (IBA) holds these services once a month at Tsukiji temple (see ch 8), where it has been based since its founding in 1949. Talks are generally given by ministers affiliated with the IBA, but sometimes guest speakers are invited. If you would like more information, please send a fax to the above number addressed to The International Buddhist Association.

Hours: 5:30 PM–7 PM the final Sat of each month (except Aug).

Access: Tsukiji temple is just outside Tsukiji Stn, Exit 1 (Hibiya Line). Meetings are held in the building to the far right of the main temple (Dai Ichi Dendo Kaikan) as you enter the compound. There will be signs in English inside directing you to the meeting room.

RISSHO KOSEI-KAI

立正佼成会

2–11–1 Wada, Suginami-ku, Tokyo 166–0012

☎ 3383–1111, 5341–1124 (Overseas Mission Section).

Fax: 5341–1224

東京都杉並区和田2-11-1　立正佼成会海外布教課　〒166-0012

Dharma seminars, or free lectures in English, Korean, or Japanese covering various aspects of Buddhism and how to apply its teachings to your daily life, are offered by the Rissho Kosei-kai (see ch 8).

Hours: Offered four times each year on Sun afternoons. Call for schedule.
Access: They will supply you with a map to the seminar.

THE TIBET HOUSE
チベット ハウス

> No. 5 Hayama Building, 5F
> 5–11–30 Shinjuku, Shinjuku-ku, Tokyo 160–0022
> ☎ 3353–4094
> 東京都新宿区新宿5-11-30　第5葉山ビル5階　〒160-0022

The Tibet House has an excellent library. In addition to books on Tibet and Tibetan Buddhism, good general books on Buddhism such as *The Buddhist Handbook: A Complete Guide to Buddhist Schools, Teaching, Practice, and History*, by John Snelling; and *The Teachings of Buddha* (published by the Buddhist Promoting Foundation) can be found here. Books can be read at tables or borrowed for up to a week. (See ch 13 for hours and access.)

Note: The center also offers weekly classes in English on Tibetan Buddhist Studies for a ¥1,500 donation per lesson.

■ Shinto

THE INTERNATIONAL SHINTO FOUNDATION
神道国際学会　（Shinto Kokusai Gakkai）

> 6–30–3 Hirai, Edogawa-ku, Tokyo 132–0035
> ☎ 3610–3975 (Phone and Fax)
> 東京都江戸川区平井6-30-3　〒132-0035
> ✐ http://www.shinto.org. E-mail to shinto@alpha-web.or.jp

This organization was formed in 1994 to spread an understanding of Shinto (which has often been misunderstood due to a lack of available information) throughout the world. In 1996 they opened a center at the United Nations Plaza in New York.

They offer free seminars on topics relating to Shinto, which are bilingual and include both Japanese and foreign speakers.

LECTURES,
CLASSES, AND
EDUCATION

For information on upcoming seminars or publications based on previous talks, fax your mailing address (English or Japanese) to the above number.

Hours: Hours are irregular, so it is best to send questions by fax or e-mail and someone will get back to you.

THE ASSOCIATION OF SHINTO SHRINES

神社本庁 （Jinja-Honcho）

    1–1–2 Yoyogi, Shibuya-ku, Tokyo 151–0053

    ☎ 3379–8016 (International Dept on Tues and Thurs)

    東京都渋谷区代々木1-1-2　〒151-0053

The Association of Shinto Shrines has put together beautifully illustrated booklets and pamphlets that explain the basics of Shinto in English. They will send these to you free of charge on request.

Hours: 9 AM–5 PM Mon–Fri, 9 AM–noon Sat. Clsd Sun and national hols.

KOKUGAKUIN UNIVERSITY SHINTO MUSEUM

国学院大学神道資料館

（Kokugakuin Daigaku Shinto Shiryokan）

    Tokiwamatsu No. 3 Building, 1F

    4–10–28 Higashi, Shibuya-ku, Tokyo 150–8440

    ☎ 5466–0210

    東京都渋谷区東4-10-28　常盤3号館ビル1階　〒150-8440

NOTE: There are not many English books available on the subject, but *Shinto: The Kami Way* by Dr. Sokyo Ono is an excellent overall introduction to Shinto.

This museum contains items connected with Shinto and its rites, rituals, and history. (See ch 10—University Museums for details.)

LEARN TO MEDITATE

BRAHMA KUMARIS RAJA YOGA CENTER

ブラハム クマリス ラジャ ヨガセンター

Harmony House, 2F

c/o Meguro, 201, 14–10 Sarugakucho, Shibuya-ku, Tokyo 150

☎ 5458–8065 (Lee James)

東京都渋谷区猿楽町14-10目黒方201　〒150

Have you been meaning to learn to meditate, but just haven't gotten around to it? Well, you will be happy to hear that free meditation lessons are available from the Brahma Kumaris Raja Yoga Center, an organization affiliated with the United Nations. An initial series of five, one-hour introductory classes based on ancient Indian practices are taught in English by Australian Lee James, who has been practicing and teaching with the center for the past thirteen years. After finishing the introductory lessons, you can join the regular meditation sessions, which are held at various times, and are also free of charge. Call for hours and map.

Access: A 3-to-5-min walk from Daikanyama Stn (Toyoko Line).

JAPANESE CLASSICAL DANCE LESSONS

HANA NO KAI

花の会

1–24–8 Nakacho, Meguro-ku, Tokyo 153

☎ 3719–2868 (Leave a message in English or send a fax)

東京都目黒区中町1-24-8　〒153

Have you ever watched a traditional Japanese dance performance and admired the grace and elegance of the dancers as they appeared to slide effortlessly across the floor? Well now you

can learn some of their secrets at a free lesson given in the art of *kamigata-mai*. Developed in Kyoto during the Edo period (1600–1868) by a choreographer of the imperial court, this slow, graceful dance style is similar to Japanese court dancing and is studied by both men and women. You will be taught basic movements such as how to sit, walk, and use your fan expressively. And you can easily learn a short and popular traditional dance entitled "*Takasago*," which is often performed on auspicious occasions.

Master Yuka Yoshimura teaches in a "mirror image" style, while her English-speaking assistants offer individual guidance. If you would like to take a lesson, you are asked to bring a pair of white socks or Japanese *tabi* and, if possible, a *yukata* (cotton kimono). Fans are supplied.

Hana no Kai is an organization of traditional Japanese dancers who offer free dance lessons and performances twice a year to promote their art (see ch 11). The class is taught at a Buddhist temple down one of Tokyo's tiny back streets, leaving no doubt in your mind that you are having a truly Japanese experience.

NOTE: If you wish to continue studying, it is possible to join a regular Sat afternoon class that meets twice a month (details and cost are available from Hana no Kai).

Hours: The free dance class is held 2:30 PM–4 PM on a Sat afternoon in March, June, Sept, and Dec. Special times can be arranged for groups of ten or more.

Access: The Yotsuya Shinjoin temple is a 5-min walk from Yotsuya Stn (JR Chuo or Sobu lines or Marunouchi Subway Line). A map will be sent to you if you plan to attend.

ACTING CLASSES

THE LIGHT COMPANY
ライト カンパニー
Fukushi Center
☎ 5458–8065 (Lee James)

Australian actor Lee James founded "The Light Company" in Tokyo in 1995. The international theater group has already performed in several shows both locally and overseas, including the popular Edinburgh Festival in Scotland. Lee James is a graduate of the National Institute of Dramatic Art in Australia, where he worked in TV, film, dance theater, and Shakespeare before coming to Japan.

He has opened his company's weekly acting workshops to the public free-of-charge. The classes usually include improvisation, singing, intoning (voice exercises), moving, dancing, and script study. When asked why he is offering his classes to participants other than his regular company members, he simply replies, "I don't have an answer." If you are interested in partaking of this great opportunity, please contact Lee James at the above number for details and directions.

Hours: 6 PM–9 PM most Wed evenings.
Access: 8 min from Toritsu Daigaku Stn (Toyoko Line). Lee will furnish a map upon request.

POETRY WORKSHOPS

ERI HARA'S POETRY WORKSHOPS
原恵理のポエトリー ワークショップ
　　Tokyo Women's Plaza, 1F Lobby
　　5–53–67 Jingumae, Shibuya-ku, Tokyo 150–0001
　　☎ 044–953–8106 (Eri Hara),
　　　5467–1711 (Tokyo Women's Plaza)
　　東京都渋谷区神宮前5-53-67　東京ウィメンズ プラザ1階
　　〒150-0001

One Sunday each month lovers of poetry get together to share their thoughts and their compositions in English, either orally or in written form—your choice.

The monthly workshops are organized by Eri Hara, who began writing poetry in New York City. The idea of the workshop

LECTURES,
CLASSES, AND
EDUCATION

was born from her desire to re-create the same "spontaneous, friendly, and creative atmosphere" that she experienced while living in the Big Apple. She feels that writing poetry should not be particularly difficult, and should not be the exclusive realm of professional writers. It should be for everyone who wants to express themselves.

Hours: 1:30 PM–4/5 PM one Sun each month.

Access: 5 min from Omotesando Stn, Exit B2 (Ginza, Hanzomon, and Chiyoda lines). Walk straight down Aoyama-dori past Kinokuniya Supermarket and Citibank. The Tokyo Women's Plaza is at the end of the passageway just before the United Nations University Building, at street level.

INSTRUCTION IN THE JAPANESE LANGUAGE

LANGUAGE EXCHANGE OPPORTUNITIES

A great way to learn Japanese is through language exchange. What this means is that you and another person get together and teach each other your native tongues. That way, the lessons end up being free for both of you. It is a pretty good deal, considering how expensive language instruction can be. Check *Tokyo Classified's* weekly "Language Exchange" column as well as the bulletin boards at the supermarkets, churches, and other places where the foreign population congregates. See Bulletin Boards and Shopping Services in ch 1.

WARD OFFICES AND INTERNATIONAL FRIENDSHIP ASSOCIATIONS

Many of Tokyo's ward (*ku*) offices and International Friendship Associations offer free classes in the Japanese language, with just a small fee charged for study materials. (See International Friendship Associations below for details on their programs.)

TOKYO VOLUNTEER CENTER

東京ボランティア センター

Central Plaza Building, 10F

1–1 Kaguragashi, Shinjuku-ku, Tokyo 162–0823

☎ 3235–1171 Ms. Kawamura and Ms. Sato speak English

東京都新宿区神楽河岸1-1　セントラル プラザ10階　〒162-0823

The Tokyo Volunteer Center maintains a listing of volunteers who will teach the Japanese language to non-Japanese for free. Phone or stop by for information.

Hours: 9 AM–8 PM wkdys, 9 AM–5 PM Sat. Clsd Sun.

Access: Next door to JR Iidabashi Stn, West Exit (Sobu Line). Cross bridge to the right. You will immediately see Fuji Bank on the 1F of a 20-story building (Central Plaza) next to the station. The center is on the 10F. From Iidabashi subway stn (Tozai, Yurakucho, and Nanboku lines), Exit B2b will bring you directly inside the building.

VARIOUS CLASSES AND EVENTS

INTERNATIONAL FRIENDSHIP ASSOCIATIONS

A number of organizations, including Tokyo's ward (*ku*) and city offices, have formed International Friendship Associations or Cultural Exchange Programs. Their purpose is to sponsor events and classes that offer cultural insights into Japan and make living in Tokyo easier for non-Japanese residents. Their offerings might include language classes, local tours, or events intended to kindle an interest in specific Japanese arts such as cooking, dance, or haiku poetry. Check with your local ward office and read the notices in the foreign-language publications for current offerings of the various associations. If the area in which you live doesn't offer such a program, another area's association might be willing to "adopt" you.

NOTE: Many of the events are free, but some ask a very small fee to cover material expenses.

LECTURES, CLASSES, AND EDUCATION

TOKYO METROPOLITAN FOUNDATION FOR
HISTORY AND CULTURE

東京都歴史文化財団 （Tokyo-to Rekishi Bunka Zaidan）
c/o Teien Bijutsukan (Teien Art Museum), 5–21–9
Shiroganedai, Minato-ku, Tokyo 108–0071
☎ 3443–0020. Fax: 3443–3227
東京都港区白金台5-21-9　東京都庭園美術館内　〒108-0071

This foundation presents a free talk and performance for foreign residents of Tokyo each year. A recent event was "Back to Edo Street," a Japanese vaudeville show held at the Edo Tokyo Museum's auditorium. It featured an English lecture on the traditional Japanese arts still alive today, followed by a performance featuring these arts against the backdrop of a typical Edo street scene. One highlight was the "Kuruma Ningyo of Hachioji," during which puppeteers operating the large dolls from within zoomed around the stage on wheels attached to the underside of their puppets.

Dates, times, and venues vary, so watch for information about their annual event (usually in March, but not always) in the foreign-language publications.

13

FREE READS
AND
OTHER GREAT
RESOURCES

LIBRARIES AND READING ROOMS

General Libraries

- *American Center Reference Service*
- *Asia-Pacific Culture Center for UNESCO*
- *Australia-Japan Foundation Library*
- *British Council Library and Information Center*
- *Canadian Embassy Research and Information Center*
- *Hibiya Library*
- *Institute of Developing Economies (IDE) Library*
- *Japan Foundation Library*
- *Japan Foundation Asia Center Library*
- *JETRO Library* (Trade and Investment)
- *National Diet Library*
- *Tokyo Metropolitan Central Library*
- *Toyo Bunko* (Oriental Studies Library)
- *United Nations Information Centre*
- *World Magazine Gallery*

Art and Music Libraries

- *Japan Traditional Craft Center Library*
- *Tokyo Metropolitan Art Museum Reading Room*
- *Tokyo Metropolitan Festival Hall Music Library and Listening Room*

Small, Specialized Libraries

- *Bible Library*—Some Very Old Bibles and Related Material
- *Bicycle Culture Center*—Bicycle and Cycling Information
- *Edo-Tokyo Museum A/V Library*—Edo Culture
- *Japan Ecology Center*—Environment, Health, and Food Safety
- *Saké Plaza*—Saké, Wines, and Whiskeys
- *Library Aqua* —Water, Design, and Architecture
- *National Film Center Library*—Film-related publications
- *Plaza Equus*—Information on Horses
- *TEPIA Foundation Library*—State-of-the-Art Technology
- *Tibet House*—Buddhism and Tibetan Culture
- *Tokyo Gas Ginza Pocket Park*—Architecture
- *TOTO Recipe*—Food and Cooking

Other Language Libraries

FRENCH

    Bibliothèque de la Maison Franco-Japonaise

    Institut Franco-Japonais de Tokyo "Mediathèque"

GERMAN

    Goethe Institute Tokyo

ITALIAN

    Istituto Italiano di Cultura—Tokyo

SPANISH

    Centro de Estudios Hispanicos—Universidad Sofia

EMBASSY LIBRARIES

BROWSING IN FOREIGN-LANGUAGE BOOKSTORES

- *Aoyama Book Center* (Roppongi, Aoyama)
- *Biblos Bookstore* (Takadanobaba)
- *Book Club Kai* (Aoyama)
- *Books Sanseido* (Kanda)
- *Christian Literature Crusade/CLC Bookstore* (Ochanomizu)
- *Fiona Bookstore* (Jiyugaoka)
- *Good Day Books* (Ebisu)
- *Jena* (Ginza)
- *Kinokuniya Bookstore* (Shinjuku, Shibuya)
- *Laox Computer Kan* (Akihabara)
- *Maruzen* (Nihonbashi, Hibiya, Ochanomizu, Bunkamura)
- *National Azabu Supermarket Bookstore* (Hiroo)
- *On Sundays* (Aoyama)
- *Taiseido Bookstore* (Shibuya)
- *Tower Records Bookstore* (Shibuya)
- *Yaesu Book Center* (Tokyo Station)
- *Used Bookstores* (Kanda)

INTRODUCTION

In the fast-paced world in which we live today, it is very easy to get caught up in the day-to-day things necessary for survival. Sometimes it's a good idea to take a break and go somewhere where we can leave life's stresses far behind. I have found that libraries and reading rooms are perfect places to do this. Unfortunately, many of us stop going to libraries when we finish our formal schooling. But there they remain for us, great sources of information and knowledge—and entertainment too.

Libraries today contain a huge volume of material in many forms—audio tapes, videos, CD-ROMs, laser disks, and computer data banks—to name a few. But let us not forget about books. In this "age of communication," with electronic information constantly clamoring for our attention, we sometimes tend to forget that we have an imagination capable of creating its own images. Books can help us to stretch those underused creative impulses and give us new perspectives on life. So rediscover libraries and reading rooms. You will be glad you did.

By extension, visiting a bookstore can be an equally rewarding experience, so I have included a list of foreign-language bookstores in Tokyo for your browsing pleasure. And who knows? You might find that great read you've been looking for.

LIBRARIES AND READING ROOMS

GENERAL LIBRARIES

AMERICAN CENTER REFERENCE SERVICE

アメリカン センター資料室 （Amerikan Senta Shiryoshitsu）

ABC Kaikan Building, 11F

2–6–3 Shiba Koen, Minato-ku, Tokyo 105–0011

☎ 3436–0901

東京都港区芝公園2-6-3　ABC会館11階　〒105-0011

Reference Library. About 8,000 publications (books, magazines, newspapers) dealing with the United States and U.S.-Japan relations are housed here. They also have a large collection of videos with five viewing booths. Approximately 450 periodicals are available on ProQuest "image-ROM."

Hours: 10:30 AM–6:30 PM Mon–Fri. Clsd wknds and both Japanese and American hols.

Access: A 3-min walk from Shiba Koen Stn, Exit A3 (Mita Line). Turn and walk in the opposite direction along Hibiya-dori. The ABC Building is on the near right corner of the second street. (There is a big ABC sign on the top of the building.)

ASIA-PACIFIC CULTURE CENTER FOR UNESCO
(UNESCO Asia Culture Center Library)

ユネスコ アジア文化センター ライブラリー

（UNESCO Ajia Bunka Senta Raiburari）

Japan Publishers' Building, 3F

6 Fukuromachi, Shinjuku-ku, Tokyo 162–0828

☎ 3269–4446

東京都新宿区袋町6　日本出版会館3階　〒162-0828

Lending Library. About 27,000 picture books (for children and adults) containing information on more than twenty Asia-Pacific countries are housed here. Most books are in English, with some in Japanese or in the language of the country of origin. Video tapes, cassettes, records, and CDs on the Asia-Pacific area are also available.

FREE READS
AND OTHER
GREAT RESOURCES

Hours: 10 AM–5 PM Mon–Fri. Clsd on wknds and hols, and April 28 (the anniversary of the center).

Access: About 8 min from JR Iidabashi Stn, West Exit (Sobu Line). Cross the bridge to the right and walk straight up Kagurazaka shoppin_ .treet for about 5 min. After you pass the Bishamonten temple on your left, turn left (a bookstore will be on the corner). The center is about 3 min up this street on the right side, just after the bend in the road. It is also accessible via Iidabashi subway stn (Tozai, Yurakucho, and Nanboku lines).

AUSTRALIA-JAPAN FOUNDATION LIBRARY

豪日交流基金オーストラリア図書館
（Gonichi Koryu Kikin Osutoraria Toshokan）
    Australian Embassy Chancery, 1F
    2–1–14 Mita, Minato-ku, Tokyo 108–0073
    ☎ 5232–4005
    東京都港区三田2-1-14　オーストラリア大使館1階　〒108-0073

Lending Library. The library stocks about 8,000 books dealing with Australia and Australia-Japan relationships. About 200 magazines and periodicals are available, and a few newspapers as well. Most of the material is in English, with some in Japanese. Materials can be borrowed at no charge.

Hours: 10 AM–5:30 PM Mon–Fri. Clsd wknds and hols.

Access: The library is located inside the Australian Embassy. Take the No. 6 bus that runs between Shinbashi and Shibuya Stn from the East Exit of Shibuya Stn. Get off at the Ninohashi stop and walk across the bridge under the highway. Continue up the hill for about 3 min and you will see the embassy on the right side. It is also about a 15-min walk from Shiba Koen Stn (Mita Line).

BRITISH COUNCIL LIBRARY AND INFORMATION CENTER

ブリティッシュ カウンシル図書館
    Kenkyusha Eigo Center Building, 1F
    1–2 Kagurazaka, Shinjuku-ku, Tokyo 162–0825
    ☎ 3235–8031
    東京都新宿区神楽坂1-2　研究社英語センタービル1階
    〒162-0825

Reference Library (lends to members). The library contains 10,000 publications from Great Britain. Books, periodicals, newspapers, CDs, and both audio tapes and videotapes dealing with the United Kingdom are available. All material is in English.

NOTE: Users must be 18 years of age or older.

Hours: 10 AM–8 PM Mon–Fri. Clsd wknds and both Japanese and British hols.

Access: 4 min from JR Iidabashi Stn, West Exit (Sobu Line). Walk right across the bridge from the exit and cross at the traffic signal. Turn left and walk along Sotobori-dori toward Ichigaya. The library is on the right side, just after the second small street. Also accessible by Iidabashi subway stn (Tozai, Yurakucho, and Nanboku lines).

CANADIAN EMBASSY RESEARCH AND INFORMATION CENTER

カナダ大使館図書館 （Kanada Taishikan Toshokan）

Canadian Embassy, B2

7–3–38 Akasaka, Minato-ku, Tokyo 107–0052

☎ 3408–2101

東京都港区赤坂7-3-38　カナダ大使館地下2階　〒107-0052

Lending Library. Approximately 15,000 books relating to Canada are kept here. Most are in English. Newspapers, magazines, and 400 videos are available also. It is possible to borrow books and videos.

Hours: 10 AM–12:30 PM and 1:30 PM–4 PM Mon–Fri. Clsd wknds and hols.

Access: 5 min from Aoyama-itchome Stn (Ginza and Hanzomon lines). Take Exit 3 for Minami Aoyama. Make a right and go to the corner. Turn right and walk along Aoyama-dori until you reach the Canadian Embassy. The library is in the embassy.

HIBIYA LIBRARY

日比谷図書館 （Hibiya Toshokan）

1–4 Hibiya Koen, Chiyoda-ku, Tokyo 100–0012

☎ 3502–0101

東京都千代田区日比谷公園1-4　〒100-0012

Lending Library. Conveniently situated in lovely Hibiya Park, the Hibiya Library contains nearly 5,000 books, 40 magazines, and 10 newspapers in foreign languages (mostly English). If you are living, working, or going to school in Tokyo, you can borrow books and other things such as records, CDs, and audio tapes. Bring your ID to get a library card. A great time-saving copy service is available for a fee—drop things off to be copied and pick them up later. You can even borrow a book, sit in the park, and read it while you wait for the copying to be done.

Hours: 10 AM–8 PM wkdys, 10 AM–5 PM on wknds and hols, but some sections (newspapers, magazines, children's Audio-Visual) are not open on Sun and hols. Clsd 1st Thurs and 3rd Sun of each month, plus one more irregular day. Also clsd New Year hols, and various days throughout the year for maintenance.

Access: 2 min from Uchisaiwaicho Stn, Exit A7 (Mita Line). Look for the map in front of the police box (*koban*) on the corner of the park. It lights up when you press the buttons (labeled in English and Japanese) and will show you the location of the library. Enter from inside the park. Also accessible from Kasumigaseki Stn, Exit B1 (Marunouchi, Hibiya and Mita lines), and Hibiya Stn, Exit A14 (Hibiya, Chiyoda and Mita lines).

INSTITUTE OF DEVELOPING ECONOMIES LIBRARY

アジア経済研究所図書館 （Ajia Keizai Kenkyujo Toshokan）
Keizai Kyoryoku Center Building, 4F
42 Ichigaya Honmuracho, Shinjuku-ku, Tokyo 162–0845
☎ 3353–4231
東京都新宿区市ヶ谷本村町42　経済協力センタービル4階
〒162-0845

Reference Library. This library contains 350,000 books on the economies of developing countries. They are mostly in English, with some in French, German, Spanish, Portuguese, and Japanese. Their 2,500 magazines and 220 newspapers deal with the economies, politics, and history of the developing countries.

NOTE: Open to people 18 years of age or older.

Hours: 10 AM–5:30 PM (enter by 5 PM) Mon–Fri. Clsd wknds, hols, and the final day of the month.

Access: A 3-min walk from Akebonobashi Stn, Exit A3 (Toei Shinjuku

Line). Turn left from the exit and walk along the main street until you reach an intersection. On your left side you will see the two IDE buildings (eight and six stories). Cross over and enter the six-story building and register at the desk.

JAPAN FOUNDATION LIBRARY

国際交流基金図書館 （Kokusai Koryu Kikin Toshokan）
　Ark Mori Building, West Wing, 20F
　1–12–32 Akasaka, Minato-ku, Tokyo 107–0052
　☎ 5562–3527
　東京都港区赤坂1-12-32　アーク森ビル西館20階　〒107-0052

Reference/Lending Library. This library is for people who want to learn more about Japan. Its collection of 50,000 books and 400 magazines/periodicals mainly concerns the humanities, culture, and social sciences—not technology. About half of these are in foreign languages (mostly English, but also in French, German, Italian, Chinese and Korean). The library carries a number of titles that would be hard to find elsewhere, such as *The American-Japan Society Bulletin, Rivers in Japan,* and *Pacific Friend.* About 3,000 Japan-related doctoral dissertations from the United States, England, and Germany are on file, and an extensive collection of videos on Japanese culture and customs can be viewed here.

Hours: 10 AM–5 PM (enter by 4:30) Mon–Fri. Clsd wknds, national and New Year hols, the final Mon of each month, and Oct 2 (anniversary of its founding).

Access: A 2-min walk from Tameike-sanno Stn, Exit 13 (Ginza and Nanboku lines). Walk straight from the exit past the ANA Hotel to the Ark Mori Bldg (the second tower in the large Ark Hills Complex). Take the elevators in the West Wing to the 20F. The library is just outside the elevators.

NOTE: Those 18 or older may use the library. If you have at least two months left on your visa, you may obtain a library card. See the next entry for the second Japan Foundation library.

JAPAN FOUNDATION ASIA CENTER LIBRARY

国際交流基金アジア センター ライブラリー

(Kokusai Koryu Kikin Ajia Senta Raiburari)

Akasaka Twin Tower Building, 1F

2–17–22 Akasaka, Minato-ku, Tokyo 107–0052

☎ 5562–3895

東京都港区赤坂2-17-22　赤坂ツインタワービル1階　〒107-0052

Reference Library. Located a few minutes away from the main Japan Foundation Library, this library focuses on Asia, particularly Southeast Asia. Operated by the Japan Foundation Asia Center, it contains about 4,600 books and numerous newspapers and magazines from Asian countries, many in English. *The Borneo Bulletin, Mongol Messenger, Cambodia Times,* and *Rising Nepal* are just a few of these. Other research material includes bulletins, leaflets, newsletters, and periodicals of cultural and research organizations that focus on this part of the world. Over 1,200 music tapes and CDs are available for listening, and videotapes (mostly in Japanese) can be viewed.

Hours: 10:30 AM–7 PM Mon–Fri. Clsd wknds, national and New Year hols, and Oct 2. (Hours and days are slightly different than those of the Japan Foundation Library.)

Access: A 1-min walk from Tameike-sanno Stn, Exit 12 (Ginza and Nanboku lines). Walk right from the exit to the end of the building from which you emerged. You will see the Akasaka Twin Towers Building directly across the street. The main entrance is to the right, just before the Japan Foundation Forum entrance. Walk all the way to the back and turn left.

JETRO (Japan External Trade Organization) LIBRARY

ジェトロ資料室　(JETRO Shiryoshitsu)

Kyodo Tsushin Building, 6F

2–2–5 Toranomon, Minato-ku, Tokyo 105–8466

☎ 3582–1775 (Library), 3587–1143 (International Lounge)

東京都港区虎ノ門2-2-5　共同通信ビル6階　〒105-8466

Reference Library. This library is very useful for people involved in or considering import-export, finance, and related fields. It contains nearly 70,000 books dealing with trade, economics, and investment. Journals, newspapers, magazines, almanacs, and directories from all over the world are available for reference. It also carries statistical information, tariff schedules, trade statistics, and other material on foreign countries.

Its International Lounge carries about 200 JETRO publications in English and European languages, and a series of videos regarding how to do business in Japan. These may be read or viewed in the lounge, and some may be borrowed.

NOTE: You must be at least 18 years old to use the library.

Hours: **Library**: 9:30 AM to 4:30 PM Mon–Fri. Clsd wknds, the 3rd Tues, and hols. **International Lounge**: 9:30 AM–noon, 1 PM–5 PM.

Access: A 7-min walk from Toranomon Stn, Exit 3 (Ginza Line). Walk straight out of the exit and follow the sidewalk as it curves to the left. (Don't cross the street here.) Continue walking for about 5 min until the road ends at a T-crossing at the Shin Nikko Building. Turn right. When you reach the main intersection, turn right again. The entrance to the building is on the right side a short way down.

NATIONAL DIET LIBRARY

国立国会図書館 （Kokuritsu Kokkai Toshokan）
1–10–1 Nagatacho, Chiyoda-ku, Tokyo 100–8924
☎ 3581–2331
東京都千代田区永田町1-10-1　〒100-8924

Reference Library. This is Japan's biggest library, similar in structure to the Library of Congress in Washington, D.C. Its main purpose is to serve the members of the Japanese Diet (Parliament), but the public may use it. It contains millions of books—about 1.5 million in foreign languages (mostly English). The system is basically closed stacks in which you submit request forms, but some areas have open stacks (such as the reference room). The 4F newspaper reading room stocks papers from around the world, and a substantial number of non-Japanese magazines are also carried.

NOTE: You must be 20 years of age or older to use the facilities. Fill out a visitor's slip at the entrance to obtain a user's card.

Hours: 9:30 AM to 5 PM Mon–Fri (enter and make requests before 4 PM). Clsd wknds (except the 3rd Sat), hols, and 3rd and 4th Mon.

Access: 2 min from Nagatacho Stn, Exit 2 (Yurakucho and Hanzomon lines). If traveling by the Hanzomon Line, exit through the

Yurakucho Line access. Go left from the station, continue across the street, and walk straight until you reach the Diet Library Building. The main user's entrance is along its far right side.

TOKYO METROPOLITAN CENTRAL LIBRARY

東京都立中央図書館 （Tokyo Toritsu Chuo Toshokan）

5–7–13 Minami Azabu, Minato-ku, Tokyo 106–0047

☎ 3442–8451

東京都港区南麻布5-7-13　〒106-0047

Reference Library. Opened to the public in 1973 as Tokyo's Central Library, this building is very user-friendly, with bilingual signs in Japanese and English throughout. The computer information is in Japanese, but the information in the card catalogues is printed in the language in which the publications are written. It contains over 1.3 million books, 10,050 magazines, and 840 newspapers. Of these, 140,000 books, 950 magazines, and 50 newspapers are in foreign languages. You can wander around and browse through publications in various languages such as French, German, Russian, and English. Audio-visual materials are also available.

NOTE: You must be 16 years or older to use the facilities.

Hours: 9:30 AM–8 PM Tues–Fri, 1 PM–8 PM Mon, 9:30 AM–5 PM Sat, Sun, and hols. (Some sections have shorter hours.) Clsd the 1st Thurs and 3rd Sun and the 25th day of each month, 20 days a year for maintenance and inventory, and New Year hols.

Access: A 7-min walk from Hiroo Stn, Exit 1 (Hibiya Subway Line). Turn left from the exit, and left again at the corner. Follow this street around and you will see the entrance to Arisugawa Park. The library is inside the park, at the very top of the hill.

TOYO BUNKO (ORIENTAL STUDIES LIBRARY)

東洋文庫 （Toyo Bunko）

2–28–21 Honkomagome, Bunkyo-ku, Tokyo 113–0021

☎ 3942–0121

東京都文京区本駒込2-28-21　〒113-0021

Reference Library. This library specializes in Asian studies, and stocks 24,000 foreign books in English and European languages. Fill out an application in the 2F reading room.

Hours: 9 AM–noon, 12:30 PM–4:30 PM Mon–Fri. Clsd wknds and hols, Nov. 19, and the final day of the month.

Access: 6 min from Komagome Stn, Exit 2 (Nanboku Line). Go straight out from the exit, cross Shinobazu-dori, and walk right. It is on the left, just before the next light.

UNITED NATIONS INFORMATION CENTRE

国連大学インフォメーション センター

United Nations University Building, 8F

5–53–70 Jingumae, Shibuya-ku, Tokyo 150–0001

☎ 5467–4451 (Ask for Mrs. Boge) ✑ www.un.org

東京都渋谷区神宮前5-53-70　国連大学ビル8階　〒150-0001

Reference/Lending Library. Information on the major United Nations organizations and their many special agencies can be found here—all in English. In addition to printed material, U.N.-related video's can either be viewed or borrowed, and photographs from their library of over 3000 items (some dating back to the origin of the U.N.) are lent free of charge for use in articles, textbooks, and other projects.

However, some material has been dispersed to the National Diet Library or the University of Tokyo Library, and some is only available at the offices of individual U.N. organizations. So please contact Mrs. Boge at the above number and she will advise you of the best place to find the material you are looking for. She also recommends that you visit the U.N. homepage (address above), where you will find information on all U.N. issues and organizations.

Hours: 10:00 AM–12:30 PM and 1:30 PM–5:30 PM (enter by 4:30). Clsd wknds and national hols.

Access: 5 min from Omotesando Stn, Exit B2 (Ginza, Hanzomon, and Chiyoda lines). Walk straight out from the exit. It is on the right side of Aoyama-dori, past Kinokuniya Supermarket and Citibank.

WORLD MAGAZINE GALLERY

ワールド マガジン ギャラリー

The Magazine House Co., 1F

3–13–10 Ginza, Chuo-ku, Tokyo 104–0061

☎ 3545–7227

東京都中央区銀座3-13-10　マガジンハウス1階　〒104-0061

Reference only. The first time I walked into the World Magazine Gallery I couldn't believe my eyes—for it is truly magazine heaven itself. The selection is vast, featuring 900 magazines from more than 50 countries from around the world. And there is no need to fill out forms and go through librarians. The magazines are out on racks and are easy to locate by area or country—some of which are Russia, Eastern Europe, Europe, the United States, Latin America, Oceania, Korea, and China. You simply choose the magazines you want to look through and take a seat at a nearby table, or you can take your selection to the 2F coffee shop. When you finish, you should return them to the correct racks.

NOTE: No, you can't take periodicals with you—sorry. But there is a black-and-white/color copy machine where you can make copies of articles for a small fee.

Hours: 11 AM–7 PM Mon–Fri. Clsd wknds, and national and New Year hols.

Access: It is located one street behind the Kabuki-za Theater, a 3-min walk from Higashi Ginza Stn, Exit 3 (Hibiya and Asakusa lines). Go straight out from the exit to the first corner and turn left. It is on the next main corner on the far left side. Look for the gray building with pink stripes running across it.

ART AND MUSIC LIBRARIES

JAPAN TRADITIONAL CRAFT CENTER LIBRARY

全国伝統的工芸品センター

（Zenkoku Dentoteki Kogeihin Senta）

    Plaza 246 Building, 2F

    3–1–1 Minami Aoyama, Minato-ku, Tokyo 107–0062

    ☎ 3403–2460

    東京都港区南青山3-1-1　プラザ246ビル2階　〒107-0062

Reference Library. The Japan Traditional Craft Center contains a library with 1,700 books (80 in English) and more than 270 videos (24 in English). I watched one entitled *Traditional Crafts in Everyday Japanese Life,* in which the influence of the ancient arts on today's lifestyle was explored in detail. It explained how everything in the Japanese household is designed to human scale, and it helped me to understand the logic and dimensions behind "men's" and "women's" sizes of teacup and other items in daily use. Many of the tapes explained the processes of making specific crafts. (See ch 9 for information on the center's exhibitions.)

Hours: 10 AM–6 PM (4 PM on the final days of an exhibition in the main room). Clsd Thurs and New Year hols.

Access:A 3-min walk from Gaienmae Stn (Ginza Line). Turn left from the ticket turnstile and go up the stairway on the right at the end of the passage. The craft center is at the first traffic signal (upstairs from Haagen-Dazs Ice Cream in the Plaza 246 Building).

TOKYO METROPOLITAN ART MUSEUM READING ROOM

東京都美術館美術図書コーナー

（Tokyo-to Bijutsukan Bijutsu Tosho Kona）

Tokyo Metropolitan Art Museum, 1F

8–36 Ueno Koen, Taito-ku, Tokyo 110–0007

☎ 3823–6921

東京都台東区上野公園8-36　東京都美術館1階　〒110-0007

Reference Library. The reading room inside the Tokyo Metropolitan Art Museum contains about 3,000 beautifully illustrated art books, many of them of the large, coffee-table variety. Whatever your taste in art, they will probably have a book to satisfy your needs on just about every art style and artist. The library also carries 12 English art magazines, including *Art in America*.

Hours: 10 AM- 5 PM Mon–Sat, 9 AM–5 PM Sun and hols. Clsd the 3rd Mon (Tues if Mon is a hol), and New Year and museum hols.

Access:3 min from JR Ueno Stn, Ueno Park Exit (Yamanote and other lines). (Get an English map of the park from the Information Center at the park entrance.) The library is on the 1F of the Tokyo Metropolitan Art Museum, located to the right of the zoo. Go up one flight from the entrance foyer, which is on B1.

TOKYO METROPOLITAN FESTIVAL HALL'S MUSIC LIBRARY AND LISTENING ROOM

東京文化会館音楽資料室

（Tokyo Bunka Kaikan Ongaku Shiryoshitsu）

Tokyo Bunka Kaikan, 4F

5–45 Ueno Koen, Taito-ku, Tokyo 110–0007

☎ 3828–2111 (Tokyo Bunka Kaikan Office)

東京都台東区上野公園5-45　東京文化会館4階　〒110-0007

Reference/Lending Library. This music library has a listening room with 30 machines on which you can play the music of your choice or watch the recorded performances of their 50,000 CDs, records, and laser disks. It also carries more than 17,000 books on music—about 1,000 in foreign languages. Some foreign magazines are available, too. When you enter the library, you will be given instructions in English on how to fill out the request form.

Hours: Noon–8 PM Tues–Sat, and noon–5 PM Sun and hols. Clsd Mon and some Sun.

Access: Directly across from JR Ueno Stn (Yamanote and other lines), Ueno Park Exit. It is at the entrance to the park on the left side—inside the Metropolitan Festival Hall (Tokyo Bunka Kaikan).

SMALL, SPECIALIZED LIBRARIES

BIBLE LIBRARY

聖書図書館 （Seisho Toshokan）
    Japan Bible Society Building, 7F
    4–5–1 Ginza, Chuo-ku, Tokyo 104–0061
    ☎ 3567–1995
    東京都中央区銀座4-5-1　日本聖書協会ビル7階　〒104-0061

Reference Library. To call this Bible library a "biblical museum" would not be too far off the mark, for it houses some unique and impressive biblical treasures. In addition to its 4,500 Bibles and biblical research books, this library (located right in the heart of Ginza) contains such precious items as the oldest existing Japanese translation of the scriptures, a 1720 German Bible that belonged to Martin Luther, a parchment Torah, and a King James Bible dating back to 1617. It also has on display an oil lamp from Lebanon and a water jug from Israel that date back to before the time of Christ. Some interesting copies are housed in the glass cases around the room, too, including a 4th-century Vatican Codex and a Gutenberg Bible dated 1455.

Hours: 10 AM–5 PM Mon–Fri. Clsd wknds, Christmas, New Year and national hols, and one week in Aug.

Access: 3 min from Ginza Stn, Exit A9 (Ginza, Marunouchi, and Hibiya lines). Go straight and make a left at the first crossing. The Bible Society Building will be on the left side at the end of the block.

BICYCLE CULTURE CENTER

自転車文化センター（Jitensha Bunka Senta）
Jitensha Kaikan No. 3 Building, 3F
1–9–3 Akasaka, Minato-ku, Tokyo 107–0052
☎ 3584–4530
東京都港区赤坂1-9-3　自転車会館3号館3階　〒107-0052

Reference Library. This comprehensive cycling library contains over 700 books on bicycling in English, French, Italian, German, and Spanish. Lots of other details on bicycling in Japan are available too—maps, courses, and places to stay along the way are some of the useful resources you can find at this great information center. On the 2F is the Bicycle Museum (see ch 10) with sixty-three unusual and interesting bicycles, including the emperor Showa's wooden-wheeled royal tricycle that dates back to 1908, a French Michaux (the first bike to arrive in Japan over 100 years ago), and a child's horse-shaped model seen in the famous paintings of Claude Monet.

Hours: 10 AM–4 PM Mon–Fri. Clsd wknds and hols.
Access: 7 min from Toranomon Stn, Exit 3 (Ginza Line). Walk straight out of the exit and follow the sidewalk as it curves to the left. (Don't cross the street here.) Continue walking for about 5 min until the road ends at a T-crossing at the Shin Nikko Building. Turn right. When you reach the main intersection, cross over. Directly across from the main entrance to the American Embassy, you will see a "Bicycle Culture Center" sign in English on the side of the building. Enter there and walk back to the No. 3 Building.

EDO-TOKYO MUSEUM A/V LIBRARY

江戸東京博物館資料室
（Edo-Tokyo Hakubutsukan Shiryoshitsu）
Edo-Tokyo Museum Building, B1
1–4–1 Yokoami, Sumida-ku, Tokyo 130–0015
☎ 3626–9974
東京都墨田区横網1-4-1　江戸東京博物館地下1階　〒130-0015

FREE READS
AND OTHER
GREAT RESOURCES

Reference Library. When you walk into this video library, you will be handed a book listing their English videos. After you make your choice, you will be assigned to one of the 28 cozy little private booths, where you punch in your newly acquired identity number, push the start button, and voila!—your video appears on the screen.

Their 40-or-so English videos cover topics dealing with the history and culture of Tokyo. First I watched a series of short films highlighting the city's one hundred most scenic spots. I then took in an exciting twenty-minute documentary on *The Taiko: Those Wonderful Japanese Drums.* Other selections feature kabuki, Noh drama, traditional music, and ikebana (flower arranging). Some videos cover broader subjects such as the *European Influence on Japanese Culture.*

The 7F also has a free exhibit entitled "HDTV Treasures from the Collection," where you can sit in a booth and peruse the museum's works (including many valuable *ukiyo-e* prints) on a high-definition television screen. You might also want to take a look in the 1F museum shop, which carries the museum's own line of traditional crafts, toys, and other items not generally found in other shops (see ch 9).

NOTE: There is a charge to see the museum's exhibitions on old Tokyo, but access to the shop and audio-visual library is free.

Hours: 10 AM–6 PM Tues–Sun (the last video request is taken at 5:30 PM). Clsd Mon (Tues if Mon is a hol), and New Year hols.

Access: 3 min from Ryogoku Stn, West Exit (JR Sobu Line). Turn right from the exit, then right again, and follow the signs. The museum is alongside the train tracks.

JAPAN ECOLOGY CENTER

ジャパン エコロジー センター

Ecology Center Building, B1
3 Fukuromachi, Shinjuku-ku, Tokyo 162–0828
☎ 5228–3370 (If no English speaking staff on duty, call back a little later)

東京都新宿区袋町3　エコロジー センタービル地下1階　〒162-0828

Reference Library. This caring little library is sponsored by the Japan Ecology Network and contains about 300 English books on important topics: the environment, health, food safety, and related subject matter. Here you can find the *Whole Earth Catalog,* recycling information, and even big picture books on animals and nature (about 4,000 more books are in Japanese). Sometimes talks are held at the center. Scientist Linda Leigh, a participant in the Biosphere 2 experiment, spoke here when she was in Japan.

The center sponsors flea markets, and they have information on 3,500 environmental groups from around the world on file (about half of these are from the United States)—as well as about 2,500 organizations in Japan.

Hours: 1 PM–6 PM Tues–Fri, and 2nd and 4th Sat.

Access: About 7 min from JR Iidabashi Stn, West Exit (Sobu Line). Cross the bridge to the right and walk straight up Kagurazaka shopping street for about 5 min. After you pass the Bishamonten temple on your left, turn left (a bookstore will be on the corner). The center is a few doors down on the right side. Take the stairway that goes down to the left (the one covered with environmental posters) to B1. It is also accessible from Iidabashi subway Stn (Tozai, Yurakucho, and Nanboku lines).

SAKÉ PLAZA

日本の酒情報館 （Nihon no Saké Joho-kan）

Nihon Shuzo Kaikan Bldg 1F/4F

1–1–21 Nishi Shinbashi, Minato-ku, Tokyo 105–0003

☎ 3519–2091

東京都港区西新橋1-1-21　日本酒造会館1階、4階　〒105-0003

Reference Library. The Japan Saké Center contains a library on the 4F with about 60 books in English and French dealing with saké, wines, whiskeys, and liquor in general. *Wines and Spirits of the World* and *Saké: A Drinker's Guide* are two of the books found in the small-but-varied selection that will be of interest to English-speaking imbibers. In total, the library has 5,000 books—mostly in Japanese.

But listen to this—the library is in the same room as the free saké sampling! So you can update your knowledge about the various brews and try your skill at rating ten types of saké in a blind taste test (simply by filling out a preference postcard)—all

NOTE: For a detailed look at saké, check out the new *Insider's Guide to Saké* by Philip Harper, a British expatriate who works in a saké brewery.

in one place. Beautiful saké labels from all around Japan decorate the hallways and staircase of the showroom, and more can be found in display books in the library. (See also ch 15.)

Hours: 10:00 AM–6:00 PM. Clsd Sat, Sun, and hols.
Access:A 5-min walk from Toranomon Stn, Exits 1 or 9 (Ginza Line). Walk straight down Sotobori-dori toward Shinbashi. Turn left at the Daiwa Bank and turn right at the gas station.

LIBRARY AQUA
ライブラリー アクア

TOTO Nogizaka Building, 5F
1–24–3 Minami Aoyama, Minato-ku, Tokyo 107–0062
☎ 3497–1010
東京都港区南青山1-24-3　TOTO乃木坂ビル5階　〒107-0062

Reference Library. This interesting library is supposed to be all about water, but its range extends far beyond the basics and includes many topics connected with water—such as gardens, architecture, and design. It carries about 250 English books, 20 English magazines, and a number of videos in English. It also carries material in French and German. Among its English videos is the BBC series *River Journeys,* which features voyages down the great rivers of the world—such as the Nile, Congo, and Mekong.

NOTE: The fabulous architectural Gallery Ma is in the same building, so you might want to pay it a visit on the 3F (see ch 14—art galleries). And if you are interested in issues of architectural magazines going back to the 1960s or 1970s, see Tokyo Gas Ginza Pocket Park Library, below.

Some of the magazines I spotted on the shelf were *The Architectural Review, Architectural Design, Interior Design, House and Garden,* and *GA Houses* and *GA Architect.* The last two are bilingual Japanese/English publications published in Japan. The French *Marie Claire Maison* and *Elle Deco,* and the German *RAS* and *DMK* are some of the European magazines carried.

Hours: 11 AM–7 PM Mon–Sat. Clsd Sun, hols, and the 3rd Thurs.
Access:Nogizaka Stn, Exit 3 (Chiyoda Line). At the top of the escalators, take the steps to your right. At street level, look back across the small road to your right and you will see a dark blue building with TOTO written on top. Take the elevator to the 5F.

NATIONAL FILM CENTER LIBRARY

ナショナル フィルムセンター ライブラリー

National Film Center Building, 4F

3–7–6 Kyobashi, Chuo-ku, Tokyo 104–0031

☎ 3561–0823 (Library)

東京都中央区京橋3-7-6　ナショナル フィルムセンタービル4階
〒104-0031

Reference Library. This is Japan's facility for the preservation and study of both Japanese and foreign films. The library contains 13,000 film-related publications. About 2,500 of these are in foreign languages—approximately half in English and the rest in French, Italian, German, Russian, Chinese, Portuguese and Spanish. Most are in closed stacks available by request (English listing of books is at desk), but there are enough English and French film magazines, and English guides and directories out in the open stacks to keep you busy for hours. Check your belongings in a locker and fill out a form at the 4F reception desk to receive an admission card. Photocopying services are available.

NOTE: The facility also screens films and houses a gallery on the 7F that features photography, graphic design, and film-related exhibitions. Both charge a small entrance fee.

Hours: 10:30 AM–6 PM. (enter by 5:30) Tue-Fri. Clsd Sat, Sun, Mon, national and New Year holidays, and shelving days.

Access: 1 min from Kyobashi Station, Exit 1 (Ginza Line). Walk straight out and soon you will see the National Film Center (name in English on building) on your right.

PLAZA EQUUS

プラザ エクウス

Shibuya Beam Building, 3F

31–2 Udagawacho, Shibuya-ku, Tokyo 150–0042

☎ 5458–4331

東京都渋谷区宇田川町31-2　渋谷ビームビル3階　〒150-0042

Reference Library. Attention, horse lovers! This library has about 900 books (200 in English) featuring horses and related subjects: the various breeds of horses and their care and training, riding techniques, steeple chasing, polo, racing, and horses around the world, to list but a few of the topics that can be explored here. Encyclopedias, guides, art books collecting the

FREE READS
AND OTHER
GREAT RESOURCES

works of famous artists who painted horses (Manet, Degas, Lautrec, and more), and even a book on horses in the movies can be found here.

In addition, the library carries a number of videos (in Japanese) on topics such as international events, famous horses, and horse festivals. (Also see ch 4.)

Hours: 11 AM–7:30 PM Wed–Mon. Clsd on Tues (Wed if Tues is a hol) and New Year hols.

Access: A 5-min walk from Shibuya Stn, Hachiko Exit (Yamanote and other lines). Walk left along Dogenzaka for about 1 min and turn right at the 109 Building (the big silver tower on the corner) onto Bunkamura-dori. Walk past three traffic lights. Then turn right at the next small street (across from Tokyu Department Store). Continue to the second corner and the Beam Building will be on the far right side. The inside escalator will take you up to the Plaza Equus Showroom and Library on the 2F and 3F.

TEPIA FOUNDATION LIBRARY

テピアプラザ

TEPIA Building, 2F

2–8–44 Kita Aoyama, Minato-ku, Tokyo 107–0061

☎ 5474–6111

東京都港区北青山2-8-44　テピアビル2階　〒107-0061

Reference Library. New media and exciting high technology are the focus of this library. It is part of TEPIA, a foundation whose sole mission is to make known the latest information from Japan's high-tech industries. It contains a mountain of information on technology that can be viewed in individual booths. Over 900 videos on high technology are available—about 80 in English, with some in French, German, Spanish, and Chinese. (Ask for a listing in English.) And with a reservation in the Hyper-Studio, you can create your own personal CD-ROM at no charge. (Also see ch 15.)

Hours: 10 AM–6 PM Mon–Fri, 10 AM–5 PM Sat and hols. Clsd Sun.

Access: A 5-min walk from Gaienmae Stn, Exit 2 (Ginza Line). Turn right from the ticket turnstile and go up the stairs. Turn right from the exit and right again at the corner. Just beyond the Prince Chichibu Memorial Rugby Ground you will see a big building on the right side with TEPIA written in large letters at the top—the library is on the 2F.

TIBET HOUSE

チベット ハウス：ダライ ラマ法王日本代表事務所
　　No. 5 Hayama Building, 5F
　　5–11–30 Shinjuku, Shinjuku-ku, Tokyo 160–0022
　　☎ 3353–4094
　　東京都新宿区新宿5-11-30　第5ハヤマビル5階　〒160-0022

Reference/Lending Library. This is the Tokyo Liaison Office of His Holiness the Dalai Lama. Its library contains 500 books on Buddhism and Tibetan culture, politics, and history—about 150 in English. In addition to books on Tibetan Buddhism, many good general books on Buddhism such as *The Buddhist Handbook: A Complete Guide to Buddhist Schools, Teaching, Practice, and History,* by John Snelling, and *The Teachings of Buddha* (published by the Buddhist Promotion Foundation) can also be found here. Books can be read at tables or borrowed for up to a week.

NOTE: The center also offers weekly classes in English on Tibetan Buddhist Studies for a ¥1,500 donation.

Hours: 10 AM–1 PM and 2 PM–5 PM Mon–Fri, 12:30 PM–5 PM Sat. Hours subject to change, so call ahead for an appointment.

Access: 4 min from Shinjuku-sanchome Stn, Exit C7 (Shinjuku or Marunouchi lines). Go straight across Yasukuni-dori (Isetan "Queen's Chef" building is on the corner). Walk right, then turn left at the second small street. The entrance will be along the side of the corner building on the left. Take the elevator to the 5F. Also a 12-min walk from Shinjuku Stn (Yamanote and other lines).

TOKYO GAS GINZA POCKET PARK

東京ガス銀座ポケットパーク
　　Tokyo Gas Building, 2F
　　7–9–15 Ginza, Chuo-ku, Tokyo 104–0061
　　☎ 3573–1401
　　東京都中央区銀座7-9-15　東京ガスビル2階　〒104-0061

Reference Library. This showroom is a great spot for architecture buffs and students who would like to explore its development. Back issues of *The Architectural Review* that date from the 1970s to current times, as well as copies of *Progressive Architecture* from the 1960s to the present, are some of the publications you can find lining the walls of their 2F architectural exhibition room (see ch 15).

NOTE: For a larger selection of material on architecture and design, be sure to pay a visit to the Library Aqua (see above).

Hours: 10:30 AM–7 PM. Clsd Wed.

Access: 5-min walk from Ginza Stn, Exit A3 (Ginza, Marunouchi, and Hibiya lines). Walk straight down Chuo-dori. The showroom is on the left side toward the end of the 3rd block.

TOTO RECIPE

TOTO 食の情報館レシピ（Toto Shoku no Johokan Resipi）

TOTO Recipe Building, 3/4F

7–8–7 Ginza, Chuo-ku, Tokyo 104–0061

☎ 3573–1010

東京都中央区銀座7-8-7　TOTOレシピビル3/4階　〒106-0061

Reference Library. This TOTO Showroom Library contains 850 books on cooking and food from around the world. Approximately 150 of these are in English (3F), and you are free to come and read them. They are not for sale, but you can make photocopies of the recipes for a small fee. A 5F art gallery features exhibitions relating to food. Coffee, tea, and cocoa are available free on every floor. (Also see ch 15.)

Hours: 11 AM–7 PM daily. Clsd 1st Wed and for New Year and summer hols.

Access: 6 min from Ginza Stn, Exit A2 (Ginza, Marunouchi, and Hibiya lines). Walk straight down Chuo-dori. The TOTO Recipe Building is on the right side of the street toward the end of the 3rd block.

OTHER LANGUAGE LIBRARIES

■ **French**

BIBLIOTHÈQUE DE LA MAISON FRANCO-JAPONAISE
(Japanese-French Center Library)

日仏会館図書室（Nichifutsu Kaikan Toshoshitsu）

Nichifutsu Kaikan, 2F

3–9–25 Ebisu, Shibuya-ku, Tokyo 150–0013

☎ 5421–7643

東京都渋谷区恵比寿3-9-25　日仏会館2階　〒150-0013

Reference Library (lends to members). This library contains 50,000 publications (most in French). Books mainly deal with art history, philosophy, social science, and religion. They also carry 200 magazines and three newspapers.

Hours: 10:30 AM–6 PM Wed and Sat. Other days 1 PM–6 PM. Clsd Sun, hols, July 14 (Bastille Day), Christmas, and New Year hols. Clsd Sat July–Sept.

Access: A 10-min walk from JR Ebisu Stn, East Exit (Yamanote Line). Take the moving "Skywalk" to the end, then turn left and walk to the next intersection. It will be on the far left corner. It is also accessible by Ebisu Stn on the Hibiya Line.

INSTITUT FRANCO-JAPONAIS DE TOKYO "MEDIATHÈQUE" (Japanese-French Institute)

東京日仏学院図書館 （Tokyo Nichifutsu Gakuin Toshoshitsu）

Tokyo Nichifutsu Gakuin, 2F

15 Ichigaya Funagawaracho, Shinjuku-ku, Tokyo 162–0826

☎ 5261–3937

東京都新宿区市ヶ谷船河原町15　東京日仏学院2階　〒162-0826

Reference Library (lends to members). This library of a French school houses 13,000 books, mainly in French. Various aspects of French culture are covered, such as literature, art, and music. The library also stocks about 600 videos, CDs, and LDs for viewing, and sometimes sponsors photo exhibitions and other art shows that feature French and Japanese artists.

Hours: Noon–7 PM Mon–Sat, noon–6 PM Sun. Clsd hols and 2 weeks in summer.

Access: 7 min from JR Iidabashi Stn, West Exit (Sobu Line). Walk right from the exit and cross the street (Sotobori-dori). Turn left and walk toward Ichigaya until you reach a gas station. Turn right and walk up the hill for about 1 min. It is on the right side. It is also accessible from Iidabashi Subway Stn on the Tozai, Yurakucho, and Nanboku lines.

■ German

GOETHE INSTITUTE TOKYO (German Culture Center)

東京ドイツ文化センター （Tokyo Doitsu Bunka Senta）
OAG Haus (Doitsu Bunka Kaikan), 2F
7–5–56 Akasaka, Minato-ku, Tokyo 107–0052
☎ 3583–7280
東京都港区赤坂7-5-56　ドイツ文化会館2階　〒107-0052

Reference/Lending Library. The Goethe Institute is a worldwide organization that promotes German culture. It maintains a library containing 18,000 books (80% are in German, 20% in Japanese) concerning German history, literature, culture, economics, art, and philosophy. The library also stocks magazines, newspapers, videos, and CDs. Computers are available for research Sometimes the library sponsors classical music concerts and other events.

NOTE: To obtain a pass to enter, show an ID card with an address. An Alien Registration Card is needed to borrow books.

Hours: Noon–6 PM Tues, Wed, Fri. Noon–8 PM on Thurs. 10 AM–4 PM Sat. Clsd Sun, Mon, hols, and all of Aug.

Access: A 7-min walk from Aoyama-itchome Stn (Ginza and Hanzomon lines). Take Exit 3 for Minami Aoyama. Turn right from the exit, then right again at the corner. Walk along Aoyama-dori past the Canadian Embassy and turn right between the park and mirrored Sogetsu Building. The OAG House is 300 m (275 yd) down the street on the left side. It also contains the German Tourist Information Center.

■ Italian

ISTITUTO ITALIANO DI CULTURA—TOKYO (Italian Cultural Center)

イタリア文化会館 （Italia Bunka Kaikan）, 2F
2–1–30 Kudan Minami, Chiyoda-ku, Tokyo 102–0074
☎ 3264–6011
東京都千代田区九段南2-1-30　2階　〒102-0074

Reference Library (lends to members). The Italian Culture Center stocks about 15,000 books (90% are in Italian, 10% in Japanese), mostly on Italian art and literature. It has been open about seventy years, and sometimes sponsors cultural programs such as lectures, concerts, and films.

Hours: 10 AM–1 PM and 2 PM–6 PM Mon–Fri. Clsd wknds and national, summer, and New Year hols.

Access: 8 min from Kudanshita Stn, Exit 2 (Hanzomon, Tozai, or Toei Shinjuku lines). Walk straight up Yasukuni-dori to the first light (Uchibori-dori). Turn left and walk 150 m (135 yd). The center is the ivy-covered building on the left side just beyond the pedestrian overpass.

■ Spanish

CENTRO DE ESTUDIOS HISPANICOS— UNIVERSIDAD SOFIA
(Center of Hispanic Studies—Sophia University)
上智大学イスパニア研究センター
(Jochi Daigaku Isupania Kenkyu Senta)

Sophia University Library Building, 6F

7–1 Kioicho, Chiyoda-ku, Tokyo 102–8554

☎ 3238–3533

東京都千代田区紀尾井町7-1　上智大学中央図書館総合研究棟6階
〒102-8554

Lending Library. This center, founded in 1959, contains about 12,000 books on Hispanic culture and society, literature, linguistics, politics, the arts, and history. There are some beautiful, coffee table–style picture books as well. Most of the material is in Spanish, but some books are in Japanese, and a few are in English. They also carry about 50 magazines.

Hours: 10 AM–noon and 1 PM–5 PM Mon–Fri.

Access: The center is on the 6F of the library on Sophia University's Yotsuya Campus, located next to Yotsuya Stn. From subway Exit 1 (Marunouchi or Nanboku lines) bear right and cross over the bridge. From the JR Sobu or Chuo lines, Kojimachi Exit, cross the main street to the right, then walk left. The main entrance to the campus is just beyond St. Ignatius Church, which is on the corner. Enter the campus and go straight back to the nine-story, white library building on the left side.

■ Embassy Libraries

In addition to the embassy libraries already mentioned that are open to the general public, keep in mind that other embassies maintain libraries that are great sources of business- and culture-related information. If you have a specific need that warrants the use of their facilities, they are generally very gracious about granting access.

Browsing in Foreign-Language Bookstores

AOYAMA BOOK CENTER
青山ブックセンター（六本木店）
> Roppongi Denki Building, 1F
> 6–1–20 Roppongi, Minato-ku, Tokyo 106–0032
> ☎ 3479–0479
> 東京都港区六本木6-1-20　六本木電気ビル1階　〒106-0032

The headquarters of this bookstore is in Aoyama (☎ 5485–5511), but this branch is located in Tokyo's late-night entertainment center of Roppongi. It is open very late, so if you miss your last train home and are looking for something to do, you could spend some time here. It carries about 1,000 English books—art books, photo books, paperbacks, magazines, and so on. There are also branches in Hiroo, Jiyugaoka, Tennozu, and Shinjuku.

Hours: 10 AM–5:30 AM Mon–Sat. 10 AM–10 PM Sun and hols.
Access: 1 min from Roppongi Stn, Exit 3 (Hibiya Line). Turn left from the exit. It is next to the Azabu police box (*koban*).

BIBLOS BOOKSTORE
洋書ビブロス
> F.I. Building, 5F
> 1–26–5 Takadanobaba, Shinjuku-ku, Tokyo 169–0075
> ☎ 3200–4531
> 東京都新宿区高田馬場1-26-5　エフアイビル5階　〒169-0075

Biblos has about 30,000 foreign publications, mostly in English. These include books on travel and languages, children's books, paperbacks, and a sizable selection of magazines that covers a wide range of topics. They also have a large resource section for teachers of English as a second language.

Hours: 10 AM–9 PM Mon–Sat. 10 AM–8 PM Sun and hols. Building clsd 3 days a year.

Access: Just across from Takadanobaba Stn, Waseda Exit (Tozai and JR Yamanote lines). Turn right from the ticket turnstile and walk across the square. The F.I. Building is the second one facing the square. Take the *elevator* to the 5F and turn right.

BOOK CLUB KAI
ブッククラブ回

2–14–1 Minami Aoyama, Minato-ku, Tokyo 107–0062

☎ 3403–1926

東京都港区南青山2-14-1　〒107-0062

They carry about 2,000 books in English on New Age–related and holistic subjects such as health, the environment, religion, and psychology. A number of English magazines are also available.

Hours: Noon–8 PM daily. Clsd New Year hols.

Access: 4 min from Gaienmae Stn (Ginza Line). Turn left from the ticket turnstile and go up the stairway on the left at the end of the passageway. Walk along Aoyama-dori toward Akasaka until you pass Doutor Coffee Shop, then turn right at the drugstore. It is 50 m (45 yd) down on the right side.

BOOKS SANSEIDO
三省堂書店　神田本店（洋書部）

5F (Foreign Books), 1–1 Kanda Jinbocho, Chiyoda-ku, Tokyo 101–0051

☎ 3293–8119

東京都千代田区神田神保町1-1　〒101-0051

Because of its proximity to a number of universities in the area, Books Sanseido carries a large stock of textbooks and paperbacks in English. They also have 10,000 foreign books on Japan, movies, music, and other topics. English and French magazines, and French newspapers are available, as well.

Hours: 10 AM–7:30 PM daily. Clsd on Tues between Aug and Nov.

Access: A 5-min walk from Jinbocho Stn, Exit A7 (Hanzomon, Mita, and Toei Shinjuku lines). Go right from the station and right again at the corner. The store is on the right side of Yasukuni-dori, just before the next big intersection. The building has a very large entryway.

CHRISTIAN LITERATURE CRUSADE/CLC ENGLISH BOOKSTORE

CLC書店（洋書部）

Ochanomizu Christian Center/OCC Building, 3F

2–1 Kanda Surugadai, Chiyoda-ku, Tokyo 101–0062

☎ 3294–0776

東京都千代田区神田駿河台2-1　OCCビル3階　〒101-0062

This store specializes in books on Christian-related topics for both adults and children. Most are in English, with some in European and Asian languages. Songbooks and tapes are available too, as well as over 50 kinds of Bibles in an impressive array of languages such as Ainu, Arabic, Burmese, Cambodian, Chinese, French, German, Korean, Spanish, Portuguese, Russian, Tagalog, Thai, and even some Indian dialects.

Hours: 10 AM–7 PM Mon–Sat (hols till 6 PM). Clsd Sun and New Year hols.

Access: 3 min from JR Ochanomizu Stn, West Exit (Sobu and Chuo lines). Turn left from the exit and walk down the main street away from the bridge. The Ochanomizu Christian Center is on the right side.

FIONA BOOKSTORE

フィオナ書店

Solofiole Jiyugaoka Building and Annex, 1F

5–41–5 Okusawa, Setagaya-ku, Tokyo 158–0083

☎ 3721–8186

東京都世田谷区奥沢5-41-5　ソルフィオーレ自由ヶ丘1階　〒158-0083

"Tokyo's Largest Selection of Children's Books in English" states their advertising. Over 40,000 titles for children and adults are available, along with art books, cookbooks, educational materials, games, CD-ROMs, and videotapes.

Hours: 11 AM–8 PM. Clsd New Year and summer hols.

Access: A 5-min walk from Jiyugaoka Stn (Toyoko Line). Go out the North Exit (at the back of the train if coming from Shibuya) and walk down the Shirakaba Shopping Street (sign is in English) that runs alongside the Sakura Bank across from the station. When the street ends at the Peacock Supermarket, turn left and cross the railroad tracks. Turn left at the 3rd small street after the tracks, and Fiona will be a few doors down on the left side. Their second and larger store is directly behind, around the side of the building.

GOOD DAY BOOKS

グッドデイ ブックス

    Asahi Building, 3F

    1–11–2 Ebisu, Shibuya-ku, Tokyo 150–0013

    ☎ 5421–0957

    東京都渋谷区恵比寿1-11-2　朝日ビル3階　〒150-0013

Good Day Books stocks over 30,000 new and used books (mostly in English) on every topic, ranging from cookbooks and New Age to business and art—and the store even accepts trade-ins for credit!

Hours: 11 AM–8 PM Mon and Wed to Sat, 11 AM–6 PM Sun and hols. Clsd Tues.

Access: A 1-min walk from JR Ebisu Stn, East Exit (Yamanote Line). Go down the stairs by the ticket gate and walk straight out to the street. Turn right when you reach the traffic signal. It is the 2nd building on the right. It is also accessible from the Hibiya Line, Ebisu Stn.

JENA

イエナ洋書店

    3F, 5–6–1 Ginza, Chuo-ku, Tokyo 104–0061

    ☎ 3571–2980

    東京都中央区銀座5-6-1　〒104-0061

About 50,000 foreign books are on the 3F at the top of the escalator. Most are in English, with some in European languages. New hardback releases, paperback novels about Japan, books to study Japanese, art and cultural topics, cookbooks, and more are available.

FREE READS
AND OTHER
GREAT RESOURCES

Hours: 11 AM–8 PM Mon–Sat, noon–7 PM Sun and hols. Clsd New Year hols.

Access: Ginza Stn, Exit B3 (Ginza, Marunouchi, and Hibiya lines). After exiting, you can see the bookstore directly across the alleyway. The entrance is on the main street.

KINOKUNIYA BOOKSTORE (Shinjuku South Store)

紀伊国屋書店 新宿南店 （洋書部）

Takashimaya Times Square Annex Building, 6F (Foreign Books)

5–24–2 Sendagaya, Shibuya-ku, Tokyo 151–0051

☎ 5361–3301

東京都渋谷区千駄ヶ谷5-24-2　高島屋タイムズ スクエア別館6階

〒151-0051

Kinokuniya Bookstore still maintains a foreign book section on the 6F of their former location on Shinjuku-dori, but in late 1996 they transferred the bulk of their foreign book department (over 100,000 international books) to the Takashimaya Times Square Annex Building, part of a huge shopping complex and entertainment center located near the South Exit of Shinjuku Station. They also have a branch in Shibuya (☎ 3463–3241), directly across the street from the JR Shibuya Station's South Exit, on the 5F of the Tokyu Plaza Building.

NOTE: Takashimaya Times Square features a 3-D IMAX Theater and Sega indoor amusement theme park among its offerings.

Hours: 10 AM–8 PM daily. Clsd one or two Wed every month.

Access: Takashimaya Times Square is adjacent to JR Shinjuku Stn's New South (Shin Minami) Exit. But it is more convenient to exit from the station's South Exit. You can see the complex as you leave the station—walk to the back of it to the Annex Building.

LAOX COMPUTER KAN

ラオックス コンピュータ館

1F, 1–7–6 Sotokanda, Chiyoda-ku, Tokyo 101–0021

☎ 5256–3111

東京都千代田区外神田1-7-6　1階　〒101-0021

This store is in the middle of Akihabara, Tokyo's electronics circus, and carries hundreds of computer books in English. Most are imported from the United States.

Hours: 10:30 AM–9 PM Mon–Fri, 10 AM–9 PM Sat, 10 AM–8 PM Sun and hols.

Access: 2 min from Akihabara Stn, Denki-gai (Electric Town) Exit (Yamanote and other lines). Walk out to Chuo-dori and turn right. Go left at the main intersection (Yamagiwa Department Store is on the corner). It is a big store just beyond the first small street on the left. The foreign books are on the back wall of the 1F.

MARUZEN

丸善（洋書部）

2/4F (Foreign Books), 2–3–10 Nihonbashi, Chuo-ku, Tokyo 103–8245

☎ 3272–7211

東京都中央区日本橋2-3-10　2/4階　〒103-8245

A very large selection of foreign books can be found on the 2F of the main store in Nihonbashi. The 4F carries children's books, art books, and hobby books in English. Maruzen also has a branch at the Press Center in Hibiya (☎ 3508–2511), one across from JR Ochanomizu Station (☎ 3295–5581), and a fabulous little shop at Bunkamura Entertainment Complex (☎ 3477–9134) in Shibuya. The latter is packed with wonderful books on the arts (about half of which are in English), and is open 10 AM–9 PM daily. Closed only Jan 1.

NOTE: The Nihonbashi store also has a nice crafts gallery on the 4F.

Hours: The Nihonbashi store is open 10 AM–7 PM Mon–Sat, 10 AM–6 PM Sun and hols. Clsd 1st and 3rd Sun.

Access: Nihonbashi Stn, Exit B3 (Ginza, Tozai, and Toei Asakusa lines). The exit comes up inside the Maruzen Building on Chuo-dori, across from Takashimaya Department Store.

NATIONAL AZABU SUPERMARKET BOOKSTORE

ナショナル 麻布 スーパーマーケット ブックストア

2F, 4–5–2 Minami Azabu, Minato-ku, Tokyo 106–0047

☎ 3442–3505

東京都港区南麻布4-5-2　〒106-0047

Located above the National Azabu Supermarket, this convenient little bookstore stocks over 4,000 English books dealing with Japanese culture, language, crafts, and lifestyle. The bookstore

FREE READS
AND OTHER
GREAT RESOURCES

also has a nice selection of cookbooks and other subjects, as well as a large variety of magazines and newspapers in English, French, German, and Italian.

Hours: 9:30 AM–7 PM daily.

Access: A 3-min walk from Hiroo Stn, Exit 1 (Hibiya Line). Turn left from the exit, and left at the corner. Follow this street around and you will see the entrance to Arisugawa Park on the corner. National Azabu Supermarket is directly across from the park. The bookstore is upstairs.

ON SUNDAYS
オン サンデイズ

The Watari Museum of Contemporary Art (Watari-um), B1/1F
3–7–6 Jingumae, Shibuya-ku, Tokyo 150–0001
☎ 3470–1424
東京都渋谷区神宮前3-7-6　ワタリウム美術館1階/地下1階　〒150-0001

This marvelous bookstore at the Watari museum is an art-lover's paradise. The store stocks about 5,000 books on art, photography, and architecture (a great number of these in English) on their B1 level. The atmosphere here is fabulous. Books are stacked on bookshelves that go up and up and up, with thin little wooden ladders running to the top that enable the staff to access them. About 10,000 postcards on art and every imaginable subject await you on the main floor—topics run from Barbie Dolls to facial hair–types (as seen in sixteen illustrated styles of moustaches and beards). It's a fun place.

NOTE: There is a charge for the museum, but the bookstore is separate and free.

Hours: 11 AM–8 PM Tues–Sun. Clsd Mon.

Access: An 8-min walk from Gaienmae Stn (Ginza Line). Turn right from the ticket turnstile and go up the stairs. Make a right from the exit and walk to the corner of the Bell Commons Building. Cross the street and turn right. Watari-um is a few minutes down on the left side.

TAISEIDO BOOKSTORE
大盛堂 （洋書部）

6F (Foreign Books), 1–22–4 Jinnan, Shibuya-ku, Tokyo 150–0041

☎ 3461–3419 (Foreign Book Dept)
東京都渋谷区神南1-22-4　6階　〒150-0041

Taiseido's foreign book corner contains about 5,000 foreign books, paperbacks, and magazines.

Hours: 10 AM–8 PM daily.

Access: A 2-min walk from Shibuya Stn, Hachiko Exit (Yamanote and other lines). You will see a big Sony television screen on the side of the 109-2 Building across from the station. Walk down the street that runs alongside the left of it. It will be on the right side of the street, across from Seibu Department Store.

TOWER RECORDS BOOKSTORE

タワーレコード渋谷店（洋書部）

Tower Records Building, 7F (Foreign Books)

1–22–14 Jinnan, Shibuya-ku, Tokyo 150–0041

☎ 3496–3661

東京都渋谷区神南1-22-14　タワーレコード7階　〒150-0041

The entire 7F of Tower Records Shibuya building is devoted to foreign books and magazines. Most of the over 80,000 books and scores of magazines are in English, with some in French and German. Tower also features newspapers from major cities around the world. Their travel, music, and arts sections are particularly plentiful, and they have a nice selection of audio books as well.

NOTE: The store is also a great playground for music lovers. For here at the largest of Tower's six Tokyo stores, you can don headsets and listen to dozens of the latest record releases for free. And the "Tower Street Studio" broadcasts live radio shows from the front window of the store.

Hours: 10 AM–10 PM daily. Clsd 10 days each year for store hols.

Access: A 3-min walk from Shibuya Stn, Hachiko Exit (Yamanote and other lines). You will see a large Sony TV screen on the side of the 109-2 Building directly in front of the station. Walk straight down the large main street that runs along its left side. Tower Records will be on the right side of this street.

YAESU BOOK CENTER

八重洲ブックセンター（洋書部）

7F (Foreign Books), 2–5–1 Yaesu, Chuo-ku, Tokyo 104–8456

☎ 3281–3606 (Foreign Books Dept)

東京都中央区八重洲2-5-1　7階　〒104-8456

Yaesu Book Center is conveniently located across from Tokyo Station and is said to be Japan's largest book store. Its foreign book section stocks over 100,000 books—mostly in English, with some in European and Asian languages. In addition to literature, art, hobbies, and travel, the store also carries books on the sciences and mathematics and maintains a large selection of computer books. It has lots of magazines and newspapers, too.

Hours: 10 AM–7:30 PM Mon–Sat and hols. Open 10 AM–6 PM the 2nd and 4th Sun of the month and clsd other Sun.

Access: 1 min from Tokyo Stn, Yaesu South Exit (Yamanote and other lines). It is on Sotobori-dori, across the street from the station and a little to the right. The name is on the building in English.

USED BOOKSTORES

And don't forget about all those wonderful used-book stores in Kanda. Foreign books are generally mixed in with the stacks piled up in front of the shops, and some stores even specialize in them. The 3F **Wonderland Bookstore** (☎ 3233–2507) carries used English magazines, comics, and paperbacks on just about every subject. **Matsumura & Company** (☎ 3295–5678) specializes in foreign art books. The hushed, scholarly atmosphere of the **Kitazawa Foreign Bookstore** (☎ 3263–0011) lets it be known that they specialize in such subjects as literature, linguistics, and history.

Ohya Shobu (☎ 3291–0062) carries original publications from the Edo period (1600–1868) and always has very old maps and art works elegantly displayed in their window. These are just a few of the many used bookstores to be found along Yasukuni-dori near Jinbocho Station (Tozai, Toei Shinjuku, and Hanzomon lines). There are many, many more waiting to be explored. And by all means, leave the main drag and check out the small back streets too.

14

PHOTO
EXHIBITIONS
AND
ART GALLERIES

PHOTO EXHIBITION SHOWROOMS

Ginza/Nihonbashi

- *Fuji Photo Salon*
- *Ginza Canon Salon*
- *Ginza Nikon Salon*
- *Kodak Photo Salon*
- *Kyocera Contax Salon*
- *Nikon Mini Gallery*
- *Zeit-Foto Salon*

Shinjuku—East

- *Konica Plaza*
- *Minolta Photo Space*

Shinjuku—West

- *Gallery One*
- *Nikon Mini Gallery*
- *Pentax Forum*
- *Shinjuku Nikon Salon*

Other Areas

Ebisu • *Studio Ebis Photo Gallery*

Hanzomon • *JCII Photo Salon*

Kanda • *Olympus Plaza*

Shibuya • *Doi Photo Plaza*, *Egg Gallery*

Toranomon • *Photo Gallery International*, *Polaroid Gallery*

ART GALLERIES

Some Ginza/Kyobashi Galleries

(Art Lovers' Paradise at Established Venues)

Ginza Area

- *Aoki Gallery*
- *Gallery Kobayashi*
- *Gallery Lunami*
- *Gallery Q & QS*
- *Ginza Graphic Gallery/ggg*
- *Kamakura Gallery*
- *Nishimura Gallery*
- *Plus Minus Gallery*
- *Sakai Kokodo Gallery*

- *Satani Gallery*
- *Shirota Gallery*
- *Yoshii Gallery*

Kyobashi Area
- *Ai Gallery*
- *Akira Ikeda Gallery Tokyo*
- *G Art Gallery*
- *Gallery K*
- *Gallery Koyanagi*
- *Galerie Tokoro*

Some Aoyama/Harajuku Galleries
(Innovative Spirit and Young Upstarts)
- *AKI-EX Gallery*
- *Gallery Tao*
- *Gallery 360°*
- *Mizuma Art Gallery*
- *Okazaki Tamako Gallery*
- *Spiral Garden*

More Nooks and Crannies to Explore
(Galleries in Other Areas)

Daikanyama • *Hillside Gallery, Asakura Gallery, Yamada Heiando Artistic Lacquerware*

Ebisu • *Contemporary Sculpture Center*

Hiroo • *Lynn Matsuoka Gallery*

Kanda • *Mita Arts Gallery, Ohya Shobo*

Nogizaka • *Gallery Ma*

Odaiba Beach Area • *Fuji Television Gallery*

Shiba Daimon • *The Tolman Collection*

Shibuya • *Bunkamura Gallery*

Shinjuku • *Gallery Shinjuku Takano, P3—Art and Environment*

Yanaka • *Artforum Yanaka, Gallery KO, SCAI/The Bathhouse*

• *Embassy-Sponsored Exhibitions*

Public Art
Odaiba Beach Area • *Searea Odaiba Art Project*

Shinjuku • *Shinjuku i-Land*

Tachikawa • *Faret Tachikawa*

PHOTO EXHIBITION SHOWROOMS

INTRODUCTION

There are a number of venues for viewing photography exhibitions in Tokyo. Camera and film companies sponsor many of these and often combine them with showrooms for their products. The two main groupings can be found in Ginza and Shinjuku, with others scattered around the city. Free postcards featuring works from the show are usually there for the taking, and the photographer is often present for the duration of the exhibition. Watch the listings—shows generally last only one or two weeks.

One great feature of photo showrooms are the courtesy bulletin boards that display information on the other exhibitions currently running in the city. But please be aware that on the final day, shows often close several hours earlier than the posted time—as is the case with many art exhibitions in Japan.

GINZA/NIHONBASHI

FUJI PHOTO SALON

富士フォトサロン

Sukiyabashi Center, 2F
5–1 Ginza, Chuo-ku, Tokyo 104–0061
☎ 3571–9411
東京都中央区銀座5-1　数寄屋橋センター2階　〒104-0061

This salon contains three exhibition areas: Fuji Photo Salon, a professional space, and a hallway gallery. The salon frequently has group exhibits with travel themes, such as life in Bora-Bora or Vietnam. A recent exhibition in the professional space showed everyday happenings taken from unusual angles—people eating on the street, a man changing shoes—fleeting moments in time captured on film. The hallway gallery often has beautiful nature shots on display. One of these was a striking exhibition of birds in flight. Exhibitions are determined by a contest held every three months for both professional and amateur photographers.

Hours: Open 10 AM–8 PM daily.

Access: 1 min from Ginza Stn, Exit C1 or C2 (Ginza, Marunouchi, and Hibiya lines). Come out either exit—turn and go back in the opposite direction. You will see the Sukiyabashi Shopping Center in front of you. The stairway on the left inside the building will take you up to the gallery.

GINZA CANON SALON
銀座キヤノンサロン

    5–9–9 Ginza, Chuo-ku, Tokyo 104–0061
    ☎ 3573–7821
    東京都中央区銀座5-9-9　〒104-0061

"Breath," a dramatic show of black-and-white close-up photography depicting leaves in their natural habitat was a recent offering at the Ginza Canon Salon. Mostly shot at night, the leaves were painstakingly lit to bring out their texture, shapes, and molding. Chosen by competition each March and September, both professional and amateur photographers display their works at this gallery.

Hours: Open 9 AM–5:30 PM Mon–Fri, 9–4 Sat. Clsd Sun and hols.

Access: 3 min from Ginza Stn, Exit A5 (Ginza, Marunouchi, and Hibiya lines). Walk straight to the 2nd corner and turn right. The entrance will be on the right side at the end of that block.

GINZA NIKON SALON
銀座ニコンサロン

    Matsushima Gankyo Building, 3F
    3–5–6 Ginza, Chuo-ku, Tokyo 104–0061
    ☎ 3562–5756
    東京都中央区銀座3-5-6　松島眼鏡ビル3階　〒104-0061

Exhibitions chosen by a panel of five artists are displayed here and cover a variety of subjects. One show was an ultra-realistic, nonglamorized look at the American Southwest. It depicted gas stations, diners, a billiard hall, and several neon-lit motels.

Unlike the other camera companies that combine their galleries with showrooms and service centers, Nikon's facilities are at separate locations (see Nikon Mini Gallery below).

Hours: Open 10:30 AM–7 PM Tues–Sun, 10:30 AM–2 PM Mon. Clsd New Year and summer hols.

Access: A 3-min walk from Ginza Stn, Exit A9 (Ginza, Marunouchi, and Hibiya lines). Go straight out from the exit. The showroom is on the left side of the next block, upstairs from Matsushima Eyeglass Store (across from Matsuya Department Store).

KODAK PHOTO SALON

コダック フォト サロン

Nikkus Ginza Building, 2F

6–11–4 Ginza, Chuo-ku, Tokyo 104–0061

☎ 3572–4411

東京都中央区銀座6-11-4　ニックス銀座ビル2階　〒104-0061

One serene exhibition here portrayed the use of stone in traditional Japanese gardens. Very large rocks represented mountains and islands, while tiny pebbles were shown as water in the abstract. Footpaths, stone bridges, lanterns, and moss-covered rocks were all beautifully photographed as well. Shows are selected by a competition held twice a year—in the spring and autumn—and cover a wide range of topics.

Hours: Open 10 AM–6 PM. Clsd Sun and hols.

Access: 3 min from Ginza Stn, Exit A5 (Ginza, Marunouchi, and Hibiya lines). Walk straight to the 2nd corner and turn right. The entrance will be on the right side at the beginning of the 2nd block.

KYOCERA CONTAX SALON

京セラ コンタックス サロン

Tokyo Kyukyodo Building, 5/6F

5–7–4 Ginza, Chuo-ku, Tokyo 104–0061

☎ 3572–1921

東京都中央区銀座5-7-4　東京鳩居堂ビル5/6階　〒104-0061

A recent exhibition here was on Pagan—Myanmar's (Burma) architectural treasure of the 11th to 13th centuries containing numerous temples and pagodas that have miraculously survived to the present day. In addition to shots of the spectacular ruins, local scenes of area shopkeepers and women with their faces decorated in powdered sandalwood were included.

The main gallery on the 6F hosts exhibitions selected via a contest each October, and a smaller space surrounding the 5F showroom features works by professional photographers and Contax Club Members.

Hours: 10:30 AM–6:30 PM. Clsd Wed.

Access: Immediately to the right of Exit A2 of Ginza Stn (Ginza, Marunouchi, and Hibiya lines). Take the elevator on the outside of the Tokyo Kyukyodo Building to the 6F to reach the main exhibition gallery.

NIKON MINI GALLERY
ニコン ミニ ギャラリー

　　Nikon Nihonbashi Service Center
　　Nihonbashi First Building, 9F
　　1–2–19 Nihonbashi, Chuo-ku, Tokyo 103–0027
　　☎ 3281–6810 (Ask for Mr. Ito)
　　東京都中央区日本橋1-2-19　日本橋ファーストビル9階ニコン日本
　　橋サービスセンター　〒103-0027

Attention budding photographers: Nikon displays the photos of their customers in two "mini galleries" located in their Nihonbashi and Shinjuku service centers—for free. No exam or test is needed to hold a two-week exhibition. Just sign up and prepare your pictures for display—the center will even provide the frames if you need them. Your show will be listed in the Asahi Camera and Nihon Camera monthly Japanese photo magazines—and the more than 100 people who come to the service center every day will see your photos. This is a great opportunity to begin exhibiting your work. Check it out next time you bring your Nikon in for a free checkup and cleaning—or before.

Hours: 10 AM–6 PM Mon–Sat. Clsd Sun and national hols.

Access: 1 min from Nihonbashi Stn, Exit A4 (Tozai and Ginza lines). Walk out of the building and turn right, then turn right again at the corner. You will see the Nikon sign in front of you.

ZEIT-FOTO SALON
ツァイト フォト サロン

Yagicho Building, 5F
1–7–2 Nihonbashi Muromachi, Chuo-ku, Tokyo 103–0022
☎ 3246–1370
東京都中央区日本橋室町1-7-2　八木長ビル5階　〒103-0022

This up-scale gallery displays classic and contemporary art photos by Japanese and foreign professional photographers. One recent show featured the intricate carvings found on gothic cathedrals and various other ornately decorated structures. Black-and-white panoramic views of the South African landscape were the focus of another.

Hours: 10:30 AM–6:30 PM wkdys, 10:30 AM–5:30 PM Sat. Clsd Sun and hols.

Access: 1-min walk from Mitsukoshi-mae Stn, Exit A1 (Hanzomon and Ginza lines). Turn and walk in the opposite direction. Make the first left down the small street and enter the first doorway on your right. Take the elevator to the 5F.

SHINJUKU—EAST

KONICA PLAZA (Photo Gallery and Camera Museum)
コニカ プラザ

Shinjuku Takano Building, 4F
3–26–11 Shinjuku, Shinjuku-ku, Tokyo 106–0022
☎ 3225–5001
東京都新宿区新宿3-26-11　新宿タカノビル4階　〒106-0022

The Konica Plaza covers an entire floor, and includes a camera museum and two photo galleries. The larger West Gallery is often used by a number of professional photographic organizations as a venue for their shows. Other exhibitions are selected through contests held each March and September. One show featured extremely large photos of Tokyoites lounging in their tiny Tokyo apartments. Although I did feel a bit like a Peeping Tom, it was fascinating to observe the different environments that individuals created for themselves in such a limited space. Another exhibition followed the adventures of Japanese quintuplets from birth to their high-school graduation on Tokunoshima Island. The East Gallery is rented to photographers to display their works, which often include international subject matter.

The free camera museum displays about 200 items, rotated periodically from the company's large permanent collection. Ranging in size from tiny "spy cameras" to large aerial-photography models, some date back to the 1800s. Cameras from a number of countries can be seen here too—I saw some from France, Germany, Spain, Russia, the United States, Korea, and China.

Hours: 10:30 AM–8 PM daily. Clsd one wkdy every two months

Access: 1 min from JR Shinjuku Stn, East Exit (Yamanote and other lines). Turn right and walk down Shinjuku-dori. The Takano Building is located on the right side of the street just behind Yodobashi Camera, which fronts the station.

MINOLTA PHOTO SPACE

ミノルタ サービス ステーション

Kawase Building, 3F

3–17–5 Shinjuku, Shinjuku-ku, Tokyo 160–0022

☎ 3356–6281

東京都新宿区新宿3-17-5　カワセビル3階　〒160-0022

Minolta's main exhibition area is known as the Photo Space. Professional and amateur photographers who have passed a monthly exam display their works here. At one show, the events leading up to a boxing match were documented in black-and-white photos. Executed with a great deal of sensitivity, the exhibition included a dramatic shot of a pair of training shoes with laces askew sitting in the middle of a large empty room.

A smaller exhibition lines the walls of the adjoining Minolta showroom and small camera museum. One was a display of photographic effects that can be achieved on a computer. You can play with all the cameras sitting out and browse through their collection of photo magazines and books. The ever-present courtesy bulletin board displays postcards of other photo exhibitions showing around town.

Hours: 10 AM–6 PM Mon–Sat. Clsd Sun and hols.

Access: Directly upstairs from Shinjuku-sanchome Stn, Exit B6 (Marunouchi Line), or a 2-min walk from JR Shinjuku Stn, East Exit (Yamanote and other lines). Turn right and walk down Shinjuku-dori toward Isetan Department Store. It is on the left side. Look for the blue Minolta logo in front.

SHINJUKU—WEST

GALLERY ONE

ギャラリー ワン

Shinjuku Park Tower Building, 1F

3–7–1 Nishi Shinjuku, Shinjuku-ku, Tokyo 163–1001

☎ 5322–6492 (Gallery), 5322–6633 (Office)

東京都新宿区西新宿3-7-1　新宿パークタワー1階　〒163-1001

One of the newer additions to the photo gallery scene, Gallery One is a permanent space on the main floor of the Shinjuku Park Tower Building. It is also the planning area for temporary exhibition spaces Galleries Two and Three, which are set up ad hoc in the building's spacious foyer from time to time. Exhibitions usually consist of photographs, but at times other art forms are displayed.

Some very interesting exhibitions have appeared here. One entitled "Colored Beauty" consisted of panels of large, blown-up photographs of brightly colored people—in various shades of green, blue, red, and yellow. It definitely made you sit up and take notice.

NOTE: The TSS Gas Showroom (see ch 15) is across the foyer of this huge 52-story building, which also houses the top-ranked Park Hyatt Hotel on its upper floors.

Hours: 11 AM–7 PM daily.

Access: A 12-min walk from JR Shinjuku Stn, South Exit (Yamanote and other lines). Turn right from the station and head toward the 52-story Shinjuku Park Tower Building looming ahead of you. It will be on the right side just beyond the road overpass. The Tokyo Gas Building is just before it—they are attached at the lobby level inside. Also accessible via Nishi Shinjuku Stn (Marunouchi Line).

NIKON MINI GALLERY

ニコン ミニ ギャラリー

> Nikon Shinjuku Service Center
> Shinjuku NS Building, 5F
> 2–4–1 Nishi Shinjuku, Shinjuku-ku, Tokyo 163–0890
> ☎ 5321–4466 (Ask for Mr. Kawada)
> 東京都新宿区西新宿2-4-1　新宿NSビル5階　ニコン新宿サービス
> センター　〒163-0890

See Nikon Mini Gallery in the Ginza/Nihonbashi section of this chapter for information on exhibitions and how Nikon users can display their photographs for free.

Hours: 10 AM–6 PM daily except New Year hols, the 4th Sun and the following Mon of Feb, the 1st Sun and the following Mon of Aug.

Access: A 10-min walk from Shinjuku Stn, South Exit (Yamanote and other lines). Turn right from the exit and walk to the 5th traffic light. Turn right (don't cross the street yet). Walk one block to the next light, then cross to your left. You will be in front of the building. Also accessible by Nishi Shinjuku Stn (Marunouchi Line).

NOTE: The very large, unusual clock in the lobby of this building is run completely by water power.

PENTAX FORUM

ペンタックス フォーラム

> Shinjuku Mitsui Building, 1F
> 2–1–1 Nishi Shinjuku, Shinjuku-ku, Tokyo 163–0401
> ☎ 3348–2941
> 東京都新宿区西新宿2-1-1　新宿三井ビル　1階　〒163-0401

Nature photography from around the world is usually featured in the Pentax Forum. During a recent show, photographs of tropical birds were accompanied by cheerful chirping and other bird sounds in the background. Another time breathtaking shots of a night train winding its way through the Japan Alps were shown. All exhibitions are determined by examinations.

Many hands-on Pentax products can be seen in the next-door showroom, including very large telescopic zoom lenses through which you can view the "nature" of the surrounding Nishi Shinjuku area. A display case in the middle of the room contains some very special items—an exquisite camera of gold

PHOTO EXHIBITIONS
AND ART GALLERIES

and alligator skin, and an interesting plastic see-through model.

Hours: 10:30 AM–6:30 PM daily.

Access:A 7-min walk from JR Shinjuku Stn, West Exit (Yamanote and other lines). Follow the signs through the underground passageway to the high-rise district. The Shinjuku Mitsui Building is on the right as you emerge from the tunnel. Also accessible via Nishi Shinjuku Stn (Marunouchi Line).

SHINJUKU NIKON SALON
新宿ニコン サロン

Keio Plaza Hotel, 3F Lobby

2–2–1 Nishi Shinjuku, Shinjuku-ku, Tokyo 160–8330

☎ 3344–0565

東京都新宿区西新宿2-2-1　京王プラザホテル ロビーフロアー
〒160-8330

This gallery often displays artistic photos with an abstract flair, with emphasis on the design elements of the picture. A recent show entitled "Moss Cosmos" explored the various kinds of moss and their growth patterns, while another defined the architectural aspects of European buildings. Selections are made from exams given once a month. Unlike most other camera company–sponsored photo galleries, the Nikon camera showroom and service centers are at separate locations. (See the above entry on the Nikon Mini Gallery.)

Hours: Open 10 AM–7 PM daily.

Access:A 7-min walk from JR Shinjuku Stn, West Exit (Yamanote and other lines). Follow the signs through the underground passageway to the high-rise district. When you emerge, the Keio Plaza Hotel will be on your left. It is inside the hotel adjacent to the 3F lobby lounge. Also accessible via Nishi Shinjuku Stn (Marunouchi Line).

OTHER AREAS

■ Ebisu

STUDIO EBIS PHOTO GALLERY

スタジオ エビス フォト ギャラリー

Studio Ebis Building, 2F
1–9–2 Ebisu, Shibuya-ku, Tokyo 150–0013
☎ 3444–5522
東京都渋谷区恵比寿1-9-2　スタジオ エビス ビル2階　〒150-0013

Studio Ebis is located in a complex containing eight studios where print ads and other types of photography are shot. The gallery seems to serve as a showcase for photographers' experimental techniques. One recent show featured colored images of water superimposed over the scenery of Spain and Portugal, while another displayed photos partially covered with oil paint and broken glass. It is an interesting gallery in the middle of an area that has become quite popular lately. Yebisu Garden Place (see ch 3) is just a few minutes away.

Hours: 10 AM–7 PM. Clsd 2nd and 4th Sun and hols.
Access: A 2-min walk from JR Ebisu Stn (Yamanote Line), East Exit. Go down the stairs by the ticket gate and walk straight out to the street. Turn left at the signal. The gallery is 50 m (45 yd) down on the left side, past the Subway sandwich shop. It is also accessible from Hibiya Line's Ebisu Stn.

■ Hanzomon

JCII PHOTO SALON

JCII フォト サロン

JCII Building, 1F
25 Ichibancho, Chiyoda-ku, Tokyo 102–0082
☎ 3261–0300
東京都千代田区一番町25　ジェイシーアイアイビル1階
〒102-0082

JCII's (Japan Camera Inspection Institute) main-floor photo gallery displays the works of Japanese professional photographers. The shows often feature old photographs of historic value.

PHOTO EXHIBITIONS
AND ART GALLERIES

Some exhibitions simply document events of days gone by, while others feature photographs that appeared in international publications such as *Life* magazine. One exhibition displayed shots that captured the 1930s lifestyle of a small Western town in the United States.

NOTE: There is also a camera museum in B1 (¥300).

Hours: 10 AM–5 PM Tues–Sun. Clsd Mon.

Access: 2 min from Hanzomon Stn, Exit 4 (Hanzomon Line) Turn right from the station and right again before Sakura Bank. The JCII Building is on the right side.

■ Kanda

OLYMPUS PLAZA
オリンパス プラザ

Ogawamachi Mitsui Building, 1F

1–3–1 Kanda Ogawamachi, Chiyoda-ku, Tokyo 101–0052

☎ 3292–1934 (Gallery), 3292–1931 (Showroom)

東京都千代田区神田小川町1-3-1　小川町三井ビル1階　〒101-0052

Striking documentary or nature shows are often the subject matter at this gallery. Previous exhibitions have featured life-sized photos and a show on the great outdoors, complete with a tent set up in the middle of the room. Selections are made from exams given twice a year.

The Olympus showroom contains various areas to explore— such as a "Digital Imaging Corner" and a "New Products Corner." During my visit, the latter featured a "Mediamask" headset that you could don and take a trip through a virtual town, whizzing through its streets and soaring above it much in the same manner as Superman. A comfortable little library corner stocked with photographic books rounds off the offerings.

Hours: The gallery is open 10 AM–6 PM Mon–Sat (the showroom from 9 AM). Clsd Sun and New Year, national, and company hols.

Access: 1 min from Ogawamachi Stn (Asakusa Line), Exit A6. From the exit, turn around and walk back in opposite direction. Soon you will see it on your left side. It is also 2 min from Awajicho Stn, Exit A4 (Marunouchi Line). Walk straight out the exit and it will be on your left.

■ Shibuya

DOI PHOTO PLAZA
ドイ フォト プラザ

Camera no Doi Head Building, 7F
1–11–3 Jinnan, Shibuya-ku, Tokyo 150–0041
☎ 3496–5141
東京都渋谷区神南1-11-3　カメラのドイ本社ビル7階　〒150-0041

This photo gallery can be found on a busy corner in central
Shibuya, where both amateur and professional groups and individuals display their works. Exhibitions are chosen through
competitions held four times a year. A show entitled "Body Language" depicted the way people express their emotions through
body movements and posture; another documented a young
Buddhist monk's daily regime.

In addition to its main gallery, Doi has a "Step Way Gallery"
that winds around the staircase from the 7F down to the 1F.
Their bulletin board is pretty special, too—detailed maps to
other exhibitions are posted on it alongside the announcements.

Hours: 10 AM–7 PM Thurs–Tues. Clsd Wed.
Access: A 4-min walk from Shibuya Stn, Hachiko Exit (Yamanote and
other lines). You will see a big Sony TV screen on the side of the
109-2 Building in front of the station. Walk down the street that
runs alongside the left of it. Doi Camera is on the far right
corner just after you pass Tower Records. The elevator up to the
7F photo gallery is located inside the store.

EGG GALLERY
エッグ ギャラリー

Egg Building, 2F
1–13–10 Jinnan, Shibuya-ku, Tokyo 150–0041
☎ 3780–5023
東京都渋谷区神南1-13-10　エッグビル2階　〒150-0041

This gallery features contemporary photography. One recent
show, "Healing Landscapes," displayed Edward Levinson's medi-
tative photographs of nature taken with a pinhole camera.
Another featured black-and-white photos in which light and

shadow were used to create flower imagery. Sometimes offerings other than photography are shown here. One such exhibition spotlighted the graphic designs of art-school students.

Hours: 11 AM–7 PM Mon–Sat. Clsd Sun.

Access: An 8-min walk from Shibuya Stn, Hachiko Exit (Yamanote and other lines). You will see a big Sony TV screen on the side of the 109–2 Building in front of the station. Walk down the street that runs alongside the left of it. Go past Tower Records on the right side and turn left at the next corner (at the Doi Camera Building). Turn right up the next small street (at Swensen's Ice Cream Parlor) and follow it around as it curves to the left. The Egg Gallery is on the right side in the block following the curve.

■ Toranomon

PHOTO GALLERY INTERNATIONAL
フォト ギャラリー インターナショナル
2–5–18 Toranomon, Minato-ku, Tokyo 105–0001
☎ 3501–9123
東京都港区虎ノ門2-5-18　〒105-0001

This cozy little gallery is located in a tiny house in a small alley, and it features works from both Japanese and foreign contributors. Black-and-white scenes of Paris and its people, desertscapes from Egypt and the American Southwest, and artistic photos of crystals and snow by a Hokkaido photographer were some recent showings. They also have a branch in Shibaura (☎ 3455–7827).

Hours: 11 AM–7 PM Mon–Fri. Clsd Sat, Sun, and hols.

Access: 4 min from Toranomon Stn, Exit 2 (Ginza Line). Go straight out from the exit to the first traffic signal (Toranomon-itchome). Cross the street and go right, then turn left down the first small alley. You will see the gallery sign in English on the left.

POLAROID GALLERY
ポラロイド ギャラリー
No. 30 Mori Building, 1F
3–2–2 Toranomon, Minato-ku, Tokyo 105–0001
☎ 3438–8811
東京都港区虎ノ門3-2-2　第30森ビル1階　〒105-0001

Photographers display work taken with Polaroid products here. One very original exhibition consisted of shots that documented various people's lifestyles through images of objects and settings—without ever actually showing the people. A show entitled "Nouvelle" featured tinted black-and-white glamor shots of women, done in the nostalgic style of the 1930s and 1940s.

Hours: 9 AM–5 PM Mon–Fri. Clsd Sat, Sun, and hols.

Access: A 5-min walk from Toranomon Stn, Exit 2 (Ginza Line). Walk straight for about 4 min until you reach the san-chome intersection (Japan Sword is on the left corner). Turn and walk right. On the left side you will see a green-and-white sign that looks like a square billiard ball with a No. 30 in the center. The gallery is on the main floor of that building.

ART GALLERIES

INTRODUCTION

Tokyo is an art-filled city. It has never been described as being a beautiful city, since the frantic rebuilding following earthquakes, fires, war, and spurts in the economy has created a kind of hodgepodge metropolis. But it is replete with art—and art lovers. Note the three-deep crowds at all the traveling art exhibitions that make their way to Tokyo each year.

And you don't have to go to pricey exhibitions to enjoy art in Tokyo. There is an easier and better way. Take in the art galleries, which some estimates have put at 1,000. Many are clustered together in central sections of the city, making gallery-hopping easy for residents and visitors alike. Look for the free little bilingual maps of gallery locations with listings of current exhibitions given out in some of the galleries.

Ginza/Kyobashi

Ginza made its mark as the center of art and fashion in prewar times. The fashion scene has since moved on to trendy Aoyama, but Ginza still maintains its place in the art world, and houses many respected and established galleries. It (together with neighboring Kyobashi) easily qualifies as the main gallery center of the city. For within the area roughly bordered by Showa-dori to the south and the Shuto Expressway on the other three sides, there are 300 to 400 galleries, with a particularly heavy concentration in Ginza's 5-chome through 8-chome neighborhoods (between Chuo-dori and Sotobori-dori streets). *But please be aware that not all of the galleries are on a main floor with big signs out front. Some of the precious little gems are located on higher or lower floors—look for tiny little roll-out signs in front.*

Aoyama/Harajuku

The fashionable Aoyama/Harajuku section of the city also

contains a high concentration of galleries. It came into its own during the "bubble economy" days of the 1980s, when many new buildings designed by celebrated architects were constructed here. Today it is the main fashion center of Tokyo, with many fun and interesting galleries mixed in with the shops and restaurants that populate its maze of narrow lanes. The art scene is centered around Omotesando Station and in the streets branching off from Omotesando Avenue stretching to Harajuku Station.

You never know what you are going to run across here. On a stroll down a back street one day I happened upon **Fairy** (☎ 3499–5541), a small gallery dedicated to the art of ballet; the four-storied **Galeria Building** that houses galleries on every floor (including Latin art); **Mizuma** (see below); and **Las Chicas** (☎ 3407–6865), a combination gallery/outdoor cafe that displays works throughout the entire building. If these were the offerings on just one small street—imagine the possibilities of what you might find on your own personal wanderings.

More Nooks and Crannies

Galleries are scattered throughout other areas of the city, too. I have included a sampling here, and soon you will discover your own favorites. The art listings in the English-language publications describe current exhibitions, and opening parties are sometimes written up—and open to all. Meeting the artists while you view their work and sip refreshments can make for some very special evenings.

And believe it or not, there is an art foundation—**Za Moca**—that offers free exhibition space in Tokyo for avant-garde artists (both local and foreign), and provides free living accommodations for visiting artists as well. They even throw great parties to launch each exhibition! The foundation supports the avant-garde culture in every form, including all visual and performing arts, and lends the works at no charge to museums around the world. For information, call or fax **Za Moca** at ☎ 3460–0680.

NOTE: If you are interested in pursuing the Tokyo gallery scene in greater depth, there is an excellent English book entitled *Tokyo Contemporary Art Guide*, published by the Japan-Netherlands Institute. While not available in stores, ordering and price information can be obtained by calling the institute at ☎ 3808–2123 or faxing 3808–2033.

PHOTO EXHIBITIONS
AND ART GALLERIES

SOME GINZA/KYOBASHI GALLERIES

■ Ginza Area

AOKI GALLERY

青木ギャラリー

Shimada Building, 2F

3–5–16 Ginza, Chuo-ku, Tokyo 104–0061

☎ 3535–6858

東京都中央区銀座3-5-16　島田ビル2階　〒104-0061

Surrealist works have been presented at this gallery since 1961. Mainly paintings are on display, but sometimes dolls and other interesting works by Japanese, German, and Austrian artists are exhibited.

Hours: 10:30 AM–6:30 PM. Clsd Sun and hols.

Access: 4 min from Ginza Stn, Exit A9 (various subway lines). Walk to the corner and make a left, then take the 1st right. The gallery is on the right side about halfway down the block. Please note that several small buildings next to each other have the same address here—so keep looking. Please don't give up as I did on my first try to find this gallery.

GALLERY KOBAYASHI

小林画廊

Yamato Building, B1

3–8–12 Ginza, Chuo-ku, Tokyo 104–0061

☎ 3561–0515

東京都中央区銀座3-8-12　ヤマトビル地下1階　〒104-0061

This gallery is known for presenting original contemporary shows of young Japanese artists in various art forms—painting, prints, sculpture, relief, and installations. Sometimes they participate in cultural exchange programs with Australian and New Zealand galleries.

Hours: 11:30 AM–7 PM. Clsd Sun.

Access: 3 min from Ginza Stn, Exit A8 (various subway lines). Walk straight for one block, then turn right. Turn left at the 2nd small street. It is the 2nd building on the right side. Go down to B1.

GALLERY LUNAMI

ルナミ画廊

Zenrin Building, 3F

4–8–11 Ginza, Chuo-ku, Tokyo 104–0061

☎ 3535–3065

東京都中央区銀座4-8-11　善隣ビル3階　〒104-0061

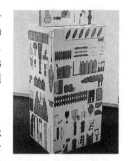

This gallery presents exhibitions of promising young contemporary artists, both foreign and Japanese. A variety of art forms can be seen here, such as paintings, photography, and sculpture. Australian Johan Davis is one of the artists who participates in their international exchange program with Australian and European galleries.

Hours: 11:30 AM–7 PM Mon–Sat. Clsd Sun.

Access: 3 min from Ginza Stn, Exit A6 (various subway lines). Walk straight down Harumi-dori and turn left at the 2nd corner (at Shinwa Bank). Gallery Lunami is in the 3rd building on the right side.

GALLERY Q & QS

ギャラリーQ アンド QS

Tosei Building, B2

8–10–7 Ginza, Chuo-ku, Tokyo 104–0061

☎ 3573–2808

東京都中央区銀座8-10-7　東成ビル地下2階　〒104-0061

This small but internationally active gallery shows works by new contemporary Japanese, Korean, and Chinese artists. The two galleries on the B2 level are both under the same management and present a great variety of offerings—paintings, sculpture, installation art, videos, and even performance art.

Hours: 11 AM–7 PM. Clsd Sun and hols.

Access: 5 min from Ginza Stn, Exit A3 (various subway lines). Walk along Chuo-dori toward Shinbashi. Turn left at the 3rd corner, and go right at the 2nd small street after that. The gallery will be on the right side toward the end of the block.

GINZA GRAPHIC GALLERY/ggg

銀座グラフィック ギャラリー

DNP Ginza Building, B1/1F
7–7–2 Ginza, Chuo-ku, Tokyo 104–0061
☎ 3571–5206
東京都中央区銀座7-7-2　DNP銀座ビル1階/地下1階　〒104-0061

For lovers of graphic design, this is the place to go. Dai Nippon, one of the world's largest printing companies, sponsors this showcase for contemporary graphic design. The gallery participates in international design shows and sometimes displays graphic design from the Netherlands, France, Hungary, and other countries. Graphics from the 1960s and 1970s can be seen here at times, as well.

Hours: 11 AM–7 PM Mon–Fri, 11 AM–6 PM Sat. Clsd Sun and hols.
Access: 5 min from Ginza Stn, Exit A2 (various subway lines). Walk straight along Chuo-dori toward Shinbashi. Turn right at the 2nd corner. The gallery is on the next corner on the left side.

KAMAKURA GALLERY

鎌倉画廊

Hirakata Building, 1F
7–10–8 Ginza, Chuo-ku, Tokyo 104–0061
☎ 3574–8307
東京都中央区銀座7-10-8　平方ビル1階　〒104-0061

This gallery deals exclusively with conceptual and minimal art. They display installations, paintings, and objects. Well-known Korean-born Lee U-Fan shows here, along with other prominent Japanese and foreign artists.

Hours: 11:30 AM–7 PM. Clsd Sun and hols.
Access: 5 min from Ginza Stn, Exit A3 (various subway lines). Walk along Chuo-dori toward Shinbashi. Turn left at the 2nd corner (at Lion Beer Hall). Turn right at the 2nd small street. The gallery will be on the right side at street level close to the next corner.

NISHIMURA GALLERY

西村画廊

Nishi Ginza Building, B1

4–3–13 Ginza, Chuo-ku, Tokyo 104-0061

☎ 3567–3906

東京都中央区銀座4-3-13　西銀座ビル地下1階　〒104-0061

The works of well-known contemporary artists can be seen at this gallery. Both Japanese and foreign artists are represented in various art forms—photographs, prints, drawings, sculpture, and paintings. David Hockney is one of the artists whose work they carry.

Hours: 10:30 AM–6:30 PM. Clsd Sun, Mon, and hols.

Access: 1 min from Ginza Stn, Exit B4 (various subway lines). When you surface, you will see Fuji Bank on your right. Turn down the street running alongside it (Namiki-dori), and Nishimura Gallery will be a few doors down on the right (Final Stage boutique is on the 1F). Go down to B1.

PLUS MINUS GALLERY

プラス マイナス ギャラリー

TEPCO Ginza Building, 2F

6–11–1 Ginza, Chuo-ku, Tokyo 104–0061

☎ 3575–0456

東京都中央区銀座6-11-1　テプコ銀座館2階　〒104-0061

This fun little gallery sponsored by TEPCO (Tokyo Electric Power Company) specializes in installation art, sculpture, and objects—no paintings or photos. It is now incorporated into the TEPCO Showroom building in the heart of Ginza, which has a number of interactive exhibits to play with. Don't miss the salt-water fish tank on the main floor with holes in the side to stick your hand in and feel the fish brush up against your fingers as they swim by! (See ch 15, TEPCO Visitors Center)

Hours: 10:30 AM–6:30 PM daily except Wed (Clsd Thurs if Wed is a hol).

Access: A 3-min walk from Ginza Stn, Exit A3 (various subway lines). Go straight out and turn left at the first street. The TEPCO building will be on the far right corner of the next block.

PHOTO EXHIBITIONS
AND ART GALLERIES

SAKAI KOKODO GALLERY

酒井好古堂

Murasaki Building, 1F
1–2–14 Yurakucho, Chiyoda-ku, Tokyo 100–0006
☎ 3591–4678
東京都千代田区有楽町1-2-14　紫ビル1階　〒100-0006

This small gallery, a stone's throw from the Imperial Hotel, has specialized in *ukiyo-e* (traditional woodblock prints) for over 100 years (since 1870). It is affiliated with the Japan Ukiyo-e Museum, which is located several hours outside Tokyo. Look for their free English pamphlet that explains how *ukiyo-e* are printed.

Hours: 11 AM–6 PM daily. Clsd noon–1 PM for lunch
Access: 5 min from Ginza Stn, Exit C1 (various subway lines). Walk straight out from the exit and turn left down the small street immediately on the other side of the train tracks. Turn right at the next large street, and the gallery will be the 2nd building on the right. The entrance is set back from the street but the name is on the door in English. Also accessible from the JR Yurakucho Stn (Hibiya Exit) and Hibiya Subway Stn (Exit A4).

SATANI GALLERY

佐谷画廊

No. 2 Asahi Building, B1
4–2–6 Ginza, Chuo-ku, Tokyo 104–0061
☎ 3564–6733
東京都中央区銀座4-2-6　第2朝日ビル地下1階　〒104-0061

Paintings, sculpture, and installations by respected artists are some of the works that can be seen at this gallery. They also handle well-known European artists like Joan Miró, Paul Klee, and Man Ray, and important Japanese artists such as Arakawa, Naofumi Maruyama, and Masato Kobayashi.

Hours: 11 AM–6 PM. Clsd Sun and hols.
Access: 2 min from Ginza Stn, Exit C6 (various subway lines). Make an immediate right down the small street outside of the exit. The building is on the left side at the end of that block. Go down to B1.

SHIROTA GALLERY

シロタ画廊

Takahashi Building, B1

7–10–8 Ginza, Chuo-ku, Tokyo 104–0061

☎ 3572–7971

東京都中央区銀座7-10-8　高橋ビル地下1階　〒104-0061

Print lovers can see the works of important contemporary Japanese print-makers here. The gallery also handles the art of such noted artists as Andy Warhol and Roy Lichtenstein. Sometimes other works, such as sculpture or paintings, are presented.

Hours: 11 AM–7 PM. Clsd Sun and hols.

Access: 5 min from Ginza Stn, Exit A3 (various subway lines). Walk straight along Chuo-dori and turn left at the 2nd corner (Lion Restaurant on corner), then right at the next corner. The entrance is on the left side near the next corner.

YOSHII GALLERY

吉井画廊

Kyoto Shinbun Building, 2F

8–2–8 Ginza, Chuo-ku, Tokyo 104–0061

☎ 3572–5726

東京都中央区銀座8-2-8　京都新聞ビル2階　〒104-0061

If you are a fan of French art, you will probably want to visit the Yoshii Gallery. Their French paintings (and a few American works as well) range from Impressionism through the present. The gallery was founded thirty years ago here in Ginza, but today they have branches in Paris and New York as well. They also have a smaller gallery directly across the street at ground level that exhibits modern French works.

Hours: 10 AM–7 PM Mon–Sat. Clsd Sun and hols.

Access: 5 min from Ginza Stn, Exit C2 (various subway lines). Walk to the corner and turn right on Sotobori-dori. The gallery is in the 4th block on the right side, across from the Nikko Hotel. There is a sign on the building in English. Also accessible from Shinbashi Stn (Yamanote and other lines).

■ Kyobashi Area

AI GALLERY

藍画廊

Shin Kyobashi Building, 1F

3–3–8 Kyobashi, Chuo-ku, Tokyo 104–0031

☎ 3274–4729

東京都中央区京橋3-38-8　新京橋ビル1階　〒104-0031

This little gallery exhibits a variety of works by emerging Japanese and Korean artists. Shows might include paintings, sculpture, or installation exhibitions. Check out the Kyobashi Gallery and Gallery Tsubaki just across the lane, too.

Hours: 11:30 AM–7 PM Mon–Fri, 11:30 AM–6 PM Sat. Clsd Sun.

Access: 2 min from Kyobashi Stn, Exit 2 (Ginza Line). Go straight out of the exit and cross Chuo-dori to the right at the 1st traffic signal. Continue down the small lane directly in front of you. A triangular-shaped building will be on your left. Enter the gallery through the side door of this building.

AKIRA IKEDA GALLERY TOKYO

アキライケダ ギャラリー東京

Jitsugyo no Nihon-sha Takaracho Building, 1F

2–17–1 Kyobashi, Chuo-ku, Tokyo 104–0031

☎ 3567–5090

東京都中央区京橋2-17-1　実業の日本社宝町ビル1階　〒104-0031

This gallery shows the works of important Japanese, American, and European artists. Exhibitions of paintings, sculpture, and installations are sometimes split between the Tokyo gallery and its larger space in Yokosuka. Robert Rauschenberg and Jiro Takamatsu are on its roster of artists, as is Italian artist Pino Pascali. The gallery has been in Tokyo since 1982, and moved to its present location in 1995. There are also branches in Nagoya and New York.

Hours: 10 AM–6 PM. Clsd Sun, Mon, and hols.

Access: A 5-min walk from Kyobashi Stn, Exit 4 (Ginza Line). Go straight to the main intersection (Showa-dori). Cross the street and turn left, then turn right at the 2nd street. The gallery is on the far left side of the next corner. Enter through the foyer of the building. Also 2 min from Takaracho Stn, Exit A2 (Toei Asakusa Line).

G ART GALLERY
ジー アート ギャラリー

> Ginza 18 Building, B1
> 2–5–18 Ginza, Chuo-ku, Tokyo 104–0061
> ☎ 3562–5858
> 東京都中央区銀座2-5-18　銀座18ビル地下1階　〒104-0061

Experimental work is shown in this rental gallery, usually by young, emerging artists in their twenties and thirties. As you descend to the gallery, you can see the works from the open staircase.

Hours: 11 AM–6:30 PM (5 PM on final day). Clsd irregularly.

Access: A 5-min walk from Kyobashi Stn, Exit 3 (Ginza Line). At street level, turn and go back to the corner. Turn right, pass under the highway, and turn right again. At the 2nd street corner, go left. It is on the left side at the beginning of the following block. It is also immediately to the left of Exit 5 of Ginza-itchome Stn (Yurakucho Line).

GALLERY K
ギャラリー K

> No. 2 Ginryoku Building, 3F
> 1–9–6 Ginza, Chuo-ku, Tokyo 104–0061
> ☎ 3563–4578
> 東京都中央区銀座1-9-6　第2銀緑ビル3階　〒104-0061

Each January and August, this caring little gallery run by a committee sponsors a nonprofit exhibition that uses art in a very special way—to raise people's awareness of problems in the world today, and hopefully instill in them a sense of responsibility to do something about them. Some past themes have been the children of Chernobyl, the mentally disabled, refugees from the former Yugoslavia, and AIDS awareness. In addition to sponsoring the exhibitions, they donate to each cause in other ways as well. The rest of the year they hold exhibitions of contemporary paintings, sculpture, installations, and other forms of art.

PHOTO EXHIBITIONS
AND ART GALLERIES

Hours: 11 AM–7 PM Mon–Sat (6 PM on the final day). Clsd Sun.

Access: 4 min from Kyobashi Stn, Exit 2 (Ginza Line) Walk straight out, pass under the highway, and turn left. Turn right at the 2nd corner and the gallery will be the fifth building on the right. The address 9–6 is on the front.

GALLERY KOYANAGI

ギャラリー小柳

Koyanagi Building, 1F

1–7–5 Ginza, Chuo-ku, Tokyo 104–0061

☎ 3561–1896

東京都中央区銀座1-7-5　小柳ビル1階　〒104-0061

The works of well-known and emerging contemporary artists can be seen here. Both Japanese and foreign artists are represented in various art forms—paintings, photographs, drawings, sculpture, installations, and videos.

Hours: 11 AM–7 PM. Clsd Sun and hols.

Access: 3 min from Kyobashi Stn, Exit 3 (Ginza Line). At street level, turn and go back to the corner and turn right. After you pass under the highway, it will be the second building on the right, after Tokyo Mitsubishi Bank.

GALERIE TOKORO

ギャルリーところ

Ginza A Building, B1

1–6–2 Ginza, Chuo-ku, Tokyo 104–0061

☎ 3563–3696

東京都中央区銀座1--6-2　銀座Aビル地下1階　〒104-0061

Galerie Tokoro displays the works of famous European, American, and Japanese artists such as Constantin Brancusi, George Segal, Peit Mondrian, and Vasily Kandinsky. Posters of previous exhibitions held here line the wall as you enter. And not to be forgotten are the works of Japanese artist Tomio Miki, whose drawings and sculptures of his ear (yes, his ear), ranging from minute to grandiose, can often be found gracing the gallery's sweeping 3 m by 62 m (10 by 200 ft) main exhibition wall.

Hours: 10 AM–6 PM. Clsd Sat, Sun and national, New Year, and summer hols.

Access: 3 min from Kyobashi Stn, Exit 3 (Ginza Line). At street level, turn and go back to the corner. Turn right, pass under the highway, and turn right. At the 1st small street go left. The gallery entrance is the stairway going down immediately on the right side.

SOME AOYAMA/HARAJUKU GALLERIES

AKI-EX GALLERY

アキ EX ギャラリー

Minami Aoyama City House, 2F

5–4–44 Minami Aoyama, Minato-ku, Tokyo 107–0062

☎ 3499–4267

東京都港区南青山5-4-44　南青山シティハウス2階　〒107-0062

This gallery is a hoot. The owner likes unusual works that make a strong impression. And that they do. One April, 500 *Hina Matsuri* (Girls' Day) dolls were on display—breaking with the tradition of doing it at the appointed time in March. But that's not all. Instead of traditional dolls in ancient court dress, you were greeted by row after row of molded dolls, painted a bright shocking pink and sporting sparkling rhinestone eyes! The show was called "Fat Time." Japanese contemporary art of all types can be seen here—including painting, photography, installation art, and objects.

Hours: 11:30 AM–7 PM Mon–Sat. Clsd Sun and hols.

Access: A 5-min walk from Omotesando Stn, Exit B1 (Ginza, Hanzomon, and Chiyoda lines). Go straight to the corner and make a left. Walk down Kotto-dori (away from Kinokuniya Supermarket), and make another left at the 2nd light. Turn right at the 2nd small street. There is a sign for the gallery there and you will be able to see the building at the end of the street. The gallery is on the 2nd floor, above the Ex-Lounge restaurant. If the entrance to the upstairs is locked, someone from the restaurant can let you in.

GALLERY TAO

ギャラリー TAO

Maple House, B1

4–8–6 Jingumae, Shibuya-ku, Tokyo 150–0001

☎ 3403–1190

東京都渋谷区神宮前4-8-6　メープルハウス地下1階　〒150-0001

Located between Omotesando and Harajuku is Gallery Tao—a delightful showcase for ceramic art. One lighthearted show that put a smile on everyone's face featured 500 small ceramic lions—each one unique. They were created by an Okinawan artist who enjoyed chatting (in English) about them. Another exhibition consisted of white, rounded sculptures with very soft, organic appearances. Both Japanese and foreign artists show here. Don't let the directions put you off—it's really quite easy to find—and worth it.

Hours: 11 AM–7 PM Mon–Sat. Clsd Sun.

Access: 5 min from Omotesando Stn, Exit A2 (Ginza, Hanzomon, and Chiyoda lines). Go straight out from the exit and turn right down the 1st small street (at McDonald's). Turn left at the end of the street (at Royal Host) and then make the 1st right followed by the 1st left (Maisen Tonkatsu Restaurant is on the corner). Gallery Tao is the pink building on the right side, adjacent to the restaurant.

GALLERY 360°

ギャラリー360°

2F, 5–1–27 Minami Aoyama, Minato-ku, Tokyo 107–0062

☎ 3406–5823

東京都港区南青山5-1-27　2階　〒107-0062

This light and cheery little contemporary art gallery overlooks the corner of Omotesando Station and essentially features international artists. Opened in 1982 as a "center for communication through the medium of contemporary art," it features minimal and conceptual works. Goods, objects, crafts, installation art, and sometimes woodblock prints are displayed. One show, "Art and Necessities," showed how interesting design concepts were incorporated into everyday objects such as shopping bags and watches. And of course, there were some unusual offerings too, such as a derby hat with a mini-chessboard on top!

Hours: 11 AM–7 PM Mon–Sat. Clsd Sun and hols.

Access: 3 min from Omotesando Stn, Exit B3 (Ginza, Hanzomon, and Chiyoda lines). Make a right from the exit. It is just past Andersen's Bakery.

MIZUMA ART GALLERY

ミヅマ アート ギャラリー

Twin S Building, 1F

5–46–13 Jingumae, Shibuya-ku, Tokyo 150–0001

☎ 3499–0226

東京都渋谷区神宮前5-46-13　ツインエスビル1階　〒150-0001

This gallery was established in 1984 in another area, but moved to this location in 1994. The works of Japanese and foreign artists covering a wide variety of styles and subject matter are exhibited here, each personally selected by the owner. A spiritual installation entitled "Karappo" (Emptiness) was one such offering. In this show, most of the gallery was taken up by the "One Hundred Stone Sutra," a large circle of stones that gradually increased in size as they encircled the Buddhist sutras written directly on the floor. Other sutras were represented by smaller displays of natural materials that were striking in their simplicity.

NOTE: For other galleries on this street, see the introduction to this section.

Hours: 11 AM–7 PM Mon–Sat. Clsd Sun and hols.

Access: A 5-min walk from Omotesando Stn, Exit B2 (Ginza, Hanzomon, and Chiyoda lines). Walk straight from the exit, passing Kinokuniya Supermarket, and turn right at Citibank. The gallery is about 3 min down the street on the right side.

OKAZAKI TAMAKO GALLERY

岡崎珠子画廊

Harajuku Greenland Building, 2F, #202

1–21–1 Jingumae, Shibuya-ku, Tokyo 150–0001

☎ 3470–2298

東京都渋谷区神宮前1-21-1　原宿グリーンランドビル2階202号　〒150-0001

Way over on the other perimeter of this art area, deep in Hara-juku-ville, lies this somewhat offbeat gallery. One long-running show consisted of a spiritual trilogy in which a series of what the artist felt were "universal sounds" were written on large blue pieces of paper arranged on the wall. The gallery is very active in both international and local events and shows works by its own artists—conceptual art as well as contemporary mixed-media, objects, and paintings.

Hours: 11 AM–7 PM Mon–Sat. Clsd Sun and hols.
Access: A 3-min walk from JR Harajuku Stn, Takeshita-dori Exit (Yamanote Line). Cross the street in front of the station and turn left. When you come to the 2nd small street, turn right. The gallery is in a green building on the right side about halfway down the road. It is set back slightly and "Harajuku Greenland" is written on the front in English. Take the outside steps on the right to the 2F.

SPIRAL GARDEN
スパイラル ガーデン
Spiral Building, 1F
5–6–23 Minami Aoyama, Minato-ku, Tokyo 107–0062
☎ 3498–1171
東京都港区南青山5-6-23　スパイラル ビル1階　〒107-0062

This is perhaps the best-known gallery in the area. Opened in 1985, the building itself is a showpiece, with its gallery in the center of—and often part of—a spiral ramp that leads to the 2F. It features contemporary art—photography, paintings, and sometimes installations. Yoko Ono is among the artists who have shown here. One exhibition was on the heart and soul of trees, and featured a series of objects carved from natural wood. They were surrounded by oversized, slightly out-of-focus forest photographs that resembled Impressionist paintings.

NOTE: Spiral Garden Gallery is free most of the time, but once in a while they charge for special exhibitions.

Hours: 11 AM–8 PM daily. Clsd New Year and summer hols.
Access: 1 min from Omotesando Stn, Exit B1 (Ginza, Hanzomon, and Chiyoda lines). Come up from the station and turn around. You will see the Spiral Building.

MORE NOOKS AND CRANNIES TO EXPLORE

■ Daikanyama

HILLSIDE GALLERY (Art Front Gallery)
ヒルサイド ギャラリー (アート フロント ギャラリー)

Hillside Terrace Building A, 1F

29–18 Sarugakucho, Shibuya-ku, Tokyo 150–0033

☎ 3476–4795 (Gallery, in Japanese),

3476–4868 (Office, in English)

東京都渋谷区猿楽町29-18　ヒルサイドテラスビルA 1階
〒150-0033

This gallery is located in Daikanyama, another of Tokyo's trendy little areas, and is known for its innovative exhibitions of Japanese sculpture, paintings, and installation art. Each artist is personally chosen by the president of the gallery, Fram Kitagawa, who is very active on both the Tokyo and the international art scenes. The gallery also represents a number of famous international artists, such as Christo and Claes Oldenburg. Mr. Kitagawa was the planner and coordinator of the ambitious Faret Tachikawa outdoor public sculpture project (see below). A map (in English) of Faret Tachikawa is available at the gallery, or the staff can direct you to a location where you might obtain one.

You might want to combine a visit to the gallery with a walk around Daikanyama afterward. If it is a weekend, just follow the crowds through the small streets lined with interesting shops and eclectic restaurants.

Hours: 11 AM–6 PM daily. Clsd New Year hols and between exhibitions. The office is open 9 AM–6 PM Mon–Fri for information. Generally someone can answer your questions in English.

Access: A 3-min walk from Daikanyama Stn, Main Exit (Tokyu Toyoko Line—local stop). Go straight out of the station and turn right when the road ends. Turn left at the major street and take the overpass across Kyu Yamate-dori (the larger street). As you descend to the right, the gallery is in front of you on the corner of the Hillside Terrace Complex.

PHOTO EXHIBITIONS
AND ART GALLERIES

Other Galleries in the Hillside Terrace Complex

Other galleries and craft shops are located within Hillside Terrace as well. Maps scattered throughout the complex give their locations. For fans of lacquer ware, **Yamada Heiando Artistic Lacquerware** (Building G) is not to be missed. Tables, dishes, screens, trays, boxes, and chests are among the treasures that await you inside. The sign outside reads: "Artistic Lacquerware and Industrial Artworks by appointment to the Imperial Household" (☎ 3464–5541).

And be sure to wander through the spacious and elegant **Asakura Gallery** (Building F), where you can view objects attractively displayed in this multi-level space. The final room is a glass-enclosed combination gallery/coffee shop (☎ 5489–3648).

■ Ebisu

CONTEMPORARY SCULPTURE CENTER

現代彫刻センター（Gendai Chokoku Center）

> Yebisu Garden Place, Nibankan Building, 1F
> 4–20–2 Ebisu, Shibuya-ku, Tokyo 150–0013
> ☎ 5423–3001
> 東京都渋谷区恵比寿4-20-2　恵比寿ガーデンテラス2番館1階
> 〒150-0013

A striking exhibition of Auguste Rodin bronzes was one recent show here. Another time sculptures of metal and paper generally void of color allowed the viewer to concentrate on their "Light, Shadow, and Reflection"—as the exhibition was called. Exhibitions of the permanent collection and guest artists are presented at this gallery.

Hours: 10 AM–6 PM. Clsd Sun and hols.

Access: Yebisu Garden Place (see ch 3) is located at the end of the Skywalk that starts at the East Exit of JR Ebisu Stn (Yamanote Line). The gallery is on the 1F of the Nibankan Building, behind Mitsukoshi Department Store.

■ Hiroo

LYNN MATSUOKA GALLERY
リン マツオカ ギャラリー

Aries Court, 101
2–9–10 Moto Azabu, Minato-ku, Tokyo 106–0046
☎ 3443–1443
東京都港区元麻布2-9-10　アリスコート101　〒106-0046

Lynn Matsuoka is an American woman who was married to a
sumo wrestler. She has become quite famous for her paintings of
sumo and kabuki life. Her studio is generally open by appointment only, but about six or seven times a year she holds an open
house. If you don't see it advertised, you might call to ask when
the next one is scheduled.

Hours: During open houses and by appointment.
Access: 8 min from Hiroo Stn, Exit 1 (Hibiya Line). Turn left from the
exit, and left at the corner. Follow this street around until you
see the National Azabu Supermarket and Arisugawa Park. Walk
up the road that runs between them to the end of the park's
baseball field and continue across the street. The gallery is here
at this T-crossing.

■ Kanda

MITA ARTS GALLERY
三田アート画廊

Ivy Building, 4F
1–10 Kanda Jinbocho, Chiyoda-ku, Tokyo 101–0051
☎ 3294–4554
東京都地千代田区神田神保町1-10　アイビービル4階　〒101-0051

David Caplan arrived in Japan in 1962 with no background in
art. But he immediately fell in love with *ukiyo-e*, Edo-period
(1600–1868) prints and paintings depicting scenes of the entertainment quarters and famous people of the day—such as
kabuki actors and sumo wrestlers. And as fate would have it, he
remained here to become a major figure on the Tokyo art scene
and an expert on *ukiyo-e* art. He is now executive director of the

Japan Ukiyo-e Society, and a member of the board of directors of the Ukiyo-e Dealers Association of Japan. In 1995 he opened Mita Arts Gallery, where he offers *ukiyo-e* works as well as modern prints and paintings, and gives free appraisals. Several times a year the gallery holds special exhibitions.

Hours: 10:30 AM–6:30 PM Tues–Sat. Clsd Sun and Mon.
Access:Next to Jinbocho Stn, Exit A5 (Hanzomon, Mita, and Toei Shinjuku lines). The gallery is just to the left of the exit.

OHYA SHOBU
大屋書房

1–1 Kanda Jinbocho, Chiyoda-ku, Tokyo 101–0051
☎ 3291–0062
東京都千代田区神田神保町1-1　〒101-0051

Ohya Shobu claims to carry the "world's largest stock" of *ukiyo-e* prints, as well as a nice collection of old maps and books. Located in the center of the used book area of Kanda (see ch 13), it is a wonderful store that feels like someone's attic—with all kinds of good stuff to look through. The gallery has original publications from the Edo period (1600–1868) handwritten in beautiful calligraphy, and woodblock prints hanging on its walls. Some very special ones are by Utamaro, Hiroshige, and Hokusai—including fifteen volumes of the latter's *manga* picture books. You can't miss the place—old world maps, books, and lovely works of art are always elegantly displayed in the front window.

Hours: 10:30 AM–6:30 PM Mon–Sat. Clsd Sun and some hols.
Access:5 min from Jinbocho Stn, Exit A7 (Hanzomon, Mita, and Toei Shinjuku lines). Make a right from the station exit, and another right at the corner. It is on Yasukuni-dori where the road bends.

■ Nogizaka

GALLERY MA

ギャラリー間

TOTO Nogizaka Building, 3F

1–24–3 Minami Aoyama, Minato-ku, Tokyo 107–0062

☎ 3402–1010

東京都港区南青山1-24-3　TOTO乃木坂ビル3階　〒107-0062

Gallery Ma isn't like any other gallery around town, for it serves as a free forum where top Japanese and international architects can express their ideas and convey their concepts of life through installation works exhibited here.

A very unusual and sprawling prototype of an ideal city created by a Japanese husband and British wife team was featured at one show. Spanish architect Felix Candela's award-winning dome shells capable of surviving 8.1 Richter-scale earthquakes were seen here another time. "Public Body in Crisis" was a group show that expressed the exhibitors' concern with the dissolution of public life, and offered some solutions for improving the situation.

NOTE: Gallery GA (☎ 3403–1581) is also a top architectural gallery in Tokyo, but charges ¥500 admission.

Hours: 11 AM–7 PM. Clsd Sun and hols.

Access: Nogizaka Stn, Exit 3 (Chiyoda Line). At the top of the escalators, take the steps to your right. At street level, look back across the small road to your right and you will see a dark blue building with TOTO written on top. Take the elevator to the 3F.

■ Odaiba Beach Area

FUJI TELEVISION GALLERY

フジテレビギャラリー

Fuji Television Headquarters Building

Media Tower, 7F

2–4–8 Daiba, Minato-ku, Tokyo 135–0091

☎ 5500–5930

東京都港区台場2-4-8　フジテレビ本社メディアタワー7階

〒135-0091

The Fuji Television Gallery sponsors original contemporary art shows of Japanese and foreign artists in a variety of art forms,

PHOTO EXHIBITIONS
AND ART GALLERIES

NOTE: You can visit the "Sphere" skydeck on the 24F afterward for a spectacular view of the entire area (¥500). Access it via the special elevators that depart from the 7F roof garden. The "Sphere" skydeck is open 10 AM to 10 PM (last elevator up at 9:30 PM). Clsd Mon (Tues if Mon is a hol).

such as painting, prints, sculpture, and installation art. After twenty-six years in the Akebonobashi area, in 1997 the gallery relocated to Fuji Television's new headquarters in the recently developed Odaiba area. (See ch 3—Odaiba Beach Area, for other nearby attractions.)

Hours: The gallery is open 11 AM–7 PM. Clsd Sun and hols.

Access: The Fuji Television Building is located next to Daiba Stn on the Yurikamome Transit System, which originates at Shinbashi Stn (Yamanote and other lines). Take the covered escalator to the 7F.

■ Shiba Daimon

THE TOLMAN COLLECTION

トールマン コレクション

2–2–18 Shiba Daimon, Minato-ku, Tokyo 105–0012

☎ 3434–1300

東京都港区芝大門2-2-18　〒105-0012

When you slide open the traditional Japanese door of this gallery you will immediately be greeted by the smell of tatami. A staff member will welcome you and show you around this former geisha house. According to owner Norman Tolman, the gallery presents "avant-garde Japanese art in a traditional setting." And the combination seems to have worked. For the gallery, which is more than twenty-five years old, has become as famous as some of the artists it represents. This includes one of Japan's most well known female artists, Toko Shinoda, whose abstract Impressionist works hang in Tokyo's Imperial Palace.

Norman and Mary Tolman have written four books on Japanese prints, and have been nominated for a Japan Foundation award for their work in introducing Japanese art to the rest of the world. They carry a wide variety of artistic styles and techniques in their collection—all signed and numbered limited editions.

Hours: 11 AM–7 PM Wed–Mon. Clsd Tues.

Access: 3 min from Daimon Stn, Exit A3 (Asakusa Line). Go left from the station and left at the corner. Walk to the 3rd small street and turn left (at Sanwa Bank). The gallery is on the left side, halfway down the block. Look for the sign in front in English. They will also be happy to fax you a map if you call ahead.

■ Shibuya

BUNKAMURA GALLERY
文化村ギャラリー

Bunkamura Building, Main Lobby
2–24–1 Dogenzaka, Shibuya-ku, Tokyo 150–0043
☎ 3477–9174
東京都渋谷区道玄坂2-24-1　文化村メインロビー　〒150-0043

The Bunkamura Gallery is a free little oasis located on the main floor of the large Bunkamura entertainment complex, where concert halls, movie theaters, and the like abound. It is not to be confused with the complex's museum downstairs (that charges an admission). The gallery has quality shows in a variety of media—which might include photography, etchings, drawings, paintings, woodblock prints, or installation works.

A 120-print exhibition featuring the work of Marc Chagall was held here recently. Etchings by Yayoi Kusama, who has been called one of Japan's most acclaimed postwar artists, was another offering. Fifty photos on Parisian life by French photographer Jean Philippe Charnonnier were also on display, including his shots of the "Liberation of Paris." Once or twice a year the gallery holds an auction of modern contemporary art.

Hours: 10 AM–7:30 PM daily. Clsd during exhibitions preparation and New Year hols.

Access: A 7-min walk from Shibuya Stn, Hachiko Exit (Yamanote and other lines). Walk left along Dogenzaka for about 1 min and turn right at the 109 Building (the big silver tower on the corner) onto Bunkamura-dori. Turn left at the 3rd traffic signal, just before Tokyu Department Store. The entrance to Bunkamura is on the right side at the end of the block. The gallery is on the 1F on the left side.

■ Shinjuku

GALLERY SHINJUKU TAKANO
ギャラリー新宿高野

Shinjuku Takano No. 2 Building, 3F
3–30–11 Shinjuku, Shinjuku-ku, Tokyo–160–-0022
☎ 3352–8893
東京都新宿区新宿3-3-0-11　新宿高野第2ビル3階　〒160-0022

This gallery has exhibitions of just about every type of art—ceramics, sculpture, paintings, prints, drawings, woodblock prints, and even crafts. This popular and convenient little gallery, located just across the street from Isetan Department Store in Shinjuku, displays the works of both Japanese and international artists.

Hours: 11 AM–7 PM. Clsd Wed.

Access: On Shinjuku-dori, directly across from Shinjuku-sanchome Stn, Exit A5 (Marunouchi and Shinjuku lines). When leaving the subway level, walk up the steps to the left—don't enter Mitsukoshi Department Store. When you reach the street level, the entrance to the building's elevators is directly across the alley. It is also a 5-min walk from JR Shinjuku Stn, East Exit (Yamanote and other lines).

P3—ART AND ENVIRONMENT
P3—アート エンバイロメント

Tochoji Temple, B1
4–34 Yotsuya, Shinjuku-ku, Tokyo 160–0004
☎ 3353–6866 (Gallery)
東京都新宿区四ツ谷4-34　東長寺地下1階　〒160-0004

This very special art space is located in the basement of a Buddhist temple that was founded in 1594. The gallery was created when the temple was rebuilt in 1989, and exhibits experimental art of Japanese and international artists—usually with a meaningful theme connected with the spiritual, the environment, or the betterment of society. It is quite large—250 sq m (2,700 sq ft) with a 5-m (16.5-ft) high ceiling. Previously called the Alternative Museum, the gallery has had shows featuring innovative music and sound installations, live performances, and interactive video displays. They have exhibitions about six times a year, each about a month long.

Don't leave without seeing the upstairs temple with the water garden in front (created in 1996 to be a new kind of cemetery). The temple also offers free lessons in *zazen* (Zen meditation) in Japanese and sponsors an Asian festival each autumn, at which entertainment from many Asian countries is featured. The name P3, by the way, is a play on two factors: the first being that the earth is the third p(lanet) from the sun, and the second a nod to their beginnings on the 3F of a p(re-fab) building.

NOTE: Admission is free about half the time. They don't always have an exhibition on, so please check first (in Japanese).

Hours: Generally 11 AM–7 PM Tues–Sun. Clsd Mon and between shows. Times may vary according to each exhibition, so it's best to call.

Access: 8-min walk from Shinjuku Gyoenmae Stn, Exit 2 (Marunouchi Line). Turn left from the exit and walk to the major intersection (Yotsuya 4-chome). Cross the street, turn left, and walk until you come to the temple on your right side. The gallery is just beyond the corner temple graveyard.

■ Yanaka

ARTFORUM YANAKA

アートフォーラム谷中

6–4–7 Yanaka, Taito-ku, Tokyo 110–0001

☎ 3824–0804

東京都台東区谷中6-4-7　〒110-0001

This light, triangular space with large windows features an eclectic variety of exhibitions—paintings, installations, ceramics, and other art forms. If there is a show going on, you can combine it with a trip to SCAI/The Bathhouse (see later entry), then wander around one of Tokyo's most traditional neighborhoods and take in all the old houses, little shops, and numerous temples.

Hours: 11 AM–7 PM. Clsd Sun, Mon, irregularly.

Access: JR Nippori Stn, South Exit (Yamanote Line). Directions same as SCAI (below) until you reach the traffic light at the end of the road. Cross the street and walk to the right. Look for the building with bamboo growing out front on the 2nd corner.

GALLERY KO

ギャラリー工

7–4–10 Yanaka, Taito-ku, Tokyo 110–0001

☎ 3823–5171

東京都台東区谷中7-4-10　〒110-0001

This is a cozy little corner space that exhibits drawings, paintings, photos, and ceramics upstairs (with little handmade items for sale downstairs, where everything seems to be scaled down to a smaller size). One exhibition featured sketches of cats in unusual poses that brought smiles to the faces of everyone who visited the show.

Hours: 11:30 AM–7 PM. Clsd Mon and Tues.
Access: JR Nippori Stn, South Exit (Yamanote Line). Directions same as for SCAI (below) until you reach the traffic light at the end of the road. It is on that near right corner.

SCAI/THE BATHHOUSE
(Shiraishi Contemporary Art Inc)

白石コンテンポラリーアート

Kashiwayu-Ato, 6–1–23 Yanaka, Taito-ku, Tokyo 110–0001

☎ 3821–1144

東京都台東区谷中6-2-12　柏湯跡　〒110-0001

This gallery was originally a bathhouse (ca 18th century), and it still looks like one. As a bathhouse it was frequented by artists, and later became a popular backdrop for television dramas before becoming an art gallery in 1994. Now it is a space for exhibitions of Japanese and international artists. It also happens to be smack in the middle of one of Tokyo's most fascinating areas—Yanaka. This historic section of Tokyo has survived fairly well intact from Edo times (1600–1868), fending off the devastation of earthquakes, fires, and war. A visit to the gallery should definitely include a look around the area, for it is almost like stepping back in time to the days of the shoguns.

Hours: Noon–7 PM. Clsd Sun, Mon, and hols.
Access: JR Nippori Stn, South Exit (Yamanote Line). Walk left from the station and go up the stairs on your left to the cemetery. Once

inside, follow the road to the left. When the road ends at the traffic light at the far end, turn left. The gallery will be at the next traffic light on the far right corner. It is also accessible via Nezu Stn, Exit 1 (Chiyoda Line).

EMBASSY-SPONSORED EXHIBITIONS

A number of the embassies in Tokyo sponsor free exhibitions. The Canadian Embassy has a permanent gallery on the same level as its library (see ch 13). Other embassies periodically sponsor shows as well (generally the works of their nationals), held either on embassy premises or at outside venues. Watch the foreign-language publications for listings. You might also check with your embassy to see if it participates in such programs.

PUBLIC ART

■ Odaiba Beach Area

SEAREA ODAIBA ART PROJECT

シーリアお台場アート プロジェクト

c/o SCAI—The Bathhouse (Shiraishi Contemporary Art)
Kashiwayu-Ato, 6–1–23 Yanaka, Taito-ku, Tokyo 110–0001
☎ 3821–1144
東京都台東区谷中6-1-23　柏湯跡　〒110-0001

This 1996 public art project is part of the development of Tokyo's new Odaiba Beach Area (see ch 3). Located among the outdoor cafes of "Sunset Beach Restaurant Row," Shigeo Fukuda's white sculptures on colored pedestals perform clever changing acts right before your eyes when viewed from different angles. The blue *Spirit of the West* changes from A to Z, the green *Spirit of the East* switches from A to N (the first and last letters on the Japanese *kana* script), and the red *Spirit of Hope* moves from zero to the sign for infinity.

Shoichiro Higuchi's two *Twisted Headband* sculptures are made of intertwining hollow stainless steel tubes painted bright orange and yellow. They were created to encourage interaction between sculpture and humans, and children are welcome to climb over and play inside them.

French artist Daniel Buren's *25 Porticos* is a series of squared-off arches that welcome visitors to Odaiba and lead them down to the beach area from a spot near the train station exit. They are painted in bright yellow, green, red, and white stripes for a light, uplifting feeling. With the exception of *Twisted Headband*, all pieces are lit up at night.

Hours: 24 hours.

Access: All the works are located near the Odaiba Kaihin Koen Stn (Yurikamome Line). Exit the station on the water side. The *Spirit* sculptures are located along Sunset Beach Restaurant Row. From the station, take the steps to the right down to street level. The first piece in the *Spirit* series is at the next corner. The other two are in the middle and the end of the restaurant row. *Twisted Headband's* orange sculpture is at the bottom of the same set of steps, and the yellow version is just beyond the beginning of *25 Porticos*, which is located on the Central Plaza, just to the left of the exit.

■ Shinjuku

SHINJUKU i-LAND
新宿アイランド

Shinjuku i-Land Tower Building
6–3–5 Nishi Shinjuku, Shinjuku-ku, Tokyo 163–1390
☎ 5323–2829
東京都新宿区西新宿6-3-5　新宿アイランドタワー　〒163-1390

If you like big, bold sculpture, you should pay a visit to Shinjuku i-Land. Ten works by well-known Japanese and international artists, such as Luciano Fabro and Roy Lichtenstein, grace the interior and exterior of this new multipurpose development (opened in 1995). Its entrance is clearly marked by Robert Indiana's large, red *LOVE* sculpture (pronunciation of the long "i" sound in English is *ai*—the Japanese word for "love"). This has been hailed as a refreshing "island" in the midst of all the stark high-rise buildings of the Nishi Shinjuku area.

Hours: Outside always open, inside open daily 10 AM–10 PM.

Access: Shinjuku i-Land is next door to the Hilton Hotel—above Nishi Shinjuku Stn (Marunouchi Line). Follow the direct access signs from inside the station. Or it's a 12-min walk from JR Shinjuku Stn, West Exit (Yamanote and other lines).

■ Tachikawa

FARET TACHIKAWA
ファーレ立川

    c/o Art Front Gallery
    Hillside Terrace Building A, 1F
    29–18 Sarugakucho, Shibuya-ku, Tokyo 150–0033
    ☎ 3476–4868 (Art Front Gallery)
    東京都渋谷区猿楽町29-18　ヒルサイドテラスA1階　〒150-0033

If you liked Shinjuku i-Land, you are going to love Faret Tachikawa. It is not as centrally located, but once you get there you will find over 100 public works of art waiting for you. Ninety-two artists from thirty-six countries participated in this massive undertaking to bring their art to this delightful redevelopment of a former American military base.

    Some fun pieces are Jean-Pierre Raynaud's (France) *Giant Flowerpot;* Robert Rauschenberg's (USA) *Bicycloid,* a neon bicycle sign that really marks the location of the bicycle parking lot; and Niu Bo's (China) *Reverse Side of a Target,* a playful piece with arrows sticking out of its backside. Other works are meant to light up your life—literally. For as dusk settles in, some of the artwork switches on to illuminate the walkways and buildings with playful splashes of color. Some pieces double as street lamps. You will want to see many of the works in the daylight, of course, but if you visit toward the end of the day you can catch the illuminated ones as well.

Note: I highly recommend that you do a little research before you go in order to get the most from your visit, since there is so much you can miss if you don't know it is there. Call the Art Front Gallery (project planner and coordinator) at the number mentioned above for information and places to pick up free English maps. And be sure to allow yourself at least two hours there.

Hours: Information is available 9 AM–6 PM Mon–Fri at the above number. The works are outdoors and accessible 24 hours a day.

Access: 3 min from Tachikawa Stn, North Exit (Chuo Line). Walk straight up the main street (Kitaguchi-odori Street) away from the station. Just beyond the next intersection (Midorikawa-dori Street) you will see a park and fountain on your left. Enter between them and start exploring.

PHOTO EXHIBITIONS
AND ART GALLERIES

15

SUPER
SHOWROOMS

VISIT A SHOWROOM

- *Amlux Toyota Auto Salon*—"Largest car showroom in the world"
- *ASEAN Centre*—Get to know our Southeast Asian neighbors
- *Cosmetic Garden—Shiseido*—Play with makeup all day long
- *Fujita Vente*—Healthy environment and lots of fun and games
- *Gas Science Center*—Take a tour and see a fabulous view
- *Ginza Sony Building*—State-of-the-art electronic fun
- *Glass Exhibition and Information Center*—The glass in your life
- *Honda Welcome Plaza*—From motorcycles to racing cars
- *INAX*—Natural Materials, galleries, model kitchens, and bathrooms (2 showrooms)
- *Informuse*—Uses of paper and beyond!
- *Saké Plaza*—Learn all about it (hic!)
- *NAIS Showroom Shinjuku*—Light up your life and relax your weary bod
- *NEC Showroom C&C Plaza*—Play with technology
- *Plaza Equus*—Horses and racing
  PREFECTURAL INFORMATION
  Prefectural Showrooms—Life outside the big city
  Furusato Plaza Tokyo—Japanese hometowns
- *Rice Information Showroom*—Japan's staple
- *Takinami Glass Factory*—100 years of glass-making
- *TEPCO Electric Energy Museum*—Everything you've ever wanted to know about electricity
- *TEPCO Electric Power Company Visitors Center*—Virtual Magic
- *TEPIA Plaza*—Technology Utopia
- *Tokyo Gas Ginza Pocket Park*—Architectural showcase
- *TOTO*—Dream kitchens, bathrooms, and food, food, food (2 showrooms)
- *TSS*—Tokyo Gas Shinjuku Showroom
- *World Import Mart*—Products from just about everywhere
- *Yamaha Showroom and Store*—Music lovers' paradise

INTRODUCTION

*W*ho would ever have thought that going to showrooms could be a major source of entertainment? In many countries this is not the case, but in Japan, companies and organizations knock themselves out to let you know what they're all about. And this does not mean just trying to sell you their products, either. It is more subtle than that: their philosophy is often the focus of the showroom. For in Japan, image comes first.

Here are some showrooms you might enjoy visiting. They cover a wide range of interests and include a lot of hands-on displays. Some actually seem to be more entertainment centers and galleries for arts and crafts than showrooms. But they were all created for you, the consumer, to come and visit—free from any sales pressure. They are great places to while away a few hours, especially when the weather outside threatens to put a damper on outdoor activities.

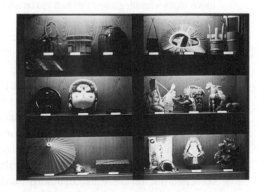

Visit a showroom

AMLUX TOYOTA AUTO SALON

アムラックス トヨタ オートサロン

3–3–5 Higashi Ikebukuro, Toshima-ku, Tokyo 170–0013

☎ 5391–5900

東京都豊島区東池袋3-3-5　〒170-0013

The Amlux Toyota Auto Salon claims to be the largest car show-room in the world, and it probably is. It features five floors of about seventy user-friendly vehicles that you can thoroughly check out. Each floor is dedicated to a specific driving theme, such as outdoor lifestyle, city driving, or luxury cruising.

It is quite easy to spend several hours on the 1F alone—for it is a real entertainment center. A number of delightful temporary exhibits, many of them hands-on, can be found here. The "Dome Factory" was a quick visit to the Toyota factory without the long train ride. Here, you could watch an authentic assembly-line robot "dance" to classical music as it worked, and a 3-D movie (complete with glasses) that took you on a realistic tour of the Toyota plant.

But the main event is definitely the Amlux Theater, an inverted silver dome that seems to defy gravity as it floats upside-down in the middle of the room. You can go up inside it and watch free 20-minute travel films (in English with Japanese sub-titles). And that's not all—a "body sonic" seat-vibrator and a kind of "smell-o-vision" aroma sensory system pull you right up into its high-resolution travel experience. The Grand Canyon, Las Vegas, and a nameless South Sea island have been some pre-viously featured destinations. The whole showroom has a very open, futuristic feel to it, enhanced by what sounds like "New Age space music" playing throughout the building.

Hours: 11 AM–8 PM Tues–Sat, 10 AM–7:30 PM Sun and national hols. Clsd on Mon unless it is a hol, then clsd Tues instead.

Access: A 7-min walk from Ikebukuro Stn, East Exit, No. 35 staircase

(Yamanote and other lines). Walk straight out from the exit along Green-odori street to the first corner. Turn left and go up the street that veers off at about a 45-degree angle. Straight ahead you will see a tall blue building with an archway on the top. This is Amlux. You can enter at street level just beyond the highway.

ASEAN CENTRE
(ASEAN Promotion Centre on Trade, Investment, and Tourism)
アジアセンター

Central Building, 1/2F
4–10–3 Ginza, Chuo-ku, Tokyo 104–0061
☎ 3546–2131 (Tourism) 3546–2011 (General Affairs)
東京都中央区銀座4-10-3　セントラルビル1/2階　〒104-0061

Are you interested in traveling to, or perhaps doing business with, the countries of Southeast Asia? If the answer is yes, then you might want to pay a visit to the ASEAN (Association of Southeast Asian Nations) Centre.

Tourism and business information on the six ASEAN member-countries of Brunei, Indonesia, Malaysia, the Philippines, Singapore, and Thailand is available here. Three to four exhibitions a year are also held in the bi-level exhibition hall—generally accompanied by meetings and promotional events. At a recent food and beverage show, some 500 visitors enjoyed the free samples and cooking demonstrations. Other themes have been fashion goods, building materials, and interior decoration. At the information corner on the main floor, English-language newspapers from the countries represented by the center are set out on racks for general reading. Printed information in both English and Japanese is available, and tourism videos can be viewed (with Japanese narration). At the printing of this book, ASEAN member Vietnam had not yet joined the ASEAN Centre. So they suggested that you contact the Vietnamese Embassy (☎ 3466–3313) for information. Other ASEAN members will be joining the center in the near future. Call for an update.

Hours: 9:30 AM–5:30 PM Mon–Fri. Clsd wknds and national and New Year hols.

SUPER SHOWROOMS

Access: A 2-min walk from Higashi Ginza Stn, Exit A2 (Hibiya or Toei Asakusa lines). From the exit, turn around and go back to the corner (Showa-dori), then turn left. The center is on the left side toward the end of the block. Access the "information corner" through the main exhibition hall on the 1F.

COSMETIC GARDEN—SHISEIDO

コスメティック ガーデン (C) 資生堂

Harajuku Piazza Building, 1F
4–26–18 Jingumae, Shibuya-ku, Tokyo 150–0001
☎ 5474–1534
東京都渋谷区神宮前4-26-18　原宿ピアザビル1階　〒150-0001

Listen up, ladies. Here is a place where you can try out makeup and other beauty products to your heart's content—guilt-free. There is no sales person in sight—guaranteed. In fact, you couldn't buy anything here even if you wanted to. This show-room is strictly for sampling.

The various offerings include makeup, fragrances, and hair, nail, and body products. Each has its own section, with single-use applicators provided at each station. The makeup areas are equipped with plenty of mirrors for checking the results. The nail section provides sitting stations and counter space where you can apply nail polish found in swiveling overhead racks. If you don't like a color, just wipe it off and try another. Cans of quick-dry spray are provided to set your final, finished manicure.

So the next time you have the urge to experiment with a new look, head for Shiseido's Cosmetic Garden. Go with a clean face and try everything. Just don't expect to have the place to yourself, for it may be buzzing with ladies who have already discovered its presence. But not to worry, it is so well laid out that it never really feels crowded. So go ahead and experiment, or create a "new you"—absolutely free!

NOTE: Complimentary beauty counseling sessions are available in Japanese if you can find a friend to translate for you.

Hours: 11:00 AM–7:30 PM Tues–Sun. Clsd Mon and 2nd Tues.
Access: A 2-min walk from Meiji Jingumae Stn, Exit 5 (Chiyoda Line). Turn around after surfacing and walk back to the corner (Meiji-dori). Cross the street and continue in the same direction along

Omotesando Ave for about 2 min. The Cosmetic Garden will be on the left side, near the pedestrian overpass.

FUJITA VENTE
フジタ バンテ

Fujita Corporation Head Office
4–6–15 Sendagaya, Shibuya-ku, Tokyo 151–0051
☎ 3796–2486 (Vente), 3402–1911 (Fujita Corp Office)
東京都渋谷区千駄ヶ谷4-6-15　株式会社フジタ　〒151-0051

"What a wonderful space this is" was the first thought that came to mind when I walked into the Fujita Urban Oasis. It is an experiment in healthy living—and one of the nicest environments in all of Tokyo. A fish tank and abundant greenery demonstrate how the components of an ecosystem can interact with each other to create healthy surroundings. There is even a suspended "floating tree" that grows without soil. And in the background, the strains of a grand (player) piano fill the air with beautiful classical music at this, the head office of Fujita, a major Japanese construction company.

A wonderful free toy museum with exhibitions from the London Toy and Model Museum is found on the 1F. The 2F houses a Hi-Vision Theater and the Vente Museum that features original exhibitions and events of art and comparative culture. At their annual "World Picture Book Exhibition," over 4,000 books from about 75 countries are on display for visitors to browse through.

In the fabulous B1 Amusement Space, a friendly little robot wheels its way around, talking to all the people it comes into contact with. Twenty interactive games feature state-of-the-art technology. My favorite was the "Melodian" automatic piano that asks you to play a few notes, then plays back a piece it has composed using your simple melody as its base. You can also create original forms out of swirling lights on the high-tech potters wheel or relax on a "Bodysonic" sofa. If you can't understand a game, one of the Vente people will explain it. If you want to be sure that an English-speaking staff member will be on duty, call ahead.

NOTE: The Vente Museum is generally free, but once in a while there is a charge for a special exhibition.

Hours: 10 AM–6 PM. Clsd Thurs (Fri if hol) and New Year and summer hols.

Access: A 5-min walk from JR Yoyogi Stn, West Exit (Yamanote Line). When you come out of the exit, you will see a police box (*koban*). Turn left down the small street that runs in front of it. At the very end of the street you will see a tall white building— this is the Fujita headquarters. Enter from the right side. The information counter there will have English pamphlets on the building and the amusement space.

GAS SCIENCE CENTER

ガスの科学館 （Gasu no Kagakukan）

Tokyo Gas Compound

6–3–16, Toyosu, Koto-ku, Tokyo 135–0061

☎ 3534–1111

東京都江東区豊洲6-3-16　東京ガス豊洲工場内　〒135-0061

A stunning view is included as part of the tour of this show-room, which has interesting gas-related displays. (See ch 16 for details.)

GINZA SONY BUILDING

銀座ソニービル

5–3–1 Ginza, Chuo-ku, Tokyo 104–0061

☎ 3573–2371

東京都中央区銀座5-3-1　〒104-0061

This Ginza landmark building is an eye-opener. Their outdoor display space at Sukiyabashi Crossing, one of Tokyo's busiest intersections, features ever-changing events: a 1,000-tulip give-away in the early spring, a male-model fashion show, and a giant aquarium full of fish from Okinawa. And that is just for starters. Inside you will find floor after floor of fun exhibits and activities. Although some of the displays are temporary, the ones listed here are relatively permanent. **Play Station**—This eerie dark space is brimming with mirrors and glass, where all eyes are glued to giant screens projecting the latest interactive computer games. Visitors can play them all. Needless to say, this is a popular spot. **High Vision Theatre**—This plush, 47-seat movie theater screens recent films for free each Saturday and Sunday afternoon at 4:30 PM. Just apply for a ticket to the movie you want to see by phone (☎ 3573–5234, fax 3573–7439), or in person, and you will be mailed a postcard that admits one or two people. If demand exceeds seating, winners are selected by lottery. The rest of the time, the theater features short films on a variety of topics. I saw an animated short created with high-definition computer graphics that previewed possible products of the future, including a car that could travel on both land and water. **Synapse**— A kind of museum of Sony products, but with a twist. Everything is encased in see-through plastic so that you can study their inner workings. **Space HDVS**—This is Sony's 3-D theater. Wander in and take a trip to Tahiti or see a number of other programs they screen at frequent intervals on their large-screen HDVS (High-Definition Video System).

Hours: 11 AM–7 PM daily except for New Year hols.
Access: On the corner of Sukiyabashi Crossing. At Ginza Stn, upstairs from Exit B9 (Ginza, Marunouchi, and Hibiya lines).

GLASS EXHIBITION AND INFORMATION CENTER

現代ガラスの博物館 （Gendai Garasu no Hakubutsukan）

Nihon Glass Kogyo Center Building, 1F

3–1–9 Shinbashi, Minato-ku, Tokyo 105–0004

☎ 3591–6016

東京都港区新橋3-1-9　日本ガラス工業センタービル1階
〒105-0004

I never realized that glass was so versatile until I visited this showroom. At the entrance you are greeted by the strains of beautiful music coming from two clear glass speakers. The song playing is composed of sounds of glass items being tapped and rubbed in various ways—accompanied by a full orchestra.

The center's permanent exhibition demonstrates the many ways that glass can be used at home, in industry, and in everyday life. We are all aware of how beautiful crystal glass can be, but did you know that technology now uses glass in such products as artificial bones and teeth, optical fibers, micro rod lenses, and liquid-crystal TV and computer screens? And what would we ever have done without camera lenses or eyeglasses? The center of the room is reserved for temporary exhibitions. One of these was a collection of interesting and unusual Japanese bottles dating back to 1870. Another showed the many uses of mirrors.

In one corner you can try your hand at diamond-point engraving. If you want a souvenir of your handiwork to take home, bring your own glass item to engrave for free. Or you can purchase one of their ashtrays to work on for a minimal fee of ¥100.

The descriptions are in Japanese, but the displays are visual and generally easy to understand. There is also a series of glass puzzles that you can play with. The showroom is the first of its kind in Japan, jointly sponsored by the Glass Manufacturers Association of Japan and six related associations.

Hours: 10 AM to 5 PM. Clsd Sun and national and New Year hols.

Access: A 5-min walk from JR Shinbashi Stn, Karasumori Exit (Yamanote and other lines). Turn right from the ticket turnstile and continue straight out the main street (Karasumori-dori) until you reach Hibiya-dori (3rd traffic light). Turn left and it will be the 7th building from the corner on the left side.

HONDA WELCOME PLAZA

ホンダ ウェルカム プラザ

2–1–1 Minami Aoyama, Minato-ku, Tokyo 107–0062

☎ 3423–4118

東京都港区南青山2-1-1　〒107-0062

Crawl in, on, over, and around Honda products of every size, shape, and form at the Honda Welcome Plaza, for all the latest Honda cars, vans, and other four-wheeled vehicles can be seen and explored here. A jazzy racing car is usually on exhibit, but this is the only one you can't climb into, sorry! New technology (such as Honda's navigational system) is generally on display for you to check out, and special temporary exhibits are often featured, too.

But the real stars of the show here are the fourteen or so

motorcycles ranging from your basic black to dazzling combinations of sporty colors. Bikes, choppers, motor scooters, motorcycles—they are all here for you to scrutinize and mount. There is even a "Raccoon" electric bicycle with a 220-watt motor that can be used either as a bicycle or as a motor bike.

An "information corner stage" features a twelve-unit multivision display screen where you can watch road races and other events. This is where new models are introduced—complete with all the PR hoopla and events connected with premieres.

Hours: 10 AM–6 PM daily.

Access: At Aoyama-itchome Stn (Ginza and Hanzomon lines). Take Exit 3 for Minami Aoyama and cross the street to the corner showroom.

INAX GALLERIES & SHOWROOM

イナックス ギャラリー

INAX Archi Plaza Building, 2F
3–6–18 Kyobashi, Chuo-ku, Tokyo 104–0031
☎ 5250–6560 (Showroom), 5250–6530 (Gallery)
東京都中央区京橋3-6-18　イナックス アーチプラザ2階
〒104-0031

INAX also sponsors two galleries at its Ginza Showroom. In Gallery 1, architecture-related exhibitions are usually seen. One demonstrated how the famous Spanish architect Antonio Gaudi came up with some of his unusual shapes for buildings and other works—by hanging chains and viewing them upside down to capture their loose, draping form. Gallery 2 generally features contemporary artworks. Tile work and model bathrooms can be seen in the upstairs showrooms.

NOTE: On the 1F as you enter is a small but well-stocked bookstore featuring art, design, and architecture books from the United States, Europe, and Japan. Exhibition catalogs of past shows can also be found here.

Hours: 10 AM–6 PM. Clsd Sun and hols. (Showroom clsd Sat, Sun, and hols)

Access: A 1-min walk from Kyobashi Stn, Exit 2 (Ginza Line). Go straight out of the exit and walk along Chuo-dori. The INAX Archi Plaza Building is on the left corner just before the traffic light.

INAX SHINJUKU SHOWROOM

イナックス新宿ショールーム

L-Tower Building, 20/21F

1–6–1 Nishi Shinjuku, Shinjuku-ku, Tokyo 160–1520

☎ 3340–1700

東京都新宿区西新宿1-6-1　エルタワービル20/21階　〒160-1520

INAX also has a showroom/gallery in Shinjuku, with a fabulous view from its entryway (see ch 16 for details). In addition to featuring lovely model kitchens and bathrooms, this showroom houses Galeria Ceramica just inside the reception area on the 20F. One exhibition held here featured see-through ceramic vases that appeared to be as delicate as lace. Another showcased Islamic tiles and bowls.

Hours: 10 AM–6 PM daily except for the 1st Wed of each month.

Access: Across from Shinjuku Stn, West Exit (Yamanote and other lines). The L-Tower Building is on the corner just beyond the Odakyu Halc Building. Take the escalator to the 2F to board elevators.

INFORMUSE

インフォミューズ

1–36–7 Nihonbashi Kakigaracho, Chuo-ku, Tokyo 103–0014

☎ 3665–1834

東京都中央区日本橋蛎殻町1-36-7　〒103-0014

Informuse is probably the most unusual showroom you will ever run across. It is hard to locate unless you are looking for it, but once you find it and ascend the single, plastic see-through step, you are in another realm. You walk along a wooden plank through a long, narrow entryway, and descend into a dark, cave-like room—which houses the exhibition. Appearing to be much more a gallery than a showroom, its main purpose is to demonstrate creative uses for paper.

An award-winning depiction of the Japanese Diet Building made up of 2,000 minute *kanji* and kana characters was the star of the show at Takahashi Noboru's exhibition of typographical photos created from computer graphics. The big picture was visible from a distance, but closer inspection revealed the startling details—that the composition consisted of countless tiny *kanji* characters in subtle shades of light and dark, each a word or part of a word relating to politics. Informuse can be counted on for inventive and entertaining shows.

Hours: Noon to 7 PM Mon–Fri. Clsd wknds and hols.
Access: 1 min from Suitengumae Stn (Hanzomon Line). Take the moving walkway to Exit 3. Go up the steps and walk straight out for about 1 min. It is in a gray building on the left, across the street from the Royal Park Hotel. The entryway looks like a cave with holes in it, and the plastic step at the doorway contains the tiniest of letters that spell out "Informuse."

SAKÉ PLAZA

日本の酒情報館 （Nihon no Saké Joho-kan）
Nihon Shuzo Kaikan Bldg 1F/4F
1–1–21 Nishi Shinbashi, Minato-ku, Tokyo 105–0003
☎ 3519–2091
東京都港区西新橋1-1-21　日本酒造会館1階、4階　〒105-0003

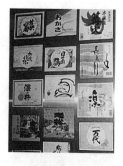

This showroom was created by the Japan Saké Brewers Association to educate people about *saké* (Japanese rice wine). A giant map on the main floor lights up to show visitors where Japan's 5,000 varieties of saké are produced—which covers just about the whole country. A display with miniature workers in the window portrays the various steps in the saké-making process, which is really quite complex.

But the real fun begins on the 4F, where you can taste ten (count them, ten) different kinds of saké —and all you have to do for this privilege is to rank the saké according to your preference on a postcard. Just so you don't get totally confused, the ranking is done in two sections of five samplings each The card is later mailed to you, grading you from a "novice" to an "expert." There is also a library on the 4F (ch 13) with about 50 books in English and French on saké and imbibing in general. (About 4,000 more are in Japanese.)

The staircase and halls of the showroom are decorated with

beautiful saké labels. Many more are displayed in books in the library, which elevates them to the art form that they really are. Some free literature is available in English, including a booklet entitled *This Is Saké* that gives a short history of the brew and explains the various ways to drink it. Either hot or cold is okay—but it should always be done with respect. And for those who still want to learn more, check out the new *Insider's Guide to Saké* by Philip Harper, a British national who has worked in the saké brewing industry for more than six years.

Hours: 10:00 AM–6:00 PM. Clsd Sat, Sun, and hols.

Access: A 5-min walk from Toranomon Stn, Exits 1 or 9 (Ginza Line). Walk straight down Sotobori-dori toward Shinbashi. Turn left at the Daiwa Bank and turn right at the gas station.

NAIS SHOWROOM SHINJUKU

ナショナル ショールーム新宿 (National A&I Systems)
Shinjuku Monolith Building, 3–5F
2–3–1 Nishi Shinjuku, Shinjuku-ku, Tokyo 163–0903
☎ 5381–8211
東京都新宿区西新宿2-3-1　新宿モノリスビル3–5階　〒163-0903

Don't miss this one, but be sure to save it for the end of the day. Basically, this showroom demonstrates how modern appliances and lighting can help improve your lifestyle in Japan—and thousands are on display here in Matsushita's three-level showroom. In model rooms along "Lighting Avenue," you can play with remote controls to lower chandeliers from ceiling mounts and to dramatically change a room's atmosphere by experimenting with various lighting effects.

Start at the 5F, for once you reach the 3F, you will not want to leave. Why? Simply because the "NAIS Life Space" contains a number of wonderful ways to soothe aching muscles and revitalize sagging spirits. In the Fitness Club area, there's a great foot massage machine that can be adjusted to vibrate faster or slower, harder or softer—absolute paradise if you have been on your feet all day. Or you can slip into a pair of "boots" that air-inflate and massage your leg all the way up to your knee. You can even lie down on a roller mat and have your whole body "rolled." Then, after you try out all of these toys, more than half a dozen massage chairs await you by the escalators. Sink into one and let its robotic magic fingers give you a shiatsu massage, kneading the kinks out of your neck, and periodically running all the way up and down your spine.

Hours: 10 AM–6 PM daily. Clsd 3rd Sun in Feb and New Year and summer hols.

Access: A 7-min walk from Shinjuku Stn, West Exit (Yamanote and other lines). Follow the signs through the underground passageway to the high-rise district. Turn left when you exit the tunnel. The Monolith Building is one street over, beyond the Keio Plaza Hotel. Also accessible from Nishi Shinjuku Stn (Marunouchi Line).

NEC SHOWROOM C&C PLAZA

NECショールーム C アンド C プラザ

Hibiya Kokusai Building, B1

2–2–3 Uchisaiwaicho, Chiyoda-ku, Tokyo 100–0011

☎ 3595–0511 (Call in advance for an English tour)

東京都千代田区内幸町2-2-3　日比谷国際ビル地下1階
〒100-0011

As you enter the NEC computer and communications showroom you will be greeted by a colorful fish tank filled with lively fish— but there's a twist. The fish swimming around inside the tank have been determined by a laser disk playing on the 32-in Hi-Vision screen inside the frame of the tank. And that's just the first stop on your little tour of this showroom's computer wizardry.

Next you will be taken to see NEC's newest computers— complete with all the latest features. The "save function" allows you to take an image from the TV and modify it on the computer, and the "karaoke function" comes with a plug-in mike and stereo speakers—with or without an echo sound.

In the Multimedia Corner, my photo was taken with a digital camera and modified with various software until it was virtually unrecognizable. In the Digital Interface Musical Instrument

Corner, I learned how to create a musical composition on the computer screen and then on the attached keyboard. I had 300 sounds from which to choose. In addition to the various instruments, delightful sound effects were available—footsteps, creaking doors, animal noises, laughing or screaming people—all in any key I wanted. (I composed a whole song of dog barks!) It was great fun, but it was also a learning experience. For in addition to working with notes, rests, and chords, I learned about mixing tracks and other essential steps that go into creating a real musical composition.

The NEC Showroom is not only informative, it is also extremely entertaining. I highly recommend calling ahead for an English tour, which basically means being shown how all the fun toys work.

Hours: 9 AM–5 PM Mon–Fri. Clsd wknds and hols.

Access: In front of Uchisaiwaicho Stn, Exit A6 (Mita Line). Don't go all the way to the street. Instead, make a right from the top of the station escalator and enter "Hibiya City," where an escalator on the right side will take you up to B1. Cross the plaza and NEC will be inside the double glass doors to the right on the other side. The showroom is the first entrance on the left

PLAZA EQUUS

プラザ エクウス

Shibuya Beam Building, 2/3F

31–2 Udagawacho, Shibuya-ku, Tokyo 150–0042

☎ 5458–4331

東京都渋谷区宇田川町31-2　渋谷ビームビル2/3階　〒150-0042

Plaza Equus is the Japan Racing Association's (JRA) showcase in central Tokyo that features race viewing, exhibitions, an art gallery, and a horse library. (See the horses section in ch 4 for details.)

PREFECTURAL INFORMATION

Since the burst of the "bubble economy" in the early 1990s people in Japan have become increasingly interested in the simpler things in life. A back-to-basics movement has taken hold in the country, and an interest in a healthier, less-complicated lifestyle has emerged in a big way.

But, you might ask, where can these things be found? The answer lies in the areas outside of Tokyo in the country's 47 prefectures—where the pace of life is not as frantic and the air is cleaner. Yes, the lifestyle of these outerlying areas of Japan is winning over many city dwellers. So to meet their growing need for information, fairs and festivals are popping up all over the city in venues such as Tokyo Dome, while folkloric arts festivals are held in the Nihon Seinenkan Hall yearly (see ch 11). Permanent resource facilities are also now available in the form of the prefectural showrooms listed below.

PREFECTURAL SHOWROOMS

Tetsudo Kaikan Building, 9F
(Above Daimaru Department Store at Tokyo Stn)
1–9–1 Marunouchi, Chiyoda-ku, Tokyo 100–0005
☎ Each showroom has its own telephone number
東京都千代田区丸ノ内1-9-1　鉄道会館ビル9階　〒100-0005

Kokusai Kanko Kaikan Building, 1–4F (Kanko Center)
(Next door to Daimaru Department Store, Tokyo Stn)
1–8–3 Marunouchi, Chiyoda-ku, Tokyo 100–0005
☎ Each showroom has its own telephone number
東京都千代田区丸ノ内1-8-3　国際観光会館ビル1–4階観光センター
〒100-0005

A preview of Japan's 47 prefectures awaits you at this showroom collective. Colorful posters, brochures, and displays of regional crafts and products can be found here. You will be impressed by the distinctive nature of the goods on display. The dolls from the various regions differ so greatly that it was hard to believe they come from places so close to one another. And masks are everywhere. The showrooms are virtual havens for mask-lovers.

It is fun to compare the pottery, too. Some prefectures' wares are rounded, while others are squarish. Some are brightly colored and others rely on earthy tones. Among the numerous other goods displayed are jewelry, carvings, lanterns, animals (mythological and otherwise), festival items, food products, and local brews. Illustrated English brochures are available to take home and study before finalizing any travel plans you might have to a particular prefecture.

Ten showrooms are located on the 9F of the Daimaru Department Store building at Tokyo Station, but this is only the tip of the iceberg. In the building right next door (the Kokusai Kanko Kaikan), there are about thirty more of these treasure houses of information on life outside the big city.

Hours: Generally 9 AM–5 PM Mon–Fri. Some showroom hours may vary slightly.

Access: Both buildings are located at the Yaesu side of Tokyo Stn. You can get to the **Tetsudo Kaikan Building** (which also contains Daimaru Dept Store) from inside the station. Take the elevator inside Daimaru to the 9F, where you will find the prefectural showrooms lined up in a row. **Kokusai Kanko Kaikan** (next door) borders the left side of the square as you exit the station. Floors one to four make up the "sightseeing center," and the names of the showrooms on each floor are written in English on the doorway to the central stairwell. (Yes, there is an elevator, too.)

FURUSATO PLAZA TOKYO

ふるさとプラザ東京

LaForet Harajuku Building, Part II, B1/1F

1–8–10 Jingumae, Shibuya-ku, Tokyo 150–0001

☎ 5413–2310

東京都渋谷区神宮前1-8-10　ラフォーレ原宿パート2　1/地下1階
〒150-0001

If you feel you haven't gained enough insight into the character of the various regions of Japan and its inhabitants yet, then head on over to the other side of Tokyo to Furusato Plaza to sample the Japanese countryside. ("Furusato" is an affectionate term, tinged with nostalgia, for "hometown.") It is an inviting open-to-the-street event space with a large, nine-section wall screen showing scenes of festivals and events held throughout the country. The 1F contains the front of a thatched-roof country house, complete with a robotic cow that chews its cud, moos, and flicks its tail as you approach. Step into the "house" and you are in the Information Corner, where a small but interesting array of crafts, wines, foods, and other regional products is on display. If you or a friend can read Japanese, information on over 2,500 communities from all around Japan can be accessed through computers, and numerous brochures describing activities such as whale-watching, camping, and castle-visiting line the walls.

The downstairs B1 level, the 7 Lucky Gods Arcade, is set up like an old Japanese village, consisting of tiny shops selling local goods from the various prefectures and manned by people wearing colorful *happi* coats. If your timing is right, you may even be offered samples of their products. A wonderful wooden cat hangs off the edge of a map of the "village," dangling a large, oval-shaped gold coin from its paw. Furusato Plaza is sponsored by the Furusato Information Center in affiliation with the Ministry of Agriculture, Forestry, and Fisheries (MAFF).

NOTE: The restaurant on B2 features food and saké from the various prefectures.

Hours: 10 AM–7 PM daily. (Some shop hours may vary slightly.) Clsd 2nd Mon and final day of each month.

Access: A 3-min walk from Meiji Jingumae Stn, Exit 5 (Chiyoda Line). Turn around after surfacing and walk back to the corner (Meiji-dori). Make a left and walk past the main LaForet Building. Continue along Meiji-dori until you come to LaForet Part II on the left side. It is invitingly open to the street.

RICE INFORMATION SHOWROOM

お米ギャラリー（Okome Gallery）

Crest Building, 1F

5–11–4 Ginza, Chuo-ku, Tokyo 104–0061

☎ 3248–4131

東京都中央区銀座5-11-4　クレストビル1階　〒104-0061

The Okome Gallery is small, comfortable, and friendly. Their literature reads, "Please make use of this gallery, not only for gathering information on rice, but also as a place for meeting and relaxing." Tables and chairs are set up in the middle of the room, and a lifesized diorama along one wall documents the

various growing stages of rice. The progression from seedlings to mature plants ready for harvest is depicted with realistic examples. Samples of the various types of rice grown in Japan show how much these can vary in color (black, red, white), shape (elongated, round, oval), and size.

A large map indicates which types of rice are grown in which regions of the country, and a nine-screen Multivision Video System shows films about rice cultivation, the Japanese diet, and other rice-related topics. The gallery was established by several rice organizations with the support of the Ministry of Agriculture, Forestry, and Fisheries (MAFF) to document the important role rice plays in the diet and daily life of the Japanese people.

Most of the displays are in Japanese, but a colorful English pamphlet available at the information counter contains explanations. There is a small library on rice and the Japanese diet, with some literature in English. Cooking classes, seminars, variety shows, and public relations events are held year-round in the event zone—many of which are free. Most are in Japanese, but some cooking classes and other special events are held in English. A large selection of Japanese recipe cards with mouth-watering pictures of rice dishes are there for the taking, too. You could always get someone to translate the ones you want to try.

NOTE: The snack area sells rice balls made from Japan's most popular types of rice. Rice products made from unusual varieties of rice—such as black, red, and scented—are also sold at the center.

Hours: 10 AM–6 PM Tues–Sun. Clsd Mon and national hols.

Access: In front of Higashi Ginza Stn, Exit A1 (Hibiya or Asakusa lines). It is the white building with the pyramid-shaped roof set back from the street. Or a 3-min walk from Ginza Stn, Exit A5 (Ginza, Marunouchi or Hibiya lines). Walk straight out from the exit down Harumi-dori. It will be on the right side.

TAKINAMI GLASS FACTORY
瀧波硝子（Takinami Garasu）

1–18–19 Taihei, Sumida-ku, Tokyo 130–0012

☎ 3622–4141

東京都墨田区大平1-18-19　〒130-0012

The Takinami Glass Factory has been open since 1897—over 100 years. Today it consists of a large building that encompasses a factory, large showroom, museum, and glass-making classroom.

The Takinami showroom/shop spans two floors and the offerings run from very exquisite to kitsch. In one corner was a unique see-through spinning-glass globe of the earth and delicate tiny glass roses. Cut crystal, art deco objects, figurines, paperweights, pendants, and rings are a few of the many other items here. This huge showroom is like a museum of glassware itself.

The Glass Museum features various glass-making techniques. (See ch 10.) A door just inside the entrance leads to a viewing platform overlooking the factory. From here you can watch workers molding objects from molten glass extracted from huge furnaces. But be forewarned—it's hot in there! In one corner of another floor you can watch classes in glass making—from behind cool window panes.

NOTE: For a fee you can even create your own works of glass between 10 AM–4:30 PM, or sign up for a regular class. The Takinami Glass Factory is one of the "Little Museums of Sumida-ku" (see ch 3).

Hours: 10 AM–6:30 PM daily. Clsd 2nd Mon of each month and New Year hols. The glass factory closes at 5 PM.

Access: A 12-to-15-min walk from Kinshicho Stn, North Exit (JR Sobu Line). Turn right from the exit and left at the main street (Yotsume-dori). Walk north for about 6 min, passing Kinshi Park on your right. When you reach the Taihei 4-chome intersection (police box on corner), turn left and walk down Kuramaebashi-dori for about another 7 min to the Taihei 1-chome intersection (gas station on corner). Turn right—the factory will be a few doors down on the left side.

TEPCO ELECTRIC ENERGY MUSEUM
テプコ電力館 （TEPCO Denryokukan）

TEPCO Building
1–12–10 Jinnan, Shibuya-ku, Tokyo 150–0041
☎ 3477–1191
東京都渋谷区神南1-12-10　テプコビル　〒150-0041

Every time I visit the TEPCO Building, I can't help but think of R2-D2—the cute little robot from *Star Wars* that wheeled itself around, beeping a lot. For that is what this building looks like— the little robot grown large. And since it juts out into the street, you can't help but feel its full effect upon your approach.

SUPER SHOWROOMS

The top floors are the most technical, and it is here you can learn about thermal, hydroelectric, and nuclear power through working models, videos, and displays that include lots of hands-on participation. In one corner, for example, you can climb inside a remote-controlled manipulator and work the levers to move around material that would normally be too dangerous for human beings to come into direct contact with.

There are also many games for kids, and lots of information for housewives, too. There is even a "Housing in the Aging Society" exhibition, with special lighting that is bright but non-glaring, heated tatami mats, and other conveniences to make life more comfortable for today's senior citizens.

The 3F is all about fun. You can participate in a virtual bicycle race, pedaling your way through the "Tour de Shibuya." At the "Digital Eyes" display in the Image and Information World Corner, your image will be distorted into all kinds of strange shapes by special camera lenses. If you should want to preserve one of these images, you can print it out for ¥100.

NOTE: Every Mon morning and afternoon TEPCO screens recent movies in their upstairs 102-seat theater. Formerly free, there is now a minimal ¥100 charge.

Yes, the TEPCO museum ("TEPCO" stands for Tokyo Electric Power Company) was created to help people to understand electricity, and the result is a very entertaining place for kids and adults. A lot of the descriptions are in Japanese, but detailed English information sheets are available on each floor for the displays on that floor.

Hours: 10:30 AM–6:30 PM. Clsd Wed and New Year hols.

Access: A 5-min walk from Shibuya Stn, Hachiko Exit (Yamanote and other lines). You will see a big Sony TV screen on the side of the 109–2 Building in front of the station. Walk down the street that runs alongside the left of this. Soon you will see the TEPCO Building (remember the little robot) straight ahead on the left, jutting out where the street curves to the right.

TEPCO ELECTRIC POWER COMPANY VISITORS CENTER

テプコ銀座館 （TEPCO Ginza-kan）

TEPCO Ginza-kan

6–11–1 Ginza, Chuo-ku, Tokyo 104–0061

☎ 3575–0456

東京都中央区銀座6-11-1　テプコ銀座館　〒104-0061

As you enter this showroom, you will see a large tank filled with brightly colored salt-water fish. It is interactive—its side pockets allow you to reach in and feel the fish as they swim by and brush up against your hand. Also on the first floor are several "waterless" aquariums on the walls, where computer-generated holograms of ancient fish swim in darkness. When you reach in and "grab" the fish, they react as if they had really been touched. Some coil up in a ball, while others turn and viciously attack.

The second floor houses the Plus-Minus Gallery, a playful and unusual art exhibition space that displays three-dimensional objects exclusively—no paintings or photographs (see ch 14). One of their recent shows featured macabre, giant-sized stuffed animals. Multimedia energy displays in Japanese are on the third floor, including one on foreign lands and their energy situation. On the fourth floor is the Virtual Magic Theatre, where a member of the audience (it could be you) dons a "virtual jacket" to control the movements of the character on the screen. This free, 20-minute virtual reality presentation takes you on a journey underneath the city, then over Japan's mountaintops north to Niigata Prefecture to visit a nuclear power station. It is presented on the world's first four-section, three-dimensional visual system. The last show began at 5 PM when I visited, so you might want to check the schedule upon arrival or call ahead for times.

Hours: 10:30 AM–6:30 PM. daily except Wed (Clsd Thurs if Wed is a hol).
Access: A 3-min walk from Ginza Stn, Exit A3 (various subway lines). Go straight out and turn left at the first street. The TEPCO building will be on the far right corner of the next block.

TEPIA PLAZA
テピア プラザ

Tepia Building, 1F
2–8–44 Kita Aoyama, Minato-ku, Tokyo 107–0061
☎ 5474–6111
東京都港区北青山2-8-44　テピアビル1階　〒107-0061

"Technology Utopia" is what TEPIA stands for. And that it is indeed. For here at this foundation showroom for the hi-tech industries of Japan, future trends and technologies are introduced in easy-to-understand exhibits with lots of hands-on participation.

The theme of the "Wings to the Future" exhibition was flight. The star attraction was a helicopter simulator that you could climb into and take over the controls of —and experience the feeling of a real pilot training course.

"The New Digital Age" exhibition featured a pool game played from inside a virtual reality headset, and in another corner you could hit real golf balls and watch their flight on a large-screen "virtual golf course."

As would be expected, the 2F library contains seemingly endless information on technology, accessible via state-of-the-art audio-visual equipment. Over 900 videos on high-technology are available—about eighty in English, with some in French, German, Spanish, and Chinese. (Ask for an English listing.) And with a reservation in the Hyper-Studio, you can even create your own personal CD-ROM at no charge (see ch 13).

Hours: 10 AM–6 PM Mon–Fri, 10 AM–5 PM Sat and hols. Clsd Sun.
Access:A 5-min walk from Gaienmae Stn, Exit 2 (Ginza Line). Turn right from the ticket turnstile and go up the stairs. Turn right at the exit, and right again at the corner. Look for a big building with TEPIA written in large letters at the top. It is just beyond the Prince Chichibu Memorial Rugby Ground on the right side.

TOKYO GAS GINZA POCKET PARK
東京ガス銀座ポケットパーク
7–9–15 Ginza, Chuo-ku, Tokyo 104–0061
☎ 3573–1401
東京都中央区銀座7-9-15 〒104-0061

This spiffy little Tokyo Gas showroom features exhibitions relating to architecture and design. One show in the 1F gallery compared the look of contemporary Shanghai with that of the 1920s and 30s, and displayed posters, photographs, magazines, maps, and clothes of the earlier period. Modern China was represented by an upbeat presentation of color photo blowups and a sampling of exports from Shanghai.

The 2F Architectural Studio amplified the theme with photos of Shanghai buildings—beginning from the 1930s and ending with sketches of buildings still in the planning stages. A final presentation consisted of two large panels of Shanghai's skyline along the Bund waterfront area, one taken in 1934 and the other in 1995. Needless to say, the changes were dramatic. Another exhibition focused on Industrial Design, featuring an "S Chair," "Time Sculpture," and "Measuring Worm," among other things.

The walls of the 2F are lined with architectural magazines that should interest architecture buffs and students of the subject. Copies of *The Architectural Review* dating from the 1970s to the present and *Progressive Architecture* starting from the 1960s are some of the English magazines in the collection.

Hours: 10:30 AM–7 PM. Clsd Wed.

Access: A 5-min walk from Ginza Stn, Exit A3 (Ginza, Marunouchi, and Hibiya lines). Walk straight down Chuo-dori from the exit. The showroom is on the left side toward the end of the 3rd block.

TOTO SUPER SPACE

TOTOスーパー スペース

L-Tower Building, 26/27F
1–6–1 Nishi Shinjuku, Shinjuku-ku, Tokyo 163–1526
☎ 3345–1010
東京都新宿区西新宿1-6-1　エルタワービル26/27階　〒163-1526

Aside from its spectacular view of the "carnival" side of Shinjuku (see ch 16), this showroom showcases standard, deluxe, and the ultimate dream kitchen and bathroom settings. Walk through rustic and modern model kitchens about the same size as a whole Japanese apartment. Take a stroll down "Bathroom Avenue" to see one that drifted down to earth right out of a fairy tale. It is called "Tsubo Niwa," and consists of a bathtub on a pedestal surrounded by a garden, a large rock and a ceramic vase, natural wood shelving, a TV, and indirect lighting. I'll take it!

Hours: 10 AM–6 PM daily. Clsd the 1st Wed of the month.

Access: Shinjuku Stn, West Exit (Yamanote and other lines). The L-

Tower Building is on the corner across from the Odakyu Halc Building. Take the escalator to the 2F to board an elevator.

TSS (Tokyo Gas Shinjuku Showroom)

東京ガス新宿ショールーム

Shinjuku Park Tower Annex, 1/2F

3–7–13 Nishi Shinjuku, Shinjuku-ku, Tokyo 106–0023

☎ 5381–6000

東京都新宿区西新宿3-7-13　新宿パークタワー別館1/2階　〒106-0023

This showroom calls itself an "Experience Hall." In its model rooms and exhibitions you can learn through experience how to improve your lifestyle with the use of gas. You can, for example, experience the difference in the comfort level of a room heated in the regular way and one heated from the floor up (keeps your tootsies warmer in winter). Ideas for accident-proofing your house can also be seen here, and there is a section devoted specifically to the comfort of seniors.

In the TSS Plaza upstairs, ingenious exhibitions related to food are presented. One entitled "Tables in Films" focused on table settings from a number of well-known movies. Some were physically re-created and others were portrayed in photos, posters, and videos. Among the films represented were *2001: A Space Odyssey, Breakfast at Tiffany's, Kramer vs. Kramer,* and several popular Japanese films. Another showed a series of ethnic settings in miniature, with great attention paid to dress, kitchen, and native foods.

Hours: 10 AM–6 PM. Clsd Wed, New Year and summer hols.

Access: A 12-min walk from JR Shinjuku Stn, South Exit (Yamanote and other lines). Turn right from the station and head toward the 52-story Shinjuku Park Tower Building, which you will see looming ahead of you on the right side just beyond the road overpass. The Annex Building is just before it—they are attached at the lobby level inside. Also accessible by Nishi Shinjuku Stn (Marunouchi Line).

WORLD IMPORT MART (Trade Promotion Center)

ワールド インポート マート

Sunshine City Complex, 5–7F

3–1–3 Higashi Ikebukuro, Toshima-ku, Tokyo 170–6006

*Japan External Trade Organization (JETRO)

*Manufactured Imports Promotion Organization (MIPRO)

☎ 3988–6234—JETRO International Exhibition Hall

☎ 3971–6571—MIPRO Import Information Center

☎ 3988–2791—Imports Shopping Center "Hakurai Yokocho"

東京都豊島区東池袋3-1-3　サンシャインシティ5–7階
〒170-6006

This is a good place to view products from around the globe. Australia, Austria, Canada, Denmark, France, Greece, Italy, Spain, and the United States all have permanent showrooms here (on the 5–7F). And at the large 6F Imports Shopping Center, "Hakurai Yokocho," you can wander around and see goods from a variety of countries in Asia, Africa, Latin America, Europe, and from the United States. It is rather like an international marketplace for food products, household goods, folkcrafts, clothes, and accessories.

Countries that don't have permanent representation may hold special exhibitions in the 6F International Exhibition Hall. One such show was held by Romania, in which over fifty Romanian companies and government organizations took part.

At the MIPRO Imports Information Center (6F), over 1,500 mail-order catalogues (mostly from the United States and Europe) can be perused. MIPRO also sponsors trade fairs and workshops, and prints a number of publications dealing with the Japanese market and the import of foreign products to it. (See ch 1—Free Publications for details.)

Hours: **Imports Shopping Center**: 10:30 AM–6 PM. Clsd Mon. **JETRO International Exhibition Hall**: 10:30 AM–5:30 PM Tues–Sun (final day of exhibition until 4 PM). Clsd Mon. **MIPRO Imports Information Center**: 10:30 AM–4:30 PM Mon–Fri. Clsd wknds and 3rd Mon of the month.

Access: A 3-min walk from Higashi Ikebukuro Stn, Exit 2 (Yurakucho Line). Make a right into the 1st small road (Verno Honda on

SUPER SHOWROOMS

433

corner) and follow that around until it runs into another street. Turn left here. This street will end at the Sunshine City Complex at the No. 3 South Gate entrance. Go straight through the building until you see an overhead sign directing you to a bank of elevators on the right for the World Import Mart. It is also a 10-min walk from Ikebukuro Stn, East Exit, No. 35 Staircase (Yamanote and other lines). Go toward the Sunshine City Complex.

YAMAHA SHOWROOM AND STORE

ヤマハ ショールーム

7–9–14 Ginza, Chuo-ku, Tokyo 104–0061

☎ 3572–3133

東京都中央区銀座7-9-14　〒104-0061

If you love musical instruments, then head for the Yamaha Showroom in Ginza. Here you will find every instrument you could ever want to fulfill your fantasy of playing in a philharmonic orchestra: violins, cellos, guitars, vibes, cornets, trumpets, saxophones, trombones, oboes, clarinets, flutes, French horns—even big ole' tubas. There is also an impressive display of drums. And for those with folksier tastes—harmonicas and accordions.

A white baby grand piano is the star on the piano floor, with some stiff competition from the player piano tinkling away nearby. There are lots of CDs that you can listen to through earphones, and tons of sheet music, books on music, and musical accessories to browse through on various levels. Whatever your musical leanings, Yamaha will no doubt have something of interest for you.

Hours: 11 AM–7 PM. Clsd 2nd Tues.

Access: 6 min from Ginza Stn, Exit A3 (Ginza, Marunouchi and Hibiya lines). Walk down Chuo-dori toward Shinbashi. Yamaha is on the left side of the street toward the end of the 3rd block. Also accessible from Shinbashi Stn (Yamanote and other lines).

16

FANTASTIC
FREE VIEWS

LAND VIEWS

- *Tokyo Metropolitan Government Building Observatories*
- *Shinjuku Sumitomo Building*
- *Shinjuku Center Building*
- *Shinjuku Nomura Building*
- *Bunkyo-ku Civic Center Observatory*
- *Top of Yebisu*

WATER VIEWS

- *St. Luke's Tower*
  Bird's-eye overview
- *Tokyo Harumi Passenger Terminal*
  Boats, bridges, and life on the water
- *Tokyo Big Sight*
  (Ariake International Exhibition Center)
- *Kasai Seaside Park*
  Bird watching and strolls along the peaceful shoreline
- *Odaiba Beach Area*
  Beachside bridge view

AIRPORT VIEWS

- *Haneda Airport Observatory*
- *Narita Airport Observatory*

SOME SHOWROOMS WITH GREAT VIEWS

- *Gas Science Center*
  Tower at the end of a pier
- *L-Tower Building (TOTO Super Space and INAX)*
  Overlooking the carnival side of Shinjuku

A VERY SPECIAL VIEW

- *Omotesando during the Christmas Season*

INTRODUCTION

*F*irst-time visitors to Tokyo often comment on how the city seems to go on . . . and on . . . and on. Until recently, restrictive building safety codes ensured that the metropolitan area sustained a low, sprawling skyline. Today, however, advanced earthquake-resistant technology has made it possible to build taller structures, and from these higher vantage points the views of the city are quite spectacular. Indeed, from high above, Tokyo does appear to go on forever.

Some of the sites here are observatories designed for the sole purpose of contemplating this expansive metropolis. Others form a part of other attractions, such as showrooms, parks, terminals, and complexes. Each offers its own special perspective and each has the capacity to take your breath away with its unique overview of Tokyo—one of the largest and most complex cities in the world.

And oh yes—don't be too disappointed if you don't see Mt. Fuji your first time out. Weather conditions being what they are, Fuji-san is only visible about 100 days in a year.

LAND VIEWS

TOKYO METROPOLITAN GOVERNMENT BUILDING OBSERVATORIES (45F)

東京都庁ビル展望ロビー（45階）

2–8–1 Nishi Shinjuku, Shinjuku-ku, Tokyo 163–8001

☎ 5321–1111 (Main number for building)

東京都新宿区西新宿2-8-1　〒163-8001

This has become *the* place where visitors and residents alike head when they want to see everything Tokyo has to offer. A smooth 55-second elevator ride whisks you to the 45F, where you are treated to a fabulous view of neighboring skyscrapers, the city's parks and gardens, important Tokyo landmarks, the Boso Peninsula, the Chichibu mountain range—and, hopefully, Mt. Fuji. Plaques in the observatories label all the sights in English and Japanese.

This city hall building was designed by world-famous architect Kenzo Tange, whose numerous credits include the stainless steel St. Mary's Cathedral (see ch 8) and the Fuji Television Headquarters located in the popular Odaiba Beach area of the city (see ch 3). The twin gothic-style towers that top it off encompass two 1,000-sq-m (1,200 sq-yd) circular observatories. Artwork, fountains, exhibition halls, and sometimes special events and concerts are featured on the main floor and in the adjoining Citizens' Plaza of the building, which was completed in April of 1991.

NOTE: Each tower has a coffee shop in the middle of the observatory area.

An English pamphlet about the observatories can be found on the 45F, and a booklet on the entire building complex is available in six languages (English, French, Korean, Chinese, Spanish, and Portuguese) at the 2F Information Counter across from the elevators.

Hours: 9:30 AM–5:30 PM Tues–Fri (last elevator up at 5 PM), 9:30 AM–7:30 PM (last elevator up at 7 PM) wknds, national hols, and Oct 1 (Tokyo Metropolitan Citizen's Day). Clsd Mon (Tues if Mon is a hol) and 4th Sat of Oct for maintenance.

Access: 10-min walk from Shinjuku Stn, West Exit (Yamanote and other lines). Follow the signs through the underground passageway to the high-rise district. After emerging from the tunnel, the huge building complex can be seen on the left side—just beyond the Keio Plaza Hotel. Go up the steps and enter the building from the plaza. Elevators to the observatories will be on either side of the door. Also accessible by Nishi Shinjuku Stn (Marunouchi Line).

SHINJUKU SUMITOMO BUILDING (51F)

新宿住友ビル展望ロビー（51階）

2–6–1 Nishi Shinjuku, Shinjuku-ku, Tokyo 163–0251

☎ 3344–6941

東京都新宿区西新宿2-6-1　〒163-0251

The 51F location of the Shinjuku Sumitomo Building Observatory creates a breathtaking vantage point for viewing the city by night. More intimate than the Metropolitan Building, its late closing hour (10 PM) affords you a dazzling scene of sparkling lights that stretch as far as the eye can see after daylight has been extinguished by the magic of darkness.

The futuristic design of the building creates a light and airy atmosphere throughout. Built in 1974 by the Nikken Sekkei architectural firm, it is best-known for its unusual triangular shape and hollow center. A large 360-degree cut-away model of the building is in the observatory area—as is a virtual fish tank (behind the tank's frame is a TV screen with realistic laser disk images of swimming fish).

After you see the sights and drink in the view, you can walk up one flight to the 52F Gallery Fuji—where artwork is displayed on the walls surrounding the building's open center well. End your visit by viewing the large paintings and sculpture on the 1F and in the building plaza.

NOTE: An inexpensive cafe is on the site, as is a clever picture-taking machine that will super-impose your photo image over one of the Tokyo skyline for ¥600.

Hours: 10 AM–10 PM daily.Clsd Jan 1 and 3rd Sun of Feb and Aug.

Access: An 8-min walk from Shinjuku Stn, West Exit (Yamanote and other lines). Follow the signs through the underground passageway to the high-rise district. Sumitomo is the 2nd large building on the right after emerging from the tunnel. Also accessible by Nishi Shinjuku Stn (Marunouchi Line).

FANTASTIC FREE VIEWS

SHINJUKU CENTER BUILDING (53F)

新宿センタービル（53階）

1–25–1 Nishi Shinjuku, Shinjuku-ku, Tokyo 163–0653

☎ 3345–1281

東京都新宿区西新宿1-25-1　〒163-0653

A number of other Shinjuku skyscrapers have set aside space for the purpose of viewing the city from high above (for free!). They are not as publicized as the other places, and their observatories are somewhat simpler—but their views are wonderful, and they have fewer crowds.

At the Shinjuku Center Building, a cozy viewing area relatively isolated from the rest of the building seems to have made this a favorite spot for young lovers to come and watch the sun go down. The southwest view overlooks the large green areas of Meiji shrine and Shinjuku Gyoen (Gardens), as well as Tokyo Tower and areas beyond.

Hours: 8 AM–10:30 PM daily. Clsd Jan 1 and 1st Sun of Feb and Aug.

Access: A 7-min walk from Shinjuku Stn, West Exit (Yamanote and other lines). Follow the signs through the underground passageway (be sure to take the one on the RIGHT side) to the high-rise district. When you reach Exit N5 (at the overhead clock), enter the Center Building and ride the escalator up to the main lobby. Then take the bank of elevators going to the 53F. Also accessible by Nishi Shinjuku Stn (Marunouchi Line).

SHINJUKU NOMURA BUILDING (49/50F)

新宿野村ビル展望ロビー（49/50階）

1–26–2 Nishi Shinjuku, Shinjuku-ku, Tokyo 163–0550

☎ 3345–0611

東京都新宿区西新宿1-26-2　〒163-0550

The dramatic northwest-facing perspective from the Sky View Observatory of the Nomura Building offers a wonderful view of Mt. Fuji at sunset, weather permitting. Although the general view is now partially blocked by a nearby skyscraper, the view is still lovely and dramatic.

Hours: 11 AM–10 PM daily. Clsd Dec 31–Jan 1 and one day in Feb and Aug.

Access:A 7-min walk from Shinjuku Stn, West Exit (Yamanote and other lines). Follow the signs through the underground passageway to the high-rise district. This building is the next one over from the Shinjuku Center Building (see above), so you can follow the same directions and walk through the Center Building—the Nomura Building will be directly across the street from it. Or it is one block to the right from the end of the underground passageway, up at the street level. Also accessible by Nishi Shinjuku Stn (Marunouchi Line).

BUNKYO-KU CIVIC CENTER OBSERVATORY (25F)

文京区シビックセンター展望ラウンジ（25階）

1–16–21 Kasuga, Bunkyo-ku, Tokyo 112–0003

☎ 3812–7111

東京都文京区春日1-16-21　〒112-0003

Opened in 1995, the Bunkyo-ku Civic Center offers one of the most comprehensive views of the city thanks to its location in an area of low-lying buildings. Its 25F circular observation platform provides a wonderful 270-degree panoramic view. It's easy to get the feeling that you are standing at the center of the universe here—particularly after dark—for, as you circle the deck, it appears that all roads lead right up to the building.

Tokyo Dome, Korakuen Amusement Park and Garden, Ueno Park (see ch 3), and Rikugien Garden are in the immediate area, with Shinjuku's New York–style skyline and Ikebukuro's Sunshine City within medium range. On a clear day, Mt. Fuji makes an appearance among the mountain ranges in the distance. The observatory circumnavigates the assembly room of the Bunkyo Ward government, which can be observed through a viewing window (except when the room is being used). Tables and chairs scattered around the deck lend a casual, restful atmosphere.

The building was designed by Nikken Sekkei, the same architects who created the Sumitomo Building in Shinjuku (see above). It shares many of the same features—such as the hollow center core and a sense of light and openness. This feeling prevails throughout the entire building, for the outdoor

FANTASTIC FREE VIEWS

NOTE: On the same floor is the moderately priced Tenbo Sky Restaurant that directly overlooks Tokyo Dome.

surroundings can be seen from just about everywhere, including the glass-enclosed elevators.

Hours: Open 9 AM–8:30 PM daily. Clsd for New Year hols and 2nd Sun of Dec.

Access: It is above Korakuen Stn, Exits 5 or 6 (Marunouchi or Nanboku lines), or across the street from the station's main exit.

TOP OF YEBISU (39F)

トップ オブ エビス（39階）

Yebisu Garden Place Tower Building
4–20–3 Ebisu, Shibuya-ku, Tokyo 150–6090
☎ 5423–7111
東京都渋谷区恵比寿4-20-3　恵比寿ガーデン プレース タワービル
〒150-6090

The Top of Yebisu is located on the 39F "Restaurant Plaza" of the Yebisu Garden Place Tower Building. Since the Yebisu Garden complex contains the only tall buildings around, the view offers an impressive, unobstructed line of vision straight north to the Shibuya and Shinjuku areas of Tokyo and beyond. After dark the skyscrapers of distant West Shinjuku serve as an elegant backdrop for the colorful patch of lower-lying Shibuya lights in the foreground.

The glass elevators to the top are located at the north end of the tallest building. Take one straight up to the 39F, where you will be let out next to the viewing area. To descend, walk down one flight and take the elevator going back down.

NOTE: "Yebisu" and "Ebisu" are two spellings of the same word (the "Y" is silent). The first is the original, and the second a modified version more commonly used today. Hence you have Yebisu Garden Place and Ebisu Station.

Opened in 1994, Yebisu Garden Place contains a number of entertainment and cultural facilities (see ch 3 for details). No doubt you will want to check out many of these when you visit, but whatever you do, do not forget to ride up and see the lovely view from the Yebisu Garden Place Tower Building.

Hours: You can go up and have a look between the hours of 11:00 AM and about 11 PM, while the tower restaurants are open.

Access: A 7-min walk from JR Ebisu Stn, East Exit (Yamanote Line), via the moving Skywalk that takes you to Yebisu Garden Place. The north side of the Tower Building containing the elevators for the

Top of Yebisu are directly ahead of the Skywalk's exit. It is also accessible via the Hibiya Line's Ebisu Stn.

WATER VIEWS

ST. LUKE'S TOWER (47F)
セントルークス タワー（47階）

    St. Luke's Garden Complex
    8–1 Akashi cho, Chuo-ku, Tokyo 104–0044
    ☎ 3248–6820
    東京都中央区明石町8-1　聖路加ガーデン　〒104-0044

St. Luke's Tower's superb location alongside the Sumida River makes it the perfect place to begin your sightseeing tour of Tokyo Harbor and its environs—or for just admiring the beauty from a distance. As you ascend from the 46F elevator stop (and walk up to the 47F observatory), a sweeping bird's-eye view of the surrounding area unfolds before you.

    Once at the top, a startling and dramatic perspective of the entire waterside and its activities greets you. After you have recovered from its impact, you can begin to pick out some of the nearby attractions skirting the entrance to Tokyo Bay—the Hamarikyu Garden, the Tsukiji Wholesale Fish Market, the majestic Rainbow Bridge, and the Harumi Passenger Terminal with large ocean-going vessels docked by its side. Upon your descent back to earth, you can walk out to the waterside park that runs alongside the building at the 2F level. Here you can sit and watch the boats go by—or stroll along the water to Tsukiji Fish Market—just beyond the bridge to your right. (See ch 3.)

NOTE: The observatory looks out over the water. The view from the other side can be seen from the Luke Restaurant, reachable via an elevator from the 46F.

    Opened in May of 1994, St. Luke's Tower is located directly across the street from St. Luke's Hospital.

Hours: 9 AM–8/8:30 PM daily.
Access: An 8-min walk from Tsukiji Stn, Exit 3 (Hibiya Line). Upon exiting from the station, turn around and walk back to the corner.

Turn left and follow this street until it ends at St. Luke's Garden Complex. When you enter the building, St. Luke's Tower will be to the left side. Take the elevator to the 46F and walk up one flight.

TOKYO HARUMI PASSENGER TERMINAL (1/3/6F)

晴海客船ターミナル（Harumi Kyakusen Terminal,1/3/6階）

5–7–1 Harumi, Chuo-ku, Tokyo 104–0053

☎ 3536–8651

東京都中央区晴海5-7-1　〒104-0053

The Harumi Passenger Terminal is located on a pier surrounded by water on three sides. Its isolation serves to give the view from the terminal a misty, dreamlike quality, even on a clear day. Each level affords a floor-to-ceiling panorama of sparkling water, ocean-going vessels, and the spectacularly long expanse of the Rainbow Bridge—all combining to form an absolutely mind-boggling vista. And the partial backdrop of tall, modern buildings in the distance creates a beautiful skyline. Who could ask for anything more?

There is a very large outdoor observation deck on the 3F, and the ground level opens out onto the Waterfront Plaza, where you can stroll along the water. The ocean liners docked there are sometimes available for exploring—call ahead and check (in Japanese) if you want to be sure.

The atmosphere of the 6F observatory is completely different from the rest of the building. You may even feel that you are wandering around in a place you shouldn't be. The wind whips through your hair as you climb the steps, ramp, and platform of the large, bright orange metal structure found there. Only the discovery of a telescope made me realize that I was not walking through some bizarre, off-limits construction area. But it is fun, and the view is great.

NOTE: For ¥100, the telescope on the 6F observatory brings everything up close—but who would want to do that? A cafeteria and restaurant are also in the building, and a sightseeing boat docks nearby.

Hours: 9 AM–5 PM Mon–Fri, 9 AM–8 PM wknds and hols in summer (7 PM in winter). Clsd new year hols.

Access: Take the No. 5 Harumi-Futo (Harumi Pier) bus from Tokyo Stn, Marunouchi South Exit. Or this same bus, and also the No. 3 Harumi-Futo bus, can be boarded from bus stops along Harumi-dori in Ginza.

TOKYO "BIG SIGHT"—TOWER BUILDING (8F)

東京ビッグサイト：会議棟（8階）

Tokyo International Exhibition Center (Ariake)
3–21–1 Ariake, Koto-ku, Tokyo 135–0063
☎ 5530–1111
東京都江東区有明3-21-1　東京国際展示場　〒135-0063

Tokyo Big Sight is the city's new Ariake International Exhibition Center, located along Tokyo's newly developed waterfront area. The Tower Building—a square, funnel-shaped structure set on pillars—soars above the building's Entrance Plaza and Center Square, and is the symbol of the whole complex.

Its 8F observatory wraps around the top of the building, offering a sweeping 360-degree view of both land and water. You can stroll along the outside decks until dark, and afterward observe the dramatic night scene through a wall of glass. This state-of-the-art conference center is the largest in Japan, and contains 80,000 sq m (262,400 sq ft) of floor space. Opened in April of 1996, it was created to replace the nearby Harumi Tokyo International Fair Grounds. (See ch 3—Odaiba Beach Area, for other nearby attractions.)

NOTE: The 8F also contains a bar lounge and JW's California Grill Restaurant (☎ 5530–1221).

Hours: The outside observation platform is open 10 AM–5 PM daily (6 PM in summer), weather permitting, and the glass-enclosed interior remains open until the adjoining restaurant closes about 9 pm.

Access: A 20-min ride from Shinbashi Stn on the new, computer-run (that's right—no driver or conductor) Yurikamome Transit System that connects the waterfront area with central Tokyo. A walkway from Kokusai Tenjijo Seimon Stn leads directly to the Tower Building. Or take the No. 16 Metropolitan Bus from Tokyo Stn (various lines), Yaesu Exit, to Tokyo Big Sight Stn (takes about 35 min).

KASAI SEASIDE PARK

葛西臨海公園（Kasai Rinkai Koen）

6–2 Rinkaicho, Edogawa-ku, Tokyo 134–0086
☎ 5696–1331 (Park), 5696–4741 (Beach)
東京都江戸川区臨海町6-2　〒134-0086

FANTASTIC FREE VIEWS

As I walked across the wide bridge that leads to the Kasai Rinkai Koen for the first time, I knew I was entering someplace special. And I was right. The Viewpoint Visitors Center (and observatory) that runs alongside the water overlooks a vast expanse of shoreline, sea, and sky that you probably never dreamed existed inside Tokyo. It also contains a history of the waterfront and information on the local flora and fauna in both English and Japanese—with accompanying visuals.

Although once a thriving fishing community in Edo days (1600–1868), the Kasai waterfront deteriorated into a garbage dump as a result of pollution from factories in modern times. Fortunately, a 1989 revitalization of the shoreline has returned the area to its former beauty, and created one of the loveliest and most peaceful spots in the entire city.

At the far corner of the park is yet another wonderful view—a bird sanctuary with a circular "watching center" situated between fresh- and saltwater ponds. Free telescopes are available for tracking the birds without disturbing them, and paths wind around the ponds, with rest stations set up for subtle close-up bird-viewing.

The park covers 783,000 sq m (approximately 2.5 million sq ft), and offers a great variety of natural environments for your viewing pleasure, including a lotus pond and two offshore beaches (one for people and one for wildlife). There is no question that you will want to spend some time at Kasai Seaside Park, wandering along its serene shores and watching the beautiful sunset at the end of the day. A free English map and guide to the park is available at the Administration Center at the far right side of the entrance bridge.

NOTE: The famous Tokyo Sea Life Park is also on the grounds (¥800 adults/¥300 students). It is clsd New Year hols and Mon (Tues if Mon is a hol).

Hours: The park itself never closes. Bird Watching Center—9:30 AM–4:30 PM daily. Viewpoint Visitors Center—9:30 AM–4:30 PM daily. Beach (Nagisa Bridge)—9 AM–5 PM daily except the following: Open until 6 PM wknds June 1–July 14 and daily Aug 16–31. Open till 7 pm daily July 20–Aug 15.

Access: The park is across from JR Kasai Rinkai Koen Stn (Keiyo Line from Tokyo Stn). There is also boat service between the park and Hinode Pier near JR Hamamatsucho Stn (Yamanote and other lines). See the posted schedule at the park to take one

back or call Kasai Rinkai Koen Boatline at ☎ 5696–0287 or
Hinode Pier at ☎ 3457–7830 (in Japanese) for schedule.

ODAIBA BEACH AREA

御台場海浜公園 （Odaiba Kaihin Koen）

   1–4–1 Daiba, Minato-ku, Tokyo 135–0091

   ☎ 5531-0851 (Park Office)

   東京都港区　台場1-4-1　〒135-0091

This hot new area in Tokyo—that doesn't feel like Tokyo—has
a wonderful beachside view of the Rainbow Bridge with the city
as a backdrop, and so much more. Great view day and night, so
try to see both. (See ch 3—Odaiba Beach Area for details.)

Hours: Odaiba Kaihin Koen (Odaiba Beachside Park) is open 24 hours.
Access: Odaiba Kaihin Koen Stn on the Yurikamome Line from Shinbashi Stn. Also accessible via boat from Hinoda Pier near
JR Hamamatsucho Stn (Yamanote and other lines) or the
Asakusa area (see ch 3—Shitamachi). (Call the Hinode Pier at
☎ 3457–7830 or Tokyo Ship Corp 3841–9178 in Japanese for
information.)

AIRPORT VIEWS

HANEDA AIRPORT OBSERVATORY (6F)

羽田空港見学者用デッキ （6階）

   Haneda Airport Terminal

   3 Haneda Airport, Ota-ku, Tokyo 144–0041

   ☎ 5757–8111

   東京都大田区羽田空港3丁目　羽田空港ターミナル　〒144-0041

No, you don't have to travel all the way out to Narita International Airport to indulge your romantic fantasies of travel to
places unknown. You can watch the big jets take off and land
much closer to home at Tokyo's centrally located Haneda
Airport—with Mt. Fuji as a backdrop!

Once Tokyo's international airport, Haneda now serves as the city's base for domestic departures and arrivals. (Taiwan's China Air is the only carrier conducting international flights here now.) But the hustle and bustle of the airport hasn't changed much—excitement still fills the air as people scurry back and forth to catch flights and greet arriving passengers.

The new terminal building, opened in 1994, is dubbed "Big Bird," and its 6F outside observation deck is aptly dubbed "Bird's Eye."

Hours: The observation deck is open 5 AM–10 PM daily (except on very windy days). The first plane takes off about 6:30 AM.

Access: Take the Tokyo Monorail from JR Hamamatsu Stn (Yamanote and Keihin Tohoku lines) to the end of the line—Haneda Airport Stn. *Do not get off at Haneda Station.* Upon arrival you will already be in the terminal building. Go upstairs and take the center elevators to the 6F to reach the observation deck.

NARITA AIRPORT OBSERVATORY (5F)
成田空港見学者用デッキ（5階）

Narita Airport Terminal One

Shin Tokyo Kokusai Kuko, Narita-shi, Chiba 286–0000

☎ 0476–34–5000

千葉県成田市新東京国際空港第1旅客ターミナル　〒286-0000

I can't imagine making a special trip all the way out to Narita Airport unless you have to. But if you are going to pick someone up or see them off (or if your own flight is delayed), you could pass the time by going up and watching the planes take off and land.

The Narita Observation Deck is located on the 5F of Terminal One, where both indoor and outdoor viewing is possible. Don't expect Mt. Fuji as a backdrop here, however. A woman who has been working at the airport for five years said she saw it only once during all that time—after a snowfall when the air was extremely clear. But you will see lots of planes. Busiest times are 10 AM–11 AM and 5 PM–6 PM.

Terminal Two also has a deck, but the view is not nearly as good.

Hours: The observation deck is open 8 AM–8 PM. The runway opens about 6 AM.

Access: The least expensive express route to the airport is the Keisei Line from Nippori or Ueno. Express trains take about 1 hour.

SOME SHOWROOMS WITH GREAT VIEWS

Tokyo's super showrooms can also boast some of the best views in town. I have listed a few here. Keep your eyes open for more.

GAS SCIENCE CENTER
ガスの科学館 （Gas no Kagakukan）
Tokyo Gas Compound
6–3–16 Toyosu, Koto-ku, Tokyo 135–0061
☎ 3534–1111
東京都江東区豊洲6-3-16　東京ガス豊洲工場内　〒135-0061

It stands alone at the end of a pier on Tokyo's waterfront—a 45-m- (150-ft-) high tower with a 360-degree panoramic view of the city and waterfront. Japan's largest see-through elevator (fifty-passenger capacity) transports you to the top, giving you a great view all the way up. Once there, you can take pictures of the nearby Harumi passenger terminal and the ocean-going vessels docked by its side. You can also watch the boats go by and cross under the long span of the Rainbow Bridge. It is a wonderful sight that not everyone gets to see—only the visitors to the Gas Science Center.

This view is included as part of the tour of the center's showroom. Although the tour is conducted in Japanese, an English booklet of the center explains things well enough for you to understand what you are seeing. The topics covered include a walk through experimental greenhouses, a mini-concert performed by a gas organ, a diorama of a city of the future, an earthquake simulator in which the gas supply automatically shuts off, and a walk under a scale model of Nishi Shinjuku skyscrapers to see how the underground gas heating/cooling system for the entire area works. All were created using state-of-the-art technology and are very visual. And you are even given presents for coming. I received a bar of natural herb soap and a rose grown in the center's own garden.

Hours: The tour is offered to individuals and smaller groups on Sat afternoons (3 times a month) at 2 PM. There is no charge, but reservations are needed. (It is best to have someone call in Japanese.) Wkdys are reserved for large groups. The center is clsd on the 3rd Sat, Sun, and national, New Year, and company hols.

Access: You will get complete instructions when you make your reservation, but basically they will meet you in a company bus at Toyosu Stn on the Yurakucho Line as part of the tour.

L-TOWER BUILDING
TOTO SUPER SPACE (26/27F) and INAX (20/21F)

エルタワー ビル：TOTO スーパー スペース(26/27階),
　　　　　　　　　イナックス新宿ショールーム(20/21階)

1–6–1 Nishi Shinjuku, Shinjuku-ku, Tokyo 163–1526 (TOTO),
163–1520 (INAX)

☎ 3345–1010 (TOTO), 3340–1700 (INAX)
東京都新宿区西新宿1-6-1　〒163-1526（TOTO）
〒163-1520（イナックス）

A shocking, almost cartoonlike sight awaits you as you step out of the elevator at the TOTO Super Space showroom after dark. The dramatic floor-to-ceiling view that looks right over the top of Shinjuku train station is punctuated by the bright neon signs of Shinjuku's frolicking and rowdy east side. It is at its most impressive at night. During the day, however, the view from INAX's lower showroom in the same building offers a better glimpse of the city because the view is much wider here and the lower perspective blots out the station's train tracks, which are a little too visible from the higher floors in the daytime. Why not try both views and judge for yourself? After all, they're free. (See ch 15 for more information on TOTO and INAX showrooms.)

Hours: Both showrooms are open 10 AM–6 PM daily, except for the 1st Wed of each month.

Access: Across from JR Shinjuku Stn, West Exit (Yamanote and other lines). The L-Tower Building is on the corner just beyond the Odakyu Halc Building. Take the escalator to the 2F to board elevators.

A VERY SPECIAL VIEW

OMOTESANDO DURING THE CHRISTMAS SEASON

Wherever you go in Tokyo during the Christmas season, there is never any question of what time of the year it is. Santa Claus is everywhere, the smell of pine permeates the air, and the department stores are decked out in full yuletide apparel (starting just after Halloween in some cases). Christmas music echoes through the halls of every building and the whole city is aglow with twinkling lights.

But the most spectacular lighting display is on Omotesando (the Champs Elysees of Tokyo) when the two long rows of zelkova trees on either side of the wide avenue burst into twinkling masses of light at dusk each evening. The area fills with sightseers, and on some nights carolers move among the crowds, their cheerful songs enhancing the already wonderfully festive spirit of the season. The best spot to get an overview of this dazzling yuletide light show is from the two pedestrian bridges that cross over the avenue. But be sure to get there early, for others have already discovered this secret. Call the Tourist Information Center (☎ 3201–3331) or the Harajuku Champs Elysees Association (☎ 3406–4303, in Japanese) for more information.

Hours: 4:30 PM–11 PM nightly for two weeks before Christmas (until midnight for the last few days).

Access: At Omotesando Stn (Ginza, Hanzomon, or Chiyoda lines), Meiji
Jingumae Stn (Chiyoda Line), or JR Harajuku Stn (Yamanote
Line). The light show spans Omotesando between Harajuku Stn
and Aoyama-dori.

POSTNOTE

Now that you have indulged in all of these delightful freebies, you might be considering giving something of yourself in return. It's no secret that there is a great need in this world for volunteers, and opportunities abound wherever you live. It doesn't cost anything to try and make this world a better place, and the personal satisfaction you will get in return couldn't be bought—at any price! So why not offer your own special touch where it is needed most? If you happen to live in Tokyo, you can check out the following opportunities:

VOLUNTEERING IN TOKYO AREA DIRECTORY

c/o Jeanne Vass, 1–12–6–202 Shoto, Shibuya-ku, Tokyo 150–0046

☎ Fax: 3481–6667 or 3460–3689

東京都渋谷区松濤1-12-6-20　〒150-0046　Jeanne Vass様方
ボランティア リスト請求

The *Volunteering in Tokyo Area Directory* is a comprehensive listing of places where your unique talents may be utilized to their best advantage, and tells you how to go about turning your volunteer spirit into a reality. It is published by Foreign Executive Women (FEW), and describes over seventy nonprofit organizations that can use your help—now. The environment, crisis support, human rights, education, and animal welfare are some of the areas explored. The book is free, and can be obtained by sending ¥390 in stamps (as of this printing) to cover mailing costs to the above address.

TOKYO VOLUNTEER CENTER

東京ボランティアセンター

Central Plaza Building, 10F

1–1 Kaguragashi, Shinjuku-ku, Tokyo 162–0823

☎ 3235–1171 (Ms. Kawamura and Ms. Sato speak English)

東京都新宿区神楽河岸1-1　セントラル プラザビル10階　〒162-0823

Information is available on a number of volunteer activities such as nongovernmental organizations (NGOs) that help people in countries abroad, and a copy of the *Volunteering in Tokyo Area Directory* (see above) is available for you to look through. (They also keep a list of volunteers who will teach Japanese to foreigners for free.)

Hours: 9 AM–8 PM wkdys, 9 AM–5 PM Sat. Clsd Sun and hols
Access: Next door to JR Iidabashi Stn, West Exit (Sobu Line). Cross the bridge to the right. You will immediately see Fuji Bank on the 1F of a 20F building (Central Plaza) next to the station. The center is on the 10F. From Iidabashi Stn (Tozai, Yurakucho, and Nanboku lines), Exit B2B will bring you directly inside the building.

JAPAN INTERNATIONAL VOLUNTEER CENTER (JVC)
日本国際ボランティア センター

Maruko Building, 6F
1–20–6 Higashi Ueno, Taito-ku, Tokyo 110–0015
☎ 3834–2388 (Hiromi Nagano). Fax: 3835–0519
東京都台東区東上野1-20-6　丸子ビル6階　〒110-0015

JVC is a nonprofit organization that is always in need of foreign language–speaking volunteers. It was founded in 1980 to help the slum dwellers in Bangkok, and has since branched out in a number of directions. It is now involved with several issues, including environmental concerns, famine relief, and community development in eight overseas countries.

Hours: 10 AM–7 PM Mon–Fri
Access: 5 min from JR Okachimachi Stn. Call for directions.

TELL NET
✆ http://www.telljp.com

The official website of Tokyo English Life Line (TELL) contains information on TELL services, volunteer opportunities, TELL supporters, and charity events, as well as valuable information for the international community.

INDEX

Ginza Hachikan shrine 202
Ginza Nikon Salon 365
Ginza Pocket Park (Tokyo Gas) Showroom 430
Ginza Sony Building 414
giveaways, free 42–51
Glass Exhibition and Information Center 415
glass museum 289
glass showroom 415–16, 426
Goethe Institute Tokyo (library) 350
Gokokuji temple 188
Golden Gai 92
Good Day Books 355
government office publications 29–32, 46
government services and offerings 43
Grand Beer Hall (Ebisu) 99
graphic design gallery 382
grocery delivery services, free 48
Gyosen Park 160–61

H

Hachiro Yuasa Memorial Museum (archaeological and folk art collection) 257
Halloween 139
Hana Matsuri (Buddha's burthday) 136, 189
Hana No Kai Classical Japanese Dance Group 300, 319
hanami (cherry blossom viewing) 136, 150–51, 156, 158
Hanazono shrine 202
antique flea market at 248
Haneda Airport
information 32
observatory 449
Happoen Garden 176
Harumi Antiques 241
Hashimoto, Seiko (Diet member) 72
Heiwajima Antiques Fair 248–49
helplines 33–34
Hibiya Library 331
Hibiya Park 151
Hie shrine/Sanno Gongen 203
Higashi Itabashi Park 131, 161
High Vision Theater (Sony) 414
hiking 81–83
Hillside Gallery 393
history buffs, suggested destinations for 58–59

Hiwatari (Fire-walking Festival) 82, 195
holiday celebrations, Western 139–141
home visit 65–67
Honda Welcome Plaza 416
Honjo Bosai-kan 37
Honmonji temple 189
Horikiri Iris Garden 169
Horse Racing Museum 128, 276
horses
pony rides for kids 130–32, 145, 162
racing 125–29
shows 129–30, 145, 162
hospital information 35–36
hotel gardens 175–79
Hotel New Otani Garden 177
Hotel Okura, classical concerts in lobby 305
Hozomon "Treasure House" Gate 95, 188
human rights assistance 39–40
Human Rights Counseling Center 39

I

ICU (International Christian University) 257
identity photos, free 50
ikebana 304
Ikebukuro Bosai-kan 38
Immigration Information Center 40, 50
Imperial Collection, Museum of the 281
Imperial Household Musicians, The 298
Imperial Palace 64
Imperial Palace Cycling Course 120
Imperial Palace East Garden 166
jogging around 124
import showrooms and shopping center 433–35
INAX galleries and showrooms 417, 418, 453
Information Bureaus of Tokyo 29, 31
information centers 33–42
Informuse 418
Inokashira Park 152
insects, in museum 279
Insider's Guide to Saké, The 343, 420
Institut Franco-Japonais de Tokyo "Mediathèque" library 349
Institute for Pacific Rim Studies, Temple University Japan 312
Institute of Developing Economies Library 332
International Aikido Federation 113

INDEX OF JAPANESE PLACE NAMES

SUSAN POMPIAN holds a Bachelor of Arts in anthropology and a Master of Arts in Travel and Tourism Administration. After a number of years in the travel industry, Pompian turned to freelance writing, specializing in travel, current events, and human-interest themes. She divides her time between Tokyo and Washington, D.C.

タダで楽しむ東京ガイド
Tokyo for Free

1998年 1 月　第 1 刷発行
2004年10月　第 7 刷発行

著　者　　スーザン・ポンピアン

発行者　　畑野文夫

発行所　　講談社インターナショナル株式会社
　　　　　〒112-8652 東京都文京区音羽 1-17-14
　　　　　電話　03-3944-6493（編集部）
　　　　　　　　03-3944-6492（営業部・業務部）
　　　　　ホームページ　www.kodansha-intl.com

印刷・製本所　　共同印刷株式会社

© スーザン・ポンピアン 1998
Printed in Japan
ISBN4-7700-2053-8